PROBLEM SOLVING SURVIVAL GUIDE
Volume I: Chapters 1-12
to accompany

ACCOUNTING PRINCIPLES

11th Edition

Jerry J. Weygandt, Ph.D., C.P.A.
Arthur Andersen Alumni Professor of Accounting
University of Wisconsin - Madison
Madison, Wisconsin

Donald E. Kieso, Ph.D., C.P.A.
KPMG Peat Marwick Emeritus Professor of Accountancy
Northern Illinois University
DeKalb, Illinois

Paul D. Kimmel, Ph.D., C.P.A.
Associate Professor of Accounting
University of Wisconsin - Milwaukee
Milwaukee, Wisconsin

Marilyn F. Hunt, M.A., C.P.A.
University of Central Florida
Orlando, Florida

JOHN WILEY & SONS, INC.

ISBN-13   978-1-118-34213-8

10 9 8 7 6 5 4 3 2 1

Printed and bound at LSI

CONTENTS

Chapter 1   Accounting in Action

Chapter 2   The Recording Process

Chapter 3   Adjusting the Accounts

Chapter 4   Completing the Accounting Cycle

Chapter 5   Accounting for Merchandising Operations

Chapter 6   Inventories

Chapter 7   Accounting Information Systems

Chapter 8   Fraud, Internal Control and Cash

Chapter 9   Accounting for Receivables

Chapter 10   Plant Assets, Natural Resources, and Intangible Assets

Chapter 11   Current Liabilities and Payroll Accounting

Chapter 12   Accounting for Partnerships

PREFACE: To the Student

The purpose of this problem-solving tutorial is to help you to improve your success rate in solving accounting homework assignments and in answering accounting exam questions. For each chapter we provide you with:

OVERVIEW	To briefly introduce the chapter topics and their importance.
STUDY OBJECTIVES	To provide you with a learning framework. Explanations of these objectives also provide you with a summary of the major points covered in the chapter.
TIPS	To alert you to common pitfalls and misconceptions and to remind you of important terminology, concepts, and relationships that are relevant to answering specific questions or solving certain problems. To help you to understand the intricacies of a problematic situation and to tell you what to do in similar circumstances.
EXERCISES	To provide you with a selection of problems which are representative of homework assignments which an introductory accounting student may encounter.
MULTIPLE CHOICE	To provide you with a selection of multiple-choice questions which are representative of common exam questions covering topics in the chapter.
PURPOSES	To identify the essence of each question or exercise and to link them to study objectives.
SOLUTIONS	To show you the appropriate solution for each exercise and multiple choice question presented.
EXPLANATIONS	To give you the details of how selected solutions were derived and to explain why things are done as shown.
APPROACHES	To coach you on the particular model, computational format, or other strategy to be used to solve particular problems. To teach you how to analyze and solve multiple-choice questions.

This book will be a welcome teaching/learning aid because it provides you with the opportunity to solve accounting problems in addition to the ones assigned by your instructor without having to rely on your teacher for solutions. Many of the exercises and questions contained herein are very similar to items in your accounting principles textbook; the difference is, the ones in this book are accompanied with detailed clearly-laid out solutions.

The use of the multiple choice questions in this volume and the related suggestions on how to approach them can easily increase your ability (and confidence in your ability) to deal with exam questions of this variety.

We give special thanks to Chelsea Hunt for her editorial assistance and supportive role in the completion of this workbook. We appreciate the help of Mary Ann Benson who skillfully prepared the manuscript and performed the composition of this book. We are thankful to James Hunt for his support in this project. We also thank James Emig of Villanova University for his assistance in the accuracy review of the manuscript of this new edition.

Marilyn F. Hunt   Donald E. Kieso
Jerry J. Weygandt   Paul D. Kimmel

HOW TO STUDY ACCOUNTING

The successful study of accounting requires a different approach than most other subjects. In addition to reading a chapter, applying the material through the completion of exercises or problems is necessary to develop a true and lasting understanding of the concepts introduced in the text chapter. The study of accounting principles is a combination of theory and practice; theory describes what to do and why, and practice is the application of guidelines to actual situations. We use illustrations (practice) to demonstrate how theory works and we use theory to explain why something is done in practice. Therefore, it is impossible to separate the two in the study of accounting.

Learning accounting is a cumulative process. It is difficult to master Chapter 4 until you are thoroughly familiar with Chapters 1-3, and so on. Therefore, it is imperative that you keep up with class assignments. And because accounting is a technical subject, you must pay particular attention to terminology.

Accounting is the language of business. It is an exciting subject that provides a challenge for most business majors. Your ultimate success in life may well depend on your ability to grasp financial data. The effort you expend now will provide rewards for years to come.

We encourage you to follow the four steps for study outlined below to give yourself the best possible chance for a successful learning experience and to make the most efficient use of your time. These steps provide a system of study for each new chapter in your text.

Step 1
- Scan the study objectives in the text.
- Read the concepts for review. Look up and review any items with which you are not thoroughly familiar.
- Scan the chapter (or chapter section) rather quickly.
- Glance over the questions at the end of the chapter.

This first step will give you an overview of the material to be mastered.

Step 2
- Read the assigned pages slowly.
- Use the marginal notes to review and to locate topics within each chapter.
- Study carefully and mark for later attention any portions not clearly understood.
- Use the Demonstration Problem at the end of the text chapter.
- Pay particular attention to examples and illustrations.
- Try to formulate tentative answers to end-of-chapter questions.

During this phase, you will be filling in the "outline" you formed in Step 1. Most of the details will fall into place during this part of your study. The remaining steps are necessary, however, for a keen understanding of the subject.

Step 3
- Carefully read the **Overview, Study Objectives,** and **Tips** sections of this *Problem Solving Survival Guide* volume.
- Do the **Exercises** in the *Problem Solving Survival Guide* that pertain to the same study objectives as your homework assignments. Review the relevant **Illustrations** in this book.
- Do the **Multiple-Choice Type Questions** in the *Problem Solving Survival Guide* that pertain to the same study objectives as your homework assignments. Also do the relevant Self-Study Questions (multiple choice) at the end of the chapter in the text.

- Refer back to the sections of the chapter in the text that you marked as unclear if any. It is likely that any confusion or questions on your part will have been cleared up through your work in the *Problem Solving Survival Guide* book. If a section remains unclear, carefully reread it and rework relevant pages of the *Problem Solving Survival Guide.*
- Repeat this process for each assigned topic area.

Step 4 • Write out formal answers to homework assignments in the text.
This step is crucial because you find out whether you can independently **apply** the material you have been studying to fresh situations. You may find it necessary to go back to the text and/or *Problem Solving Survival Guide* to restudy certain sections. This is common and merely shows that the study assignments are working for you.

Additional comments pertaining to Step 3 and your usage of this *Problem Solving Survival Guide* volume are as follows:

- The **Study Objectives** and **Tips** sections along with **Illustrations** will aid your understanding and retention of the material. **Exercises** provide examples of application of the text material. These should be very valuable in giving you guidance in completing homework assignments which are often similar in nature and content.

- The **Approach** stated for an exercise or question is likely the most valuable feature of this *Problem Solving Survival Guide* volume because it tells you how to **think** through the situation at hand. This thought process can then be used for similar situations. It is impossible to illustrate every situation you may encounter. You can, however, handle new situations by simply applying what you know and making modifications where appropriate. Many students make the mistake of attempting to memorize their way through an accounting book. That too is an impossible feat. **Do not rely on memorization.** If this material is going to be useful to you, you must **think** about what you are reading and always be thinking of **why** things are as they are. If you know the reasoning for a particular accounting treatment, it will be much easier to remember that treatment and reconstruct it even weeks after your initial study of it.

- **Explanations** are provided for exercise and questions. These are very detailed so that you will thoroughly understand what is being done and why. These details will serve you well when you complete your homework assignments.

- Always make an honest effort to solve the exercises and answer the questions contained in this *Problem Solving Survival Guide* volume **before** you look at the solutions. Usage in this manner will maximize the benefits you can expect to reap from this book.

- The **Multiple-Choice Type Questions** are self-tests to give you immediate feedback on how well you understand the material. Study the **Approaches** suggested for answering these questions in the *Problem Solving Survival Guide.* Practice them when answering the multiple choice questions in the text. Apply them when taking examinations. By doing so, you will learn to calmly, methodically, and successfully process examination questions. This will definitely improve your exam scores.

- When you work an **Exercise** in the *Problem Solving Survival Guide* or in the text, always read the instructions **before** you read all of the given data. This allows you to determine what you are to accomplish. Therefore, as you now read through the data, you can begin to process it because you can determine its significance and relevance. If you read the data before the instructions, you are likely to waste your time because you will have to reread the facts once you find out what you are to do with them. Also, more importantly, you are likely to begin to anticipate what the problem is about, which will often cause you to do things other than what is requested in the question.

Good luck and best wishes for a positive learning experience!

HOW TO APPROACH A MULTIPLE CHOICE EXAMINATION

1. Work questions in the order in which they appear on the exam. If a question looks too long or difficult and you choose to skip over it, put a big question mark in the margin to remind yourself to return to that question after others are completed. Also put a mark in the margin for any question meriting additional review at the end of the exam period.

2. Do not look at the answer choices until you have thoroughly processed the question stem (see 3 and 4 below). The wrong answers are called "distracters". The manner in which these "distractors" are developed causes them to likely mislead you or cause you to misinterpret the question if you read them too early in the process.

3. Read each question very carefully. Start with the requirement or essence of the question first (this is usually the last sentence or last phrase of the stem of the question) so that you immediately focus on the question's intent. Now as you read through the rest of the stem and encounter data, you can tell which data are relevant. Underline keywords and important facts. Be especially careful to note exception words such as **not**. Prepare intermediary solutions as you read the question. Identify pertinent information with notations in the margin of the exam. If a set of data is the basis for two or more questions, read the requirements of each of the questions **before** reading the data and before beginning to work on the first question (sometimes the questions can be worked simultaneously or you may find it easier to work them out of order).

4. Anticipate the answer before looking at the alternative solutions. Recall the applicable definition, concept, principle, rule, model, or format. If the question deals with a computation, perform the computation. Use abbreviations to descibe each component of your computation; this will greatly aid you in following your work and staying on target with the question.

5. Read the answers and select the best answer choice. For computational questions, if the answer you have computed is not among the choices, check your math and the logic of your solution.

6. When you have completed all questions, review each question again to verify your choices. Reread the question requirement, scan the data, look at your selected answer, scan your work, and determine the reasonableness of your choice.

CHAPTER 1

. . . .

ACCOUNTING IN ACTION

OVERVIEW

You and every other member of society depend on information to function efficiently and effectively. For example, people who invest in business enterprises use economic information to guide their decisions about future financial possibilities. Information about the effects of past actions is accumulated to serve as an aid in making better decisions in the future.

As a financial information system, accounting is the process of identifying, recording, and communicating the economic events of an organization. In this chapter, we: (1) introduce the subject of accounting and GAAP (generally accepted accounting principles), (2) discuss the basic accounting equation and the effects of transactions on its elements, and (3) examine the composition of the four general purpose financial statements required for business enterprises.

SUMMARY OF LEARNING OBJECTIVES

1. **Explain what accounting is.** Accounting is an information system that identifies, records, and communicates the economic events of an organization (business or nonbusiness) to interested users.

2. **Identify the users and uses of accounting.** The major users and uses of accounting are as follows: (a) Management uses accounting information in planning, controlling, and evaluating business operations. (b) Investors (owners) decide whether to buy, hold, or sell their financial interests on the basis of accounting data. (c) Creditors (suppliers and bankers) evaluate the risks of granting credit or lending money on the basis of the accounting information. Other groups that use accounting information are taxing authorities, regulatory agencies, customers, labor unions, and economic planners.

3. **Understand why ethics is a fundamental business concept.** Ethics are the standards of conduct by which actions are judged as right or wrong. Effective financial reporting depends on sound ethical behavior.

4. **Explain generally accepted accounting principles.** Generally accepted accounting principles are a common set of standards used by accountants.

5. **Explain the monetary unit assumption and the economic entity assumption.** The monetary unit assumption requires that companies include in the accounting records only transaction data that can be expressed in terms of money. The economic entity assumption requires that the activities of each economic entity be kept separate from the activities of its owners(s) and other economic entities.

6. **State the accounting equation, and define its components.** The basic accounting equation is:

ASSETS = LIABILITIES + OWNER'S EQUITY

Assets are resources a business owns. Liabilities are claims on total assets. Owner's equity is the ownership claim on total assets.

The expanded accounting equation is:

ASSETS = LIABILITIES + OWNER'S CAPITAL – OWNER'S DRAWINGS
+ REVENUES - EXPENSES

Owner's capital is the amount of assets the owner has put into the business. Owner's drawings are the amounts of assets the owner withdraws for personal use. Revenues are increases in assets from income-earning activities; Expenses are the cost of assets consumed or services used in the process of earning revenue.

7. **Analyze the effect of business transactions on the accounting equation.** Each business transaction must have a dual effect on the basic accounting equation. For example, if an individual asset increases, there must be a corresponding (1) decrease in another asset, (2) increase in a specific liability, or (3) increase in owner's equity.

8. **Understand the four financial statements and how they are prepared.** An income statement presents the revenues and expenses of a company for a specified period of time. An owner's equity statement summarizes the changes in owner's equity that have occurred during a given period of time. A balance sheet reports the assets, liabilities, and owner's equity of a business at a specific date. A statement of cash flows summarizes information about the cash inflows (receipts) and outflows (payments) for a specific period of time.

*9. **Explain the career opportunities in accounting.** Accounting offers many different jobs in fields such as public and private accounting, governmental, and forensic accounting. Accounting is a popular major because there are many different types of jobs, with unlimited potential for career advancement.

*This material appears in the **Appendix 1A** in the text.

TIPS ON CHAPTER TOPICS

TIP: Accounting is the language of business. Thus, the more you learn and understand about accounting and its usefulness, the better you will be able to succeed in any business endeavor, regardless of your major field of study or job title.

TIP: When you encounter a transaction, always analyze it in terms of its effects on the elements of the basic accounting equation (or **balance sheet equation**). For your analysis to be complete, it must maintain balance in the basic accounting equation. The **basic accounting equation** is as follows:

ASSETS = LIABILITIES + OWNER'S EQUITY

Assets are economic resources. Liabilities and owner's equity are sources of resources; liabilities are creditor sources, and owner's equity represents owner sources (owner investments and undistributed profits).

TIP: There are three types of business organizations: proprietorships, partnerships, and corporations. Ignoring the specific type of organization of a particular entity, we can express its basic accounting equation as shown in the **TIP** above. If the entity is a corporation, the **owners' equity** is called **stockholders' equity**; if the entity is a partnership, the owners' equity is called **partners' equity**; if the entity is a proprietorship, the residual equity is called **owner's equity** or **capital**. The emphasis in this textbook is on the proprietorship form of organization.

TIP: The balance of liabilities and the balance of owner's equity at a point in time simply serve as scorecards of the total amounts of unspecified assets which have come about from creditor sources (liabilities) and owner sources (owner's equity). Thus, you can **not** determine the amount of cash (or any other specific asset) held by an entity by looking at the balance of owner's equity or liabilities. You must look at the listing of individual assets on the balance sheet to determine the amount of cash owned.

TIP: Like any other discipline, accounting has its own vocabulary. In order for you to be able to understand what you read in subsequent chapters of this book, it is imperative that you master the new terms explained in this chapter. If you are not thoroughly familiar with the basic concepts used to explain more advanced material, you will likely have an erroneous interpretation of that later material. For each chapter in your text, make it a habit to study the glossary until you master the new terms being introduced.

TIP: Accounting assumptions and principles are often referred to as accounting concepts.

TIP: Generally, accounting is based on completed transactions. As a result, salaries which have been earned by employees (whether paid or not) must be accounted for presently, however, salaries to be earned by employees and paid by the entity in future periods are not reflected in the entity's statements until the future period in which they are incurred.

TIP: Read the Preface and How to Study Accounting. These precede **Chapter 1** of this Problem Solving Survival Guide.

EXERCISE 1-1

Purpose: (L.O. 6, 7) This exercise will test your understanding of the components of the basic accounting equation.

Instructions
A list of **independent** situations appears below. Answer each question posed.

1. The total assets of Douglas Company at December 31, 2014 are $380,000 and its total liabilities are $150,000 at that same date. **Question:** What is the amount of Douglas Company's total owner's equity at December 31, 2014?

   Answer: _____

2. The total assets of Missy Company are $400,000 at December 31, 2014, and its total owner's equity is $280,000 at the same date. **Question:** What is the amount of Missy Company's total liabilities at December 31, 2014?

   Answer: _____

3. The total liabilities of Jeter Company are $128,000 at December 31, 2014. Total owner's equity for the company is $220,000 at that same date. **Question:** What is the amount of total assets for the company at December 31, 2014?

   Answer: _____

4. The total liabilities of Butler Company are $80,000. The total assets of the company are three times the amount of its total liabilities. **Question:** What is the amount of Butler Company's total owner's equity?

   Answer: _____

5. At January 1, 2014, Molly Company had total assets of $600,000 and total liabilities of $340,000. During the calendar year of 2014, total assets increased $80,000, and total liabilities decreased $30,000. **Question 1:** What was the change in owner's equity during 2014?

   Answer 1: _____

   Question 2: What was the amount of owner's equity at December 31, 2014?

   Answer 2: _____

6. At January 1, 2014, Skipper Company had total assets of $500,000 and total owner's equity of $280,000. During 2014, total assets decreased $40,000, and total liabilities decreased $22,000. **Question 1:** What was the amount of total liabilities at January 1, 2014?

Answer 1: _____

Question 2: What was the change during 2014 in total owner's equity?

Answer 2: _____

Question 3: What was the total owner's equity at December 31, 2014?

Answer 3: _____

SOLUTION TO EXERCISE 1-1

Approach: Write down the basic accounting equation:

ASSETS = LIABILITIES + OWNER'S EQUITY
or
A = L + OE

Fill in the amounts given and use your knowledge of algebra to solve for any unknown.

Explanation:
1. Assets = Liabilities + Owner's Equity
   $380,000 = $150,000 + OE
   $380,000 - $150,000 = OE
   $230,000 = OE
   <u>$230,000</u> = Owner's Equity

TIP:	Recall that algebraic rules require the change in a number's sign when moved to the other side of the equals sign. Thus, a positive $150,000 becomes a negative $150,000 when moved from the right side of the equation to the left side of the equation.

2. Assets = Liabilities + Owner's Equity
   $400,000 = L + $280,000
   $400,000 - $280,000 = L
   $120,000 = L
   <u>$120,000</u> = Liabilities

3.   Assets = Liabilities + Owner's Equity
     A = $128,000 + $220,000
     A = $348,000
     Assets = $348,000

4.   Assets = Liabilities + Owner's Equity
     3 (L) = L + OE
     3 ($80,000) = $80,000 + OE
     $240,000 = $80,000 + OE
     $240,000 - $80,000 = OE
     $160,000 = OE
     $160,000 = Owner's Equity

5.   (1) $\Delta A = \Delta L + \Delta OE$
           ↑$80,000 = ↓$30,000 + ΔOE
           ↑$80,000 + ↑$30,000 = ΔOE
           ↑$110,000 = ΔOE
           Increase of $110,000 = Change in Owner's Equity

TIP: When the ↓$30,000 is moved from the right side of the "=" to the left side of the equation, its sign changes so it becomes a ↑$30,000.

TIP: The basic accounting equation is applied at a specific point in time. When you have the facts for the equation components at two different points in time for the same entity (such as amounts as of the beginning of a year and amounts as of the end of the year), you can modify the basic accounting equation to reflect that total changes in assets equals total changes in liabilities plus total changes in owner's equity. Using the symbol Δ to designate change, the following equation also holds true:

$$\Delta A = \Delta L + \Delta OE$$

---

     (2)   Assets = Liabilities + Owner's Equity
           $600,000 = $340,000 + OE
           $600,000 - $340,000 = OE at January 1, 2014
           $260,000 = Owner's Equity at January 1, 2014

Owner's Equity at January 1, 2014	$260,000
Increase in Owner's Equity during 2014 (Answer 1)	110,000
Owner's Equity at December 31, 2014	$370,000

OR

Assets at January 1, 2014	$600,000
Increase in Assets during 2014	80,000
Total Assets at December 31, 2014	$680,000

Liabilities at January 1, 2014	$340,000
Decrease in Liabilities during 2014	(30,000)
Total Liabilities at December 31, 2014	$310,000

Assets = Liabilities + Owner's Equity
$680,000 = $310,000 + OE
$680,000 - $310,000 = OE
$370,000 = OE
$370,000 = Owner's Equity at December 31, 2014

6. (1) Assets = Liabilities + Owner's Equity
$500,000 = L + $280,000
$500,000 - $280,000 = L
$220,000 = L
$220,000 = Liabilities at January 1, 2014

(2) $\Delta A = \Delta L + \Delta OE$
$\downarrow$$40,000 = $\downarrow$$22,000 + ΔOE
$\downarrow$$40,000 + $\uparrow$$22,000 = ΔOE
$\downarrow$$18,000 = ΔOE
Decrease of $18,000 = Change in Owner's Equity during 2014

(3)
Owner's Equity at January 1, 2014	$280,000
Decrease in Owner's Equity during 2014 (Answer 2)	(18,000)
Owner's Equity at December 31, 2014	$262,000

OR

Assets at January 1, 2014	$500,000
Decrease in Assets during 2014	(40,000)
Assets at December 31, 2014	$460,000

Liabilities at January 1, 2012 (Answer 1)	$220,000
Decrease in Liabilities during 2014	(22,000)
Liabilities at December 31, 2014	$198,000

Assets = Liabilities + Owner's Equity
$460,000 = $198,000 + OE
$460,000 - $198,000 = OE
$262,000 = Owner's Equity at December 31, 2014

EXERCISE 1-2

Purpose: (L.O. 7) This exercise illustrates that:
(1) Each transaction has a dual effect on the basic accounting equation.
(2) The basic accounting equation remains in balance after each transaction is properly analyzed and recorded.

Nick Cannon owns and operates the Mariah Carey Motorcycle Repair Shop. A list of the transactions that take place in August 2014 follows:

1. August 1 Nick begins the business by depositing $5,000 of his personal funds in the business bank account.

2. August 2 Nick rents space for the shop behind a strip mall and pays August rent of $800.

3. August 3 Nick purchases supplies for cash, $3,000.

4. August 4 Nick pays Cupboard News, a local newspaper, $300 for an ad appearing in the Sunday edition.

5. August 5 Nick repairs a cycle for a customer. The customer pays cash of $1,300 for services rendered.

6. August 11 Nick repairs a cycle for a customer, Paula Deen, on credit, $500.

7. August 13 Nick purchases supplies for $900 by paying cash of $200 and charging the rest on account.

8. August 14 Nick repairs a Harley for Zonie Kinkennon, a champion rider, for $1,900. Nick collects $1,000 in cash and puts the rest on account.

9. August 22 Nick takes home supplies from the shop that had cost $100 when purchased on August 3.

10. August 24 Nick collects cash of $400 from Paula Deen.

11. August 28 Nick pays $200 to Local Electric Co. for utilities incurred during the month of August.

12. August 29 Nick repairs a cycle for Rachael Ray for $1,200 on account.

13. August 31 Nick transfers $500 from the business bank account to his personal bank account.

Instructions

Prepare a tabular analysis of the transactions above to indicate the effect of each of the transactions on the various balance sheet items. Use a "+" to indicate an increase and a "-" to indicate a decrease. Indicate the new balances after each transaction. In the owner's equity column, indicate the cause of each change in the owner's total claim on assets. Use the following column headings:

		ASSETS		=	LIABIL-ITIES	+	OWNER'S EQUITY
Transaction	Cash	+ Receivable	Accounts + Supplies	=	Accounts Payable	+	N. Cannon Capital

SOLUTION TO EXERCISE 1-2

Transaction	Cash	+	Accounts Receivable	+	Supplies	=	Accounts Payable	+	N. Cannon Capital	Explanation
(1)	+$5,000					=			+$5,000	Owner's Investment
(2)	-800								-800	Rent Expense
Balances	4,200					=			4,200	
(3)	-3,000				+$3,000					
Balances	1,200	+			3,000	=			4,200	
(4)	-300								-300	Advertising Expense
Balances	900	+			3,000	=			3,900	
(5)	+1,300								+1,300	Service Revenue
Balances	2,200	+			3,000	=			5,200	
(6)			+$ 500						+ 500	Service Revenue
Balances	2,200	+	500	+	3,000	=			5,700	
(7)	-200				+900		+$700			
Balances	2,000	+	500	+	3,900	=	700	+	5,700	
(8)	+1,000		+900						1,900	Service Revenue
Balances	3,000	+	1,400	+	3,900		700	+	7,600	
(9)					-100				-100	Owner's Drawings
Balances	3,000	+	1,400	+	3,800	=	700	+	7,500	
(10)	+400		-400							
Balances	3,400	+	1,000	+	3,800	=	700	+	7,500	
(11)	-200								-200	Utilities Expense
Balances	3,200	+	1,000	+	3,800	=	700	+	7,300	
(12)			1,200						+1,200	Service Revenue
Balances	3,200		2,200	+	3,800		700	+	8,500	
(13)	-500								- 500	Owner's Drawings
Balances	$2,700	+	$2,200	+	$3,800	=	$700	+	$8,000	

TIP: Make sure the balances at any given point in time reflect equality in the components of the basic accounting equation. If equality does not exist, the work is incomplete or some error has been made. After all transactions are analyzed Mariah Carey Repair Shop, total assets = $8,700, total liabilities = $700, and total owner's equity = $8,000. The equation is in balance.

TIP: Notice transaction number 7. Even though there were three items affected (Cash, Supplies, and Accounts Payable), the analysis of the transaction maintains balance in the basic accounting equation. Total assets increased by $700 ($900 - $200), and liabilities increased by $700.

TIP: Notice transaction number 8. Even though there were three items affected (Cash, Accounts Receivable, and Nick Cannon Capital), the analysis of the transaction maintains balance in the equation. Total assets increased by $1,900 ($1,000 + $900), and owner's equity increased by $1,900.

Approach: Take each transaction and analyze it separately. Determine if the transaction involves the following:

Assets: Assets are resources owned or controlled by a business. Thus, they are the things of value used in carrying out such activities as production, consumption, and exchange. As asset represents a future economic benefit that will eventually result in an inflow of cash to the holder.

Liabilities: Liabilities are creditor sources of resources or creditors' claims on total assets. They are existing debts and obligations which will become due in the future and will normally require an outlay of cash to be liquidated.

Owner's Equity: The ownership claim on total assets is known as owner's equity. Total assets less total liabilities equals total owner's equity. Accountants often refer to total owner's equity by use of the word **capital.** The components of owner's equity are as follows:

(1) **Invested capital**—the owner's investment in the business.
(2) **Earned capital**—business earnings retained for use in the business; net income since the inception of the business less total owner withdrawals (drawings) since the inception of the business.

    (a) **Net income** is the amount of excess of total revenues over total expenses for a particular period of time. (An excess of total expenses over total revenues for a particular period of time is referred to as **net loss.**)

    (b) **Revenues** are the gross increases in owner's equity resulting from business activities entered into for the purpose of earning income. Generally, revenues result from the sale of merchandise (sales), the performance of services (service revenue), the rental of property (rental revenue), or the lending of money (interest revenue).

    (c) **Expenses** are the costs of assets consumed or services used up in the process of earning revenue. Expenses are the decreases in owner's equity that result from operating the business. Expenses represent actual or expected cash outflows (payments).

    (d) **Drawings** occur when an owner withdraws cash or other assets for personal use. Owner withdrawals cause a decrease in total owner's equity.

If a transaction involves assets or liabilities, identify which particular asset or liability is affected and in what direction and by what amount. If a transaction involves owner's equity, identify the specific reason for that change—owner investment, owner withdrawal, revenue earned, or expense incurred. Be sure to classify each revenue and expense item by type (for example, salaries expense or rent expense). Also identify the amount and direction of each change in owner's equity.

TIP: A keen understanding of the definitions for the terms listed above (especially assets, liabilities, owner's equity, revenues, and expenses) is vitally important for your study of accounting. Proceed with your reading of the forthcoming chapters **only** after you have mastered these terms! As you progress through the book, periodically return here to review these concepts.

ILLUSTRATION 1-1
MEASUREMENT PRINCIPLES (L.O. 4)

GAAP (generally accepted accounting principles) generally uses one of two measurement principles, the **historical cost principle** or the **fair value principle**. Selection of which principle to follow generally relates to trade-offs between relevance and faithful representation. **Relevance** means that financial information is capable of making a difference in a decision. **Faithful representation** means that the numbers and descriptions match what really existed or happened—it is factual.

The **historical cost principle** (or cost principle) dictates that companies record assets at their cost and continue to report assets at their cost over the time the assets are held. For example, if Staples purchases land for $60,000, the company initially reports it in its accounting records at $60,000. But what does Staples do if, by the end of the next year, the fair value of the land has increased to $80,000? Under the historical cost principle it continues to report the land at $60,000.

The **fair value principle** indicates that assets and liabilities should be reported at fair value (the price received to sell an asset or settle a liability). Fair value information may be more useful than historical cost for certain types of assets and liabilities. For example, certain investment securities are reported at fair value because market value information is often readily available for these types of assets. In choosing between cost and fair value, the FASB uses two qualities that make accounting information useful for decision making—relevance and faithful representation. In determining which measurement principle to use, the FASB weighs the factual nature of cost figures versus the relevance of fair value. In general, the FASB indicates that most assets must follow the cost principle because market values are not representationally faithful. Only in situations where assets are actively traded, such as investment securities, is the fair value principle applied.

TIP:	The cost of an asset is measured by the fair value of the asset (or the fair value of the consideration given in the exchange) at the date the item is acquired. Therefore an asset is always recorded at cost (which is equal to fair value) at the acquisition date. It is reported at a later date at either its original cost or at its current fair value, depending on which measurement principle is employed.

ILLUSTRATION 1-2
DUEL EFFECT OF TRANSACTIONS ON THE
BASIC ACCOUNTING EQUATION (L.O. 6, 7)

Each transaction affects items in the basic accounting equation in such a manner as to maintain equality in the basic accounting equation. The possible combinations of dual effects are illustrated below with examples of transactions that fit each category of combinations. Some examples are too advanced to be comprehended at this level in your accounting study so references are made to future chapters for those items. Do not attempt to research those items at this time—just accept the fact that in the future you will more readily understand those examples. These advanced examples are included here to show you that there are illustrations of every conceivable combination of dual effects on the equation.

Effects of Transaction on Basic Equation

Examples

1. $A = L + OE$
   $\uparrow \qquad \uparrow$

   a. Owner investment of personal assets into the business.
   b. Sale of services for cash or on account.

2. $A = L + OE$
   $\downarrow \qquad \downarrow$

   a. Owner withdrawal of assets from the business for personal use.
   b. Cash payment for various expenses, such as salaries and wages expense and advertising expense. (Also, **Chapter 3,** consumption of noncash assets in operations, such as the consumption of supplies.)

3. $A = L + OE$
   $\uparrow \quad \uparrow$

   a. Acquisition of any asset on credit. Borrowing money.

4. $A = L + OE$
   $\downarrow \quad \downarrow$

   a. Paying off any debt.

5. $A = L + OE$
   $\downarrow\uparrow$

   a. Exchanging any asset for another asset, such as purchase of equipment for cash or collection of an account receivable.

6. $A = L + OE$
   $\quad \uparrow\downarrow$

   a. Exchanging one liability for another, such as settling an account payable by issuing a note payable.

7. $A = L + OE$
   $\qquad \uparrow\downarrow$

   a. (**Chapter 14**—Corporation declares a stock dividend).

ILLUSTRATION 1-1 (Continued)

8. A = L + OE
        ↓   ↑

a. Liquidating a debt by giving an ownership interest in the entity.

b. (**Chapter 3**—Entity earns revenue after cash was previously received and recorded).

9. A = L + OE
        ↑   ↓

a. (**Chapter 14**—Corporation declares cash dividends on stock).

b. (**Chapter 3**—Incurring expense—consuming benefits in carrying out operations-- before paying for the goods or services, such as repairs made to an entity's equipment before the vendor is paid.)

TIP:	**Transactions** are the economic events of an entity recorded by accountants. Some events (happenings of consequence to an entity) are not measurable in terms of money and thus do not get recorded in the accounting records. Hiring employees, placing an order for supplies, greeting a customer and quoting prices for products are examples of activities that do not by themselves constitute transactions. When an event is identified as a transaction, it must be measured (i.e., the appropriate dollar amount must be determined) before it can be recorded.
TIP:	Examine the examples. Some of them are preceded by an a. and some are preceded by a b. Notice that all of the a. type examples have no impact on the income statement; whereas all of the b. type examples do impact the income statement. All examples above impact the balance sheet.
TIP:	**A revenue type transaction** will always cause an increase in owner's equity. In addition, it will cause either an increase in assets or a decrease in liabilities (the former is the more common effect). An **expense type transaction** will always cause a decrease in owner's equity. In addition, it will cause either a decrease in assets or an increase in liabilities (the former is the more common effect).
TIP:	A single transaction may affect more than two items in the basic accounting equation and still maintain equality in the equation. For example, if a company received a $700 bill for repairs to a copier and paid $500 cash to the vendor along with a promise to pay the remaining $200 in one month, the transaction would affect the components of the equation as follows:

A   =   L   +   OE
↓$500 =   ↑$200 +   ↓$700

The equation remains in balance.

TIP:	As you progress through your accounting course(s) and possibly a career in business, you will constantly encounter new transactions and familiar transactions with a new twist. These unfamiliar situations can be addressed with confidence if you carefully analyze the effects of each transaction on the basic accounting equation.

EXERCISE 1-3

Purpose: (L.O. 8) This exercise will provide you with an illustration of an income statement, owner's equity statement, a balance sheet, and a statement of cash flows.

The Mariah Carey Repair Shop in Monrovia, California, prepares financial statements each month.

Instructions
Refer to the **Solution to Exercise 1-2** above. Use the information displayed to:
(a)   Prepare an income statement for the month of August 2014
(b)   Prepare an owner's equity statement for the month of August 2014
(c)   Prepare a balance sheet at August 31, 2014
(d)   Prepare a statement of cash flows for the month of August 2014

Approach: Think about what each statement is to report. A summary is as follows:
(a)   The **income statement** reports the results of operations for a period of time. Therefore, the income statement in this exercise reports revenues and expenses for August.
(b)   The **owner's equity statement** reports all changes in owner's equity for a period of time. It starts with the balance of owner's equity at the beginning of the period. It reports withdrawals (drawings), additional owner investments and includes the net income (or net loss) figure from the income statement to arrive at the balance of owner's equity at the end of the period.
(c)   The **balance sheet** reports on the financial position at a point in time (August 31 in this case). It reports assets, liabilities, and owner's equity. The balance of owner's equity used here comes from the owner's equity statement.
(d)   The **statement of cash flows** reports the cash inflows and cash outflows during a period of time and classifies these flows into three activities: (1) operating, (2) investing, and (3) financing.

SOLUTION TO EXERCISE 1-3

(a)

MARIAH CAREY REPAIR SHOP
Income Statement
For the Month Ended August 31, 2014

Revenues		
Service revenue		$4,900*
Expenses		
Rent expense	$800	
Advertising expense	300	
Utilities expense	200	
Total expenses		1,300
Net income		$3,600

*Computation: $1,300 + $500 + $1,900 + $1,200 = $4,900.

TIP: Even though there were four separate revenue transactions, they are reported in the aggregate on the income statement. Also notice that there is no distinction made on the income statement between cash revenue transactions and revenue transactions that are on account.

TIP: As you might be wondering, there are likely some other expenses incurred by the Mariah Carey Motorcycle Repair Shop during August that have not yet been addressed. For example, some supplies were probably consumed in making repairs. Also, expenses such as salaries and wages were likely consumed in August. These situations will be explained in **Chapter 3.**

TIP: **Drawings** are often called **owner's drawings** or simply **withdrawals.** They do **not** appear on the income statement because they are not expenses—they have no impact on operations. Withdrawals are a distribution of company profits and not a determinant of profits (net income).

(b)

MARIAH CAREY REPAIR SHOP
Owner's Equity Statement
For the Month Ended August 31, 2014

Owner's Capital, August 1, 2014	$ 0
Add: Investments	5,000
Net income for August 2014	3,600
	8,600
Less: Drawings	600*
Owner's Capital, August 31, 2014	$8,000

*Computation: $100 + $500 = $600.

(c)

MARIAH CAREY REPAIR SHOP
Balance Sheet
August 31, 2014

Assets

Cash	$2,700
Accounts receivable	2,200
Supplies	3,800
Total assets	$8,700

Liabilities and Owner's Equity

Liabilities	
Accounts payable	$ 700
Owner's Equity	
Owner's Capital	8,000
Total liabilities and owner's equity	$8,700

TIP: Supplies refers to supplies on hand. Therefore, this item is an asset.

(d)

MARIAH CAREY REPAIR SHOP
Statement of Cash Flows
For the Month Ended August 31, 2014

Cash flows from operating activities		
Cash receipts from customers		$2,700
Cash payments for expenses and supplies		(4,500)
Net cash used by operating activities		(1,800)
Cash flows from investing activities		
[None illustrated here]		
Net cash provided by investing activities		0
Cash flows from financing activities		
Investments by owner	$5,000	
Drawings by owner	(500)	
Net cash provided by financing activities		4,500
Net increase in cash		2,700
Cash at the beginning of the period		0
Cash at the end of the period		$2,700

Computations:
Cash receipts from customers: $1,300 + $1,000 + $400 = $2,700.
Cash payments for expenses and supplies: $800 + $3,000 + $300 + $200 + $200
= $4,500.

TIP:	Notice that although the owner's capital balance is $8,000, the balance of cash is far less than that. Also notice what gave rise to that $8,000 balance of owner's equity: the owner invested $5,000, the company has operated at a profit of $3,600 (total revenues exceeded total expenses) since its inception, and total company earnings ($3,600) exceed total owner's drawings ($600). Therefore, the ending owner's equity stems from owner investments of $5,000 and undistributed earnings of $3,000.
TIP:	Think about the logical order in which the financial statements are prepared: income statement then owner's equity statement and then balance sheet. That's because the income statement provides the net income figure used to compute the change in owner's equity. All changes in owner's equity are reported on the owner's equity statement to determine the ending balance for owner's equity. That ending owner's equity balance is then used as a necessary component of the balance sheet.
TIP:	Notice that everything on the balance sheet in the liabilities and owner's equity section lacks physical existence. The balance of Accounts Payable represents the total amount owed at the balance sheet date to suppliers of goods and services because of past transactions. The balance of Owner's Capital tells us the dollar amount of the entity's resources at the balance sheet date which have resulted from the owner's investments and the entity's profitable operations (i.e., profits that have not been distributed to the owner). Notice that in this particular situation the ending balance of owner's equity exceeds the amount of cash. Also, the amount of net income for the month of August exceeds the amount of cash at August 31, 2014.
TIP:	The **owner's equity statement** is often called the **statement of owner's equity.**

EXERCISE 1-4

Purpose: (L.O. 8) This exercise will give you practice in classifying items on financial statements.

_____	1.	Cash	_____ 21.	Sales revenue
_____	2.	Accounts payable	_____ 22.	Insurance expense
_____	3.	Equipment	_____ 23.	Rent expense
_____	4.	Utilities expense	_____ 24.	Rent revenue
_____	5.	Owner's capital	_____ 25.	Interest expense
_____	6.	Salaries and wages payable	_____ 26.	Interest revenue
_____	7.	Salaries and wages expense	_____ 27.	Ticket revenue
_____	8.	Advertising expense	_____ 28.	Supplies expense
_____	9.	Bonds payable	_____ 29.	Interest receivable
_____	10.	Supplies	_____ 30.	Service revenue
_____	11.	Notes payable	_____ 31.	Subscription revenue
_____	12.	Notes receivable	_____ 32.	Operating expenses
_____	13.	Owner's drawings	_____ 33.	Prepaid insurance
_____	14.	Dividend revenue	_____ 34.	Property tax expense
_____	15.	Miscellaneous expense	_____ 35.	Mortgage payable
_____	16.	Travel expense	_____ 36.	Utilities payable
_____	17.	Prepaid rent	_____ 37.	Dividends payable
_____	18.	Property taxes payable	_____ 38.	Prepaid advertising
_____	19.	Delivery expense	_____ 39.	Car rental expense
_____	20.	Income tax expense	_____ 40.	Buildings

Instructions

Indicate how each of the above should be classified on a set of financial statements. Use the following abbreviations to communicate your responses.

A	Asset on the balance sheet
L	Liability on the balance sheet
OE	Owner's equity balance on the balance sheet
D	Drawings on the owner's equity statement
R	Revenue on the income statement
E	Expense on the income statement

SOLUTION TO EXERCISE 1-4

Approach: Look for the key word or words, if any, in each individual item. For example, a list of key words or phrases follows along with the likely classifications:

Key word (phrases)	Classification
Revenue	Revenue on the income statement
Expense	Expense on the income statement
Earned	Revenue on the income statement
Incurred	Expense on the income statement
On hand	Asset on the balance sheet
Prepaid	Asset on the balance sheet
Receivable	Asset on the balance sheet
Payable	Liability on the balance sheet

1.	A	9.	L	17.	A	25.	E	33.	A
2.	L	10.	A	18.	L	26.	R	34.	E
3.	A	11.	L	19.	E	27.	R	35.	L
4.	E	12	A	20.	E	28.	E	36.	L
5.	OE	13.	D	21.	R	29.	A	37.	L
6.	L	14.	R	22.	E	30.	R	38.	A
7.	E	15.	E	23.	E	31.	R	39.	E
8.	E	16.	E	24.	R	32.	E	40.	A

TIP: Keep in mind that an asset is an item that offers probable future economic benefits. If something will assist the revenue generating process of a future accounting period, it is an asset.

TIP: You can determine the position of an entity in a particular transaction by the wording of the explanation. For example, we would use the item "bank loan payable" (a liability) if we had borrowed money from the bank. The bank would have "loan receivable" (an asset) item on their balance sheet. As another example, we would have "legal fees incurred" (an expense) on our income statement if we had used legal services. The law firm which provided the services would report a corresponding "legal fees earned" (revenue) item on its income statement.

EXERCISE 1-5

Purpose: (L.O. 6, 7, 8) This exercise reviews the basic accounting equation (A = L + OE) and the connection between the income statement and the balance sheet. The connection is a change in owner's equity due to the net income or net loss for the period.

The following data were extracted from the records of Handy Hernando, a sole proprietorship:

Total assets, beginning of the period	$250,000
Total liabilities, beginning of the period	90,000
Owner's drawings during the period	75,000
Total assets, end of the period	270,000
Total liabilities, end of the period	95,000
Owner's investment during the period	25,000

Instructions
Compute the amount of net income (or net loss) for the period. Show your computations.

SOLUTION TO EXERCISE 1-5

Approach: The question asks you to solve for net income; however, no information is given regarding revenues and expenses for the period. Only balance sheet data and transactions affecting owner's equity are given. Net income (or net loss) for a period is one reason for change in the balance of owner's equity. Write down the items that reconcile the beginning owner's equity balance with the ending owner's equity balance, enter the amounts known, compute beginning and ending owner's equity balances by use of the basic accounting equation, and then solve for the amount of net income.

Beginning owner's equity	$160,000[a]
Additional owner's investment	25,000
Owner's drawings during the period	(75,000)
Subtotal	110,000
Net income (loss) for the period	+ __X__
Ending owner's equity	$175,000[b]
Solving for X, net income =	$65,000

[a]A = L + OE
$250,000 = $90,000 + ?
Beginning owner's equity = $160,000

[b]A = L + OE
$270,000 = $95,000 + ?
Ending owner's equity = $175,000

TIP:	Solving an exercise of this type requires a lot of thought and a clear understanding of the relationships between and among the financial statements.

EXERCISE 1-6

Purpose: (S.O. 1 thru 8) This exercise will quiz you about terminology used in this chapter.

A list of accounting terms with which you should be familiar appears below.

Accounting
Assets
*Auditing
Balance sheet
Basic accounting equation
Bookkeeping
Convergence
Corporation
Drawings
Economic entity assumption
Ethics
Expanded accounting equation
Expenses
Fair value principle
Faithful representation
Financial accounting
Financial Accounting Standards Board
  (FASB)
*Forensic accounting
Generally accepted accounting principles
  (GAAP)
Historical cost principle
Income statement
International Accounting Standards Board (IASB)

International Financial Reporting
  Standards (IFRS)
Investments by owner
Liabilities
Managerial accounting
*Management consulting
Monetary unit assumption
Net income
Net loss
Owner's equity
Owner's equity statement
Partnership
*Private (or managerial) accounting
Proprietorship
*Public accounting
Relevance
Revenues
Sarbanes-Oxley Act (SOX)
Securities and Exchange Commission
  (SEC)
Statement of cash flows
*Taxation
Transactions

*These items appear in the **Appendix to Chapter 1.**

Instructions
For each item below, enter in the blank the term that is described.

1. _____The information system that identifies, records, and communicates the economic events of an organization to interested users.

2. _____An accounting principle that states that companies should record assets at their cost.

3. _____A financial statement that presents the revenues and expenses and resulting net income or net loss of a company for a specific period of time. Sometimes called the **operating statement.**

4. _____The gross increase in owner's equity resulting from business activities entered into for the purpose of earning income.

5. _____The cost of assets consumed or services used in the process of earning revenue.

6. _____Assets = Liabilities + Owner's equity.

7. _____Resources a business owns.

8. _____Creditor's claims on total assets.

9. _____The ownership claim on total assets. Sometimes called **net worth**.

10. _____A financial statement that reports the assets, liabilities, and owner's equity at a specific date. Sometimes called the **statement of financial position.**

11. _____Common standards that indicate how to report economic events.

12. _____A financial statement that summarizes the changes in owner's equity for a specific period of time.

13. _____An assumption stating that companies only include in the accounting records transaction data that can be expressed in terms of money.

14. _____An assumption that requires the activities of the entity be kept separate and distinct from the activities of its owner and all other economic activities.

15. _____The economic events of a business that are recorded by accountants.

16. _____Withdrawal of cash or other assets from an unincorporated business for the personal use of the owner(s).

17. _____A financial statement that provides information about the cash inflows (receipts) and cash outflows (payments) of an entity for a specific period of time.

18. _____The examination of financial statements by a certified public accountant in order to express an opinion as to the fairness of presentation.

19. _____An area of public accounting involving tax advice, tax planning, preparing tax returns, and representing clients before government agencies.

20. _____An area of public accounting ranging from development of accounting and computer systems to support services for marketing projects and merger and acquisition activities.

21. _____An area of accounting in which the accountant offers expert service to the general public.

22. _____The field of accounting that provides economic and financial information for managers and other internal users.

23. _____A private organization that establishes generally accepted accounting principles in the United States (GAAP)

24. _____A governmental agency that requires companies to file financial reports in accordance with generally accepted accounting principles.

25. _____The amount by which revenues exceed expenses for a specific period of time.

26. _____A business organized as a separate legal entity under state corporation law having ownership divided into transferable shares of stock.

27. _____An association of two or more persons to carry on as co-owners of a business.

28. _____A business owned by one person.

29. _____The amount of resources (assets) put into the business by the owner.

30. _____A part of accounting that involves only the recording of economic events.

31. _____The amount by which expenses exceed revenues for a specific period of time.

32. _____The standards of conduct by which one's actions are judged as right or wrong, honest or dishonest, fair or not fair.

33. _____The field of accounting that provides economic and financial information for investors, creditors, and other external users.

34. _____An area of accounting within a company that involves activities such as cost accounting, budgeting, design and support of accounting information systems, and tax planning and preparation.

35. _____An area of accounting that uses accounting, auditing, and investigative skills to conduct investigations into theft and fraud.

36. _____A law passed by Congress in 2002 to reduce unethical corporate behavior.

37. _____An accounting standard-setting body that issues standards adopted by many countries outside the United States.

38. _____Assets = Liabilities + Owner's Capital − Owner's Drawings + Revenues − Expenses.

39. _____The process of reducing the differences between GAAP and IFRS.

40. _____An accounting principle stating that assets and liabilities should be reported at fair value (the price received to sell an asset or settle a liability).

41. _____Numbers and descriptions match what really existed or happened—they are factual.

42. _____The field of accounting that provides internal reports to help users make decisions about their companies.

43. _____Financial information that is capable of making a difference in a decision.

44. _____International accounting standards set by the International Accounting Standards Board (IASB).

SOLUTION TO EXERCISE 1-6

1. Accounting
2. Historical cost principle
3. Income statement
4. Revenues
5. Expenses
6. Basic accounting equation
7. Assets
8. Liabilities
9. Owner's equity
10. Balance sheet
11. Generally accepted accounting principles
12. Owner's equity statement
13. Monetary unit assumption
14. Economic entity assumption
15. Transactions
16. Drawings
17. Statement of cash flows
18. Auditing
19. Taxation
20. Management consulting
21. Public accounting
22. Managerial accounting
23. Financial Accounting Standards Board (FASB)
24. Securities and Exchange Commission
25. Net income
26. Corporation
27. Partnership
28. Proprietorship
29. Investments by owner
30. Bookkeeping
31. Net loss
32. Ethics
33. Financial accounting
34. Private (or managerial) accounting
35. Forensic accounting
36. Sarbanes-Oxley Act (SOX)
37. International Accounting Standards Board (IASB)
38. Expanded accounting equation
39. Convergence
40. Fair value principle
41. Faithful representation
42. Managerial accounting
43. Relevance
44. International Financial Reporting Standards (IFRS)

ANALYSIS OF MULTIPLE-CHOICE TYPE QUESTIONS

1. (L.O. 4) The two organizations who are primarily responsible for establishing generally accepted accounting principles are
   a. The FASB and the FBI.
   b. The SEC and the IRS.
   c. The SEC and the FASB.
   d. The IRS and the publisher of the Wall Street Journal.

   Explanation: The Financial Accounting Standards Board (FASB) is a private organization that establishes broad reporting standards of general applicability as well as specific accounting rules. The Securities and Exchange Commission (SEC) is a governmental agency that requires companies filing financial reports with it to follow generally accepted accounting principles. In situations where no principles exist, the SEC often mandates that certain guidelines be used. In general, the FASB and the SEC work hand in hand to assure that timely and useful accounting principles are developed. (Solution = c)

2. (L.O. 5) Which accounting assumption or principle dictates that a business owner's personal expenses should not be recorded on the books of the business?
    a. Economic entity assumption.
    b. Monetary unit assumption.
    c. Historical cost principle.
    d. Basic accounting equation.

    Approach and Explanation: Briefly explain each answer selection. Compare your explanations with the question. The economic entity assumption requires that the activities of the entity be kept separate and distinct from (1) the activities of its owner, and (2) all other economic entities. The monetary unit assumption requires that only transaction data that can be expressed in terms of money be included in the accounting records and provides that all transactions and events can be measured in terms of a common denominator—units of money. The historical cost principle states that assets should be recorded at cost and indicates that cost is measured by the value exchanged at the time something is acquired. The basic accounting equation provides that total assets at a point in time equals total liabilities plus total owner's equity at the same point in time. (Solution = a.)

3. (L.O. 4) The Seller Company sold the Buyer Company a building on August 1, 2014. Buyer Company paid Seller Company $92,000 cash. The Seller Company had originally purchased the building in 2011 for $80,000. The county taxing authority showed an assessed valuation of $78,000 for the building for 2013 taxing purposes and an independent appraisal agency appraised it at $95,000 on July 15, 2014. The Buyer Company should record the building in their accounting books at:
    a. $78,000.
    b. $80,000.
    c. $92,000.
    d. $95,000.

    Approach and Explanation: Read the last sentence first. You can tell by that last sentence the Buyer is acquiring a building (an asset). Think about the **historical cost principle.** It provides that all assets be recorded at cost. Cost is measured by the value exchanged at the time something is acquired. In any exchange transaction, cost is therefore measured by the fair market value (cash equivalent value) of the consideration given or by the fair market value of the consideration received, whichever is more clearly (objectively) determinable. When cash is paid, there is no question about the cash value of the consideration given. Read the rest of the question. In this case, the cash payment of $92,000 clearly determines the cost of the building to the Buyer Company. (Solution = c.)

TIP:	The **historical cost principle** is often simply called the **cost principle.** Because of this principle, we typically report assets held at their cost, **not** their current market values. Generally, the balance sheet does not purport to reflect current market values. Cost is the value exchanged at the time something is acquired; thus cost equals the market value (sometimes called fair value or fair market value) at the date of acquisition.

4. (L.O. 8) The balance sheet is sometimes called the:
    a. Earnings statement.
    b. Operating statement.
    c. Profit and loss statement.
    d. Statement of financial position.

    Approach and Explanation: Read the question stem. Think of alternative names for the balance sheet. Then take each answer selection and see if it agrees with your response or not. Answer selections a., b., and c. are all alternative names for the income statement. Statement of financial position is a name for the balance sheet because it reports on the entity's financial position at a point in time. Statement of assets and equities might be another (but not popular) alternative name for the balance sheet. (Solution = d.)

5. (L.O. 6, 7) At January 1, 2014, Chully Company's assets totaled $70,000, and its liabilities amounted to $40,000. Net income for 2014 was $24,000 and owner's drawings amounted to $25,000. At December 31, 2014, assets totaled $90,000, and liabilities amounted to $57,000. The amount of additional owner's investment during 2014 amounted to:
    a. $0.
    b. $2,000.
    c. $3,000.
    d. $4,000.
    e. Cannot be determined from the facts given.

    Approach: Use your knowledge of the basic accounting equation and reasons for changes in owner's equity to solve.

    Explanation:

	A	=	L	+	OE	
	$70,000	=	$40,000	+	$30,000a	Balance at 1/1/14
					24,000	Net income for 2014
					(25,000)	Drawings for 2014
					+ X	Investments for 2014
	$90,000	=	$57,000	+	$33,000b	Balance at 12/31/14

    a$70,000 - $40,000 = $30,000
    b$90,000 - $57,000 = $33,000

    Solving for X: $30,000 + $24,000 - $25,000 + X = $33,000
    $29,000 + X = $33,000
    X = $33,000 - $29,000
    X = $4,000 owner investments during 2014

    (Solution = d.)

6.   (L.O. 6, 7) At January 1, 2014, King Corporation's assets totaled $76,000, and its liabilities amounted to $42,000. Net income for 2014 was $17,000, and owner's drawings amounted to $13,000. The amount of owner's equity at December 31, 2014 is:
   a. $38,000.
   b. $51,000.
   c. $80,000.
   d. $93,000.

Approach: Use your knowledge of the basic accounting equation and reasons for changes in owner's equity to solve.

Explanation:

$$A = L + OE$$
$$\$76,000 = \$42,000 + OE \text{ at } 1/1/14$$
$$\$76,000 - \$42,000 = \$34,000 \text{ OE at } 1/1/14$$

$34,000	Owner's equity at January 1, 2014
17,000	Net income for 2014
(13,000)	Drawings for 2014
0	Additional owner investments for 2014
$38,000	Owner's equity at December 31, 2014

(Solution = a.)

7.   (L.O. 7) Which of the following phrases describes the effects of the purchase of an asset on account?
   a.   Increase in assets and increase in expenses.
   b.   Increase in assets and increase in liabilities.
   c.   Increase in expenses and increase in liabilities.
   d.   Increase in liabilities and decrease in owner's equity.

Approach: Determine the effects of the transaction and write them down before you read the answer selections. Write down the basic accounting equation and analyze the effects of the transaction on the elements of the equation. If the transaction affects owner's equity, clearly state why and how.

Explanation: A = L + OE
                              ↑   ↑   (Solution = b.)

8.   (L.O. 6) Which of the following statements is **not** true about all expenses?
   a.   They result in a decrease in owner's equity.
   b.   They result from the consumption of goods and services.
   c.   They occur in the process of generating revenue.
   d.   They are the same thing as liabilities.

Approach and Explanation: Write down the definition of expense and the possible effects of an expense type transaction on the basic accounting equation. Then take each answer selection and see if it is true or not true about all expenses. An expense is the cost of an asset or other goods or services consumed in the process of generating revenue. The possible effects of an expense on the basic accounting equation are as follows:

A = L + OE
↓   ↓

OR   ↑   ↓

Liabilities are debts or obligations. A liability may arise because an asset is acquired on credit or because money is borrowed. A liability may arise in an expense transaction but not all expense transactions involve liabilities. Liabilities and expenses are **not** synonymous terms. (Solution = d.)

9.   (L.O. 7) Which of the following statements is true regarding the current period's consumption of supplies which were purchased and recorded as an asset in a prior accounting period?
a.   Total assets remain unchanged.
b.   Total owner's equity decreases.
c.   Total liabilities increase.
d.   Total assets increase.

Approach and Explanation: Write down the effects of the consumption of supplies previously on hand. The supplies were an asset when they were on hand. Now, they are an expense because they have been consumed. Therefore, assets decrease, and owner's equity decreases. (Solution = b.)

10.   (L.O. 7) Which of the following statements is true regarding the effect of the purchase of equipment for cash?
a.   Total assets decrease.
b.   Total liabilities increase.
c.   Total assets remain unchanged.
d.   Total owner's equity decreases.

Approach and Explanation: Think about the transaction. Cash (an asset) decreases. Equipment (another asset) increases by the same amount. There is no effect on liabilities or owner's equity. Look for the answer selection that fits the effects described. (Solution = c.)

$$A = L + OE$$
$$\downarrow\uparrow$$

11.   (L.O. 6) Which of the following items is an example of a liability?
a.   Salaries and wages expense.
b.   Mortgage payable.
c.   Accounts receivable.
d.   Owner's equity

Approach and Explanation: Think about the definition of a liability. Key words often associated with a liability are "debt," "obligation," or "payable." Examine each answer selection and determine its classification on financial statements. Write down your responses. Salaries and wages expense is an expense item on the income statement. Mortgage payable is a liability (Bingo!). Accounts receivable is an asset (key word is receivable). Owner's equity is owner's equity on the balance sheet. (Solution = b.)

12. (L.O. 7) The effects of a withdrawal by an owner are to
    a. Increase expenses and decrease net income.
    b. Increase expenses and decrease owner's equity.
    c. Decrease assets and decrease net income.
    d. Decrease assets and decrease owner's equity.

    Approach and Explanation: Write down the basic accounting equation and use arrows to indicate the effects of an owner withdrawal (of cash or other assets).

    $$A = L + OE$$
    $$\downarrow \qquad \downarrow$$

    Examine each answer selection and see if it fits your description. An owner withdrawal is not an expense because it does not have anything to do with carrying out operations and generating revenue; it is a distribution of profits to the owner. (Solution = d.)

*13. (L.O. 9) Which of the following terms refers to the process of reviewing the accounting records and reports to evaluate the fairness of the presentations in the reports and their compliance with established guidelines and rules?
    a. Auditing.
    b. Tax return preparation.
    c. Management consulting work.
    d. Public accounting.

    Approach and Explanation: Briefly define each answer selection. Compare your definitions with the question stem to determine your answer. Auditing services are provided by public accounting firms. An audit is an examination of the financial statements of a company by a CPA for the purpose of an expression of an opinion as to the fairness of presentation. Tax return preparation involves preparing tax returns, usually without any verification of the data to be used for completion. Management consulting work involves giving advice to management on various matters. Public accounting involves providing services to clients. As a public accountant, an individual may perform one or more of the following services: auditing, taxation, and management consulting. (Solution = a.)

TIP: The accounting profession is comprised of four major fields: public accounting, private accounting, not-for-profit accounting, and forensic accounting. In public accounting one may pursue a career in auditing, taxation, or management consulting. In private or managerial accounting, one may pursue a career in cost accounting, budgeting, general accounting, accounting information systems, tax accounting, or internal auditing. In not-for-profit accounting one may pursue a career in hospitals, universities, and foundations, or in local, state, and federal governmental units. In forensic accounting, one may work for an insurance company or other corporation, a law firm, or a government agency and use accounting, auditing, and investigative skills to conduct investigations into theft and fraud.

CHAPTER 2

. . . .

*T*HE RECORDING PROCESS

OVERVIEW

Due to the great number of transactions that occur daily in most businesses, accountants do not find it practical to present the cumulative effects of these transactions on the basic accounting equation in tabular form as we did in Exercise 2 in Chapter 1. Instead, they have developed a system by which the effects of transactions and events may conveniently be recorded, sorted, summarized, and stored until financial statements are desired. That system is the focus of this chapter.

SUMMARY OF LEARNING OBJECTIVES

1. **Explain what an account is and how it helps in the recording process.** An account is a record of increases and decreases in specific asset, liability, and owner's equity items.

2. **Define debits and credits and explain their use in recording business transactions.** The terms debit and credit are synonymous with left and right. Assets, drawings, and expenses are increased by debits and decreased by credits. Liabilities, owner's capital, and revenues are increased by credits and decreased by debits.

3. **Identify the basic steps in the recording process.** The basic steps in the recording process are: (a) analyze each transaction in terms of its effect on the accounts, (b) enter the transaction information in a journal, and (c) transfer the journal information to the appropriate accounts in the ledger.

4. **Explain what a journal is and how it helps in the recording process.** The initial accounting record of a transaction is entered in a journal before the data is entered in the accounts. A journal (a) discloses in one place the complete effect of a transaction, (b) provides a chronological record of transactions, and (c) prevents or locates errors because the debit and credit amounts for each entry can be easily compared.

5. **Explain what a ledger is and how it helps in the recording process.** The ledger is the entire group of accounts maintained by a company. The ledger provides the balance in each of the accounts as well as keeps track of changes in these balances.

6. **Explain what posting is and how it helps in the recording process.** Posting is the transfer of journal entries to the ledger accounts. This phase of the recording process accumulates the effects of journalized transactions in the individual accounts.

7. **Prepare a trial balance and explain its purposes.** A trial balance is a list of accounts and their balances at a given time. Its primary purpose is to prove the mathematical equality of debits and credits after posting. A trial balance also uncovers errors in journalizing and posting and is useful in preparing financial statements.

TIPS ON CHAPTER TOPICS

TIP: An **account** is an individual accounting record of increases and decreases in a specific asset, liability, owner's equity, revenue, or expense item. An account consists of three parts: (1) the title of the account, (2) a left or debit side, and (3) a right or credit side. In classrooms and in textbooks, we refer to this as a **T-account.** We need a separate account for each item reported in the income statement and balance sheet. When we refer to a specific account (such as Cash or Accounts Payable or Service Revenue), we capitalize its name.

The basic form of any T-account is as follows:

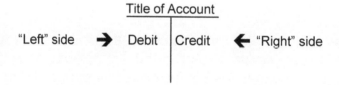

Periodically, the accounts are totaled to arrive at balances. For each account, the amounts entered on the debit side are totaled, and the amounts entered on the credit side are separately totaled. The difference between these two totals is the account's balance; the balance appears on the side that has the greater total.

TIP: **To journalize** or **journalizing** refers to the process of recording a transaction or event in a journal. **To post** or **posting** refers to the transferring of information from journal entries to the appropriate ledger accounts. The posting phase of the recording process accumulates the effects of journalized transactions in the individual accounts.

ILLUSTRATION 2-1
EXPANDED BASIC ACCOUNTING EQUATION AND DEBIT AND CREDIT RULES (L.O. 2)

Basic Equation   Assets = Liabilities + Owner's Equity

Expanded Basic Equation

	Assets	=	Liabilities	+	Owner's Capital	−	Owner's Drawings	+	Revenues	−	Expenses
Debit/Credit	Dr. | Cr.		Dr. | Cr.		Dr. | Cr.		Dr. | Cr.		Dr. | Cr.		Dr. | Cr.
Rules	+ | −		− | +		− | +		+ | −		− | +		+ | −

TIP: A "+" indicates an increase and a "−" indicates a decrease. Therefore, a transaction which causes an increase in an asset is recorded by a debit to the related asset account; a transaction which causes a decrease in the same asset is recorded by a credit to the same account.

TIP: Drill on the "debit and credit rules" until you can quickly and correctly repeat them. If you memorize the rules for an asset account, you can figure out the rules for all other types of accounts by knowing which rules are the opposite of the rules for assets and which are the same as the rules for assets.

TIP: "Debit" is a term that simply refers to the left side of any account. Thus, the debit side of an account is always the left side. "Credit" is a word that simply refers to the right side of an account. Thus, the credit side of an account is always the right side of the account. The phrase "to debit an account" means to enter an amount on the debit side of an account. Abbreviations are Dr. and Cr.

TIP: Total assets at December 31, 2014 = Total liabilities at December 31, 2014 + Owner's capital balance at January 1, 2014 − Owner's drawings **during** the year of 2014 + total Revenues earned **during** 2014 − total Expenses incurred **during** 2014. (Carefully notice the dates involved in the expanded equation.)

Owner's capital at January 1, 2014 − Owner's drawings for 2014 + Revenues for 2014 − Expenses for 2014 = Owner's capital balance at December 31, 2014. (Thus, owner's drawings, revenues, and expenses are subdivisions of the Owner's Capital account because they explain reasons why total owner's equity changes. Although all changes in owner's equity could be recorded in the Owner's Capital account, it is preferable to use separate accounts for each type of revenue, each type of expense, and owner's drawings so that detailed data on these items can be accumulated and reported.) Assets at December 31, 2014 = Liabilities at December 31, 2014 + Owner's Capital at December 31, 2014.

EXERCISE 2-1

Purpose: (L.O. 2) This exercise will test your understanding of the debit and credit rules.

A list of accounts appears below:

		Debit	Credit
1.	Cash	✓	
2.	Sales Revenue		
3.	Commissions Expense		
4.	Advertising Expense		
5.	Salaries and Wages Payable		
6.	Prepaid Insurance		
7.	Property Taxes Payable		
8.	Property Tax Expense		
9.	Owner's Drawings		
10.	Interest Revenue		
11.	Salaries and Wages Expense		
12.	Commissions Revenue		
13.	Unearned Service Revenue		
14.	Equipment		
15.	Notes Payable		
16.	Buildings		
17.	Accounts Payable		
18.	Land		
19.	Accounts Receivable		
20.	Owner's Capital		

Instructions

For each account, put a check mark (✓) in the appropriate column to indicate if it is increased by an entry in the debit (left) side of the account or by an entry in the credit (right) side of the account. The first one is done for you.

TIP:	In essence, you are being asked to identify the normal balance of each of the accounts listed. The **normal balance** of an account is the side where increases are recorded.

SOLUTION TO EXERCISE 2-1

Approach: Determine the classification of the account (asset, liability, owner's capital, drawing, revenue or expense). Think about the debit and credit rules for that classification.

	Account	Debit	Credit	Classification
1.	Cash	✓		Asset
2.	Sales Revenue		✓	Revenue
3.	Commissions Expense	✓		Expense
4.	Advertising Expense	✓		Expense
5.	Salaries and Wages Payable		✓	Liability
6.	Prepaid Insurance	✓		Asset
7.	Property Taxes Payable		✓	Liability
8.	Property Tax Expense	✓		Expense
9.	Owner's Drawings	✓		Drawing
10.	Interest Revenue		✓	Revenue
11.	Salaries and Wages Expense	✓		Expense
12.	Commissions Revenue		✓	Revenue
13.	Unearned Service Revenue		✓	Liability
14.	Equipment	✓		Asset
15.	Notes Payable		✓	Liability
16.	Buildings	✓		Asset
17.	Accounts Payable		✓	Liability
18.	Land	✓		Asset
19.	Accounts Receivable	✓		Asset
20.	Owner's Capital		✓	Owner's Equity

TIP:	Increases in assets are recorded by debits. Because liabilities and owner's equity are on the other side of the equal sign in the basic accounting equation A = L + OE, they must have debit and credit rules that are opposite of the debit and credit rules for assets. Therefore, a liability or an owner's equity account is increased by a credit entry. Revenues earned increase owner's equity so the debit and credit rules to record increases in revenue are the same as the rules to record increases in the Owner's Capital account (increases are recorded by credits). Because expenses and owner's drawings reduce owner's equity, the debit and credit rules for an expense account are opposite of the debit and credit rules for the Owner's Capital and revenue accounts.
TIP:	A separate account should exist in the ledger for each item that will appear on the financial statements.

TIP: The debit and credit rules are summarized below:

Asset Accounts	
Debit	Credit
Increase	Decrease
+	-

Liability Accounts	
Debit	Credit
Decrease	Increase
-	+

Owner's Drawings Account	
Debit	Credit
Increase	Decrease
+	-

Owner's Capital Account	
Debit	Credit
Decrease	Increase
-	+

Expense Accounts	
Debit	Credit
Increase	Decrease
+	-

Revenue Accounts	
Debit	Credit
Decrease	Increase
-	+

↑
Normal
Balance

↑
Normal
Balance

Notice that the accounts are arranged in such a way here that all of the increases
("+" signs) are on the outside and all of the decreases ("-" signs) are on the inside of this
diagram.

TIP: Another name for "debit" is "charge". Thus, "to charge an account" means to debit an
account.

EXERCISE 2-2

Purpose: (L.O. 2, 4) This exercise will give you practice in applying the debit and
credit rules.

A list of transactions appears below:
1. Dan Harrier invests $1,000 cash in his new business, Ultimate Detailing.
2. Purchases equipment for $600 cash.
3. Purchases $300 of supplies on account.
4. Rents a vehicle for the month and pays $250.
5. Pays $100 for an ad in a local newspaper.
6. Purchases gas for $20 on credit.
7. Sells services for $200 cash.
8. Sells services for $300 on account.
9. Pays $90 wages for an assistant's work.
10. Withdraws $80 for personal use.
11. Pays for use of beeper service, $30.
12. Borrows $2,000 from the Cash-N-Carry Bank in anticipation of expanding the
business.

Instructions

Indicate how you would record each transaction. What account would you debit and what account would you credit? Use the appropriate code designation. The first transaction is coded for you.

	Transaction
1.	D11, C31
2.	_____
3.	_____
4.	_____
5.	_____
6.	_____
7.	_____
8.	_____
9.	_____
10.	_____
11.	_____
12.	_____

Code

D—Debit
C—Credit

11—Cash
12—Accounts Receivable
14—Supplies
16—Equipment
21—Accounts Payable
22—Notes Payable
31—Owner's Capital
41—Owner's Drawing
51—Service Revenue
63—Beeper Expense
64—Gas Expense
65—Rent Expense
66—Advertising Expense
67—Salaries and
    Wages Expense

SOLUTION TO EXERCISE 2-2

Approach: Analyze each transaction to determine what items are increased or decreased. Translate that information into debit and credit language by applying the debit and credit rules (see **Illustration 2-1**). Visualize the resulting journal entry.

	Transaction		**Transaction**		**Transaction**
1.	D11, C31	6.	D64, C21	11.	D63, C11
2.	D16, C11	7.	D11, C51	12.	D11, C22
3.	D14, C21	8.	D12, C51		
4.	D65, C11	9.	D67, C11		
5.	D66, C11	10.	D41, C11		

TIP:	The account Supplies on Hand is often titled Supplies.

> **TIP:** The fourth transaction could be recorded by a debit to Prepaid Rent and a credit to Cash at the date the rent is paid (at the beginning of the rental month). Then, at the end of the rental month, the expired amount would be transferred to the expense account (this approach will be explained in **Chapter 3**).

EXERCISE 2-3

Purpose: (L.O. 4) This exercise will illustrate how to record transactions in the general journal.

Transactions for the Mariah Carey Motorcycle Repair Shop (from **Exercise 1-2**) for August 2014 are repeated below.

1. August 1   Nick begins the business by depositing $5,000 of his personal funds in the business bank account.

2. August 2   Nick rents space for the shop behind a strip mall and pays August rent of $800.

3. August 3   Nick purchases supplies for cash, $3,000.

4. August 4   Nick pays Cupboard News, a local newspaper, $300 for an ad appearing in the Sunday edition.

5. August 5   Nick repairs a cycle for a customer. The customer pays cash of $1,300 for services rendered.

6. August 11   Nick repairs a cycle for a customer, Paula Deen, on credit, $500.

7. August 13   Nick purchases supplies for $900 by paying cash of $200 and charging the rest on account.

8. August 14   Nick repairs a Harley for Zonie Kinkennon, a champion rider, for $1,900. Nick collects $1,000 in cash and puts the rest on account.

9. August 22   Nick takes home supplies from the shop that had cost $100 when purchased on August 3.

10. August 24   Nick collects cash of $400 from Paula Deen.

11. August 28   Nick pays $200 to Local Electric Co. for utilities incurred during the month of August.

12. August 29   Nick repairs a cycle for Rachael Ray for $1,200 on account.

13. August 31   Nick transfers $500 from the business bank account to his personal bank account.

Instructions
(a) Explain the impact of each transaction on the elements of the basic accounting equation and translate that into debit and credit forms.
(b) Journalize the transactions listed above. Include a brief explanation with each journal entry.

SOLUTION TO EXERCISE 2-3

Approach: Write down the effects of each transaction on the basic accounting equation. Think about the individual asset, liability, or owner's equity accounts involved. Apply the debit and credit rules to translate the effects into a journal entry.

TIP:	Refer to the Solution to **Exercise 1-2** for an analysis of the effects of the transaction on the individual components of the basic accounting equation. Refer to **Illustration 2-1** for the summary of the debit and the credit rules.

(a) 1.   Increase in Cash.   Debit Cash
          Increase in Common Stock.   Credit Owner's Capital

     2.   Increase in Rent Expense.   Debit Rent Expense
          Decrease in Cash.   Credit Cash

     3.   Increase in Supplies.   Debit Supplies
          Decrease in Cash.   Credit Cash

     4.   Increase in Advertising Expense.   Debit Advertising Expense
          Decrease in Cash.   Credit Cash

     5.   Increase in Cash.   Debit Cash
          Increase in Service Revenue   Credit Service Revenue

     6.   Increase in Accounts Receivable.   Debit Accounts Receivable
          Increase in Service Revenue.   Credit Service Revenue

     7.   Increase in Supplies.   Debit Supplies
          Decrease in Cash.   Credit Cash
          Increase in Accounts Payable.   Credit Accounts Payable

     8.   Increase in Cash.   Debit Cash
          Increase in Accounts Receivable.   Debit Accounts Receivable
          Increase in Service Revenue   Credit Service Revenue

     9.   Increase in Owner's Drawings.   Debit Owner's Drawings
          Decrease in Supplies.   Credit Supplies

    10.   Increase in Cash.   Debit Cash
          Decrease in Accounts Receivable.   Credit Accounts Receivable

11.	Increase in Utilities Expense. Decrease in Cash.	Debit Utilities Expense Credit Cash
12.	Increase in Accounts Receivable. Increase in Service Revenue.	Debit Accounts Receivable Credit Service Revenue
13.	Increase in Owner's Drawings. Decrease in Cash.	Debit Owner's Drawings Credit Cash

(b)

GENERAL JOURNAL   J1

	Date		Account Titles and Explanations	Ref.	Debit	Credit
	2014					
1.	Aug.	1	Cash		5,000	
			Owner's Capital			5,000
			(Owner invested cash in business)			
2.		2	Rent Expense		800	
			Cash			800
			(Paid August rent)			
3.		3	Supplies		3,000	
			Cash			3,000
			(Purchased supplies for cash)			
4.		4	Advertising Expense		300	
			Cash			300
			(Paid Cupboard News for advertising)			
5.		5	Cash		1,300	
			Service Revenue			1,300
			(Received cash for service fees earned)			
6.		11	Accounts Receivable		500	
			Service Revenue			500
			(Performed services for Paula Deen on account)			
7.		13	Supplies		900	
			Cash			200
			Accounts Payable			700
			(Purchased supplies for cash and on credit)			

GENERAL JOURNAL   J1

	Date	Account Titles and Explanations	Ref.	Debit	Credit
	2014				
8.	Aug. 14	Cash		1,000	
		Accounts Receivable		900	
		Service Revenue			1,900
		(Performed services for Zonie Kinkennon			
		for cash and on credit)			
9.	22	Owner's Drawings		100	
		Supplies			100
		(Owner withdrew supplies for personal use)			
10.	24	Cash		400	
		Accounts Receivable			400
		(Received cash from Paula Deen on account)			
11.	28	Utilities Expense		200	
		Cash			200
		(Paid Local Electric Co. for utilities)			
12.	29	Accounts Receivable		1,200	
		Service Revenue			1,200
		(Performed services on for Rachael Ray			
		on account)			
13.	31	Owner's Drawings		500	
		Cash			500
		(Owner withdrew cash for personal use)			

TIP: A journal entry must contain equal debits and credits. That is, the total amount debited to individual accounts in an entry **must equal** the total amount credited to individual accounts. Thus, the dual (two-sided) effect of each transaction is recorded in appropriate accounts. This **double-entry system** offers a means of proving the accuracy of the recorded amounts. If every transaction is recorded with equal debits and credits, then the sum of all the debits to the accounts must equal the sum of all the credits to the accounts.

TIP: A journal entry is either a **simple entry** (an entry that contains only one debit and one credit) or a **compound entry** (an entry that contains more than one debit and/or more than one credit). Entries 7 and 8 above are compound entries.

TIP: Unless otherwise indicated, the use of the term **journal** refers to the general journal. Companies may use various kinds of journals, but every entity has a general journal which is the most basic form of journal.

TIP: Unless otherwise indicated, the use of the term **ledger** refers to the **general ledger.** Companies may use various kinds of ledgers, but every company has a general ledger. The general ledger contains accounts for each of the assets, liabilities, and owner's equity of an entity.

TIP: When specific account titles are given in homework assignments such as this exercise, they should be used. When account titles are not given, you may select account titles that identify the nature and content of each account. The account titles are for specific items that appear on the balance sheet (for example, asset type accounts include Cash, Accounts Receivable, Land, and Equipment and liability accounts include Accounts Payable and Notes Payable) and on the income statement (for example, revenue type accounts include Service Revenue and Rent Revenue and expense type accounts include Salaries and Wages Expense, Supplies Expense, and Utilities Expense). The account titles used in journalizing should not contain explanations such as Cash Paid or Cash Received. When cash is received, the account Cash is debited, when cash is paid, the account Cash is credited.

TIP: To correctly record a transaction, you must carefully analyze the event and translate that analysis into debt and credit language. First, determine what items in the expanded basic accounting equation are affected by the transaction. Second, determine if those items are increased or decreased and by how much. Third, translate the increases and decreases into debits and credits.

EXERCISE 2-4

Purpose: (L.O. 6) This exercise will illustrate how to post transactions from the general journal to the general ledger.

Journal entries to record transactions for the Mariah Carey Motorcycle Repair Shop for August 2014 appear in the **Solution to Exercise 2-3.**

Instructions
Post the entries referred to above from the general journal to the following T-accounts. In the reference column of the journal, write the account number to which a debit or credit amount is posted.

Cash No. 101	Accounts Receivable No. 112	Supplies No. 126

Accounts Payable No. 201	Owner's Capital No. 301	Owner's Drawings No. 310

Service Revenue No. 400	Rent Expense No. 510	Advertising Expense No. 520

Utilities Expense   No. 732

SOLUTION TO EXERCISE 2-4

Cash		No. 101	
8/1	5,000	8/2	800
8/5	1,300	8/3	3,000
8/14	1,000	8/4	300
8/24	400	8/13	200
		8/28	200
		8/31	500

Accounts Receivable No. 112			
8/11	500	8/24	400
8/14	900		
8/29	1,200		

Supplies		No. 126	
8/3	3,000	8/22	100
8/13	900		

Accounts Payable	No. 201	
	8/13	700

Owner's Capital	No. 301	
	8/1	5,000

Owner's Drawings		No. 310
8/22	100	
8/31	500	

Service Revenue	No. 400	
	8/5	1,300
	8/11	500
	8/14	1,900
	8/29	1,200

Rent Expense		No. 510
8/2	800	

Advertising Expense No. 520		
8/4	300	

Utilities Expense	No. 732	
8/28	200	

Explanation: Posting refers to the process of transferring journal entries to the ledger accounts. This phase of the recording process accumulates the effects of journalized transactions in the individual accounts. Posting involves the following steps:

1. In the ledger, enter, in the appropriate columns of the account(s) debited, the date, journal page, and debit amount shown in the journal.
2. In the reference column of the journal, write the account number to which the debit amount was posted.
3. In the ledger, enter, in the appropriate columns of the account(s) credited, the date, journal page, and credit amount shown in the journal.
4. In the reference column of the journal, write the account number to which the credit amount was posted.

The use of the reference column in the journal serves two purposes. It allows for:
   (a)   Cross referencing between the journal and the ledger which facilitates tracing of transactions from the journal to the ledger at a later date.
   (b)   A method of noting that the posting has been completed.

When T-accounts are used, such as in this exercise, the journal page of the debit or credit amount being posted is typically omitted in the ledger.

The general journal for the Mariah Carey Motorcycle Repair Shop should appear as follows when the posting process is completed:

	Date		Account Titles and Explanations	Ref.	Debit	Credit
	2014					
1.	Aug.	1	Cash	101	5,000	
			Owner's Capital	301		5,000
			(Owner invested cash in business)			
2.		2	Rent Expense	510	800	
			Cash	101		800
			(Paid August rent)			
3.		3	Supplies	126	3,000	
			Cash	101		3,000
			(Purchased supplies for cash)			
4.		4	Advertising Expense	520	300	
			Cash	101		300
			(Paid Cupboard News for advertising)			
5.		5	Cash	101	1,300	
			Service Revenue	400		1,300
			(Received cash for service fees earned)			
6.		11	Accounts Receivable	112	500	
			Service Revenue	400		500
			(Performed services for Paula Deen on account)			
7.		13	Supplies	126	900	
			Cash	101		200
			Accounts Payable	201		700
			(Purchased supplies for cash and on credit)			

GENERAL JOURNAL — J1

GENERAL JOURNAL   J1

	Date	Account Titles and Explanations	Ref.	Debit	Credit
	2014				
8.	Aug. 14	Cash	101	1,000	
		Accounts Receivable	112	900	
		Service Revenue	400		1,900
		(Performed services for Zonie Kinkennon for cash and on credit)			
9.	22	Owner's Drawings	310	100	
		Supplies	126		100
		(Owner withdrew supplies for personal use)			
10.	24	Cash	101	400	
		Accounts Receivable	112		400
		(Received cash from Paula Deen on account)			
11.	28	Utilties Expense	732	200	
		Cash	101		200
		(Paid Local Electric Co. utilities)			
12.	29	Accounts Receivable	112	1,200	
		Service Revenue	400		1,200
		(Performed services for Rachael Ray on account)			
13.	31	Owner's Drawings	310	500	
		Cash	101		500
		(Owner withdrew cash for personal use)			

EXERCISE 2-5

Purpose: (L.O. 7) This exercise will (1) illustrate how to prepare a trial balance, and (2) will discuss the reasons for preparing a trial balance.

A trial balance is prepared after all transactions have been posted from the journal to the ledger.

Instructions
Refer to the **Solution to Exercise 2-4**
(a) Determine the balance of each account in the ledger.
(b) Prepare a trial balance.
(c) Describe a trial balance and list the reasons why it is to be prepared.

> **TIP:** To balance a T-account, a balancing line is to be drawn in the T-account; the balance is entered beneath that line on the side of the account which has the largest total. (An account balance is determined by totaling the debits and totaling the credits and taking the difference between those two totals.) If an account has only one entry in it, no balancing line is needed because that one entry readily establishes the account's balance.

SOLUTION TO EXERCISE 2-5

Cash			No. 101		Accounts Receivable		No. 112		Supplies		No. 126
8/1	5,000	8/2	800	8/11	500	8/24	400	8/3	3,000	8/22	100
8/5	1,300	8/3	3,000	8/14	900			8/13	900		
8/14	1,000	8/4	300	8/29	1,200			Bal.	3,800		
8/24	400	8/13	200	Bal.	2,200						
		8/28	200								
		8/31	500								
Bal.	2,700										

Accounts Payable		No. 201		Owner's Capital		No. 301		Owner's Drawings		No. 310
	8/13	700			8/1	5,000		8/22	100	
								8/31	500	
								Bal.	600	

Service Revenue		No. 400		Rent Expense		No. 510		Advertising Expense		No. 520
	8/5	1,300		8/2	800			8/4	300	
	8/11	500								
	8/14	1,900								
	8/29	1,200								
	Bal.	4,900								

Utilities Expense		No. 732
8/28	200	

(b)
MARIAH CAREY MOTORCYCLE REPAIR SHOP
Trial Balance
August 31, 2014

	Debit	Credit
Cash	$ 2,700	
Accounts Receivable	2,200	
Supplies	3,800	
Accounts Payable		$ 700
Owner's Capital		5,000
Owner's Drawings	600	
Service Revenue		4,900
Rent Expense	800	
Advertising Expense	300	
Utilities Expense	200	
	$10,600	$10,600

(c) A **trial balance** is a list of the accounts and their balances at a given point in time. A trial balance serves several purposes, including:

1. It proves that the ledger is in balance (that is, that total debits equal total credits in the ledger accounts). If errors are made in journalizing and posting, they may be detected in the process of preparing a trial balance.
2. It is a starting point for organizing the information to be reported on a company's financial statements.

TIP: Scan over **Exercises 2-3, 2-4,** and **2-5.** Notice the logical progression of the steps in recording, classifying, and summarizing the transactions. In **Exercise 2-3,** each transaction had to be identified and analyzed in terms of its effects on various accounts. Then the transactions were recorded in the journal. In **Exercise 2-4,** the information in the journal is transferred (posted) to the ledger. Thus, all transactions that affect individual components of the basic accounting equation are summarized together. In **Exercise 2-5,** the accounts are balanced, and a trial balance is prepared which furthers the summarization process and checks for the maintenance of equality of debits and credits in the recording and posting phases.

TIP: To sum a column of figures (such as the debt column of a trial balance) is sometimes referred to as **to foot** the column. When the summation is completed and the total is entered at the bottom of the column, the column is then said to be **footed.**

EXERCISE 2-6

Purpose: (L.O. 7) This exercise will test your ability to identify the effects of errors that commonly occur in the process of recording and posting transactions. As you will see, some errors cause the accounts to be out of balance, thus quickly identifying the existence of an error. However, some errors do **not** cause an imbalance in the accounts and are more difficult to discover.

An inexperienced bookkeeper for Nip-N-Tuck Alteration Shop made the following errors in journalizing and posting the transactions that occurred during February 2014.

1. The credit portion of a journal entry to record a $500 loan payment was posted to the ledger twice.
2. A fictitious transaction was recorded in the journal for the amount of $300.
3. A cash payment of $700 for rent was recorded in the journal by a debit of $700 to Rent Expense and a credit of $70 to Cash.
4. A debit entry of $50 to the Accounts Receivable account was incorrectly recorded as a debit entry of $50 to the Cash account.
5. A cash sale of $890 was incorrectly recorded in the journal as a cash sale of $980.
6. The debit portion of a journal entry to record a $60 credit sale was posted to the ledger, but the credit portion of this entry was not posted.
7. A $150 credit entry in the journal to the Accounts Payable account was posted as a credit to the Accounts Receivable account in the ledger.
8. An entire entry in the journal to record the $75 payment to the City of Orlando for an annual business license fee was omitted in the posting process.
9. A debit of $200 to the Equipment account was incorrectly posted as a $200 credit to the Equipment account.
10. The debit portion of a journal entry to record a $80 sale on account was posted to the ledger twice.
11. A $40 cash sale was completely omitted from the journal.
12. A $45 cash sale was recorded in the journal twice.
13. The balance in the Cash account was calculated incorrectly at $1,700. It should be $1,640.
14. A payment on account of $190 was journalized and posted as a debit to Repairs and Maintenance Expense and a credit to cash for $190.
15. A cash receipt of $80 from a customer on account was recorded twice in the journal.
16. The debit portion of a journal entry to record a cash sale was correctly posted to the ledger for $120. The credit portion of the same journal entry was posted to the Sales account in the ledger for $210.

Instructions
For each error, indicate (a) whether or not the resulting trial balance will balance. If the trial balance will not balance, indicate (b) the amount of the difference, and (c) the trial balance column that will have the larger total. Consider each error separately. Use the following form, in which error (1) is given as an example.

Error	(a) In Balance?	(b) $ Difference	(c) Larger Column
(1)	No	$500	Credit
(2)			
(3)			
(4)			
(5)			
(6)			
(7)			
(8)			
(9)			
(10)			
(11)			
(12)			
(13)			
(14)			
(15)			
(16)			

SOLUTION TO EXERCISE 2-6

Error	(a) In Balance?	(b) $ Difference	(c) Larger Column
(1)	No	$500	Credit
(2)	Yes		
(3)	No	$630	Debit
(4)	Yes		
(5)	Yes		
(6)	No	$60	Debit
(7)	Yes		
(8)	Yes		
(9)	No	$400	Credit
(10)	No	$80	Debit
(11)	Yes		
(12)	Yes		
(13)	No	$60	Debit
(14)	Yes		
(15)	Yes		
(16)	No	$90	Credit

Approach: For each error:
(a) Determine if total debits equal total credits in the journal and in the ledger. An imbalance in debits and credits in the journal and posting errors may cause an imbalance of total debits and credits in the ledger.
(b) Determine the amount of difference and larger column if the trial balance is not in balance. Errors that will cause an imbalance in the trial balance include:

1. Failure to record either the debit or credit portion (but not both portions) of a journal entry.
2. Recording the debit and credit portions of a journal entry but for unequal amounts.
3. Failure to post either the debit or credit portion of a journal entry.
4. Posting either the debit or credit portion (but not both portions) of a journal entry more than once.
5. Posting the debit and credit portions of a journal entry but for unequal amounts.
6. Incorrect computation of a ledger account balance.

EXERCISE 2-7

Purpose: (L.O. 1 thru 7) This exercise will quiz you about terminology used in this chapter.

A list of accounting terms with which you should be familiar appears below:

Account	Journalizing
Chart of accounts	Ledger
Compound entry	Normal balance
Credit	Posting
Debit	Simple entry
Double-entry system	T-account
General journal	Three-column form of account
General ledger	Trial balance
Journal	

Instructions
For each item below, enter in the blank the term that is described.

1. _____A record of increases and decreases in specific asset, liability, and owner's equity items.

2. _____The basic form of an account.

3. _____A form with columns for debit, credit, and balance amounts in an account.

4. _____A list of accounts and the account numbers which identify their relative location in the ledger.

5. _____The right side of an account.

6. _____The left side of an account.

7. _____An account balance on the side where an increase in the account is recorded.

8. _____An accounting record in which transactions are initially recorded in chronological order.

9. _____An journal entry that involves three or more accounts (more than one debit and/or more than one credit).

10. _____An journal entry that involves only two accounts (one debit and one credit).

11. _____The most basic form of journal.

12. _____The entering of transaction data in the journal.

13. _____The entire group of accounts maintained by a company.

14. _____The procedure of transferring journal entries to the ledger accounts.

15. _____A list of accounts and their balance at a given time, usually at the end of the accounting period.

16. _____The ledger that contains all of the asset, liability, and owner's equity accounts.

17. _____A system that records, in appropriate accounts, the dual effect of each transaction.

SOLUTION TO EXERCISE 2-7

1. Account
2. T-account
3. Three-column form of account
4. Chart of accounts
5. Credit
6. Debit
7. Normal balance
8. Journal
9. Compound entry
10. Simple entry
11. General journal
12. Journalizing
13. Ledger
14. Posting
15. Trial balance
16. General ledger
17. Double-entry system

ANALYSIS OF MULTIPLE-CHOICE TYPE QUESTIONS

1. (L.O. 2) The left side of an account is called:
   a. debit.
   b. journal.
   c. credit.
   d. asset.

   Explanation: The left side of any account is the debit side; the right side of any account is the credit side. (Solution = a.)

2. (L.O. 2) Credits are used to record increases in:
   a. assets, revenues, liabilities, and owner's capital.
   b. expenses, liabilities, and owner's capital.
   c. revenues, owner's drawings, and assets.
   d. revenues, liabilities, and owner's capital.

   Approach and Explanation: List the types of accounts which are increased by credits: liabilities, owner's capital, and revenues. Then look for the answer selection which matches your list. (Solution = d.)

3. (L.O. 2) Which of the following accounts is increased by credits?
   a. Cash.
   b. Supplies.
   c. Prepaid Rent.
   d. Accounts Payable.

   Approach and Explanation: List the types of accounts which are increased by credits: liabilities, owner's capital, and revenues. Identify each answer selection as an asset, liability, owner's capital, revenue or expense. Cash, supplies, and prepaid rent are all assets, and, thus, are increased by debits. Accounts payable is a liability and, thus, is increased by credits. (Solution = d.)

4. (L.O. 4) The Ref. column of the journal is used to:
   a. cross reference entries in the ledger and to indicate that posting has been completed.
   b. indicate that entries have been properly posted to the financial statements.
   c. test the equality of debits and credits in the journal.
   d. indicate the initials of the employee who performed the posting process.

   Explanation: The Ref. (Reference) column of the journal is left blank at the time a journal entry is made. At the time of posting, the ledger account number to which the amount is posted is placed in the Reference column to indicate what account received the posting. Thus, the Reference column in the journal is used to indicate whether posting has been completed and to what account an amount has been posted. (Solution = a.)

5. (L.O. 4) The payment of rent for office space solely for the current period is recorded in the accounts by a debit to:
   a. Rent Expense and a credit to Cash.
   b. Rent Expense and a credit to Owner's Capital.
   c. Cash and a credit to Accounts Payable.
   d. Cash and a credit to Rent Expense.

   Approach and Explanation: Do **not** read the answer selections until you analyze and journalize the transaction. Always start with the easiest part of the transaction. Cash was paid. Credit Cash to reduce its balance. Because the payment was for the rental of space for the current period, benefits do not extend beyond the current period; hence, an expense has been incurred. Debit Rent Expense to record the increase in expense. (Solution = a.)

6. (L.O. 4) The journal entry to record the payment for three years' rent in advance involves a debit to:
    a. Rent Expense and a credit to Prepaid Rent.
    b. Owner's Capital and a credit to Cash.
    c. Prepaid Rent and a credit to Cash.
    d. Prepaid Rent and a credit to Owner's Capital.

    Approach and Explanation: Analyze and journalize the transaction **before** you read the answer selections. Match your written response with the appropriate answer choice. Start with the easiest part of the transaction: a cash payment was made. Credit Cash to decrease the balance of that account. The payment is for benefits which are to extend beyond the current period; hence, an asset account should be increased (by a debit). The particular asset in this case is Prepaid Rent. (Solution = c.)

7. (L.O. 4) The "book of original entry" is the:
    a. journal.
    b. ledger.
    c. trial balance.
    d. transactions book.

    Approach: Complete the statement in the question stem **before** you look at the answer selections. Choose the selection which corresponds to your response. (Solution = a.)

8. (L.O. 4) The receipt of cash from a customer for services to be provided in a future accounting period is recorded by a:
    a. debit to Cash and a credit to Unearned Service Revenue.
    b. debit to Cash and a credit to Service Revenue.
    c. debit to Unearned Service Revenue and a credit to Cash.
    d. debit to Service Revenue and a credit to Cash.

    Approach and Explanation: Analyze the transaction and prepare the journal entry to record that transaction before you read the answer selections. The receipt of cash from a customer in advance of the earning of revenue causes the asset cash to increase and a liability (unearned service revenue) to increase. At a later time, the revenue will be earned; then the liability (unearned service revenue) will decrease and revenue will increase. (Solution = a.)

9. (L.O. 5) Which statement is true regarding posting?
    a. Posting must be done at the end of each week.
    b. Posting must be done after the financial statements are prepared.
    c. Posting must be done immediately after the transaction is recorded in the journal.
    d. Posting may be done at any time but must be completed before financial statements are prepared.

    Explanation: There is no set time to perform the posting process; however, financial statements cannot be prepared until all transactions are reflected in the accounts. Transactions are recorded in the accounts via the process of posting from the journal to the ledger. (Solution = d.)

10. (L.O. 7) The debit column of a trial balance amounts to $78,000; the credit column also amounts to $78,000. Which error may still exist?
    a. A journal entry contains a correct debit amount and an incorrect credit amount.
    b. A debit entry to the Accounts Receivable account in the journal is incorrectly posted as a credit to the Accounts Receivable account in the ledger.
    c. The debit portion of a journal entry is posted to the ledger twice.
    d. A cash payment on account of $240 is incorrectly recorded as a cash payment of $420.

    Approach and Explanation: Analyze each error (answer selection) and write down whether or not the error will cause the trial balance to be out of balance. Look for the selection which will **not** cause an imbalance in the trial balance (selection "d"). Both the debit and credit amounts recorded in the journal entry in selection "d" are in error. Selections "a", "b", and "c" all cause an imbalance in the trial balance. (Solution = d.)

11. (L.O. 7) A transposition error in entering one ledger account balance on the trial balance will cause a difference figure in the trial balance totals that will be evenly divisible by:
    a. 2.
    b. 7.
    c. 9.
    d. 10.

    Approach and Explanation: Set up an example for yourself to prove how this works. For instance, assume a $240 account balance is listed on the trial balance as $420. That error causes a difference of $180 which is divisible by 2, 9, and 10. Another example would be 9 entered for 90. The difference is 81 which is divisible by 9. Thus, the answer is narrowed down to the digit of 9. (Solution = c.)

12. (L.O. 7) Which of the following errors will cause an imbalance in the trial balance?
    a. Omission of a transaction in the journal.
    b. Posting an entire journal entry twice to the ledger.
    c. Posting a credit of $720 to Accounts Payable as a credit of $720 to Accounts Receivable.
    d. Listing the balance of an account with a debit balance in the credit column of the trial balance.

    Approach and Explanation: Analyze each error (answer selection) and write down whether or not the error will cause the trial balance to be out of balance. Look for the selection which will cause an imbalance (selection "d"). Selections "a", "b", and "c", do not cause an imbalance in the trial balance. (Solution = d.)

13. (L.O. 7) A trial balance that is in balance proves that:
    a. all entries have been entered in the journal correctly.
    b. total debits equal total credits in the ledger accounts.
    c. all entries have been posted from the journal to the ledger correctly.
    d. no significant errors exist in the ledger accounts.

    Explanation: A number of errors can still exist even though a trial balance is in balance. A trial balance that balances only proves that there are equal amounts of debits and credits in the ledger accounts. (Solution = b.)

CHAPTER 3

. . . .

ADJUSTING THE ACCOUNTS

OVERVIEW

In accordance with the **revenue recognition principle,** revenue is to be recognized (reported) in the period in which the performance obligation is satisfied. In accordance with the **expense recognition (matching) principle,** the expenses incurred in generating revenues should be recognized in the same period as the revenues they helped to generate. Adjusting entries are often required so that revenues and expenses are reflected on an accrual basis of accounting (revenues recognized when services are performed and expenses recognized when incurred) rather than on a cash basis of accounting. Therefore, adjusting entries reflect the accruals and deferrals of revenues and expenses. Adjusting entries are simply entries required to bring account balances up to date before financial statements can be prepared. The failure to record proper adjustments will cause errors in both the income statement and the balance sheet.

SUMMARY OF LEARNING OBJECTIVES

1. **Explain the time period assumption.** The time period assumption assumes that the economic life of a business is divided into artificial time periods of equal length. Another name for this assumption is the periodicity assumption.

2. **Explain the accrual basis of accounting.** Accrual basis accounting means that companies record events that change a company's financial statements in the periods in which these events occur, rather than in the periods in which the company receives or pays cash. Thus, companies recognize revenues when the related performance obligation is satisfied and companies recognize expenses when they are incurred.

3. **Explain the reasons for adjusting entries.** Companies make adjusting entries at the end of an accounting period. Such entries ensure that companies record revenues in the period in which the performance obligation is satisfied and recognize expenses in the period in which they are incurred.

4. **Identify the major types of adjusting entries.** The major types of adjusting entries are for deferrals (prepaid expenses and unearned revenues), and accruals (accrued revenues and accrued expenses).

5. **Prepare adjusting entries for deferrals.** Deferrals are for either prepaid expenses or unearned revenues. Companies make adjusting entries for deferrals to record the portion of the prepayment that represents the expense incurred or the revenue for services performed in the current accounting period.

6. **Prepare adjusting entries for accruals.** Accruals are for either accrued revenues or accrued expenses. Companies make adjusting entries for accruals to record revenues for services performed and expenses incurred in the current accounting period that have not been recognized through daily entries.

7. **Describe the nature and purpose of an adjusted trial balance.** An adjusted trial balance shows the balances of all accounts, including those that have been adjusted, at the end of an accounting period. Its purpose is to prove the equality of the total debit balances and total credit balances in the ledger after all adjustments.

*8. **Prepare adjusting entries for the alternative treatment of deferrals.** Companies may initially record a prepayment by a debit to an expense account. Likewise, companies may record the receipt of cash from a customer in advance (i.e., a customer prepayment or unearned revenue) by a credit to a revenue account. At the end of the period, the nominal accounts (expenses and revenues) may be overstated because of this practice and thus need adjustment. The adjusting entry to establish a prepaid expense includes a debit to an asset account and a credit to an expense account. This entry defers (puts off) the recognition of an expense until a future period in which it is incurred. An adjusting entry to establish unearned revenue involves a debit to a revenue account and a credit to a liability account. This entry defers (puts off) revenue recognition until a future period when the related performance obligation is met. (i.e., when the related services are performed).

9. **Discuss financial reporting concepts. To be judged useful, information should have the primary characteristics of relevance and faithful representation. In addition, it should be comparable, consistent, verifiable, timely, and understandable. The **monetary unit assumption** requires that companies include in the accounting records only transaction data that can be expressed in terms of money. The **economic entity assumption** states that economic events can be identified with a particular unit of accountability. The **time period assumption** states that the economic life of a business can be divided into artificial time periods and that meaningful accounting reports can be prepared for each period. The **going concern assumption** states that the company will continue in operation long enough to carry out its existing objectives and commitments. **The historical cost principle** states that companies should record assets at their cost. The **fair value principle** indicates that assets and liabilities should be reported at fair value. The **revenue recognition principle** requires that companies recognize revenue in the accounting period in which the performance obligation is satisfied. The **expense recognition principle** dictates that efforts (expenses) be matched with results (revenues). The **full disclosure principle** requires that companies disclose circumstances and events that matter to financial statement users. The **cost constraint** weighs the cost that companies incur to provide a type of information against its benefits to financial statement users.

*This material appears in **Appendix 3A** in the text.
This material appears in **Appendix 3B in the text.

TIPS ON CHAPTER TOPICS

TIP:	**This chapter is an extremely important one.** A good understanding of this chapter and an ability to think and work quickly with the concepts incorporated herein are necessary for comprehending subsequent chapters. Pay close attention when studying this chapter.
TIP:	Notice that **each adjusting entry** discussed in this chapter **involves a balance sheet account and an income statement account.**
TIP:	Notice that **none** of the adjusting entries discussed in **Chapter 3** involve the **Cash** account. Therefore, if you are instructed to record **adjusting entries,** double check your work when it is completed. If you have used the Cash account in any adjusting entry, it is very likely in error. (The only time Cash belongs in an adjusting entry is when a bank reconciliation discloses a need to adjust the Cash account—this will be explained in **Chapter 7**—or when an error has been made that involves the Cash account, in which case a correcting entry is required.)
TIP:	Keep in mind that for accrued items (accrued revenues and accrued expenses), the related cash flow **follows** the period in which the relevant revenue or expense is recognized; whereas, with prepayment type items (unearned revenues and prepaid expenses), the related cash flow **precedes** the period in which the relevant revenue or expense is recognized.
	For example, assume the accounting period is the calendar year. Consider an accrued expense such as accrued salaries at the end of 2014. An adjusting entry will be recorded at the end of 2014 so the expense will get reported on the 2014 income statement. The related cash payment to employees will take place in the following accounting period (2015, in this case). For another example, consider a prepaid expense such as the prepayment of rent in December 2014 for January 2015 occupancy. The cash payment occurs in December 2014. The expense is incurred and recognized in the following accounting period (January 2015).
TIP:	Revenue is to be recognized in the period the related performance obligation is satisfied (at which time the revenue is considered to be earned) and an expense is to be recognized in the period it is incurred. **Recognition** is the process of formally recording an item as an asset, liability, revenue, expense, or the like. A **revenue is recognized** in the period the related product or service is provided to the customer. Some revenues are earned with the passage of time; such as interest revenue which is earned as the borrower has use of the lender's funds and rent revenue which is earned as the tenant has use of a landlord's property. An **expense is incurred** (sustained) in the period in

which the benefits of goods and services are consumed in the process of generating revenue. Some expenses are incurred with the passage of time; such as interest expense which is incurred as the borrower has use of a lender's funds and insurance expense which is incurred as the time period lapses for which insurance coverage has been obtained.

TIP: If cash is **received** in a rental situation, the amount will be recorded in either a rent revenue account or an unearned rent revenue account, **not** in an expense or a prepaid expense account. Cash received for rent relates to revenue or unearned revenue. If cash is **paid** in a rental situation, the amount will be recorded in either an expense or a prepaid expense account.

TIP: You should be able to define the following four terms and describe the related adjusting entry for each. They are:

1. A **prepaid expense** is an expense that has been paid but has **not** been incurred. An adjusting entry for a deferred expense involves an EXPENSE account and an ASSET (prepaid expense) account.
2. An **unearned revenue** is a revenue that has been collected but whose related performance obligation has **not** been satisfied. An adjusting entry for an unearned revenue involves a LIABILITY (unearned revenue) account and a REVENUE account.
3. An **accrued revenue** is a revenue related to services already performed but whose related cash has **not** been received. An adjusting entry for an accrued revenue involves an ASSET (receivable) account and a REVENUE account.
4. An **accrued expense** is an expense that has been incurred but has **not** been paid. An adjusting entry for an accrued expense involves an EXPENSE account and a LIABILITY (payable) account.

TIP: A **prepaid expense** may be called a **deferred expense.** A deferred expense is so named because the recognition of expense is being deferred (put-off) to a future period; thus, a debit is carried on the balance sheet now and will be released to the income statement in a future period when the related benefits are consumed (expense is incurred).

TIP: An **unearned revenue** is often called **deferred revenue** because the recognition of revenue is being deferred to a future period; thus, a credit is carried on the balance sheet now and will be released to the income statement in a future period when the related performance obligation is satisfied.

TIP: An **adjusting entry for prepaid insurance expense** (expense paid but not incurred) involves an expense account and an asset account. The expense account is often called Insurance Expense or Expired Insurance. Possible titles for the asset account include Prepaid Insurance, Deferred Insurance Expense, Prepaid Insurance Expense, Deferred Insurance, and Unexpired Insurance.

TIP: An **adjusting entry for deferred rent revenue** (revenue collected but related services **not** yet performed) involves a liability account and a revenue account. Possible titles for the liability account include Unearned Rent Revenue, Unearned Rent, Deferred Rent Revenue, Rent Revenue Received in Advance, and Rental Income Collected in Advance. The use of Prepaid Rent Revenue as an account title is **not** appropriate because the term prepaid usually refers to the payment of cash in advance, **not** the receipt of cash in advance. The revenue account is often called Rent Revenue or Rental Income or Rent Earned.

TIP: In an **adjusting entry to record accrued interest revenue** (revenue services performed but related cash **not** yet received), the debit is to an asset account and the credit is to a revenue account. Possible names for that asset account are Interest Receivable and Accrued Interest Receivable. Possible names for the revenue account include Interest Revenue, Interest Income, and Interest Earned.

TIP: In an **adjusting entry to record accrued salaries and wages expense** (expense incurred, but not paid) the debit is to an expense account and the credit is to a liability account. The expense account is usually titled Salaries and Wages Expense. Possible names for the liability account include Salaries and Wages Payable and Accrued Salaries and Wages Payable.

TIP: In an **adjusting entry for an accrual** (accrued revenue or accrued expense), the word "accrued" is not needed in either account title. If you choose to use the word "accrued" in an account title, it is appropriate to do so only in the balance sheet account title. For example, accrued salaries of $1,000 may be recorded as follows:

Salaries and Wages Expense...	1,000	
Salaries and Wages Payable		1,000

The word "accrued" is not needed in either account title, but it could be used in the liability account title if desired (the account title would then be Accrued Salaries and Wages Payable). It would be wrong to insert the word "accrued" in the expense account title. Some people simply call the credit account "Accrued Salaries and Wages" but we advise that you include the key word "Payable" and omit the unnecessary "Accrued."

TIP: The **revenue recognition principle** is applied to determine in what period(s) to recognize revenue. Then, the **expense recognition principle (matching principle)** is applied to determine in what period(s) to recognize expense.

TIP: An **unadjusted trial balance** is referred to as either "unadjusted trial balance" or simply "trial balance."

EXERCISE 3-1

Purpose: (L.O. 6) This exercise will provide you with examples of adjusting entries for the accrual of expenses and revenues.

The following information relates to the Nippy Clothing Sales Company at the end of 2014. The accounting period is the calendar year. This is the company's first year of operations.

1. Employees are paid every Monday for the five-day work week ending on the prior Friday. Salaries amount to $2,400 per week. The accounting period ends on a Tuesday.
2. On October 1, 2014, Nippy borrowed $16,000 cash by signing a note payable due in one year at 8% interest. Interest is due when the principal is due.
3. A note for $2,000 was received from a customer in a sales transaction on May 1, 2014. The note matures in one year and bears 12% interest per annum. Interest is due when the principal is due.
4. A portion of Nippy's parking lot is used by executives of a neighboring company. A person pays $6 per day for each day's use. The parking fees (rent) are due by the fifth business day following the month of use. The fees for December 31, 2014 amount to $2,904.

Instructions
Prepare the necessary adjusting entries at December 31, 2014.

SOLUTION TO EXERCISE 3-1

1. Salaries and Wages Expense 960
        Salaries and Wages Payable 960
            (To record accrued salaries)
            ($2,400 ÷ 5 = $480); ($480 X 2 = $960)

2. Interest Expense 320
        Interest Payable.. 320
            (To record accrued interest on note payable)
            ($16,000 X 8% X 3/12 = $320)

3. Interest Receivable 160
        Interest Revenue 160
            (To record accrued interest on note receivable)
            ($2,000 X 12% X 8/12 = $160)

TIP: The **interest rate** is an annual rate unless otherwise indicated. For preparing an adjusting entry involving interest, compute interest assuming the rate given is for a whole year, unless it is evident that this is not the case. Also, assume a 360 day year, unless otherwise indicated

---

4. Accounts Receivable.. 2,904
        Rent Revenue.. 2,904
            (To accrue rent earned but not billed or collected)

Explanation: An accrued expense is an expense that has been incurred but not paid. The "incurred" part results in an increase in Expense (debit) and the "not paid" part results in an increase in Payable (credit). An accrued revenue is a revenue for which services have been performed but the related cash has not been received. The "performed" part results in an increase in Revenue (credit) and the "not received" part results in an increase in Receivable (debit).

EXERCISE 3-2

Purpose: (L.O. 5, 6, 7) This exercise provides examples of simple adjusting entries.

The unadjusted trial balance for the Mariah Carey Motorcycle Repair Shop appears below (from the **Solution to Exercise 2-5**) with information needed for adjusting entries.

MARIAH CAREY MOTORCYCLE REPAIR SHOP
Trial Balance
August 31, 2014

	Debit	Credit
Cash	$ 2,700	
Accounts Receivable	2,200	
Supplies	3,800	
Accounts Payable		$ 700
Owner's Capital		5,000
Owner's Drawings	600	
Service Revenue		4,900
Rent Expense	800	
Advertising Expense	300	
Utilities Expense	200	
	$10,600	$10,600

Additional Information:
1.   A count of supplies at August 31 shows $2,100 of unused items on hand.
2.   The shop received an utility bill of $80 for August. Payment is due by September 20. Nick decided to wait until September to make payment.

Instructions
(a)   Prepare the appropriate adjusting entries.
(b)   Prepare an adjusted trial balance at August 31, 2014.

SOLUTION TO EXERCISE 3-2

Approach: From the facts given, determine the adjustments needed to report the financial statements in accordance with generally accepted accounting principles. Look at the existing account balances. Make the appropriate entries to adjust the trial balance.

(a)   1.   Supplies Expense   1,700

                Supplies   1,700

                (To record supplies used: $3,800 - $2,100 = $1,700)

      2.   Utilities Expense   80

                Utilities Payable   80

                (To record accrued utilities)

(b)

MARIAH CAREY MOTORCYCLE REPAIR SHOP
Adjusted Trial Balance
August 31, 2014

	Debit	Credit
Cash	$ 2,700	
Accounts Receivable	2,200	
Supplies	2,100	
Accounts Payable		$ 700
Utilities Payable		80
Owner's Capital		5,000
Owner's Drawing	600	
Service Revenue		4,900
Rent Expense	800	
Advertising Expense	300	
Cleaning Expense	280	
Supplies Expense	1,700	
	$10,680	$10,680

TIP: Notice the account balances that are different on the adjusted trial when compared to the unadjusted trial balance. They are: Supplies, Supplies Expense, Utilities Expense, and Utilities Payable.

TIP: Notice that the balance of Owner's Capital on the adjusted trial balance represents the capital balance at the beginning of the period (August 1) plus additional owner investments made during the period, if any. That is, the balance here does not yet reflect the effect of this period's results of operations (revenues and expenses) on owner's equity. Also, the balance here does not yet reflect the effect of owner's drawings during this period.

TIP: Refer to the **Solution to Exercise 1-3.** The financial statements shown in that exercise were prepared **before** considering the information for the adjusting entries for supplies consumed during the period and accrued utilities expense. Those financial statements did not reflect the two necessary adjustments because the subject of financial statements was introduced in **Chapter 1** but, for purposes of simplicity, the subject of adjusting entries was **not** introduced until **Chapter 3.** Be aware now that financial statements for the Mariah Carey Motorcycle Repair Shop for August 31, 2014, should reflect the balances shown on the "Adjusted Trial Balance" above in this exercise. Thus, the correct net income figure is $1,820 ($3,600 - $1,700 - $80 = $1,820) for the income statement and the ending balance for Owner's Capital for the balance sheet is $6,220 ($8,000 - $1,700 - $80 = $6,220).

EXERCISE 3-3

Purpose: (L.O. 5) This exercise will provide you with examples of adjusting entries for prepaid expenses and unearned revenues (that is, for the deferral of expenses and revenues).

The following information relates to the Snoop Lion Magazine Company at the end of 2014. The accounting period is the calendar year.

1. An insurance premium of $8,000 was paid on April 1, 2014, and was charged to Prepaid Insurance. The premium covers a 24-month period beginning April 1, 2014.

2. The Supplies account showed a balance of $3,500 at the beginning of 2014. Supplies costing $12,000 were purchased during 2014 and debited to the asset account. Supplies of $2,200 were on hand at December 31, 2014.

3. On July 1, 2014, cash of $48,000 was received from subscribers (customers) for a 36-month subscription period beginning on that date. The receipt was recorded by a debit to Cash and a credit to Unearned Subscription Revenue.

4. At the beginning of 2014, the Unearned Service Revenue account had a balance of $75,000. During 2014, collections from advertisers of $800,000 were recorded by credits to Unearned Service Revenue. At the end of 2014, revenues received for which services are yet to be performed are computed to be $51,000.

Instructions
Using the information given above, prepare the necessary adjusting entries at December 31, 2014.

SOLUTION TO EXERCISE 3-3

1. Insurance Expense   3,000
        Prepaid Insurance   3,000
        ($8,000 X 9/24 = $3,000 expired cost)

2. Supplies Expense   13,300
        Supplies   13,300
        ($3,500 + $12,000 - $2,200 = $13,300
            supplies consumed)

3. Unearned Subscription Revenue   8,000
        Subscription Revenue   8,000
        ($48,000 X 6/36 = $8,000 earned revenue)

4. Unearned Service Revenue   824,000
        Service Revenue   824,000
        ($75,000 + $800,000 - $51,000 = $824,000
            earned revenue)

Approach and Explanation: Write down the definitions for prepaid expense and unearned revenue. Think about what is to be accomplished by each of the adjustments required in this exercise. A **prepaid expense** is an expense that has been paid but not incurred. In a case where the prepayment was recorded as an increase in an asset account (such as Prepaid Expense or Supplies), the adjusting entry will record the increase in Expense (debit) and a decrease in the recorded Asset (credit) due to the consumption of the benefits yielded by the earlier prepayment. An **unearned revenue** is a revenue that has been received for services that have **not** been performed. In a case where the cash receipt was recorded as an increase in a liability account (such as Unearned Service Revenue), the adjusting entry will record a decrease in the recorded liability Unearned Revenue (debit) and an increase in Earned Revenue (credit) due to the earning of all or a portion of the revenue represented by the earlier cash receipt.

It is helpful to sketch a T-account for the related asset or liability account. Enter the amounts reflected in that account before adjustment, enter the desired ending balance, and notice how the required adjustment is then obvious from facts reflected in your T-account. The T-accounts would appear as follows:

1.

2.

3.

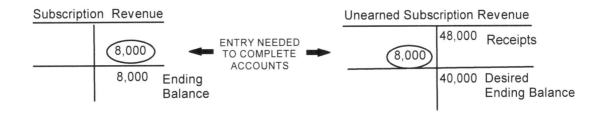

4.

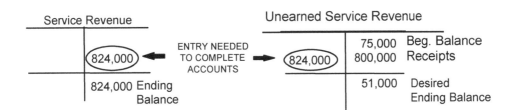

ILLUSTRATION 3-1
SUMMARY OF ADJUSTMENT RELATIONSHIPS
AND EXPLANATIONS (L.O. 4, 5, 6, 8)

Type of Adjustment	Account Relationship		Reason for Adjustment	Account Balances Before Adjustment	Adjusting Entry
1. Prepaid Expenses	Assets and Expenses	(a)	Prepaid expenses initially recorded in asset accounts have been used.	Assets overstated Expenses understated	Dr. Expenses Cr. Assets
		* (b)	Prepaid expenses initially recorded in expense accounts have not been used.	Assets understated Expenses overstated	Dr. Assets Cr. Expenses
2. Unearned Revenues	Liabilities and Revenues	(a)	Unearned revenues initially recorded in liability accounts have been earned.	Liabilities overstated Revenues understated	Dr. Liabilities Cr. Revenues
		* (b)	Unearned revenues initially recorded in revenue accounts have not been earned.	Liabilities understated Revenues overstated	Dr. Revenues Cr. Liabilities
3. Accrued Revenues	Assets and Revenues		Revenues for services performed have not been billed nor collected nor recorded.	Assets understated Revenues understated	Dr. Assets Cr. Revenues
4. Accrued Expenses	Expenses and Liabilities		Expenses incurred have not been billed nor paid nor recorded.	Expenses understated Liabilities understated	Dr. Expenses Cr. Liabilities

*This situation is addressed in Appendix 3A in the text.

Explanation:

1. When expenses are paid for before they are incurred, the payment may either be recorded by a debit to an asset account (prepaid expense) or by a debit to an expense account. At the end of the accounting period, the accounts are adjusted as needed. If the prepayment was initially recorded by use of a prepaid (asset) account, the consumed portion is transferred to an expense account in the adjusting entry. Whereas, if the prepayment was initially recorded by use of an expense account, an adjusting entry is required only if a portion of the expense remains prepaid at the end of the accounting period (in which case the unconsumed portion is transferred to an asset account). (The latter case is discussed in the **Appendix 3A** in the text.)

2. When revenues are received before they are earned, the receipt may either be recorded by a credit to a liability account (unearned revenue) or by a credit to a revenue account. At the end of the accounting period, the accounts are adjusted as needed. If the collection was initially recorded by a credit to a liability account (unearned revenue), the earned portion is transferred to a revenue account in the adjusting entry. Whereas, if the collection was initially recorded by use of a revenue account, an adjusting entry is required only if a portion of the revenue remains unearned at the end of the accounting period (in which case the unearned portion is

transferred to a liability account). (The latter case is discussed in **Appendix 3A** in the text.)

3. Revenues are often earned (performed) before they are collected. A revenue earned but not received is called an accrued revenue. If at the end of an accounting period this accrued revenue has not been recorded (which is often the case because it usually has not been billed yet), it must be recorded by way of an adjusting entry. Revenue that accrues with the passage of time (such as interest revenue) is a good example of a reason to need an accrued revenue type of adjusting entry.

4. Expenses are often incurred before they are paid. An expense incurred but not yet paid is called an accrued expense. If at the end of an accounting period this accrued expense has not been recorded (which is often the case because it usually has not been billed yet by the vendor), it must be recorded by way of an adjusting entry. Expense that accrues with the passage of time (such as interest expense) is a good example of a reason to need an accrued expense type adjusting entry.

| TIP: | Examine each type of adjustment explained above and notice the logic of the resulting entry. For example, an adjustment to recognize supplies used (when the supplies were recorded in an asset account when purchased) should reduce assets and increase expenses. |

ILLUSTRATION 3-2
ALTERNATIVE TREATMENTS OF PREPAID EXPENSES AND UNEARNED REVENUES* (L.O. 5, 8)

*This material is covered in **Appendix 3A** in the text.

PREPAID EXPENSES

When a company writes a check to pay for an item that affects expense in at least two different time periods (such as for an insurance premium or a license or dues), the bookkeeper may record the payment in one of two ways, either as a prepaid expense (asset) or as an expense. The first way is used most often in introductory accounting textbooks; the second is used most often in the real world. Regardless of the way the payment is recorded, an appropriate adjusting entry should be made at the end of the accounting period so that correct balances appear on the income statement and the balance sheet.

For example, a $1,200 payment is made on April 1, 2014, for a twelve-month insurance premium covering the time between April 1, 2014 and March 31, 2015. (Assume a calendar year reporting period.) A comparison of the two possible approaches appears below:

	Prepayment (Cash Paid) Initially Debited to Asset Account		OR	Prepayment (Cash Paid) Initially Debited to Expense Account	

Apr. 1	Prepaid Insurance
	    Cash
		1,200
		
				Apr. 1	Insurance Expense 1,200
					    Cash

		1,200			1,200

Dec. 31	Insurance Expense
	    Prepaid Insurance
		900
		
				Dec. 31	Prepaid Insurance 300
					    Insurance Expense

		900			300

After posting the entries, the accounts appear as follows:

Prepaid Insurance				
4/1	1,200	12/31 Adj.	900	
12/31 Bal.	300			

Prepaid Insurance		
12/31 Adj.	300	

Insurance Expense		
12/31 Adj.	900	

Insurance Expense			
4/1	1,200	12/31 Adj.	300
12/31 Bal.	900		

Notice that regardless of the path, you end up at the same place—with a balance of $300 in Prepaid Insurance and a balance of $900 in Insurance Expense. That was your objective—to report balances in accordance with the accrual basis of accounting.

UNEARNED REVENUES

When a company receives cash from a customer in advance of performing the services to earn the related revenue, the bookkeeper may record the receipt in one of two ways, either as an unearned revenue (liability) or as an earned (performed) revenue. The first way is used most often in introductory accounting textbooks; the second is used most often in the real world. Regardless of the way the receipt is recorded, an appropriate adjusting entry should be made at the end of the accounting period so that correct balances appear on the income statement and the balance sheet.

For example, $1,200 is received on May 1, 2014, for a twelve-month magazine subscription covering the time between May 1, 2014 and April 30, 2015. (Assume a calendar year reporting period.) A comparison of the two possible approaches appears below:

Unearned Revenue (Cash Received) Initially Credited to Liability Account			OR	Unearned Revenue (Cash Received) Initially Credited to Revenue Account		
May 1 Cash	1,200			May 1 Cash	1,200	
Unearned Subscription Revenue		1,200		Subscription Revenue		1,200
Dec. 31 Unearned Subscription Revenue	800			Dec. 31 Subscription Revenue	400	
Subscription Revenue		800		Unearned Subscription Revenue		400

After posting the entries, the accounts appear as follows:

Unearned Subscription Revenue					Unearned Subscription Revenue			
12/31 Adj.	800	5/1	1,200				12/31 Adj.	400
		12/31 Bal.	400					

Subscription Revenue					Subscription Revenue			
		12/31 Adj.	800		12/31 Adj. 400		5/1	1,200
							12/31 Bal.	800

Notice that the account balances are the same regardless of the approach used; that is, Unearned Subscription Revenue is $400, and Subscription Revenue is $800 at December 31.

EXERCISE 3-4

Purpose: (L.O. 5, 6, 7) This exercise will illustrate the preparation of adjusting entries from an unadjusted trial balance and additional data.

The following list of accounts and their balances represents the unadjusted trial balance of Lady Gaga's Equipment Rentals at December 31, 2014 the end of the annual accounting period.

LADY GAGA'S EQUIPMENT RENTALS
Trial Balance
December 31, 2014

	Debit	Credit
Cash	$ 6,500	
Prepaid Insurance	4,320	
Supplies	13,200	
Land	12,000	
Buildings	50,000	
Equipment	130,000	
Accumulated Depreciation—Buildings		$ 10,000
Accumulated Depreciation—Equipment		52,000
Notes Payable		50,000
Accounts Payable		9,310
Unearned Rent Revenue		10,200
Owner's Capital		30,660
Owner's Drawings	31,000	
Rent Revenue		161,960
Salaries and Wages Expense	70,600	
Interest Expense	3,500	
Miscellaneous Expense	3,010	
	$324,130	$324,130

Additional data:
1. On November 1, 2014, Lady Gaga received $10,200 rent from a lessee for a 12-month equipment lease beginning on that date and credited Unearned Rent Revenue for the entire collection.
2. Per a physical observation at December 31, 2014, Lady Gaga determines that supplies costing $2,200 were on hand at the balance sheet date. The cost of supplies is debited to an asset account when purchased.
3. Prepaid Insurance contains the premium cost of a policy that is for a 3-year term and was taken out on May 1, 2014.
4. The cost of the buildings is being depreciated at a rate of 5% per year.
5. The cost of the equipment is being depreciated at a rate of 10% per year.
6. The note payable bears interest at 12% per year. Interest is payable each August 1. The $50,000 principal is due in full on August 1, 2019.
7. At December 31, 2014, Lady Gaga has some equipment in the hands of renters who have used the equipment but have not yet been billed. They will make a payment of $1,400 on January 2, 2015.

8. Employees are paid total salaries of $3,200 every other Friday for a two-week period ending on that payday. December 31, 2014 falls on a Wednesday. The last payday of the year is the last Friday in the year. The work week is Monday through Friday.

Instructions

Prepare the year-end adjusting entries in general journal form using the information above.

SOLUTION TO EXERCISE 3-4

1.	Unearned Rent Revenue...	1,700	
	Rent Revenue..		1,700
	(To record rent revenue earned: $10,200 X 2/12 = $1,700)		
2.	Supplies Expense	11,000	
	Supplies..		11,000
	(To record supplies used: $13,200 - $2,200 = $11,000)		
3.	Insurance Expense	960	
	Prepaid Insurance		960
	(To record insurance expired: $4,320 X 8/36 = $960)		
4.	Depreciation Expense	2,500	
	Accumulated Depreciation—Buildings............................		2,500
	(To record annual depreciation on building: $50,000 X 5% = $2,500)		
5.	Depreciation Expense	13,000	
	Accumulated Depreciation—Equipment		13,000
	(To record annual depreciation on equipment: $130,000 X 10% = $13,000)		
6.	Interest Expense	2,500	
	Interest Payable..		2,500
	(To record interest accrued on note: $50,000 X 12% X 5/12 = $2,500)		
7.	Accounts Receivable..	1,400	
	Rent Revenue..		1,400
	(To record accrued revenue)		
8.	Salaries and Wages Expense	960	
	Salaries and Wages Payable		960
	(To record accrued salaries: $3,200 X 3/10 = $960)		

Approach and Explanation: Identify each item as involving: (1) a prepaid expense, (2) an unearned revenue, (3) an accrued revenue, or (4) an accrued expense. From the facts, determine the existing account balances. Read the facts carefully to determine the desired account balances for financial statements in accordance with generally accepted accounting principles (cost principle, revenue recognition principle, expense recognition principle, etc.). Determine the adjusting entries necessary to bring existing account balances to the appropriate account balances.

1. On November 1, 2014, cash was received and recorded as follows:

Cash	10,200	
Unearned Rent Revenue		10,200

    This situation involves unearned revenue. At December 31, 2014, before adjustment, there is an Unearned Rent Revenue account with a balance of $10,200. The amount unearned at that date is $10,200 X 10/12 = $8,500. Therefore, an adjusting entry is necessary to transfer the $1,700 earned from the Unearned Rent Revenue account to an earned revenue account.

2. This situation involves a prepaid expense. All supplies are charged to an asset account, Supplies, when purchased. Therefore, Supplies has an unadjusted balance of $13,200, which reflects the balance at the beginning of the year plus the cost of all supplies acquired during the year. Supplies of $2,200 are to appear on the balance sheet. Thus, $11,000 of consumed supplies must be transferred from the asset account to an expense account in an adjusting entry.

3. This item involves a prepaid expense. The Prepaid Insurance account reflects a $4,320 balance which represents the cost of a three-year premium. That three-year period began on May 1, 2014. Therefore, eight of the total 36 months have gone by and the cost of the eight month's coverage ($960) has expired. The expired portion must be transferred from the asset account to an expense account. This will leave 28 months of coverage ($4,320 X 28/36 = $3,360 or $4,320 - $960 = $3,360) in the asset account, Prepaid Insurance.

4. This item involves a long-term prepaid expense. A long-lived tangible item such as buildings or equipment represents a bundle of benefits when it is acquired. These benefits are to be used up (consumed) over the course of the asset's estimated service life.

    Depreciation is a term that refers to the process of allocating the cost of a long-lived tangible asset to the periods benefited from its use. The process of depreciation is necessary to comply with the expense recognition principle. The buildings or equipment are used to generate revenue during the period. Consequently, a portion of the bundle of benefits represented by the asset is consumed. There is a cost associated with those consumed benefits. This cost is to be matched with the revenues it helped generate. Thus, an expense is recorded (Depreciation Expense), and an asset is reduced. It is customary, however, to make use of a contra asset account, Accumulated Depreciation, rather than to credit the asset account itself.

5. See the explanation for 4. above. Notice that a credit to Accumulated Depreciation has the same impact as a credit to the account being depreciated (Equipment, for example). Thus, total assets are reduced by the journal entry to record depreciation.

6. This situation involves an accrued expense. Interest is a function of debt balance, interest rate, and time. Interest is due and payable at the end of an interest period.

The last interest payment date was August 1, 2014. Thus, interest incurred and not yet paid or payable amounts to five months worth or $2,500 ($50,000 X 12% X 5/12 = $2,500). The accrued interest is recorded by an increase to the Interest Expense account and a credit to a liability account, Interest Payable. (Note the balance before adjustment in the Interest Expense account represents seven months of interest. On August 1, 2014, an interest payment of $6,000 was made and $3,500 of that represented the interest from January 1, 2014 through July 31, 2014. The other $2,500 paid for interest would have been accrued earlier at the end of 2013.)

7. This situation involves an accrual of revenue. Revenue has been earned but has not yet been billed or recorded or received. The earned part is recorded in the adjusting entry by a credit to Rent Revenue. The part not received is recorded by a debit to Accounts Receivable. Thus, the appropriate adjusting entry increases assets and revenues earned.

8. This item involves an accrued expense. An accrued expense is an expense incurred but not yet paid. The salary for the last three work days of the year has been incurred because the employees have contributed their labor services for a period of time that has passed. The employees will not be paid until nine calendar days after the balance sheet date. The accrued expense is recorded at the balance sheet date by a debit to an expense account and a credit to a liability account.

TIP:	Scan down Lady Gaga's unadjusted trial balance again. Think about what you would expect to see on an adjusted trial balance. The adjusted trial appears below for your study. Verify that the balances are what you would expect them to be.

LADY GAGA'S EQUIPMENT RENTALS
Adjusted Trial Balance
December 31, 2014

	Debit	Credit
Cash	$ 6,500	
* Accounts Receivable	1,400	
Prepaid Insurance	3,360	
Supplies	2,200	
Land	12,000	
Buildings	50,000	
Equipment	130,000	
Accumulated Depreciation—Buildings		$ 12,500
Accumulated Depreciation—Equipment		65,000
Notes Payable		50,000
Accounts Payable		9,310
* Interest Payable		2,500
* Salaries and Wages Payable		640
Unearned Rent Revenue		8,500
Owner's Capital		30,660
Owner's Drawing	31,000	
Rent Revenue		165,060
Salaries and Wages Expense	71,240	
Interest Expense	6,000	
* Supplies Expense	11,000	
* Insurance Expense	960	
* Depreciation Expense	15,500	
* Miscellaneous Expense	3,010	
	$344,170	$344,170

* Note that the accounts are listed in the order that they appear in the chart of accounts, i.e, assets, liabilities, owner's equity, revenues, and expenses.

TIP:	Now that the adjusted trial balance is complete, think about where the account balances are to go in the preparation of financial statements. Study the following diagrams to verify your conclusions. (It is assumed that there were no additional owner investments during 2014.)

LADY GAGA'S EQUIPMENT RENTALS
Adjusted Trial Balance
December 31, 2014

Account	Debit	Credit
Cash	$ 6,500	
Accounts Receivable	1,400	
Prepaid Insurance	3,360	
Supplies	2,200	
Land	12,000	
Buildings	50,000	
Equipment	130,000	
Accumulated Depreciation—Buildings		$ 12,500
Accumulated Depreciation—Equipment		65,000
Notes Payable		50,000
Accounts Payable		9,310
Interest Payable		2,500
Salaries and Wages Payable		640
Unearned Rent Revenue		8,500
Owner's Capital		30,660
Owner's Drawing	31,000	
Rent Revenue		165,060
Salaries and Wages Expense	71,240	
Interest Expense	6,000	
Supplies Expense	11,000	
Insurance Expense	960	
Depreciation Expense—Building	2,500	
Depreciation Expense—Equipment	13,000	
Miscellaneous Expense	3,010	
	$344,170	$344,170

LADY GAGA'S EQUIPMENT RENTALS
Income Statement
For the Year Ended December 31, 2014

Revenues		
Rent revenue		$165,060
Expenses		
Salaries and wages expense	$71,240	
Interest expense	6,000	
Supplies expense	11,000	
Insurance expense	960	
Depreciation expense—building	2,500	
Depreciation expense—equipment	13,000	
Miscellaneous expense	3,010	
Total expenses		107,710
Net income		$ 57,350

LADY GAGA'S EQUIPMENT RENTALS
Owner's Equity Statement
For the Year Ended December 31, 2014

Owner's Capital, January 1	$30,660
Add: Net income	57,350
	88,010
Less: Drawings	31,000
Owner's Capital, December 31	$57,010

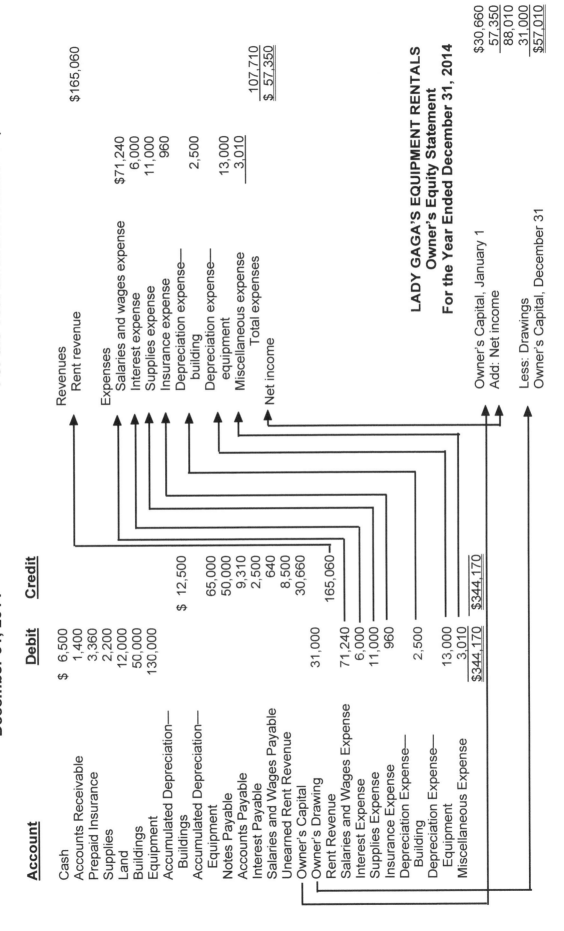

LADY GAGA'S EQUIPMENT RENTALS
Adjusted Trial Balance
December 31, 2014

Account	Debit	Credit
Cash	$ 6,500	
Accounts Receivable	1,400	
Prepaid Insurance	3,360	
Supplies	2,200	
Land	12,000	
Buildings	50,000	
Equipment	130,000	
Accumulated Depreciation—Buildings		$12,500
Accumulated Depreciation—Equipment		65,000
Notes Payable		50,000
Accounts Payable		9,310
Interest Payable		2,500
Salaries and Wages Payable		640
Unearned Rent Revenue		8,500
Owner's Capital		30,660
Owner's Drawing	31,000	
Rent Revenue		165,060
Salaries and Wages Expense	71,240	
Interest Expense	6,000	
Supplies Expense	11,000	
Insurance Expense	960	
Depreciation Expense	15,500	
Miscellaneous Expense	3,010	
	$344,170	$344,170

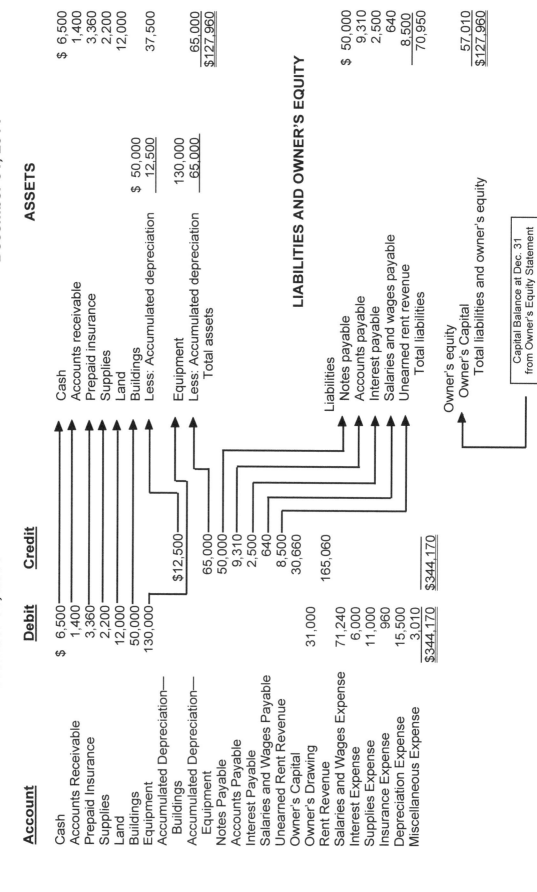

LADY GAGA'S EQUIPMENT RENTALS
Balance Sheet
December 31, 2014

ASSETS

Cash		$ 6,500
Accounts receivable		1,400
Prepaid insurance		3,360
Supplies		2,200
Land		12,000
Buildings	$ 50,000	
Less: Accumulated depreciation	12,500	37,500
Equipment	130,000	
Less: Accumulated depreciation	65,000	65,000
Total assets		$127,960

LIABILITIES AND OWNER'S EQUITY

Liabilities		
Notes payable	$ 50,000	
Accounts payable	9,310	
Interest payable	2,500	
Salaries and wages payable	640	
Unearned rent revenue	8,500	
Total liabilities		70,950
Owner's equity		
Owner's Capital		57,010
Total liabilities and owner's equity		$127,960

Capital Balance at Dec. 31
from Owner's Equity Statement

EXERCISE 3-5

Purpose: (L.O. 4) This exercise will help you develop skill in recognizing circumstances involving accrual of revenue, accrual of expense, unearned revenue, and prepaid expense.

Instructions

Assume it is now Tuesday, December 31, 2014. For each of the situations below, indicate whether (a) An accrued revenue, or (b) An accrued expense, or (c) An unearned revenue, or (d) A prepaid expense or (e) neither an accrual nor a prepayment is involved. You may use the designated letters (a), (b), (c), (d), and (e) to indicate your answers. The accounting period is the calendar year of 2014.

Answers		Situations
_____	1.	A check was written on June 2, 2014, for $6,000 to pay for an insurance policy which covers the period June 1, 2014 through May 31, 2015. An asset was debited.
_____	2.	At December 31, 2014, the company reviews tenants' records and notes that rent of $3,000 has been earned but not received.
_____	3.	The company has some revenue that has been received but has not been earned as of December 31, 2014.
_____	4.	Property taxes for the period July 1, 2014 through June 30, 2015 amount to $9,000 and are due by July 31, 2015.
_____	5.	$1,200 was received from a tenant on December 20, 2014, to cover the months of December 2014, January 2015, and February 2015.
_____	6.	At Jan. 1, 2014, office supplies on hand were valued at $220. During the year, purchases of office supplies amounted to $800. On Dec. 31, a count of supplies discloses $230 worth to be on hand.
_____	7.	The company wrote a check on Dec. 14 for $100 to pay for an ad which appeared in the Dec. 10 newspaper.
_____	8.	The company employs an office clerk and pays him $300 every Friday for the week ending on that payday. December 31, 2014 falls on a Wednesday.
_____	9.	Charges for local telephone service were paid on Dec. 1 for the month of December. Another payment is due on Jan. 1 for local telephone service for January.
_____	10.	An employee was hired on December 31, 2014, and is to begin work on Jan. 2.

SOLUTION TO EXERCISE 3-5

1.	d		6.	d
2.	a		7.	e
3.	c		8.	b
4.	b		9.	e
5.	c		10.	e

EXERCISE 3-6

Purpose: (L.O. 5, 6, 7) This exercise will test your ability to detect adjusting entries by comparing an adjusted trial balance with an unadjusted trial balance.

The trial balance and the subsequent adjusted trial balance at December 31, 2014, for the Bradley Company appear below. The accounting period coincides with the calendar year.

BRADLEY COMPANY
Trial Balance
December 31, 2014

	Before Adjustment		After Adjustment	
	Debit	**Credit**	**Debit**	**Credit**
Cash	$ 20,000		$ 20,000	
Accounts Receivable	8,000		8,700	
Note Receivable (8%)	10,000		10,000	
Interest Receivable	0		200	
Prepaid Rent	8,400		1,200	
Prepaid Insurance	3,200		800	
Supplies	2,000		300	
Equipment	12,000		12,000	
Accumulated Depreciation —Equipment		$ 3,000		$ 4,000
Accounts Payable		3,400		3,400
Unearned Service Revenue		5,000		1,300
Salaries and Wages Payable		0		1,800
Owner's Capital		52,000		52,000
Owner's Drawing	36,000		36,000	
Service Revenue		82,100		86,500
Interest Revenue		0		200
Salaries and Wages Expense	45,900		47,700	
Rent Expense	0		7,200	
Insurance Expense	0		2,400	
Supplies Expense	0		1,700	
Depreciation Expense	0		1,000	
	$145,500	$145,500	$149,200	$149,200

Instructions
(a) Journalize the adjusting entries recorded on December 31, 2014.
(b) Answer the following questions:
   1. How many months was the note receivable outstanding during 2014?
   2. If the rent is a constant amount each month, how many months rent is prepaid as of December 31, 2014?
   3. How much is the monthly insurance expense assuming the monthly amount has remained unchanged during the whole year?
   4. If the depreciation is a constant amount each year, for how many years has the office equipment been in use?
   5. Assuming the balance of Salaries and Wages Payable at January 1, 2014 was $0, how much cash was paid to employees during 2014?

SOLUTION TO EXERCISE 3-6

(a) 1.   Accounts Receivable.. 700
            Service Revenue   700
               (To record revenue earned but not yet billed or collected)

   2.   Interest Receivable 200
            Interest Revenue   200
               (To accrue interest revenue on a note receivable)

   3.   Rent Expense... 7,200
            Prepaid Rent   7,200
               (To record rent expired)

   4.   Insurance Expense 2,400
            Prepaid Insurance   2,400
               (To record expired insurance)

   5.   Supplies Expense 1,700
            Supplies...   1,700
               (To record supplies consumed)

   6.   Depreciation Expense 1,000
            Accumulated Depreciation—Equipment..................   1,000
               (To record depreciation on Equipment)

   7.   Unearned Service Revenue 3,700
            Service Revenue   3,700
               (To record revenue earned)

   8.   Salaries and Wages Expense 1,800
            Salaries and Wages Payable   1,800
               (To accrue salaries incurred but not paid or recorded)

> **TIP:** Watch that your journal entries utilize the exact account titles appearing in the adjusted trial balance.

(b) 1.   3 months.   4.   4 years.
     2.   2 months prepaid rent.   5. $45,900.
     3. $200 per month.

Explanations:

1. Face   X   Rate   X   Time   =   Interest Earned
    $10,000   X   8%   X   T/12   = $200
     $800   X   T/12   = $200
    T/12 = $200/$800
    T = 3 months

2. Rent Expense = $7,200
    $7,200 ÷ 12 months = $600 expense per month
    Prepaid Rent = $1,200
    $1,200 ÷ $600 = 2 months prepaid rent

3. Insurance Expense = $2,400
    $2,400 ÷ 12 months = $200 per month

4. Depreciation Expense for 2010 = $1,000
    Accumulated Depreciation = $4,000
    $4,000 ÷ $1,000 = 4 years of service thus far

5.

Salaries and Wages Expense			Salaries and Wages Payable	
Paid	45,900		1/1/14	0
Adj.	1,800		Adj.	1,800
Total Sal.	47,700		12/31/14 Bal.	1,800

   $47,700 - $1,800 = $45,900 cash paid.

EXERCISE 3-7

Purpose: (L.O. 2) This exercise illustrates the different results that are obtained when the accrual and the cash methods of accounting are used.

Annabelle's Specialty Service Shop conducted the following transactions during the first week in March.
1. Purchased supplies for $1,800. Paid 20% down; remaining 80% to be paid in 10 days.
2. Paid $30 for newspaper advertising to appear this week.
3. Collected $1,400 from customers on account.
4. Performed services at a $1,620 charge to a customer's account.
5. Paid $600 rent for the month of March.
6. Performed services for $280 cash.
7. Paid part-time sales clerk $40 wages for the week.
8. Wrote a check for $100 to the owner for her personal use.
9. Consumed supplies of $1,400.

Instructions
(a) Compute the net income for the week, using the cash-basis of accounting.
(b) Compute the net income for the week, using the accrual-basis of accounting.
Show your computations in good form.

SOLUTION TO EXERCISE 3-7

(a)   **Cash-Basis**

Cash received from customers ($1,400 + $280)		$1,680
Less: Payment for supplies ($1,800 X 20%)................	$360	
Payment for advertising	30	
Payment for rent..	600	
Payment to employee	40	1,030
Net income (cash method)		$ 650

> **TIP:** Using the **cash-basis of accounting,** revenues are recognized (recorded and reported) in the period in which they are **received** and expenses are recognized in the period in which they are **paid.** The cash basis is **not** a generally accepted accounting method for income statement reporting. However, the cash basis income figure does appear on the statement of cash flows by the caption "net cash provided (used) by operating activities."

(b)   **Accrual-Basis**

Service revenue ($1,620 + $280)		$1,900
Less: Operating expenses		
Supplies expense...	$1,400	
Advertising expense..	30	
Rent expense ($600 ÷ 4)...............................	150	
Salaries and wages expense	40	1,620
Net income (accrual method)		$ 280

> **TIP:** Withdrawals by owner ($100) do **not** enter into the income computations.
>
> **TIP:** Using the **accrual-basis of accounting,** revenues are recognized in the period in which the related services are performed and expenses are recognized in the period in which they are **incurred.**

EXERCISE 3-8

Purpose: (L.O. 5, 8) This exercise will provide you with examples of adjusting entries for:

(1) Prepaid expenses when cash payments are recorded in an asset account.

(2) Prepaid expenses when cash payments are recorded in an expense account.

(3) Unearned revenues when cash receipts are recorded in a liability account.

(4) Unearned revenues when cash receipts are recorded in a revenue account.

Thus, this exercise will compare the alternative treatment approach for prepaid expenses and unearned revenues explained in the **Appendix 3A** in your text (see **Illustration 3-2** in this *Problem Solving Survival Guide*) with the approach explained in the chapter.

Each situation described below is **independent** of the others.

(1) Supplies are recorded in an asset account when acquired. There were $400 of supplies on hand at the beginning of the period. Cash purchases of supplies during the period amounted to $900. A count of supplies at the end of the period shows $320 worth to be on hand.

(2) Supplies are recorded in an expense account when acquired. There were $400 of supplies on hand at the beginning of the period. Cash purchases of supplies during the period amount to $900. A count of supplies at the end of the period shows $320 worth to be on hand.

(3) Receipts from customers for magazine subscriptions are recorded as a liability when cash is collected in advance of delivery. The beginning balance in the liability account was $6,700. During the period, $54,000 was received for subscriptions. At the end of the period, it was determined that the balance of the Unearned Subscription Revenue account should be $8,000.

(4) Receipts from customers for magazine subscriptions are recorded as revenue when cash is collected in advance of delivery. The beginning balance in the liability account was $6,700. During the period, $54,000 was received for subscriptions. At the end of the period, it was determined that the balance of the Unearned Subscription Revenue account should be $8,000.

Instructions

For each of the independent situations above:

(a) Prepare the appropriate adjusting entry in general journal form.
(b) Indicate the amount of revenue or expense which will appear on the income statement for the period.
(c) Indicate the balance of the applicable asset or liability account at the end of the period.
(d) Indicate the amount of cash received or paid during the period.
(e) Indicate the change in the applicable asset or liability account from the beginning of the period to the end of the period.

TIP:	It would be helpful to draw T-accounts for each situation. Enter the information given as it would be, or needs to be, reflected in the accounts. Solve for the adjusting entry that would be necessary to "reconcile" the facts given.

SOLUTION TO EXERCISE 3-8

(1) (a) Supplies Expense 980
     Supplies... 980
   (b) Supplies Expense $980
   (c) Supplies $320
   (d) Cash paid $900
   (e) Decrease in Supplies $ 80

Approach:

	Supplies	
Beg.Bal.	400	(980) ⟵ ENTRY NEEDED TO COMPLETE ACCOUNTS
Acquisitions	900	
Desired Ending Balance	0 320	
	0	

Supplies Expense

(980) ⟶ ENTRY NEEDED TO COMPLETE ACCOUNTS ⟶ (980)

Ending Balance 980

(2) (a) Supplies Expense 80
     Supplies... 80
   (b) Supplies Expense $980
   (c) Supplies $320
   (d) Cash paid $900
   (e) Decrease in Supplies $ 80

Approach:

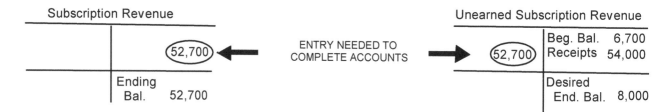

	Supplies		
Beg. Bal.	400		
		80	ENTRY NEEDED TO COMPLETE ACCOUNTS
Desired Ending Bal.	320		

Supplies Expense		
Acquisitions	900	
	80	
Ending Bal.	980	

> **TIP:** Compare situation (2) with situation (1). Notice the facts are the same **except** for the account debited for acquisitions of supplies. The solution is the same **except** for the adjusting entry required.

(3) (a) Unearned Subscription Revenue 52,700
        Subscription Revenue 52,700
    (b) Subscription Revenue $52,700
    (c) Unearned Subscription Revenue $ 8,000
    (d) Cash received $54,000
    (e) Increase in Unearned Subscription Revenue $ 1,300

Approach:

Subscription Revenue		
	52,700	ENTRY NEEDED TO COMPLETE ACCOUNTS
Ending Bal.	52,700	

Unearned Subscription Revenue		
	52,700	Beg. Bal. 6,700
		Receipts 54,000
		Desired End. Bal. 8,000

(4) (a) Subscription Revenue 1,300
        Unearned Subscription Revenue 1,300
    (b) Subscription Revenue $52,700
    (c) Unearned Subscription Revenue $ 8,000
    (d) Cash received $54,000
    (e) Increase in Unearned Subscription Revenue $ 1,300

Approach:

Unearned Subscription Revenue		
Beg. Bal.	6,700	
	1,300	ENTRY NEEDED TO COMPLETE ACCOUNTS
Desired Ending Bal.	8,000	

Subscription Revenue		
		Receipts 54,000
	1,300	
		Ending Bal. 52,700

> **TIP:** Compare situation (4) with situation (3). Notice the facts are the same **except** for the account credited for receipt of revenue in advance of the period in which the revenue is earned. The solution is the same **except** for the adjusting entry required.

EXERCISE 3-9

Purpose: (L.O. 1 thru 8)   This exercise will quiz you about terminology used in this chapter.

A list of accounting terms with which you should be familiar appears below:

Accrual-basis of accounting	Depreciation
Accruals	Expense recognition principle
Accrued expenses	(matching principle)
Accrued revenues	Fiscal year
Adjusted trial balance	Interim periods
Adjusting entries	Prepaid expenses (prepayments)
Book value	Revenue recognition principle
Calendar year	Time period assumption
Cash-basis accounting	Unearned revenues
Contra asset account	Useful life
Deferrals	

Instructions
For each item below, enter in the blank the term that is described.

1. _____Accounting basis in which companies record transactions that change a company's financial statements in the periods in which the events occur. Thus, revenues are recognized when earned and expenses are recognized when incurred, regardless of when cash is received or paid.

2. _____Accounting basis in which companies record a revenue when they receive cash and an expense when they pay cash.

3. _____An assumption that accountants can divide the economic life of a business into artificial time periods.

4. _____The principle that companies recognize revenue in the accounting period in which the performance obligation is satisfied.

5. _____The principle that companies match efforts (expenses) with accomplishments (revenues).

6. _____Adjusting entries for either accrued revenues or accrued expenses.

7. _____Adjusting entries for either prepaid expenses or unearned revenues.

8. _____Expenses incurred but not yet paid in cash or recorded. They result in accrued liabilities.

9. _____Revenues for services performed but not yet received in cash or recorded. They result in accrued receivables.

10. _____Expenses paid in cash and reported as assets before the related goods and services are used up or consumed (often called **deferred expenses**).

11. _____Cash is received and a liability is recorded before services are performed for the customer (often called **deferred revenues).**

12. _____Entries made at the end of an accounting period to comply with the revenue recognition and expense recognition principles.

13. _____A list of accounts and their balances after all adjustments have been made.

14. _____The difference between the cost of a depreciable asset and its related accumulated depreciation (often called **carrying value** or **carrying amount).**

15. _____An accounting period that extends from January 1 to December 31.

16. _____An account that is offset against an asset account on the balance sheet.

17. _____The length of service of a productive facility (often called **service life).**

18. _____The allocation of the cost of a plant asset to expense over its useful life in a rational and systematic manner.

19. _____An accounting period that is one year in length.

20. _____Monthly or quarterly accounting time periods.

SOLUTION TO EXERCISE 3-9

1. Accrual-basis of accounting
2. Cash-basis accounting
3. Time period assumption
4. Revenue recognition principle
5. Expense recognition principle (matching principle)
6. Accruals
7. Deferrals
8. Accrued expenses
9. Accrued revenues
10. Prepaid expenses (prepayments)

11. Unearned revenues
12. Adjusting entries
13. Adjusted trial balance
14. Book value
15. Calendar year
16. Contra asset account
17. Useful life
18. Depreciation
19. Fiscal year
20. Interim periods

*EXERCISE 3-10

Purpose: (L.O. 9) This exercise will review the qualitative characteristics that make accounting information useful for decision making purposes and the basic accounting assumptions principles, and constraints.

A list of accounting terms with which you should be familiar appears below (some refer to qualitative characteristics of accounting information and some pertain to the basic accounting assumptions, principles, and constraints.):

a. Comparability
b. Consistency
c. Cost constraint
d. Economic entity assumption
e. Expense recognition principle
f. Fair value principle
g. Faithful representation
h. Full disclosure principle
i. Going concern assumption

j. Historical cost principle
k. Materiality
l. Monetary unit assumption
m. Relevance
n. Revenue recognition principle
o. Timely
p. Time period assumption
q. Understandability
r. Verifiable

Instructions

For each of the following statements, identify (by corresponding letter) the appropriate qualitative characteristic(s) or basic accounting concept being described or that is **most directly related** to the given phrase or statement. Each code letter may be used more than once.

_____ 1. Two fundamental qualities that make accounting information useful for decision-making purposes.

_____ 2. Information that is capable of making a difference in a decision is said to have this fundamental quality.

_____ 3. Information that is complete and reasonably free of error and bias is said to have this fundamental quality.

_____ 4. Five enhancing qualities that are related to both relevance and faithful representation.

_____ 5. An entity is to apply the same accounting methods to similar events for successive accounting periods; that is, when an entity selects one method from a list of alternative acceptable methods, that same method is used period after period.

_____ 6. Information is measured and reported in a similar manner for different enterprises.

_____ 7. Neutrality is an ingredient of this fundamental quality of accounting information.

_____ 8. Requires the information cannot be selected to favor one set of interested parties over another.

_____ 9. When information provides a basis for forecasting annual earnings for future periods, it is said to have predictive value which is an ingredient of this fundamental quality of accounting information.

_____10. Information that has confirmatory value confirms or corrects users' prior expectations and is an ingredient of this fundamental quality.

_____11. Information must be available to decision makers before it loses its capacity to influence their decisions.

_____12. Imperative for providing comparisons of a single firm from period to period.

_____13. Enhancing quality being employed when companies in the same industry are using the same accounting principles.

_____14. A company cannot suppress information just because such disclosure is embarrassing or damaging to the entity.

_____15. The amounts and descriptions in financial statement should agree with the elements or events that these amounts and descriptions purport to represent due to this fundamental quality of information.

_____16. This quality requires information to be free of personal bias.

_____17. Requires a high degree of consensus among individuals on a given measurement.

_____18. Independent measurers, using the same measurement method, obtain similar results.

_____19. Both the nature and/or magnitude of the item must be considered in determining if an item could influence decisions of a user.

_____20. Information has this quality if it is presented in a clear and concise fashion so that reasonably informed users of that information can interpret it and comprehend its meaning.

_____21. Revenue should be recognized when services are performed.

_____22. According to this principle, all information necessary to ensure that the financial statements are **not** misleading should be reported.

_____23. This concept eliminates the "liquidation concept" in viewing business affairs.

_____24. Measurement of the standing and progress of entities should be made at regular intervals rather than at the end of the business's life.

_____25. The recorded amount of an acquired item should be the cost of the item at the date of acquisition.

_____26. The president of a business should **not** loan his spouse the company's credit card for personal gasoline purchases.

_____27. Expenses should be recognized in the same period that the related revenues are recognized.

_____28. This concept is often exemplified by numerous notes to the financial statements.

_____29. If a revenue is deferred to a future period, the related costs of generating that revenue should be deferred to the same future period.

_____30. Only things that can be expressed in terms of money are included in the accounting records.

_____31. The cost of an item should be measured by the amount of the resources expended to acquire it.

_____32. Accruals and deferrals are often necessary in order to report expenses in the proper time periods.

_____33. Each accounting unit is considered separate and distinct from all other accounting units.

_____34. An accountant assumes that a business will continue indefinitely.

_____35. In order to justify requiring a particular measurement or disclosure, the benefits perceived to be derived from it must exceed the costs expected to be associated with it.

_____36. Reporting must be done at defined time intervals. The time intervals are of equal length.

_____37. This principle indicates that assets and liabilities should be reported at fair value.

SOLUTION TO EXERCISE 3-10

1.	m and g	16.	g	31.	j	
2.	m	17.	r	32.	e	
3.	g	18.	r	33.	d	
4.	a, b, r, o, and q	19.	k	34.	i	
5.	b	20.	q	35.	c	
6.	a	21.	n	36.	p	
7.	g	22.	h	37.	f	
8.	g	23.	i			
9.	m	24.	p			
10.	m	25.	j			
11.	o	26.	d			
12.	b	27.	e			
13.	a	28.	h			
14.	g and h	29.	e			
15.	g	30.	l			

ANALYSIS OF MULTIPLE-CHOICE TYPE QUESTIONS

1. (L.O. 2) Which of the following statements best describes the expense recognition principle?
   a. Total debits to expense accounts should equal total credits to revenue accounts.
   b. Total debits must be matched with total credits in the ledger accounts.
   c. Amounts on the balance sheet must be matched with amounts reported on the income statement.
   d. Expenses should be recognized in the same period that the related revenues are recognized.

   Approach and Explanation: Mentally define the expense recognition principle **before** you read the answer selections. Jot down the key words of your definition. The **revenue recognition principle** gives us guidance to determine when to recognize (record and report) revenue. The **expense recognition principle** then dictates that the expenses incurred in generating the revenue earned during the current period should be recognized in the same period as the revenue it helped to create. Answer selections "a" and "c" are nonsensical responses. Answer selection "b" refers to the fact that there is a equality of debits and credits in the ledger but that equality is due to the basic accounting equation and the double-entry accounting system, not the matching principle. (Solution = d.)

2. (L.O. 2) Which of the following statements is associated with the accrual-basis of accounting?
   a. The timing of cash receipts and disbursements is emphasized.
   b. A minimum amount of record keeping is required.
   c. This method is used less frequently by businesses than the cash method of accounting.
   d. Revenues are recognized in the period they are earned (when the related services are performed), regardless of the time period the cash is received.

   Approach and Explanation: Mentally define the accrual basis of accounting. Write down the key words and phrases of your definition. Compare each answer selection with your definition and choose the one that best matches. Using **accrual-basis accounting,** events that change a company's financial statements are recorded in the periods in which the events occur. Thus, revenues are recognized in the period in which the related services are performed and expenses are recognized in the period in which they are incurred, regardless of when the related cash is received or paid. Answer selections "a" and "b" refer to the cash basis of accounting which is not GAAP. (Solution = d.)

3. (L.O. 2) The McKiernan Company made cash sales of services of $5,000 and credit sales of services of $4,200 during the month of July. The company incurred expenses of $6,000 during July of which $2,000 was paid in cash and the remainder was expected to be paid in August. Using the accrual method of accounting, net income for July amounts to:
   a. $7,200.
   b. $5,200.
   c. $3,200.
   d. $200.

   Approach and Explanation: Write down the essence of the accrual method: revenues are recorded when earned and expenses are recorded when incurred. Look for the figures to fit the description. Cash sales of $5,000 plus credit sales of $4,200 equals $9,200 total revenue earned during July. Revenues earned of $9,200 minus expenses incurred of $6,000 equals net income of $3,200. (Solution = c.)

4. (L.O. 2) Accruals of expenses are often necessary to:
   a. comply with the expense recognition (matching) principle.
   b. comply with the cost principle.
   c. make the balance sheet balance.
   d. ensure that revenues exceed expenses.

   Explanation: Accruals of expenses are often necessary to comply with accrual-basis accounting which stems from the revenue recognition and expense recognition principles. (Solution = a.)

5. (L.O. 4) Which of the following adjusting entries will cause an increase in revenues and a decrease in liabilities?
   a. Entry to record an accrued expense.
   b. Entry to record an accrued revenue.
   c. Entry to record the consumed portion of an expense paid in advance and initially recorded as an asset.
   d. Entry to record the earned portion of revenue received in advance and initially recorded as unearned revenue.

   Approach and Explanation: For each answer selection, write down the sketch of the adjusting entry described and the effects of each half of the entry. Compare the stem of the question with your analysis to determine the correct answer. (Solution = d.)

   The entry to record an accrued expense:

Dr.	Expenses	
	Cr.	Liabilities

   The effects of the entry are to increase expenses and to increase liabilities.

   The entry to record an accrued revenue:

Dr.	Assets	
	Cr.	Revenues

   The effects of the entry are to increase assets and to increase revenues.

   The entry to record the consumed portion of a prepaid expense initially recorded as an asset is:

Dr.	Expenses	
	Cr.	Assets

   The effects of the entry are to increase expenses and to decrease assets.

   The entry to record the earned portion of unearned revenue initially recorded as a liability is:

Dr.	Liabilities	
	Cr.	Revenues

   The effects of the entry are to decrease liabilities and to increase revenues.

6.   (L.O. 5) The term "book value" of an asset refers to:
    a.   the market value of a used asset.
    b.   the original cost of an asset minus the amount of depreciation accumulated to date.
    c.   an asset's original cost value.
    d.   an asset's assessed value for tax purposes.

Explanation: **Book value** (often called **carrying value** or **undepreciated cost**) is the difference between the cost of a depreciable asset and its related accumulated depreciation. (Solution = b.)

7.   (L.O. 5) The balance in the Accumulated Depreciation account that relates to a building represents the amount of:
    a.   the asset's remaining unallocated cost.
    b.   depreciation expense for the building for the current period.
    c.   total depreciation recorded to date for the building.
    d.   reduction in market value experienced to date on the building.

Explanation: **Depreciation** is the process of allocating the cost of a long-lived asset to expense over the periods benefited by use of the asset. This cost allocation process is performed to comply with the expense recognition (matching) principle. The depreciation recorded for a single period (for example, the current period) is referred to as **depreciation expense.** The total depreciation recorded on the asset since its acquisition is referred to as **accumulated depreciation.** (Solution = c.)

8.   (L.O. 5) An adjusting entry to allocate a previously recorded asset to expense involves a debit to an:
    a.   asset account and a credit to Cash.
    b.   expense account and a credit to Cash.
    c.   expense account and a credit to an asset account.
    d.   asset account and a credit to an expense account.

Approach and Explanation: Write down the sketch of an adjusting entry to transfer an asset to expense. Compare each answer selection with your entry and choose the one that matches.
     Dr.   Expenses
        Cr.   Assets   (Solution = c.)

9.   (L.O. 5) Which of the following accounts is a contra account?
    a.   Accounts Payable.
    b.   Building.
    c.   Unearned Service Revenue.
    d.   Accumulated Depreciation.

Explanation: A **contra account** is one whose normal balance is opposite of the normal balance of the account to which it relates. A contra account is offset against the account to which it relates in order to properly value that item for financial reporting purposes. In recording depreciation, the account Accumulated Depreciation is used instead of crediting the asset account itself in order to permit disclosure of both the original cost of the asset and the total cost that has expired to date. (Solution = d.)

10. (L.O. 6) An accrued expense is an expense that:
    a. has been incurred but has not been paid.
    b. has been paid but has not been incurred.
    c. has been incurred for which payment is to be made in installments.
    d. will never be paid.

    Approach and Explanation: Write down a definition for accrued expense. Compare each answer selection with your definition and choose the best match. Expenses may be paid for in the same period in which they are incurred or they may be paid for in the period before or in the period after the one in which they are incurred. An **accrued expense** refers to an expense that has been incurred but has not yet been paid. It will be paid for in a period subsequent to the period in which it was incurred. (Solution = a.)

11. (L.O. 6) An adjusting entry to record an accrued expense involves a debit to a(an):
    a. expense account and a credit to a prepaid account.
    b. expense account and a credit to Cash.
    c. expense account and a credit to a liability account.
    d. liability account and a credit to an expense account.

    Approach and Explanation: Write down a definition for accrued expense and the types of accounts involved in an adjusting entry to accrue an expense. Find the answer selection that describes your entry.

    Dr.   Expenses
        Cr.   Liabilities

    Notice the logic of the entry. An **accrued expense** is an expense incurred but not yet paid. Thus, you record the incurrence by increasing an expense account and you record the "not paid" aspect by increasing a liability account. (Solution = c.)

12. (L.O. 6) The failure to properly record an adjusting entry to accrue an expense will result in an:
    a. understatement of expenses and an understatement of liabilities.
    b. understatement of expenses and an overstatement of liabilities.
    c. understatement of expenses and an overstatement of assets.
    d. overstatement of expenses and an understatement of assets.

    Approach and Explanation: Write down the adjusting entry to record an accrued expense. Analyze the effects of the entry. This will help you to determine the effects of the failure to properly make that entry.

    Dr.   Expenses
        Cr.   Liabilities

    This entry increases expenses and liabilities. Therefore, the failure to make this entry would result in an understatement of expenses and an understatement of liabilities. (Solution = a.)

*13. (L.O. 8) An adjusting entry contains a debit to Prepaid Advertising and a credit to Advertising Expense. The purpose of this entry is to:
  a. defer advertising cost to a future period in which it will be incurred.
  b. accrue advertising expense to the current period.
  c. reduce a prepaid item.
  d. report a revenue item.

Approach and Explanation: Think about the impact of the entry described. A debit to a prepaid account increases assets; a credit to an expense reduces expenses. Thus, the entry reduces expenses this period and increases prepaids so that an expense is deferred to a future period. Apparently, when the cash payment was made earlier, it was recorded by the alternative treatment; whereby, a debit was recorded to Advertising Expense and a credit was made to Cash. Thus, the adjusting entry will put the appropriate amount of asset on the books for the amount of expense to be deferred to a future period. (Solution = a.)

**14. (L.O. 9) Which of the following accounting concepts requires that information reported in financial statements cannot be selected to favor one set of interested parties over another?
  a. Consistency.
  b. Fair value principle.
  c. Full disclosure principle.
  d. Faithful representation.

Explanation: For information to be useful to investors and creditors for making decisions about providing capital, the information must possess two fundamental qualities: relevance and faithful representation. **Faithful representation** means that information accurately depicts what really happened. To provide a faithful representation, information must be complete, neutral (not biased toward one position or another), and free from error. **Consistency** refers to the concept that requires a company to use the same accounting principles and methods year after year. **Fair value principle** states that (certain) assets and liabilities should be reported at fair value. **Full disclosure principle** requires that a company report all circumstances and events that may make a difference to a reader of the financial statements in decisions they make. (Solution = d.)

CHAPTER 4

. . . .

COMPLETING THE ACCOUNTING CYCLE

OVERVIEW

During the accounting period, transactions are recorded daily in the journal. At convenient times, information is posted from the journal to the ledger. At the end of the accounting period, the accountant summarizes the effects of the many recorded transactions, adjusts the accounts, and prepares financial statements. To help organize the information, the accountant uses an organized piece of scratch paper called a worksheet. The worksheet is a simple tool and is an optional step in the accounting cycle. Its preparation and uses are discussed in this chapter. After financial statements are drafted, the nominal (or temporary) accounts must be prepared for the accumulation of data pertaining to transactions in the following accounting period. Closing entries are journalized and posted to do just that; they are a required step in the accounting cycle and are discussed in this chapter. At the beginning of the subsequent (new) accounting period, reversing entries may be prepared in order to facilitate the recording of cash receipts and disbursements that relate to adjusting entries of the prior period. Reversing entries are an optional step in the accounting cycle and are discussed in the appendix to this chapter.

SUMMARY OF LEARNING OBJECTIVES

1. **Prepare a worksheet.** The steps in preparing a worksheet are as follows: (a) Prepare a trial balance on the worksheet (b) Enter the adjustments in the adjustment columns. (c) Enter adjusted balances in the adjusted trial balance columns. (d) Extend adjusted trial balance amounts to appropriate financial statement columns. (e) Total the statement columns, compute net income (or net loss), and complete the worksheet.

2. **Explain the process of closing the books.** Closing the books occurs at the end of an accounting period. The process is to journalize and post closing entries and then rule (underline) and balance all accounts. In closing the books, companies make separate entries to close revenues to Income Summary, expenses to Income Summary, Income Summary to owner's capital, and owner's drawings to owner's capital. Only temporary accounts are closed.

3. **Describe the content and purpose of a post-closing trial balance.** A post-closing trial balance contains the balances in permanent accounts that are carried forward to the next accounting period. The purpose of this trial balance is to prove the equality of these balances.

4. **State the required steps in the accounting cycle.** The required steps in the accounting cycle are: (1) analyze business transactions, (2) journalize the transactions, (3) post to ledger accounts, (4) prepare a trial balance, (5) journalize and post adjusting entries, (6) prepare an adjusted trial balance, (7) prepare financial statements, (8) journalize and post closing entries, and (9) prepare a post-closing trial balance.

5. **Explain the approaches to preparing correcting entries.** One way to determine the correcting entry is to compare the incorrect entry with the correct entry. After comparison, the company makes a correcting entry to correct the accounts. An alternative approach is to reverse the incorrect entry and then prepare the correct entry.

6. **Identify the sections of a classified balance sheet.** A classified balance sheet categorizes assets as current assets; long-term investments; property, plant, and equipment; or intangibles. A classified balance sheet categorizes liabilities as either current or long-term. There is also an owner's (owners') equity section, which varies with the form of business organization.

*7. **Prepare reversing entries.** Reversing entries are the opposite of the adjusting entries made in the preceding period. A company can choose to use or not use reversing entries. When reversing entries are used, they are made at the beginning of a new accounting period to simplify the recording of later transactions related to specific adjusting entries. In most cases, only accrual type adjusting entries are reversed.

*This material appears in **Appendix 4A** in the text.

EXERCISE 4-1

Purpose: (L.O. 1) This exercise will allow you to quickly check your knowledge of how items are extended on a worksheet.

A partial worksheet for the Maxwell Smart Investigative Services Company appears below. (The accounts are not listed in their usual order, the worksheet is only partially illustrated, and the Trial Balance and Adjustments columns have been omitted.)

MAXWELL SMART INVESTIGATIVE SERVICES
Worksheet
For the Year Ended December 31, 2014

Account	Adjusted Trial Balance		Income Statement		Balance Sheet	
	Debit	Credit	Debit	Credit	Debit	Credit
Salaries and Wages Payable		X				X
Prepaid Insurance						
Accumulated Depreciation—Equipment						
Unearned Service Revenue						
Rent Expense						
Service Revenue						
Prepaid Rent						
Owner's Drawings						
Maintenance and Repairs Expense						
Interest Receivable						
Accounts Receivable						
Advertising Expense						
Depreciation Expense						
Land						
Equipment						
Salaries and Wages Expense						
Mortgage Payable						
Cash						
Internet Service Expense						
Utilities Expense						
Net Income						

Instructions

For each account, place an "X" in the appropriate Adjusted Trial Balance column pair to indicate whether the account balance will appear in the Debit or Credit column (assume a normal balance in each account) on the worksheet. Also for each account, place an "X" in the appropriate Income Statement or Balance Sheet column to indicate the column to which the balance should be extended. The first one is done for you.

SOLUTION TO EXERCISE 4-1

MAXWELL SMART INVESTIGATIVE SERVICES
Worksheet
For the Year Ended December 31, 2014

Account	Adjusted Trial Balance		Income Statement		Balance Sheet	
	Debit	Credit	Debit	Credit	Debit	Credit
Salaries and Wages Payable		X				X
Prepaid Insurance	X				X	
Accumulated Depreciation—Equipment		X				X
Unearned Service Revenue		X				X
Rent Expense	X		X			
Service Revenue		X		X		
Prepaid Rent	X				X	
Owner's Drawing	X				X	
Maintenance and Repairs Expense	X					
Interest Receivable	X				X	
Accounts Receivable	X				X	
Advertising Expense	X		X			
Depreciation Expense	X		X			
Land	X				X	
Equipment	X				X	
Salaries and Wages Expense	X		X			
Mortgage Payable		X				X
Cash	X				X	
Internet Service Expense	X		X			
Utilities Expense	X		X			
Net Income[a]			X			X

[a]In the process of completing a worksheet, each of the statement columns must be totaled. The net income or loss for the period is then found by computing the difference between the totals of the two income statement columns. If total credits exceed total debits, net income has resulted. In such a case, the words "net income" are inserted in the account title space. The amount then is entered in the income statement debit column and the balance sheet credit column. The debit amount balances the income statement columns and the credit amount balances the balance sheet columns. In addition, the credit in the balance sheet column indicates the increase in owner's equity resulting from net income. Conversely, if total debits in the income statement columns exceed total credits, a net loss has occurred. The amount of the net loss is entered in the income statement credit column and the balance sheet debit column.

EXERCISE 4-2

Purpose: (L.O. 1) This exercise illustrates the function of a worksheet.

Carl's Video Service has a fiscal year ending on April 30. The following information is available:

(a)   Supplies on hand at April 30, 2014, amount to $1,600.
(b)   Wages incurred but not paid at April 30, 2014, amount to $320.
(c)   The $540 balance in the Prepaid Insurance account represents a payment for 12 months that began on August 1, 2013.
(d)   The note payable bears interest of 6% per year and was issued on December 1, 2013.
(e)   The estimated amount of utilities consumed but unpaid as of year end amounts to $400.
(f)   Depreciation on equipment for the year amounts to $3,000.

Instructions
Complete the worksheet for Carl's Video Service for the year ended April 30, 2014. The trial balance has already been put on the worksheet for you.

TIP:	Remember to cross-reference (key) your adjustments by use of the appropriate letters.
TIP:	Before beginning a worksheet, think about the steps involved in its completion: Step 1: Prepare a trial balance on the worksheet. Step 2: Enter the adjustments in the adjustments columns. Step 3: Enter adjusted balances in the adjusted trial balance columns. Step 4: Extend adjusted trial balance amounts to appropriate financial statement columns. Step 5: Total the statement columns, compute the net income (or net loss), and complete the worksheet.
TIP:	The debit and credit columns for every column pair must be equal before you can proceed to the next column pair. (This pertains to the first three column pairs.)
TIP:	Every amount appearing in the adjusted trial balance column pair must be extended to one of the four statement columns. Debit amounts go to a debit column further to the right and credit amounts go to a credit column further to the right of the adjusted trial balance column pair.
TIP:	When a dollar amount is added to balance the income statement column pair of columns, the same amount must be added in an opposite debit or credit column in the balance sheet column pair. This amount in a balance sheet column indicates the impact of net income (or net loss) on owner's equity.

CARL'S VIDEO SERVICE
Worksheet
For the Year Ended April 30, 2014

Account Titles	Trial Balance		Adjustments		Adjusted Trial Balance		Income Statement		Balance Sheet	
	Dr.	Cr.	Dr.	Cr.	Dr.	Cr.	Dr.	Cr.	Dr.	Cr.
Cash	1,000									
Accounts Receivable	1,800									
Supplies	9,100									
Prepaid Insurance	540									
Equipment	24,000									
Accum. Depreciation—Equip.		6,000								
Accounts Payable		2,000								
Notes Payable (due 11/30/16)		4,000								
Owner's Capital		20,560								
Owner's Drawing	21,700									
Service Revenue		43,500								
Salaries and Wages Expense	10,380									
Rent Expense	4,800									
Utilities Expense	2,170									
Advertising Expense	490									
Miscellaneous Expense	80									
Totals	76,060	76,060								

SOLUTION TO EXERCISE 4-2

CARL'S VIDEO SERVICE
Worksheet
For the Year Ended April 30, 2014

Account Titles	Trial Balance Dr.	Trial Balance Cr.	Adjustments Dr.	Adjustments Cr.	Adjusted Trial Balance Dr.	Adjusted Trial Balance Cr.	Income Statement Dr.	Income Statement Cr.	Balance Sheet Dr.	Balance Sheet Cr.
Cash	1,000				1,000				1,000	
Accounts Receivable	1,800				1,800				1,800	
Supplies	9,100			(a) 7,500	1,600				1,600	
Prepaid Insurance	540			(c) 405	135				135	
Equipment	24,000				24,000				24,000	
Accum. Depreciation—Equip.		6,000		(f) 3,000		9,000				9,000
Accounts Payable		2,000				2,000				2,000
Notes Payable (due 11/30/16)		4,000				4,000				4,000
Owner's Capital		20,560				20,560				20,560
Owner's Drawing	21,700				21,700				21,700	
Service Revenue		43,500				43,500		43,500		
Salaries & Wages Expense	10,380		(b) 320		10,700		10,700			
Rent Expense	4,800				4,800		4,800			
Utilities Expense	2,170		(e) 400		2,570		2,570			
Advertising Expense	490				490		490			
Miscellaneous Expense	80				80		80			
Totals	76,060	76,060								
Supplies Exp.			(a) 7,500		7,500		7,500			
Salaries & Wages Payable				(b) 320		320				320
Insurance Expense			(c) 405		405		405			
Interest Expense			(d) 100		100		100			
Interest Payable				(d) 100		100				100
Utilities Payable				(e) 400		400				400
Depreciation Expense			(f) 3,000		3,000		3,000			
Totals			11,725	11,725	79,880	79,880	29,645	43,500	50,235	36,380
Net Income							13,855			13,855
							43,500	43,500	50,235	50,235

(a) $9,100-$1,600 = $7,500 supplies consumed
(b) $540 X 9/12 = $405 insurance expired
(c) $4,000 X 6% X 5/12 = $100 interest accrued

TIP:	All five pairs of columns must balance for a worksheet to be complete.
TIP:	The amount shown for owner's capital on the completed worksheet is the account balance before considering drawings and net income (or net loss) for the accounting period.

EXERCISE 4-3

Purpose: (L.O. 1, 6) This exercise will illustrate the preparation of financial statements from information contained in the worksheet.

A worksheet is a tool used by most accountants to aid in the organization of data for the preparation of financial statements.

Instructions
Refer to the **Solution to Exercise 4-2.** Use the completed worksheet for Carl's Video Service to:
(a) Prepare an income statement for the year ending April 30, 2014.
(b) Prepare an owner's equity statement for the year ending April 30, 2014.
(c) Prepare a classified balance sheet at April 30, 2014.

SOLUTION TO EXERCISE 4-3

(a)

CARL'S VIDEO SERVICE
Income Statement
For the Year Ended April 30, 2014

Revenues		
Service revenue		$43,500
Expenses		
Salaries and wages expense	$10,700	
Supplies expense	7,500	
Rent expense	4,800	
Depreciation expense	3,000	
Utilities expense	2,570	
Advertising expense	490	
Insurance expense	405	
Interest expense	100	
Miscellaneous expense	80	
Total expenses		29,645
Net income		$13,855

(b)

CARL'S VIDEO SERVICE
Owner's Equity Statement
For the Year Ending April 30, 2014

Owner's Capital, May 1, 2013	$20,560
Add: Net income	13,855
	34,415
Less: Drawings	21,700
Owner's Capital, April 30, 2014	$12,715

(c)

CARL'S VIDEO SERVICE
Balance Sheet
April 30, 2014

Assets

Current assets		
Cash		$1,000
Accounts receivable		1,800
Supplies		1,600
Prepaid insurance		135
Total current assets		4,535
Property, plant, and equipment		
Equipment	$24,000	
Less: Accumulated depreciation	9,000	
Total property, plant, and equipment		15,000
Total assets		$19,535

Liabilities and Owner's Equity

Current liabilities	
Accounts payable	$ 2,000
Salaries and wages payable	320
Utilities payable	400
Interest payable	100
Total current liabilities	2,820
Long-term liabilities	
Notes payable	4,000
Total liabilities	6,820
Owner's equity	
Owner's Capital	12,715
Total liabilities and owner's equity	$19,535

TIP: Recall the order of items listed within categories on the financial statements. Although not mandatory, expenses are usually listed in descending order of amounts (with miscellaneous expenses always being the last in the list). Current assets are to be listed in order of liquidity. Current liabilities have no certain order but typically notes payable (short-term notes payable or current portion of long-term notes payable) and accounts payable are listed first and the rest are often listed in descending order.

EXERCISE 4-4

Purpose: (L.O. 2) This exercise will give you practice in identifying those accounts which are closed at the end of the accounting period and those accounts which are not closed.

Instructions

The following accounts were taken from the financial statements of a local business. Indicate whether each of the following accounts would or would not be closed at the end of the accounting period by placing an "X" in the appropriate column.

TIP: Remember the general rule: All nominal accounts (revenues, expenses, and owner's drawing) are closed and all real accounts (assets, liabilities, and owner's capital) are **not** closed. Therefore, to determine if an account will be closed or not closed, analyze the classification of the account.

TIP: Ten of the following are nominal or temporary accounts; nine are real or permanent accounts.

Accounts	Closed	Not Closed
1. Accounts Receivable		
2. Rental Revenue		
3. Repairs Expense		
4. Building		
5. Depreciation Expense		
6. Accumulated Depreciation		
7. Notes Payable		
8. Interest Payable		
9. Service Revenue Earned		
10. Salaries and Wages Expense		
11. Revenue Received in Advance[a]		
12. Furniture		
13. Prepaid Insurance		
14. Insurance Expense		
15. Advertising Expense		
16. Eric Nelson, Capital		
17. Eric Nelson, Drawing		
18. Interest Revenue		
19. Internet Service Expense		

[a]Another title for Unearned Revenue.

SOLUTION TO EXERCISE 4-4

Accounts	Closed	Not Closed
1. Accounts Receivable		X
2. Rental Revenue	X	
3. Repairs Expense	X	
4. Building		X
5. Depreciation Expense	X	
6. Accumulated Depreciation		X
7. Notes Payable		X
8. Interest Payable		X
9. Service Revenue Earned	X	
10. Salaries and Wages Expense	X	
11. Revenue Received in Advance[a]		X
12. Furniture		X
13. Prepaid Insurance		X
14. Insurance Expense	X	
15. Advertising Expense	X	
16. Eric Nelson, Capital		X
17. Eric Nelson, Drawing	X	
18. Interest Revenue	X	
19. Internet Service Expense	X	

EXERCISE 4-5

Purpose: (L.O. 2, 3) This exercise illustrates the preparation of closing entries and a post-closing trial balance, and discusses the importance of both.

The recording and posting of closing entries is a required step in the accounting cycle.

Instructions
Refer to the **Solution to Exercise 4-2.**
(a) Prepare the closing entries for Carl's Video Service at April 30, 2014.
(b) Discuss the two reasons why closing entries are prepared.
(c) Prepare a post-closing trial balance for Carl's Video Service.
(d) Explain why a post-closing trial balance is prepared and indicate what type of accounts will appear on the post-closing trial.

SOLUTION TO EXERCISE 4-5

(a)	Service Revenue	43,500	
	Income Summary		43,500
	(To close revenue account)		
	Income Summary	29,645	
	Salaries and Wages Expense		10,700
	Rent Expense		4,800
	Utilities Expense		2,570
	Advertising Expense		490
	Miscellaneous Expense		80
	Supplies Expense		7,500
	Insurance Expense		405
	Interest Expense		100
	Depreciation Expense		3,000
	(To close expense accounts)		
	Income Summary	13,855	
	Owner's Capital		13,855
	(To close net income to capital)		
	Owner's Capital	21,700	
	Owner's Drawings		21,700
	(To close drawings to capital)		

> **TIP:** The Income Summary account is used only in the closing process. Before it is closed, the balance in this account must equal the net income or net loss figure for the period.
>
> The amounts above would be reflected in the Income Summary account as follows:
>
> Income Summary
>
> | | |
> |---|---|
> | 29,645 | 43,500 |
> | | 13,855 Balance |
> | To close 13,855 | |
>
> **TIP:** Where do you look for the accounts (and their amounts) to be closed? If a worksheet is used, you can use the amounts listed in the Income Statement column pair and the balance of the owner's drawings account. If a worksheet is not used, you must refer to the temporary accounts (after adjustment) in the ledger to determine the balances to be closed.

(b) The major reason closing entries are needed is that they prepare the temporary (nominal) accounts for the recording of transactions of the next accounting period. Closing entries produce a zero balance in each of the temporary accounts so that they can be used to accumulate data pertaining to the next accounting period. Because of closing entries, the revenues of 2014 are not commingled with the revenues of the prior period (2013). A second reason closing entries are needed is that the owner's capital account will reflect a true balance only after closing entries have been completed. Closing entries formally recognize in the ledger the transfer of net income (or loss) and owner's drawings to owner's capital as shown in the owner's equity statement.

(c)

CARL'S VIDEO SERVICE
Post-Closing Trial Balance
April 30, 2014

	Debit	Credit
Cash	$ 1,000	
Accounts Receivable	1,800	
Supplies	1,600	
Prepaid Insurance	135	
Equipment	24,000	
Accumulated Depreciation—Equipment		$ 9,000
Accounts Payable		2,000
Salaries and Wages Payable		320
Utilities Payable		400
Interest Payable		100
Notes Payable		4,000
Owner's Capital		12,715
Totals	$28,535	$28,535

> **TIP:** Notice that although all of the balance sheet accounts appear on this post-closing trial balance, the total asset figure does not correspond to the total of the debit column on this trial. The reason for the difference is the placement of the Accumulated Depreciation account. Although its balance appears in the credit column of the trial balance, its balance is a reduction within the asset section of the balance sheet.

(d) The purpose of a post-closing trial balance is to prove the equality of the permanent (real) accounts after the closing entries have been recorded and posted. The accounts appearing on a post-closing trial are the ones having balances that are carried forward into the next accounting period which can be described as the **real accounts** or the **permanent accounts** or the **balance sheet accounts.**

EXERCISE 4-6

Purpose: (L.O. 4) This exercise will review the proper sequence of the required steps in the accounting cycle.

The required steps in the accounting cycle are listed in random order below.

_____ a. Prepare an adjusted trial balance.

_____ b. Analyze business transactions.

_____ c. Prepare a post-closing trial balance.

_____ d. Prepare a trial balance.

_____ e. Prepare financial statements.

_____ f. Post to ledger accounts.

_____ g. Journalize and post adjusting entries.

_____ h. Journalize and post closing entries.

_____ i. Journalize the transactions.

Instructions
Indicate the proper sequence of the steps by numbering them "1," "2," and so forth in the spaces provided.

> **TIP:** As you work through this exercise, concentrate on the logical step progression and the flow of information in the data gathering process.

SOLUTION TO EXERCISE 4-6

a. 6   c. 9   e. 7   g. 5   i. 2
b. 1   d. 4   f. 3   h. 8

EXERCISE 4-7

Purpose: (L.O. 1, 4) This exercise reviews the procedures involved in the accounting cycle when the two optional steps, a worksheet and reversing entries, are employed.

Ten steps in the accounting cycle for a company which uses a worksheet and reversing entries are listed in random order below.

_____   a.   Journalize and post closing entries.

_____   b.   Prepare financial statements from the worksheet.

_____   c.   Prepare a post-closing trial balance.

_____   d.   Balance the ledger accounts and prepare a trial balance on the worksheet.

_____   e.   Journalize and post adjustments made on the worksheet.

_____   f.   Record transactions in the journal.

_____   g.   Journalize and post reversing entries.

_____   h.   Post from journal to the ledger.

_____   i.   Complete the worksheet (adjusting entries, adjusted trial balance and extend amounts to financial statement columns).

_____   j.   Analyze business transactions.

Instructions
Arrange the ten procedures carried out in the accounting cycle in the order in which they should be performed by numbering them "1," "2," and so forth in the spaces provided.

TIP:	As you work through this exercise, concentrate on the logical progression and the flow of information in the data gathering process.

SOLUTION TO EXERCISE 4-7

a. 8   c. 9   e. 7   g. 10   i. 5
b. 6   d. 4   f. 2   h. 3   j. 1

ILLUSTRATION 4-1
BALANCE SHEET CLASSIFICATIONS (L.O. 6)

Current assets—includes cash and items which are expected to be converted to cash or sold or consumed within the next year (or operating cycle, whichever is longer).

Long-term investments—includes assets such as investments in stocks and bonds of other companies which can be realized in cash, but conversion into cash is not expected within the next year (or operating cycle, whichever is longer).

Property, plant, and equipment—includes long-lived tangible assets (land, building, equipment, and machinery) that are currently being used in operations (used to produce goods and services for customers). Assets in this category are often referred to as **plant assets** or **fixed assets.** They are **not** held for resale.

Intangible assets—includes assets that lack physical substance, such as patent, copyright, trademark, or trade names that give the holder exclusive right of use for a specified period of time. Their value to a company is generally derived from the rights or privileges granted by governmental authority.

Current liabilities—includes obligations that are due within a year **and** are expected to require the use of existing current assets (or the creation of other current liabilities) to liquidate them such as accounts payable, short-term notes payable, interest payable, and unearned service revenue.

Long-term liabilities—includes obligations that do not meet the criteria to be classified as current liabilities such as bonds payable, mortgages payable, long-term notes payable, lease liabilities, and obligations under employee pension plans.

Owner's equity—includes the owner's contributions and profits retained for use in the business. For a proprietorship, there is one capital account. For a partnership, there is a capital account for each partner. For a corporation, owner's equity is called **stockholders' equity** and includes two subclassifications—Capital Stock and Retained Earnings.

TIP:	Memorize the definition of current assets. **Current assets** are cash and other assets that are expected to be converted into cash, sold, or consumed (used up) within one year or the operating cycle, whichever is longer. Think about how various examples of current assets meet this definition. Accounts receivable are current assets because they will be converted to cash shortly after the balance sheet date; inventory (to be discussed in the next chapter) is a current asset because it will be sold within the year that follows the balance sheet date; prepaid insurance is a current asset because it will be consumed (used up) within the next year.

ILLUSTRATION 4-1 (Continued)

TIP:	A normal **operating cycle** is the length of time required to go from cash back to cash. That is, for an entity which sells products, the operating cycle is the time required to take cash out to buy inventory then sell the inventory and receive cash (either from a cash sale or the collection of an account receivable stemming from a credit sale). Unless otherwise indicated, always assume the operating cycle is less than a year so the one-year test is used as the cutoff between current and noncurrent.
TIP:	Memorize the definition of current liabilities. **Current liabilities** are obligations that the company is to pay within the coming year or its operating cycle, whichever is longer. Current liabilities are debts which are expected to require the use of current assets (or the incurrence of other current liabilities) within the year following the balance sheet date.
TIP:	In a classified balance sheet, any asset that is not classified as a current asset is a **noncurrent asset.** There are three noncurrent asset classifications: long-term investments; property, plant and equipment; and intangible assets. Some entities add another noncurrent section titled "other assets" to use for assets that don't fit well into other classifications.
TIP:	In a classified balance sheet, liabilities are classified either as current or noncurrent liabilities. The noncurrent liabilities are usually titled "long-term liabilities."
TIP:	It is extremely important that items are properly classified on a balance sheet. Errors in classification can result in incorrect ratio analyses (to be discussed in **Chapter 18**) which may lead to misrepresentations of the meaning of the information conveyed and can affect decisions that are based on those analyses.
TIP:	Current assets are listed in the order of their liquidity, with the most liquid ones being listed first. (**Liquidity** refers to the ease with which an asset can be converted to cash.) Current liabilities are not listed in any prescribed order; however, notes payable (short-term) is usually listed first followed by accounts payable (and the remainder of the current liabilities are often listed in descending order of amount).
TIP:	"Short-term" is synonymous with "current" and "long-term" is synonymous with "noncurrent." Therefore, "short-term debt" can be used to refer to "current liabilities". Asset classifications are typically titled current and noncurrent; whereas, liability classifications are typically titled current and long-term.
TIP:	All **noncurrent assets** (assets in classifications other than "current assets") are resources that are not expected to be converted into cash or fully consumed in operations within one year or the operating cycle, whichever is longer.
TIP:	Long-term investments are investments made by the business; they are **not** investments by the owner in the business. Investments by the owner in the business are reported as part of owner's equity on the balance sheet of the business.

EXERCISE 4-8

Purpose: (L.O. 6) This exercise will allow you to practice identifying the classification of accounts on a classified balance sheet.

A list of the balance sheet classifications appears below along with a list of account titles for the Steve Martin Corporation.

Classifications

CA	Current Assets	CL	Current Liabilities
INV	Long-Term Investments	LTL	Long-Term Liabilities
PPE	Property, Plant and Equipment	OE	Owner's Equity
ITG	Intangible Assets	NRBS	Not Reported on the Balance Sheet

Accounts

_____ 1. Accounts Receivable

_____ 2. Salaries and Wages Payable

_____ 3. Notes Payable (due in 4 Years)

_____ 4. Office Equipment

_____ 5. Notes Payable (due in 6 months)

_____ 6. Patents

_____ 7. Notes Payable (due in 4 months)

_____ 8. Bonds Payable (due in 20 years)

_____ 9. Notes Receivable (due in 3 years)

_____ 10. Mortgages Payable (due in 5 years)

_____ 11. Salaries and Wages Expense

_____ 12. Prepaid Insurance

_____ 13. Delivery Trucks

_____ 14. Copyrights

_____ 15. Cash

_____ 16. Utilities Expense

_____ 17. Depreciation Expense

_____ 18. Unearned Rent Revenue

_____ 19. Interest Receivable

_____ 20. Rent Revenue

_____ 21. Owner's Capital

_____ 22. Buildings

_____ 23. Prepaid Advertising

_____ 24. Prepaid Property Taxes

_____ 25. Investment in Orlando Aviation Authority Bonds

_____ 26. Property Taxes Payable   _____ 30. Franchises

_____ 27. Short-term Investment   _____ 31. Unearned Subscription
                                                              Revenue
_____ 28. Land
                                                   _____ 32. Utilities Payable
_____ 29. Parking Lots and Driveways

Instructions

Indicate which balance sheet classification is the most appropriate for reporting each account listed above by selecting the abbreviation of the corresponding section. If the account is not a real (permanent) account, use the abbreviation NRBS for Not Reported on the Balance Sheet.

Approach: Mentally review the brief descriptions of each classification. (See **Illustration 4-1.**) Use these descriptions to aid your analysis.

SOLUTION TO EXERCISE 4-8

Item #	Solution	Item #	Solution	Item #	Solution	Item #	Solution
1.	CA	9.	INV	17.	NRBS	25.	INV
2.	CL	10.	LTL	18.	CL	26.	CL
3.	LTL	11.	NRBS	19.	CA	27.	CA
4.	PPE	12.	CA	20.	NRBS	28.	PPE
5.	CL	13.	PPE	21.	OE	29.	PPE
6.	ITG	14.	ITG	22.	PPE	30.	ITG
7.	CL	15.	CA	23.	CA	31.	CL
8.	LTL	16.	NRBS	24.	CA	32.	CL

Selected Explanations:

a. Salaries and Wages Expense (Item #11), Utilities Expense (Item #16), Depreciation Expense (Item #17), and Rent Revenue (Item #20) are all income statement accounts. Hence, they are nominal or temporary accounts and do **not** belong on the balance sheet.

b. Prepaid items such as Prepaid Insurance (Item #12), Prepaid Advertising (Item #23), and Prepaid Property Taxes (Item #24) are generally expected to be consumed within the next year or operating cycle, whichever is longer; hence, they are current assets.

c. Unearned Rent Revenue (Item #18), unless otherwise indicated, should be treated as if it will be earned within the year following the balance sheet date; hence, it is a current liability. If evidence existed to show the unearned amount was not expected to be earned in the next year, it would be classified as a long-term (noncurrent) liability. The same reasoning applies to Unearned Subscription Revenue (Item #31).

d.   Interest payments are typically due monthly, quarterly, semiannually, or at least annually. Hence, we expect to collect the amount in Interest Receivable (Item #19) within the next year (unless evidence exists to the contrary).

e.   Investments such as Investment in Orlando Aviation Authority Bonds (Item #25) should be assumed to be held for a long-term purpose (unless there is evidence to the contrary); hence, they are classified as long-term investments. If an investment is held for sale and is expected to be sold within the next year as is (Item #27), it should be classified as a current asset.

EXERCISE 4-9

Purpose: (L.O. 5) This exercise will illustrate how to correct errors made in the recording process.

The following errors were discovered in the books of the Cool Way AC Repair Shop.

1.   A cash payment of $120 for repairs on a typewriter was recorded by a debit to Equipment and a credit to Cash.

2.   A cash payment of $70 for office supplies was recorded by a debit to Supplies and a credit to Accounts Payable.

3.   An owner's drawing was recorded by a debit to Salaries and Wages Expense and a credit to Cash for $700.

4.   A cash payment of $150 for an ad appearing in Sunday's edition of the local newspaper was recorded by a debit to Utilities Expense and a credit to Cash for $150.

5.   A $500 cash receipt from a customer on account was recorded by a debit to Cash for $50 and a credit to Service Revenue for $50.

6.   The first interest payment made this accounting period (on a note payable) was for $1,000, which included $300 of interest accrued at the end of the last accounting period. The payment was recorded by a debit to Interest Expense for $1,000 and a credit to Cash for $1,000. (No reversing entries were made at the beginning of this accounting period.)

7.   A $300 cash sale of services was recorded by a debit to Accounts Receivable for $300 and a credit to Service Revenue for $300.

8.   A cash payment of $2,000 for some new tools was recorded by a debit to Equipment for $200 and a credit to Cash for $200.

Instructions

Prepare an analysis of each error showing

(a)   the incorrect entry,

(b)   the correct entry, and

(c)   the correcting entry.

SOLUTION TO EXERCISE 4-9

1.   (a)   **Incorrect entry:**

Equipment	120	
Cash		120

(b)   **Correct entry:**

Maintenance and Repairs Expense	120	
Cash		120

(c)   **Correcting entry:**

Maintenance and Repairs Expense	120	
Equipment		120

2.   (a)   **Incorrect entry:**

Supplies	70	
Accounts Payable		70

(b)   **Correct entry:**

Supplies	70	
Cash		70

(c)   **Correcting entry:**

Accounts Payable	70	
Cash		70

3.   (a)   **Incorrect entry:**

Salaries and Wages Expense	700	
Cash		700

(b)   **Correct entry:**

Owner's Drawing	700	
Cash		700

(c) **Correcting entry:**

Owner's Drawing	700	
Salaries and Wages Expense		700

4. (a) **Incorrect entry:**

Utilities Expense	150	
Cash		150

(b) **Correct entry:**

Advertising Expense	150	
Cash		150

(c) **Correcting entry:**

Advertising Expense	150	
Utilities Expense		150

5. (a) **Incorrect entry:**

Cash	50	
Service Revenue		50

(b) **Correct entry:**

Cash	500	
Accounts Receivable		500

(c) **Correcting entry:**

Service Revenue	50	
Cash	450	
Accounts Receivable		500

TIP:	This one is tricky because both the amount and an account were in error in the original entry.

6. (a) **Incorrect entry:**

Interest Expense	1,000	
Cash		1,000

(b) **Correct entry:**

Interest Payable	300	
Interest Expense	700	
Cash		1,000

(c) **Correcting entry:**

Interest Payable	300	
Interest Expense		300

7. (a) **Incorrect entry:**

Accounts Receivable	300	
Service Revenue		300

(b) **Correct entry:**
Cash.. 300
    Service Revenue 300

(c) **Correcting entry:**
Cash.. 300
    Accounts Receivable 300

8. (a) **Incorrect entry:**
Equipment 200
    Cash 200

(b) **Correct entry:**
Equipment 2,000
    Cash 2,000

(c) **Correcting entry:**
Equipment 1,800
    Cash 1,800

Approach: Compare the correct entry with the incorrect entry to determine the accounts which need to be increased or decreased in the correcting entry to arrive at their correct balances.

Alternate Approach: If you are not usually successful in identifying the appropriate correcting entry by using the approach above, a simpler approach may be to reverse the incorrect entry and prepare the correct entry. These two entries together constitute the correction. For example, refer to error number 3. The correction could be made by the following:

Reversal of the erroneous entry:
Cash.. 700
    Salaries and Wages Expense.................................. 700

Correct entry:
Owner's Drawing.. 700
    Cash 700

Notice that these two entries are the equivalent to the single correcting entry given earlier in the solution as:

Owner's Drawing 700
    Salaries and Wages Expense............................ 700

You can readily tell this because in the two entry (second) approach, the debit to Cash for $700 offsets the credit to Cash for $700 which leaves only the remainder of the entries having an impact on account balances. That remainder is a debit to Owner's Drawing and a credit to Salaries and Wages Expense for $700.

EXERCISE 4-10

Purpose: (L.O. 1 thru 7) This exercise will quiz you about terminology used in this chapter.

A list of accounting terms with which you should be familiar appears below:

Classified balance sheet	Long-term liabilities
Closing entries	Operating cycle
Correcting entries	Permanent (real) accounts
Current assets	Post-closing trial balance
Current liabilities	Property, plant, and equipment
Income Summary	Reversing entry
Intangible assets	Stockholders' equity
Liquidity	Temporary (nominal) accounts
Long-term investments	Worksheet

Instructions

For each item below, enter in the blank the term that is described.

1. _____A multiple-column form that may be used in making adjusting entries and in preparing financial statements.

2. _____Entries made at the end of an accounting period to transfer the balance of temporary accounts to a permanent owner's equity account, owner's capital.

3. _____A list of permanent accounts and their balances after a company has journalized and posted closing entries.

4. _____Revenue, expense, and drawing accounts whose balances a company transfers to owner's capital at the end of an accounting period.

5. _____Balance sheet accounts whose balances companies carry forward to the next accounting period.

6. _____A temporary account used in closing revenue and expense accounts.

7. _____An entry, made at the beginning of a new accounting period, that is the exact opposite of the related adjusting entry made in the previous period.

8. _____The average time that it takes to purchase inventory, sell it on account, and then collect cash from customers.

9. _____Cash and other resources that a company expects to convert to cash or use up within one year.

10. _____Generally, investments in stocks and bonds of other companies that companies normally hold for many years. Also includes long-term assets such as land and buildings, not currently being used in operations.

11. _____Assets with relatively long useful lives, currently being used in operations.

12. _____Noncurrent assets that do not have physical substance.

13. _____Obligations that a company expects to pay from existing current assets within the coming year.

14. _____Obligations that a company expects to pay after one year.

15. _____Owners' equity of a corporation; the ownership claim of shareholders on total assets.

16. _____The ability of a company to pay obligations expected to become due within the next year.

17. _____Entries to correct errors made in recording transactions.

18. _____A balance sheet that contains a number of standard classifications or sections.

SOLUTION TO EXERCISE 4-10

1. Worksheet
2. Closing entries
3. Post-closing trial balance
4. Temporary accounts (or nominal accounts)
5. Permanent accounts (or real accounts)
6. Income Summary
7. Reversing entry
8. Operating cycle
9. Current assets
10. Long-term investments
11. Property, plant and equipment
12. Intangible assets
13. Current liabilities
14. Long-term liabilities
15. Stockholders' equity
16. Liquidity
17. Correcting entries
18. Classified balance sheet

ILLUSTRATION 4-2
USE OF REVERSING ENTRIES VERSUS
NO REVERSING ENTRIES USED* (L.O. 7)

---

*This material is covered in **Appendix 4A** in the text.

Reversing entries are most often used to reverse two types of adjusting entries: accrued revenues and accrued expenses.

As an example of the flow of information through the accounts when using reversing entries versus the flow when no reversing entries are used, consider the following information and the resulting entries and account balances. Notice that you arrive at the same account balances, regardless of your path, by the time financial statements are to be prepared.

Data:
A three-year note receivable for $12,000 was accepted on May 1, 2014. It carries a 10% interest rate. The interest is to be collected every 6 months so the first interest receipt was on November 1, 2014 and the second interest receipt is scheduled for May 1, 2015. The annual accounting period ends on December 31, 2014. Two months of accrued interest exists at year end.

Entries:

When Reversing Entries Are Not Used			When Reversing Entries Are Used		

Receipt Entry--Nov. 1, 2014

Cash	600		Cash	600	
Interest Revenue		600	Interest Revenue		600

Adjusting Entry--Dec. 31, 2014

Interest Receivable	200		Interest Receivable	200	
Interest Revenue		200	Interest Revenue		200

Closing Entry--Dec. 31, 2014

Interest Revenue	800		Interest Revenue	800	
Income Summary		800	Income Summary		800

Reversing Entry--Jan. 1, 2015

None			Interest Revenue	200	
			Interest Receivable		200

ILLUSTRATION 4-2 (Continued)

When Reversing Entries Are Not Used			When Reversing Entries Are Used		

Receipt Entry--May 1, 2015

Cash	600		
Interest Receivable		200	
Interest Revenue		400	

Receipt Entry--May 1, 2015

Cash	600	
Interest Revenue		600

Receipt Entry--Nov. 1, 2015

Cash	600	
Interest Revenue		600

Receipt Entry--Nov. 1, 2015

Cash	600	
Interest Revenue		600

The posting of the entries through Nov. 1, 2015 is reflected as follows:

Interest Receivable				
12/31/14 Adj.	200	**5/1/15 Rec.**	**200**	

Interest Receivable				
12/31/14 Adj.	200	**1/1/15 Rev.**	**200**	

Interest Revenue			
12/31/14 Closing	800	11/1/14 Rec.	600
		12/31/14 Adj.	200
	800		800
		5/1/15 Rec.	**400**
		11/1/15 Rec.	600

Interest Revenue			
12/31/14 Closing	800	11/1/14 Rec.	600
		12/31/14 Adj.	200
	800		800
1/1/15 Rev.	**200**	**5/1/15 Rec.**	**600**
		11/1/15 Rec.	600

TIP: The differences are highlighted in bold print. Notice that by the end of the day on December 31, 2014, the account balances are the same regardless of which alternative is chosen. Also, by the end of the day on May 1, 2015, the account balances are once again the same under both approaches. (Abbreviations are: Rec. = Receipt; Rev. = Reversing; Adj. = Adjusting.)

TIP: Notice how reversing entries allowed the bookkeeper to record the receipt of $600 on May 1, expediently like the November 1, 2014 receipt (debit to Cash for $600 and a credit to Interest Revenue for $600) without looking in the records to determine if the receipt is partially for revenue earned in a prior period or not. (Think of the time savings if you collect varying amounts of accrued interest from hundreds of different sources.)

*EXERCISE 4-11

Purpose: (L.O. 7) This exercise will provide practice in determining which adjusting entries may be reversed.

The following represent adjusting entries prepared for the Office Furniture Design Company.

_____	1.	Interest Expense	700	
		Interest Payable		700
_____	2.	Depreciation Expense	1,100	
		Accumulated Depreciation-Equipment		1,100
_____	3.	Accounts Receivable..	600	
		Rent Revenue		600
_____	4.	Insurance Expense	400	
		Prepaid Insurance		400
_____	5.	Accounts Receivable..	300	
		Service Revenue		300
_____	6.	Supplies Expense	200	
		Supplies...		200
_____	7.	Salaries and Wages Expense	1,000	
		Salaries and Wages Payable		1,000
_____	8.	Unearned Subscription Revenue	1,200	
		Subscription Revenue		1,200

Instructions
For each adjusting entry above (prepared at December 31, 2014), indicate if it would be appropriate to reverse the entry at the beginning of 2015. Indicate your answer by writing **yes** or **no** in the space provided.

SOLUTION TO EXERCISE 4-11

1. Yes   5. Yes
2. No   6. No
3. Yes   7. Yes
4. No   8. No

Explanation:

1. An expense accrual type adjustment can always be reversed. The reversing entry will eliminate the payable balance established by the adjustment and create a credit balance (an abnormal balance) in the expense account at the beginning of the new period. Thus, when the related cash is paid for the interest, the payment can be recorded by a credit to Cash and a debit to Interest Expense for the entire amount paid. (The abnormal balance in the expense account which was created by the reversing entry is eliminated with the posting of the cash payment entry.) This entry to record the cash payment is simpler than the alternate route of using no reversal and recording a portion of the payment (representing the accrued amount) by a debit to a payable account and the remainder (incurred in the new period) by a debit to the expense account.

2. An adjusting entry to record depreciation should **never** be reversed. It would not make sense to reverse this adjustment because to do so would reduce the depreciation to date (accumulated depreciation).

3. A revenue accrual type adjustment can always be reversed. The reversing entry will eliminate the receivable balance established by the adjustment and create a debit balance (an abnormal balance) in the revenue account at the beginning of the new period. Thus, when the related cash is collected from the tenant, the receipt can be recorded by a debit to Cash and a credit to Rent Revenue for the entire amount received. (The abnormal balance in the revenue account is eliminated with the posting of the cash collection entry.) This entry to record the cash receipt is simpler than the alternate route of using no reversal and recording a portion of the collection (representing the accrued amount) by a credit to the receivable account and the remainder (earned in the new period) by a credit to the revenue account.

4. An adjusting entry to transfer the expired portion of the insurance premium from an asset account (prepaid) to an expense account should **never** be reversed. A reversing entry would put the expired portion back into an asset account.

5. An adjusting entry to record accrued revenue can always be reversed. Refer to the logic explained for item 3. above.

6. An adjusting entry to transfer the cost of consumed supplies from an asset account to an expense account should never be reversed. Refer to the logic explained for item 4. above.

7. An adjusting entry to record accrued expense can always be reversed. Refer to the logic explained for item 1. above.

8. An adjusting entry to transfer the earned portion of the revenue collected in advance from the unearned account to an earned account should **never** be reversed. A reversing entry would put the earned portion back into an unearned (liability) account, which would **not** make sense because that portion of the cash received has been earned and no liability remains for that portion.

ANALYSIS OF MULTIPLE-CHOICE QUESTIONS

1.   (L.O. 2) Which of the following accounts is a nominal (temporary) account?
a.   Cash.
b.   Prepaid Rent.
c.   Accumulated Depreciation.
d.   Advertising Expense.

Approach and Explanation: Write down the definition of a nominal (or temporary) account. A **nominal account** is an account which is closed at the end of an accounting period. Think of what types of accounts get closed—revenues, expenses, owner's drawing. Think of what types of accounts never get closed—asset, liability, and owner's equity. Identify the classification of each of the accounts mentioned:

Cash	Asset
Prepaid Rent	Asset
Accumulated Depreciation	Contra Asset
Advertising Expense	Expense

When judging if an account is temporary or permanent (real), a contra account is classified in the same manner (temporary or permanent) as the account to which it relates. Hence, a contra asset account is a real account. (Solution = d.)

2.   (L.O. 2) Certain accounts are closed at the end of an accounting period in order to:
a.   reduce the number of items that get reported in the general purpose financial statements.
b.   prepare those accounts for recording of transactions of the subsequent accounting period.
c.   reduce the number of accounts that appear in the ledger.
d.   transfer the effect of transactions recorded in real accounts to the owner's capital account.

Approach and Explanation: Review the two reasons for preparing closing entries: (1) closing entries prepare the temporary accounts for the recording of transactions of the succeeding accounting period, and (2) closing entries transfer the net income (or net loss) amount and owner's drawings to owner's capital as shown in the owner's equity statement. Net income is determined by the balances in revenue and expense accounts (collectively called nominal or temporary accounts). (Solution = b.)

3.   (L.O. 2) A journal entry to close the Service Revenue account in the closing process will involve a debit to:
a.   Service Revenue and a credit to Income Summary.
b.   Income Summary and a credit to Service Revenue.
c.   Owner's Capital and a credit to Service Revenue.
d.   Service Revenue and a credit to Cash.

Approach and Explanation: Think of the normal balance of the account to be closed. Revenue accounts have a normal credit balance. A closing entry will involve the opposite action to that account; therefore, debit the Service Revenue account. All closing entries for income statement accounts involve the Income Summary account; therefore, credit Income Summary. (Solution = a.)

4. (L.O. 2) If a business has profitable operations for the period, the balance of the Income Summary account will be closed by:

a. a debit to Income Summary and a credit to Owner's Capital.
b. a debit to Owner's Capital and a credit to Income Summary.
c. debits to the expense accounts, credits to the revenue accounts, and a credit to the Income Summary account.
d. debits to the revenue accounts, credits to the expense accounts, and a credit to the Income Summary account.

Approach and Explanation: Keep in mind that assets have normal debit balances and owner's equity has the opposite (credit) normal balance. Revenues increase owner's equity so revenue accounts have normal credit balances and expense accounts have normal debit balances. Revenue accounts are closed by debits to those revenue accounts and credits to Income Summary; expense accounts are closed by credits to those expense accounts and debits to Income Summary. When revenues exceed expenses, the entity is profitable and the Income Summary account therefore has a credit balance before closing. The Income Summary account is closed, in those conditions, by a debit to Income Summary (for its balance) and a credit to the Owner's Capital account. (Solution = a.)

5. (L.O. 3) Which of the following groups of accounts have balances after the books have been closed at the end of an accounting period?

a. All asset and revenue accounts.
b. All expense and liability accounts.
c. All asset, liability, owner's capital, revenue, and expense accounts.
d. All asset, liability, and owner's capital accounts.

Approach and Explanation: Think of which accounts get closed. They are the temporary or nominal accounts (which include all revenue, expense and owner's drawing accounts). The real accounts are not closed (asset, liability, and owner's capital accounts). (Solution = d.)

6. (L.O. 1) Before computing the net income figure for the period, the total of the income statement debit column of a worksheet is $42,000 and the total of the income statement credit column is $40,000. This indicates that:

a. there was a net loss of $2,000 for the period.
b. there was a net income of $2,000 for the period.
c. the Income Summary account will be closed by a debit to that Income Summary account.
d. an error has been made in preparing the worksheet.

Explanation: Debits on the income statement reduce net income; credits on the income statement increase income. An excess of debits over credits on the income statement results in a net loss. A net loss will cause a debit balance in the Income Summary account so that account will be closed by a credit. (Solution = a.)

7. (L.O. 1) The preparation of a worksheet at the end of an accounting period will:
   a. eliminate the need for journalizing and posting adjusting entries.
   b. replace the preparation of individual financial statements.
   c. eliminate the need for preparing closing entries and a post-closing trial balance.
   d. serve as an aid to the accountant in organizing the data required for the preparation of financial statements.

   Explanation: The worksheet is an optional step in the accounting cycle. It does **not** eliminate the need for adjusting entries, financial statements, or closing entries. These are prepared in the same manner whether or not a worksheet is prepared. (Solution = d.)

8. (L.O. 1) In completing a worksheet, the account Depreciation Expense requires an amount in the adjusted trial balance column pair and also an amount in the:
   a. Income Statement debit column.
   b. Income Statement credit column.
   c. Balance Sheet debit column.
   d. Balance Sheet credit column.

   Explanation: Depreciation expense is to appear on the income statement as a reduction in net income (debit). (Solution = a.)

9. (L.O. 1) In completing a worksheet, the account Prepaid Insurance requires an amount in the adjusted trial balance column pair and also an amount in the:
   a. Income Statement debit column.
   b. Income Statement credit column.
   c. Balance Sheet debit column.
   d. Balance Sheet credit column.

   Approach and Explanation: Think about the statement on which the Prepaid Insurance account will appear and where. Prepaid Insurance will appear on the balance sheet as an asset (debit). (Solution = c.)

10. (L.O. 1) When revenues exceed expenses for a period, the worksheet will require the net income figure to be entered in the following columns to properly complete the worksheet.
    a. income statement debit column and balance sheet credit column.
    b. income statement credit column and balance sheet debit column.
    c. income statement debit column and balance sheet debit column.
    d. income statement credit column and balance sheet credit column.

    Explanation: Revenue accounts have credit balances; expense accounts have debit balances. Due to worksheet technique, when revenues exceed expenses (credits in income statement column exceed debits in income statement column on worksheet), a debit is needed in the income statement column pair to balance that pair. That debit is the net income figure. Debits have to equal credits. The corresponding credit is to the balance sheet column pair. (Solution = a.)

11. (L.O. 5) A piece of equipment was acquired for cash this period and was incorrectly recorded by a debit to Maintenance and Repairs Expense. The correcting entry should:
    a. increase assets and reduce expenses.
    b. increase expenses and reduce assets.
    c. increase liabilities and increase assets.
    d. reduce assets and reduce expenses.

    Approach and Explanation: Write down the incorrect entry (debit to Maintenance and Repairs Expense and a credit to Cash) and the correct entry (debit to Equipment and a credit to Cash). Compare the two entries and identify the errors (Maintenance and Repairs Expense is overstated and Equipment is understated). Prepare the correcting entry (debit to Equipment and a credit to Maintenance and Repairs Expense). Notice that the effect of the correcting entry is to reduce expenses and to increase assets. (This solution ignores the depreciation that should also be recorded for the period.) (Solution = a.)

12. (L.O. 7) Which of the following adjusting entries could be reversed at the beginning of the following accounting period?
    a. The entry to record depreciation for the period.
    b. The entry to record accrued revenue.
    c. The entry to transfer the expired portion of the supplies from an asset account to an expense account.
    d. The entry to transfer the earned portion of revenue received in advance from a liability account to a revenue account.

    Approach and Explanation: Think about the adjusting entries that can be reversed. Accrual type adjusting entries can always be reversed (the procedure is optional). Prepayment type adjusting entries are usually not reversed. Selection "a" is incorrect because depreciation entries are never reversed. Selection "c" is incorrect because a reversing entry would put expired costs back into an asset account. Selection "d" is incorrect because a reversing entry would put earned revenue back into a liability account. (Solution = b.)

CHAPTER 5

. . . .

ACCOUNTING FOR MERCHANDISING OPERATIONS

OVERVIEW

A service entity performs services for its customers to earn service revenue. A merchandising entity sells products to its customers to earn sales revenue. Both types of entities incur expenses in generating revenue. Thus, both must match expenses incurred with revenues earned. This chapter will acquaint you with the income statement for a merchandising entity. The major differences between the income statement for a service type firm and the income statement for a merchandising firm lie with the data reported for net sales revenue and cost of goods sold expense for the merchandiser. Both the single-step and the multiple-step formats for the income statement are discussed in this chapter.

A merchandiser must account for the purchase and sale of its inventory items. The perpetual system is discussed in this chapter and the periodic system is explained in an appendix to this chapter.

SUMMARY OF LEARNING OBJECTIVES

1. **Identify the differences between service and merchandising companies.** Because of the presence of inventory, a merchandising company has sales revenue, cost of goods sold, and gross profit. To account for inventory, a merchandising company must choose between a perpetual inventory system and a periodic inventory system.

2. **Explain the recording of purchases under a perpetual inventory system.** The company debits the Inventory account for all purchases of merchandise, freight-in and other costs, and credits it for purchase discounts and purchase returns and allowances.

3. **Explain the recording of sales revenues under a perpetual inventory system.** When a merchandising company sells inventory, it debits Accounts Receivable (or Cash), and credits Sales Revenue for the **selling price** of the merchandise. At the same time, it debits Cost of Goods Sold and credits Inventory for the **cost** of the

inventory items sold. Sales Returns and Allowances and Sales Discounts are debited.

4. **Explain the steps in the accounting cycle for a merchandising company.** Each of the required steps in the accounting cycle for a service company applies to a merchandising company. A worksheet is again an optional step. Under a perpetual inventory system, the company must adjust the Inventory account to agree with the physical count.

5. **Distinguish between a multiple-step and a single-step income statement.** A multiple-step income statement shows numerous steps in determining net income, including nonoperating activities sections. A single-step income statement classifies all data under two categories, revenues or expenses, and determines net income in one step.

*6. **Prepare a worksheet for a merchandising company.** The steps in preparing a worksheet for a merchandising company are the same as for a service company. The unique accounts for a merchandiser are Inventory, Sales Revenue, Sales Returns and Allowances, Sales Discounts, and Cost of Goods Sold.

7. **Explain the reporting of purchases and sales of inventory under a periodic inventory system. In recording purchases under a periodic system, companies must use entries for (a) cash and credit purchases, (b) purchase returns and allowances, (c) purchase discounts, and (d) freight costs. In recording sales, companies must make entries for (a) cash and credit sales, (b) sales returns and allowances, and (c) sales discounts.

*This material is covered in **Appendix 5A** in the text.

This material is covered in **Appendix 5B in the text.

TIPS ON CHAPTER TOPICS

TIP: Sales revenue is recorded and reported in the period that it is earned. Sales revenue is earned in the period in which the related products are sold. For a given sales transaction, the related cash may or may not be received in the same time period as the sale. If the sale occurs before the cash is received, the business has an account receivable until the point of collection. If the cash receipt occurs before the sale, the business has a liability (which is often called unearned revenue) until the point in time when the revenue is earned.

TIP: Be careful to distinguish between a purchase type transaction and a sales type transaction. When one entity has a purchase, another entity has a sale. **Always describe the transaction from the viewpoint of the party for whom you are accounting.** For example, if Intel sells a computer chip to IBM, Intel has a sale and IBM has a purchase. When IBM sells a computer to Ray Sturm, IBM has a sale and Ray Sturm has a purchase.

TIP: Purchases of merchandise inventory are recorded by debiting the Inventory account (assuming the perpetual inventory system is used). Purchases of equipment are recorded by debits to Equipment. Purchases of supplies are recorded by debits to the Supplies account.

TIP: One of two basic systems may be used to keep track of inventory costs: (1) the perpetual inventory system, or (2) the periodic inventory system.

Under a **perpetual inventory system,** the cost of each inventory item is debited to the Inventory account when it is purchased. **At the time of sale,** the cost of an item is transferred from the Inventory account to the Cost of Goods Sold account. Thus, the Cost of Goods Sold account is continually updated **so, at all times,** it reflects the cost of merchandise sold during the period and the balance of the Inventory account **at all times** reflects the cost of merchandise on hand. (The perpetual system is discussed in this chapter.)

Under a **periodic inventory system,** no attempt is made to keep detailed inventory records of the goods on hand throughout the accounting period. The cost of goods sold is determined **only** at the end of the period when a physical inventory count is taken to determine the quantity of goods on hand and their related cost. (The details of the periodic system are discussed in **Appendix 5B** in the text).

TIP: When a perpetual inventory system is used, the balance of the Inventory account at the end of the accounting period reflects the cost of inventory on hand at the balance sheet date. This balance is verified by physically counting the merchandise and identifying its historical cost. If shrinkage or theft has occurred, an adjustment of the ending Inventory balance is necessary.

TIP: The following T-account displays the information which is reflected in the Inventory account when the **perpetual inventory system** is used:

Inventory	
Beginning Balance	
Purchases	Purchase Discounts
Freight-in	Purchase Returns and
	Allowances
	Cost of Goods Sold
Ending Balance	

By looking at the entries in the T-account above, we can see that the net cost of goods purchased during a period is added to the balance of the Inventory account. (That is, purchases are added, returns and discounts related to purchases are deducted, and freight-in is added.) The cost of goods sold during a period is removed from the Inventory account so that the cost of the inventory on hand at the end of the accounting period is the balance that remains in the Inventory account. That balance is called ending inventory.

Thus, the following relationships exist:

	Purchases
-	Purchase Returns and Allowances
-	Purchase Discounts
=	Net Purchases
+	Freight-In
=	Cost of Goods Purchased
	Beginning Inventory Balance
+	Cost of Goods Purchased
=	Cost of Goods Available for Sale
-	Cost of Goods Sold
=	Ending Inventory Balance

TIP: **Freight-in** is often called **transportation-in.** Freight-in refers to freight charges incurred to transport merchandise from the supplier's location to the merchandiser's warehouse. Freight-out refers to transportation charges incurred to transport merchandise from the merchandiser's warehouse to the customer's (consumer's) location. **Freight-out** is often called **transportation-out.** Freight-in is a component of the cost of inventory acquired (and thus becomes part of the cost of goods sold when items are sold), while freight-out is classified as a selling expense (which is part of operating expenses).

TIP: The cost of an inventory item includes all costs necessary to acquire the item and get it ready for resale. Thus, if inventory is purchased FOB shipping point, freight-in is recorded by a debit to Inventory (assuming the perpetual inventory system is in use). Thus, when the inventory item is ultimately sold, the freight-in is included in the cost of goods sold figure on the income statement. Any freight-out is an operating expense.

TIP: An **invoice** is a document prepared by the seller that shows the relevant information about a sale. From the seller's perspective, this document is a **sales invoice;** from the buyer's perspective, it is a **purchase invoice.**

ILLUSTRATION 5-1
COMPUTATION MODELS FOR COMPONENTS OF
A MULTIPLE-STEP INCOME STATEMENT (L.O. 1, 5, 7)

    Sales Revenue
-    Sales Returns and Allowances
-    <u>Sales Discounts</u>
=   Net Sales

    Net Sales
-    <u>Cost of Goods Sold</u>
=   Gross Profit

    Gross Profit
-    <u>Operating Expenses</u>
=   Income (Loss) from Operations

    Income (Loss) from Operations
+   Other Revenues and Gains
-    <u>Other Expenses and Losses</u>
=   Net Income (Loss)

TIP: An entity often has two types of sales: cash sales and credit sales. **Credit sales** are often called **sales on account** or **charge sales** or **sales on credit.** Both cash sales and credit sales are recorded in the Sales Revenue account and are reported by the caption Sales Revenue or Sales on the income statement.

TIP: Even if a credit customer has paid the balance of his account, there are several reasons why the amount of cash collected from the customer may not equal the amount of the related sales revenue. Three of these reasons are discussed in this chapter; they are sales returns, sales allowances, and sales discounts.

TIP: The normal balance of the **Sales Returns and Allowances** account is a debit balance. It is **not** an expense account. Its balance is reported as a deduction from the sales revenue figure on the income statement; hence, it is classified as a **contra-revenue** account. Although the amounts of sales returns and allowances could be directly debited to the Sales Revenue account, most businesses prefer to use a separate Sales Returns and Allowances account in order for management to readily notice if these items get unreasonably large.

TIP: **Cost of goods sold** is an expense item. For most retail companies, it is the largest expense displayed on the income statement.

TIP: **Gross profit** is often called **gross margin.**

TIP: The Sales Revenue account (sometimes simply titled Sales) is used only to record the sale of goods held for resale (inventory). The sale of an asset not held for sale in the ordinary course of business does not affect the Sales Revenue account. For example, assume two items are sold for cash of $10,000 each. The first item is an inventory item with a cost of $6,000. The second item is a plot of land which was purchased years ago for $6,000 and held as a future store site. Assuming a **perpetual inventory system** (rather than a periodic inventory system) is used, the sale of the inventory item would be recorded as follows:

Cash...	10,000	
Sales Revenue.......................................		10,000
Cost of Goods Sold..	6,000	
Inventory...		6,000

A gross profit of $4,000 would be reflected on the income statement because of the sales figure of $10,000 and the expense (cost of goods sold) of $6,000.

The sale of the land would be recorded as follows:

Cash	10,000	
Land		6,000
Gain on Sale of Land.................................		4,000

The gain would be reflected as a nonoperating item on the income statement; thus it is included under the Other Revenues and Gains caption.

TIP: Operating expenses are incurred in the process of generating sales revenue. They include both selling and administrative expenses. Examples include: sales commissions expense, advertising expense, freight-out, insurance, depreciation, and utilities.

TIP: The transactions related to a company's primary operating activities are summarized by the caption "Income (Loss) from Operations." Nonoperating activities consist of (1) revenues and expenses from auxiliary operations and (2) gains and losses that are unrelated to the company's operations. The results of nonoperating activities are shown in two sections: **"Other revenues and gains"** and **"Other expenses and losses."**

EXERCISE 5-1

Purpose: (L.O. 1) This exercise will help you to identify the relationships among the components involved in measuring net income for a merchandising company.

The following information applies to The Sports Shop for 2014:

Sales revenue	$748,000
Sales returns	10,000
Sales discounts	7,000
Cost of goods sold	388,000
Sales commissions expense	107,700
Advertising expense	16,800
Salaries and wages expense	100,000
Utilities expense	25,000
Insurance expense	6,000
Freight-out	8,000
Interest revenue	5,500
Interest expense	7,200

Instructions
(a) Compute net sales for 2014.
(b) Compute gross profit for 2014.
(c) Compute total operating expenses for 2014.
(d) Compute net income for 2014.

SOLUTION TO EXERCISE 5-1

Explanations:

(a)	Sales revenue	$748,000
	Sales returns	(10,000)
	Sales discounts	(7,000)
	Net sales	$731,000
(b)	Net sales	$731,000
	Cost of goods sold	(388,000)
	Gross profit	$343,000
(c)	Sales commissions expense	$107,700
	Advertising expense	16,800
	Freight-out	8,000
	Salaries and wages expense	100,000
	Utilities expense	25,000
	Insurance expense	6,000
	Total operating expenses	$263,500
(d)	Gross profit	$343,000
	Total operating expenses	(263,500)
	Other revenue—interest revenue	5,500
	Other expense—interest expense	(7,200)
	Net income	$ 77,800

Approach for parts (a), (b) and (d): Write down the elements of the computations for net sales, gross profit, and net income. **Refer to Illustration 5-1.** Enter the data given and solve.

Approach for part (c): Examine the items not used to compute net sales and gross profit. Identify the items that are operating expenses and think about whether they are involved with the selling function (selling expenses such as salaries for the sales force, sales commissions, advertising, freight-out, and depreciation of sales counters, showroom, and store equipment) or not (administrative expenses such as officer salaries, rent, and insurance). Nonoperating items are other revenues, gains, other expenses, and losses.

> **TIP:** Some companies subdivide the operating expenses into the subclassifications of selling expenses and administrative expenses. Administrative expenses are often called general and administrative expenses. (However, for homework purposes, do not do this subdivision unless specifically instructed to do so). **Selling expenses** include expenses associated with the making of sales, such as salaries for the sales force, sales commissions, advertising, freight delivery, and depreciation of sales counters, showroom, and store equipment. **General and administrative expenses** include expenses relating to general operating activities such as rent, officer salaries, personnel management, insurance, accounting, and store security.

ILLUSTRATION 5-2
DAILY RECURRING AND ADJUSTING AND CLOSING ENTRIES FOR A MERCHANDISING ENTITY USING A PERPETUAL INVENTORY SYSTEM (L.O. 2, 3, 4)

The following are the typical entries for a merchandising entity employing a perpetual inventory system:

Transactions	Daily Recurring Entries	Dr.	Cr.	Effect on A = L + OE
Selling merchandise to customers	Cash or Accounts Receivable	XX		↑
	Sales Revenue		XX	↑
	Cost of Goods Sold	XX		↓
	Inventory		XX ↓	
Paying freight costs on sales FOB destination	Freight-Out	XX		↓
	Cash		XX ↓	
Granting sales returns (or allowances) to customers	Sales Returns and Allowances	XX		↓
	Cash or Accounts Receivable		XX ↓	
Granting sales returns (not allowances) to customers	Inventory	XX		↑
	Cost of Goods Sold		XX	↑
Receiving payment from customers within discount period	Cash	XX		↑
	Sales Discounts	XX		↓
	Accounts Receivable		XX ↓	
Receiving payment from customers after discount period	Cash	XX		↑
	Accounts Receivable		XX ↓	
Purchasing merchandise for resale	Inventory	XX		↑
	Cash (or Accounts Payable)		XX ↓ or ↑	
Paying freight costs on merchandise purchased; FOB shipping point	Inventory	XX		↑
	Cash		XX ↓	
Receiving purchase returns or allowances from suppliers	Cash (or Accounts Payable)	XX		↑ or ↓
	Inventory		XX ↓	
Paying suppliers within discount period	Accounts Payable	XX		↓
	Inventory		XX ↓	
	Cash		XX ↓	
Paying suppliers after discount period	Accounts Payable	XX		↓
	Cash		XX ↓	

ILLUSTRATION 5-2 (Continued)

Events	Adjusting Entry	Dr.	Cr.	Effect on A = L + OE
Adjust because booked amount is higher than the inventory amount deter-mined to be on hand	Cost of Goods Sold Inventory	XX	XX	↓ ↓

Closing Entries

Events		Dr.	Cr.	Effect on A = L + OE
Closing accounts with credit balances	Sales Revenue Income Summary	XX	XX	↓ ↑

Closing accounts with debit balances	Income Summary
	    Sales Returns and Allowances
	    Sales Discounts
	    Cost of Goods Sold
	    Freight-out
	    Expenses (various operating
	        expenses)
		XX	XX
			XX
			XX
			XX
			
			XX
				↓
				↑
				↑
				↑
				↑
				
				↑

> **TIP:** Notice that the first five transactions in this Illustration involve activities related to the sale of merchandise inventory; whereas, each of the second group of five transactions involves activities related to the purchase of merchandise inventory.

EXERCISE 5-2

Purpose: (L.O. 2) This exercise reviews the journal entries to record purchases of merchandise inventory under a perpetual inventory system.

A list of transactions for the Luke Bryan Memorabilia Sales Company appears below. A perpetual inventory system is used.

July 1 Purchased merchandise from Oliver Company for $3,000 cash.
       2 Purchased merchandise from Yearwood Company, $5,000, FOB shipping point, terms 2/10, n/30.
       6 Paid freight on July 2 purchase, $125.
      10 Paid Yearwood Company the amount owed.
      11 Purchased merchandise from McBride Company, $7,000, FOB destination, terms 1/10, n/30.
      23 Paid McBride Company the amount owed.

Aug. 7 Purchased merchandise from Dun Company, $4,000, FOB destination, terms 2/10, n/30.
       9 Returned one-fourth of the merchandise acquired in the August 7 transaction to Dun Company because of detected defects.
      16 Paid Dun Company the balance owed.

Instructions
Prepare the journal entries to record these transactions on the books of the Luke Bryan Memorabilia Sales Company.

SOLUTION TO EXERCISE 5-2

July	1	Inventory	3,000	
		Cash		3,000
		(To record cash purchases)		

	2	Inventory	5,000	
		Accounts Payable...		5,000
		(To record goods purchased on account, terms 2/10, n/30)		

	6	Inventory	125	
		Cash		125
		(To record payment of freight, terms FOB shipping point)		

	10	Accounts Payable	5,000	
		Inventory..		100
		Cash		4,900
		(To record payment within discount period)		
		($5,000 X .02 = $100; $5,000 - $100 = $4,900)		

	11	Inventory	7,000	
		Accounts Payable...		7,000
		(To record goods purchased on account, terms 1/10, n/30)		

	23	Accounts Payable	7,000	
		Cash		7,000
		(To record payment with no discount taken)		

Aug.	7	Inventory	4,000	
		Accounts Payable...		4,000
		(To record goods purchased on account, terms 2/10, n/30)		

	9	Accounts Payable	1,000	
		Inventory..		1,000
		(To record allowance for damaged goods)		
		(1/4 X $4,000 = $1,000)		

	16	Accounts Payable	3,000	
		Inventory..		60
		Cash		2,940
		(To record payment within discount period)		
		($4,000 - $1,000 returned = $3,000; $3,000 X .02 = $60 discount; $3,000 - $60 = $2,940 payment)		

> **TIP:** Freight terms are expressed as either FOB shipping point or FOB destination. The letters **FOB** mean **free on board.** Thus, **FOB shipping point** means that goods are placed free on board the carrier by the seller, and the buyer pays the freight. Conversely, **FOB destination** means that the goods are placed free on board for the buyer's place of business, and the seller pays the freight.
>
> **TIP:** A purchase discount is computed on the amount purchased less any purchase returns or purchase allowances.

EXERCISE 5-3

Purpose: (L.O. 3) This exercise reviews the journal entries to record sales of merchandise inventory under a perpetual inventory system.

A list of transactions for the Luke Bryan Memorabilia Sales Company appears below. A perpetual inventory system is used.

July   17   Sold merchandise with a cost of $300 to Eric Nelson for $520 cash.
     18   Sold merchandise with a cost of $340 to Guy Sellars for $580, terms 2/10, n/30.
     23   Issued a credit memo for $80 to Guy Sellars because of a sales allowance granted to him due to the inferior quality of goods sold to him on July 18.
     26   Received payment from Guy Sellars for amount due for sale of July 18.
     27   Sold merchandise to Jason Zahner, $200, terms n/30. The merchandise cost $120.
Aug.   25   Received payment in full from Jason Zahner.
     26   Sold merchandise with a cost of $460 to Michele Blackburn for $800, terms 2/10, n/30.
     28   Issued a credit memo for $150 to Michele Blackburn because she returned a portion of the goods sold to her on Aug. 26; the returned merchandise had a cost of $90.
Sept.   4   Collected balance of account from Michele Blackburn.
     5   Sold merchandise to Andrea Brotherly, $600, terms 2/10, n/30. The merchandise cost $350.
     22   Received payment from Andrea Brotherly for amount due for sale of Sept. 5.
     23   Sold merchandise costing $220 to Herman Ichner for $400, terms 2/10, n/30.
Oct.   10   Received payment from Herman Ichner for sale of September 23.

Instructions
Prepare the journal entries to record these transactions on the books of the Luke Bryan Memorabilia Sales Company.

SOLUTION TO EXERCISE 5-3

July	17	Cash..	520	
		Sales Revenue		520
		(To record cash sales)		
		Cost of Goods Sold	300	
		Inventory..		300
		(To record cost of merchandise sold)		
	18	Accounts Receivable....................................	580	
		Sales Revenue		580
		(To record sales on account, terms 2/10, n/30)		
		Cost of Goods Sold	340	
		Inventory..		340
		(To record cost of merchandise sold)		
	23	Sales Returns and Allowances...................................	80	
		Accounts Receivable		80
		(To record allowance because of inferior goods)		

TIP:	There is no entry affecting Inventory because there was no return of merchandise; there was a sales allowance granted.

	26	Cash..	490	
		Sales Discounts..	10	
		Accounts Receivable		500
		(To record collection within discount period)		
		($580 - $80 allowance = $500; $500 X .02 = $10; $500 - $10 = $490)		
	27	Accounts Receivable...	200	
		Sales Revenue		200
		(To record sales on account, terms n/30)		
		Cost of Goods Sold	120	
		Inventory..		120
		(To record cost of merchandise sold)		
Aug.	25	Cash..	200	
		Accounts Receivable		200
		(To record collection on account)		

Aug. 26	Accounts Receivable	800	
	Sales Revenue		800
	(To record sales on account, terms 2/10, n/30)		
	Cost of Goods Sold	460	
	Inventory		460
	(To record cost of merchandise sold)		
28	Sales Returns and Allowances	150	
	Accounts Receivable		150
	(To record return of goods)		
	Inventory...	90	
	Cost of Goods Sold...		90
	(To record cost of goods returned)		

TIP:	This entry assumes the goods returned were still in good condition.

Sept. 4	Cash...	637	
	Sales Discounts..	13	
	Accounts Receivable		650
	(To record collection within discount period)		
	($800 - $150 = $650)		
	($650 X .02 = $13; $650 - $13 = $637)		
5	Accounts Receivable	600	
	Sales Revenue		600
	(To record sales on account, terms 2/10, n/30)		
	Cost of Goods Sold	350	
	Inventory		350
	(To record cost of merchandise sold)		
22	Cash...	600	
	Accounts Receivable		600
	(To record collection, not within the discount period)		

TIP:	The amount was collected after the end of discount period so no discount is allowed.

23	Accounts Receivable	400	
	Sales Revenue		400
	(To record sales on account, terms 2/10, n/30)		
	Cost of Goods Sold	220	
	Inventory		220
	(To record cost of merchandise sold)		
Oct. 10	Cash...	400	
	Accounts Receivable		400
	(To record collection with no discount taken)		

TIP: The terms of a credit sale may include an offer for a cash discount, called a sales discount, to the customer for prompt payment of the balance due. Credit terms of 2/10, n/30, which is read "two-ten, net thirty" means that a 2% cash discount may be taken on the invoice price (less any returns or allowances) if payment is made within 10 days of the invoice date (the discount period); otherwise, the invoice price less any returns or allowances is due 30 days from the invoice date. Alternatively, the discount period may extend to a specified number of days following the month in which the sale occurs. For example, 1/10 EOM (end-of-month) means that a 1% discount is available if the invoice is paid within the first 10 days of the next month. Payment terms of n/30 means no discount is offered and the invoice price is due within 30 days of the invoice date.

EXERCISE 5-4

Purpose: (L.O. 1, 2, 3, *7) This exercise reviews the elements of the net sales, cost of goods sold, gross profit, total operating expenses, and net income computations for a merchandising company.

Instructions
Compute the missing amounts for each of the independent situations below.

(a) Beginning inventory $22,000
    Purchases 79,000
    Purchase returns 3,000
    Sales allowances 2,000
    Ending inventory 23,500
    Cost of goods sold _____

(d) Beginning inventory $ 14,000
    Ending inventory 17,000
    Net sales 105,000
    Gross profit 41,000
    Cost of goods purchased _____

(b) Net sales $140,000
    Beginning inventory 20,000
    Purchases 80,000
    Purchase returns 2,000
    Cost of goods sold 83,500
    Ending inventory _____

(e) Cost of goods purchased $82,000
    Ending inventory 21,000
    Net income 8,000
    Total operating expenses 44,000
    Net sales 140,000
    Gross profit _____
    Cost of goods sold _____
    Beginning inventory _____

(c) Cost of goods available
    for sale $42,000
    Beginning inventory 12,000
    Purchase returns and
    allowances 1,100
    Purchases (gross) _____

(f)			(g)		
Beginning inventory	$10,000		Sales revenue		$100,000
Purchases	62,000		Sales returns		7,000
Freight-out	2,100		Net sales		90,000
Freight-in	1,800		Sales discounts		_____
Purchase returns	3,100				
Ending inventory	13,500				
Cost of goods purchased	_____				

TIP: Be careful to distinguish between purchase allowances and sales allowances. **Sales allowances** are reductions in sales prices allowed to customers. **Purchase allowances** are reductions in the purchase prices of merchandise from suppliers. Sales allowances are a contra revenue item; purchase allowances reduce the balance of the Inventory account (when the perpetual system is used to record inventory purchases). Likewise, be careful to distinguish between (a) sales returns and purchase returns, and (b) sales discounts and purchase discounts. Returns and discounts processed for customers are related to sales; returns and discounts honored by suppliers of merchandise inventory are related to purchases.

SOLUTION TO EXERCISE 5-4

Approach: Use the computation models in **Illustration 5-1** and the data that flows through the Inventory account. Fill in the information given. Solve for the unknown.

(a)			
Beginning inventory			$22,000
Purchases		$79,000	
Purchase returns and allowances		(3,000)	
Purchase discounts		(-0-)	
Net purchases		76,000	
Freight-in		-0-	
Cost of goods purchased			76,000
Cost of goods available for sale			98,000
Cost of goods sold			(X)
Ending inventory			$23,500

Solving for X: $98,000 - X = $23,500
$98,000 - $23,500 = $74,500
X = **$74,500** **Cost of goods sold**

TIP: Sales allowances have **no** impact on the balance of the Inventory account, the cost of merchandise purchased, or the cost of goods sold computation.

(b) | | | |
|---|---:|---:|
| Beginning inventory | | $20,000 |
| Purchases | $80,000 | |
| Purchase returns and allowances | (2,000) | |
| Purchase discounts | (-0-) | |
| Net purchases | 78,000 | |
| Freight-in | -0- | |
| Cost of goods purchased | | 78,000 |
| Cost of goods available for sale | | 98,000 |
| Cost of goods sold | | 83,500 |
| Ending inventory | | $ (X) |

Solving for X: $98,000 - $83,500 = X
               X = **$14,500** = **Ending Inventory**

TIP: Net sales is irrelevant information for the question at hand.

(c) | | | |
|---|---:|---:|
| Beginning inventory | | $12,000 |
| Purchases | $ X | |
| Purchase returns and allowances | (1,100) | |
| Purchase discounts | (-0-) | |
| Net purchases | Y | |
| Freight-in | -0- | |
| Cost of goods purchased | | Z |
| Cost of goods available for sale | | $42,000 |

Solving for Z: $12,000 + Z = $42,000
               Z = $42,000 - $12,000
               Z = $30,000 = Cost of goods purchased

Solving for Y: Y + $0 = $30,000
               Y = $30,000 = Net purchases

Solving for X: X - $1,100 - $0 = $30,000
               X = $30,000 + $1,100
               X = **$31,100** = **Purchases**

(d) | | |
|---|---:|
| Beginning inventory | $14,000 |
| Cost of goods purchased | X |
| Cost of goods available for sale | Y |
| Cost of goods sold | (Z) |
| Ending inventory | 17,000 |
| | |
| Net sales | 105,000 |
| Cost of goods sold | (Z) |
| Gross profit | $ 41,000 |

Solving for Z: $105,000 - Z = $41,000
              Z = $105,000 - $41,000
              Z = $64,000 = Cost of goods sold

Solving for Y: Y - $64,000 = $17,000
              Y = $17,000 + $64,000
              Y = $81,000 = Cost of goods available for sale

Solving for X: $14,000 + X = $81,000
              X = $81,000 - $14,000
              X = **$67,000** = **Cost of goods purchased**

(e) Net sales $140,000
     Cost of goods sold   (W)
     Gross profit   X
     Operating expenses   (44,000)
     Net income $ 8,000

     Beginning inventory $ Y
     Cost of goods purchased   82,000
     Cost of goods available for sale   Z
     Cost of goods sold   (W)
     Ending inventory $21,000

Solving for X: X - $44,000 = $8,000
              X = $8,000 + $44,000
              X = **$52,000** = **Gross profit**

Solving for W: $140,000 - W = $52,000
              $140,000 - $52,000 = W
              W = **$88,000** = **Cost of goods sold**

Solving for Z: Z - $88,000 = $21,000
              Z = $21,000 + $88,000
              Z = $109,000 = Cost of goods available for sale

Solving for Y: Y + $82,000 = $109,000
              Y = $109,000 - $82,000
              Y = **$27,000** = **Beginning Inventory**

(f) Purchases $62,000
    Purchase returns and allowances   (3,100)
    Purchase discounts   (-0-)
    Net purchases   58,900
    Freight-in   1,800
    Cost of goods purchased $ X

Solving for X: $58,900 + $1,800 = X
        X = **$60,700** = **Cost of goods purchased**

TIP:	The beginning and ending inventory amounts have no effect on the computation of the cost of goods purchased. Freight-out is a selling expense and, therefore, does not affect the computation of the cost of goods purchased.

(g) Sales revenue $100,000
    Sales returns and allowances   (7,000)
    Sales discounts   (X)
    Net sales $ 90,000

Solving for X: $100,000 - $7,000 - X = $90,000
        $100,000 - $7,000 - $90,000 = X
        X = **$3,000** = **Sales discounts**

EXERCISE 5-5

Purpose: (L.O. 5) This exercise will allow you to practice preparing an income statement and to contrast the multiple-step format and the single-step format for this statement.

The accountant for Steve Bradley Golf Products has compiled the following information from the company's records as a basis for an income statement for the year ended December 31, 2014.

Rent revenue	$ 29,000
Interest expense	18,000
Salaries and wages expense	134,900
Supplies expense	10,000
Other operating expenses	1,700
Sales revenue	970,000
Freight-out	7,600
Advertising expense	15,800
Depreciation expense	65,000
Sales returns and allowances	7,000
Rent expense	120,000
Cost of goods sold	446,000
Sales discounts	2,000
Owner's Drawings	85,000

Instructions

(a) Prepare a multiple-step income statement.
(b) Prepare a single-step income statement.

SOLUTION TO EXERCISE 5-5

(a)

STEVE BRADLEY GOLF PRODUCTS
Income Statement
For the Year Ended December 31, 2014

Sales revenues			
Sales revenue			$970,000
Less: Sales returns and allowances	$7,000		
Sales discounts	2,000		9,000
Net sales			961,000
Cost of goods sold			446,000
Gross profit			515,000
Operating expenses			
Salaries and wages expense	134,900		
Rent expense	120,000		
Depreciation	65,000		
Advertising expense	15,800		
Supplies expense	10,000		
Freight-out	7,600		
Other operating expenses	1,700		
Total operating expenses			355,000
Income from operations			160,000
Other revenues and gains			
Rent revenue		29,000	
Other expenses and losses			
Interest expense		18,000	11,000
Net income			$171,000

(b)

STEVE BRADLEY GOLF PRODUCTS
Income Statement
For the Year Ended December 31, 2014

Net sales	$ 961,000	
Rent revenue	29,000	
Total revenues		$990,000
Expenses		
Cost of goods sold	446,000	
Operating expenses	355,000	
Interest expense	18,000	
Total expenses		819,000
Net income		$171,000

TIP: A merchandising business has various types of expenses. Common expense categories are as follows: (1) cost of goods sold, (2) selling, (3) administrative, (4) interest, and (5) income taxes. Collectively, selling expenses and administrative expenses are usually called operating expenses; they may be separately displayed or combined for one line item as illustrated above. Refer to the multiple-step income statement [part (a) above]. Notice where each of these types of expenses appear on a multiple-step income statement. (Income tax expense will be illustrated in a later chapter.)

TIP: Nonoperating activities consist of (1) revenues and expenses that result from secondary or auxiliary operations and (2) gains and losses that are unrelated to the company's operations. The results of nonoperating activities are shown in two sections on a multiple-step income statement: Other Revenues and Gains and Other Expenses and Losses. Items classified in the **Other Revenues and Gains** section of a multiple-step income statement include rent revenue, investment revenues (interest revenue and dividend revenue), unusual inflows (such as prizes received), and gains on the sale of assets **not** classified as inventory. Items classified in the **Other Expenses and Losses** section of a multiple-step income statement include financing expenses (interest expense), unusual outflows (such as casualty losses and litigation losses), and losses on the sale or abandonment of assets **not** classified as inventory (such as loss on the sale of property, plant and equipment).

TIP: The term **revenue** is a gross concept and the term **income** is usually used as a net concept. Thus, net income results after expenses are offset against revenues. Sometimes the word income is used interchangeably with revenue in describing other types of revenues (such as interest income and rental income); it is best, however, if the term "revenue" instead of "income" is used in those contexts.

EXERCISE 5-6

Purpose: (L.O. 4) This exercise will review closing entries for a merchandising enterprise.

Closing entries are recorded at the end of an accounting period to prepare the temporary accounts for the subsequent accounting period. For example, assume the calendar year is the accounting period for a company. At the end of 2014, the Sales Revenue account balance is closed so that the Sales Revenue account begins the year of 2015 with a zero balance. Therefore, at the end of 2015, the balance in the Sales Revenue account will reflect only sales that took place in that single year (2015).

Closing entries also update the balance of the Owner's Capital account.

Instructions
Refer to the facts in **Exercise 5-5** and its Solution. Prepare the closing entries for Steve Bradley Golf Products for the year ending December 31, 2014.

SOLUTION TO EXERCISE 5-6

Sales Revenue...	970,000	
Rent Revenue	29,000	
Income Summary		999,000
(To close temporary accounts with credit balances)		
Income Summary	828,000	
Sales Returns and Allowances.....................................		7,000
Sales Discounts		2,000
Cost of Goods Sold		446,000
Rent Expense..		120,000
Salaries and Wages Expense		134,900
Depreciation Expense		65,000
Advertising Expense...		15,800
Supplies Expense..		10,000
Freight-out..		7,600
Other Operating Expenses..		1,700
Interest Expense		18,000
(To close income statement accounts with debit balances)		
Income Summary	171,000	
Owner's Capital...		171,000
(To transfer net income to capital)		
Owner's Capital..	85,000	
Owner's Drawings		85,000
(To close drawings to capital)		

TIP: The closing process for a merchandiser includes the following:

   (1) entry to (a) debit Sales Revenue for its ending balance, debit any other revenue or gain accounts for their ending balances, and (b) credit Income Summary. This entry closes the temporary account(s) with credit balance(s).

   (2) entry to (a) credit contra sales items (Sales Returns and Allowances and Sales Discounts) for their ending balances, (b) credit operating expense accounts for their ending balances, and (c) credit interest expense and any other expense or loss accounts for their ending balances, and (d) debit Income Summary.

   (3) entry to close the balance of the Income Summary account to the Owner's Capital account.

   (4) entry to credit the Owner's Drawing account for its ending balance and debit the Owner's Capital account. This entry closes the Owner's Drawing account to the Owner's Capital account.

**ILLUSTRATION 5-3
COMPUTATION MODELS FOR COMPONENTS OF
A MULTIPLE-STEP INCOME STATEMENT WHEN THE PERIODIC
INVENTORY SYSTEM IS USED (L.O. **7)

Net Sales
- Cost of Goods Sold
= Gross Profit

Sales Revenue
- Sales Returns and Allowances
- Sales Discounts
= Net Sales

Gross Profit
- Operating Expenses
= Income (Loss) from Operations

Beginning Inventory
+ Cost of Goods Purchased
= Cost of Goods Available for Sale
- Ending Inventory
= Cost of Goods Sold

Income (Loss) from Operations
+ Other Revenues and Gains
- Other Expenses and Losses
= Net Income (Loss)

Purchases
- Purchase Returns and Allowances
- Purchase Discounts
= Net Purchases
+ Freight-In
= Cost of Goods Purchased

TIP: You should memorize all of the models in this Illustration. Think about the logic of each computation. Visualize the transactions that give rise to the account balances used in these computations. This should make the memorization process easier and more effective.

TIP: The **Freight-In** account is often called **Transportation-In.** Freight-In is used to record freight charges incurred to transport merchandise from the supplier's location to the merchandiser's warehouse. Freight-Out is used to record transportation charges incurred to transport merchandise from the merchandiser's warehouse to the customer's (consumer's) location. **Freight-Out** is often called **Transportation-Out.** Freight-In is a component of the cost of goods sold computation, while Freight-Out is classified as a selling expense (which is part of operating expenses).

TIP: **Ending Inventory** refers to the inventory balance reported at a balance sheet date (for example, December 31, 2014). The ending inventory for 2014 is the beginning inventory for 2015.

ILLUSTRATION 5-3 (Continued)

TIP:	The **cost of goods purchased** is to include all costs necessary to acquire merchandise during the period and get it to the place and condition for its intended purpose (resale). Thus, freight charges borne by the purchasing entity are added to the invoice price of purchases, and purchase discounts and purchase returns and allowances are deducted in arriving at the net cost of merchandise acquisitions for the period. Purchase Discounts and Purchase Returns and Allowances are thus contra accounts to Purchases.
TIP:	Think about the components of the **cost of goods sold computation** before you attempt to memorize them; it will make it much easier to recall these items in the future. A merchandiser will begin a period (the year of 2014, for example) with some merchandise inventory on hand (beginning inventory). Add to that the merchandise purchased during the period (to arrive at total goods available for sale). Deduct from that total the goods that are still on hand at the end of the period (ending inventory) to arrive at the goods that are gone (goods sold). This calculation can be done in terms of units (quantity) or cost. To do it in terms of cost: cost of the beginning inventory plus the cost of goods purchased minus the cost of the ending inventory equals the cost of goods sold. The cost of goods purchased is determined by taking the cost of gross purchases (purchases) and deducting the merchandise that was returned to the supplier (purchase returns) and any reductions in price allowed by the supplier for defective items (purchase allowances) or for prompt payment (purchase discounts) and adding the cost of transporting it from the supplier to the merchandiser's location (freight-in). The cost of the ending inventory is determined by a physical count of goods on hand and applying unit costs to those goods.

ILLUSTRATION 5-4
PERPETUAL VS. PERIODIC INVENTORY SYSTEMS (L.O. 2, 3, **7)

Features of
A Perpetual System

1. Purchases of merchandise for resale are debited to Inventory rather than to Purchases.
2. Freight-in, purchase returns and allowances, and purchase discounts are recorded in the Inventory account rather than in separate accounts.
3. Cost of goods sold is recognized for each sale by debiting the account, Cost of Goods Sold, and crediting Inventory at the time of sale.
4. The Cost of Goods Sold account and the Inventory account are continuously updated for acquisitions and withdrawal of inventory during the period. Thus, at any point during the accounting period (assuming all postings are up to date), the balance of the Inventory account reflects the cost of the items that should be on hand at that point in time, and the Cost of Goods Sold account reflects the cost of the goods sold during the period.
5. Inventory is a control account that is supported by a subsidiary ledger of individual inventory records. The subsidiary records show the quantity and cost of each type of inventory on hand.

Features of
A Periodic System

1. Purchases of merchandise for resale are debited to Purchases.
2. The Freight-In, Purchase Returns and Allowances, and Purchase Discounts accounts are separate accounts which are used to record information about inventory acquisitions during the accounting period.
3. Cost of goods sold is recognized only at the end of the accounting period when the (1) ending inventory amount (determined by physical count, pricing, and extensions) is recorded in the Inventory account, (2) the Purchases, Freight-In, Purchase Returns and Allowances, and Purchase Discounts account balances are closed to the Cost of Goods Sold account, and (3) the beginning inventory amount is transferred from the Inventory account to the Cost of Goods Sold account.
4. All during the accounting period, the Inventory account reflects the cost of the inventory items on hand at the beginning of the accounting period (beginning inventory). The Inventory account is **not** updated for acquisitions and withdrawals of inventory during the period; it is updated only at the end of the period to reflect the cost of the items on hand at the balance sheet date.

TIP: When the perpetual system is used, purchases of merchandise inventory are charged to the Inventory account (a real or permanent account). When the periodic system is used, four temporary (nominal) accounts are used to record the net cost of purchases (Purchases, Purchase Returns and Allowances, Purchase Discounts, and Freight-In); the balances in these temporary accounts must be closed (reduced to zero at the end of the accounting period) so that information about the cost of goods sold in the next accounting period can be properly accumulated.

EXAMPLE

Perpetual System	**Periodic System**

1.   Start with 8 units in beginning inventory at a cost of $2,000 each.

The inventory accounts shows the inventory on hand at $16,000.	The inventory accounts shows the inventory on hand at $16,000.

2.   Purchase 12 items on account at $2,000 each.

Inventory	24,000		Purchases	24,000	
Accounts Payable		24,000	Accounts Payable		24,000

3.   Return 1 defective item for $2,000 credit.

Accounts Payable	2,000		Accounts Payable	2,000	
Inventory		2,000	Purchase Returns and Allowances		2,000

4.   Sell 16 items on account for $3,000 each.

Accounts Receivable	48,000		Accounts Receivable	48,000	
Sales Revenue		48,000	Sales Revenue		48,000
Cost of Goods Sold	32,000				
Inventory		32,000			

5.   Receive 1 item back from customer as a sales return. Give customer credit on his account.

Sales Returns and Allowances	3,000		Sales Returns and Allowances	3,000	
Accounts Receivable		3,000	Accounts Receivable		3,000
Inventory	2,000				
Cost of Goods Sold		2,000			

6.   Prepare end of period entries for inventory related accounts (4 units on hand at $2,000 each).

No entries are necessary:	**Closing entries are necessary:**
The account, Inventory, shows the ending balance, $8,000 ($16,000 + $24,000 - $2,000 - $32,000 + $2,000). If the ending Inventory on hand did not agree with the book balance for Inventory, an adjusting entry would be used to bring the book balance into agreement with the actual inventory on hand (as determined by a physical count).	

Cost of Goods Sold	16,000	
Inventory (Beginning)		16,000
Inventory (Ending)	8,000	
Cost of Goods Sold		8,000
Cost of Goods Sold	24,000	
Purchases		24,000
Purchase Returns and Allowances	2,000	
Cost of Goods Sold		2,000

****ILLUSTRATION 5-5**
DAILY RECURRING AND CLOSING ENTRIES FOR A
MERCHANDISING ENTITY USING A PERIODIC
INVENTORY SYSTEM (L.O. **7)

				Effect on	
Transactions	**Daily Recurring Entries**	**Dr.**	**Cr.**	**A = L + OE**	
Selling merchandise to customers	Cash or Accounts Receivable	XX		↑	
	Sales Revenue		XX		↑
Paying freight costs on sales	Freight-Out	XX			↓
FOB destination	Cash		XX	↓	
Granting sales returns or	Sales Returns and Allowances	XX			↓
allowances to customers	Cash or Accounts Receivable		XX	↓	
Receiving payment from cus-	Cash	XX		↑	
tomers within discount period	Sales Discounts	XX			↓
	Accounts Receivable		XX	↓	
Receiving payment from	Cash	XX		↑	
customers after discount period	Accounts Receivable		XX	↓	
Purchasing merchandise for resale	Purchases	XX			↓[a]
	Cash (or Accounts Payable)		XX	↓ or ↑	
Paying freight costs on	Freight-In	XX			↓[a]
merchandise purchased;	Cash		XX	↓	
FOB shipping point					
Receiving purchase returns or	Cash (or Accounts Payable)	XX		↑ or ↓	
allowances from suppliers	Purchase Returns and				
	Allowances		XX		↑
Paying suppliers within discount	Accounts Payable	XX		↓	
period	Purchase Discounts		XX		↑
	Cash		XX	↓	
Paying suppliers after discount	Accounts Payable	XX		↓	
period	Cash		XX	↓	

[a]Increases in Purchases and Freight-In cause decreases in owner's equity because purchases and freight-in are positive components of the cost of goods sold computation. Cost of goods sold is an expense; therefore, an increase in cost of goods sold will cause a decrease in owner's equity. If the goods purchased have not been sold by the end of the accounting period, the journal entry to establish the amount of the ending inventory in the Inventory account will include the relevant freight charges and will be a debit to Inventory and a credit to Cost of Goods Sold. This latter entry causes an increase in assets and an increase in owner's equity.

ILLUSTRATION 5-5 (Continued)

Event	Closing Entries	Dr.	Cr.	Effect on A = L + OE
Recording ending inventory	Inventory (End.)	XX		↑
and transferring components	Purchase Returns and Allow-			
of cost of good sold to the	ances	XX		↓
Cost of Goods Sold account	Purchase Discounts	XX		↓
	Cost of Goods Sold		XX	↑
	Cost of Goods Sold	XX		↓
	Inventory (Beg.)		XX	↑
	Purchases		XX	↑
	Freight-In		XX	↑

> **TIP:** Compare **Illustration 5-5** (entries for a periodic system) with **Illustration 5-2** (entries for a perpetual system). Note the differences and think about the reasons for the differences.

*EXERCISE 5-7

Purpose: (L.O. 7) This exercise reviews the journal entries to record purchases of merchandise inventory under a periodic inventory system.

A list of transactions for the Randy Travis Sales Company appears below. A periodic inventory system is used.

July	1	Purchased merchandise from Oliver Company for $3,000 cash.
	2	Purchased merchandise from Yearwood Company, $5,000, FOB shipping point, terms 2/10, n/30.
	6	Paid freight on July 2 purchase, $125.
	10	Paid Yearwood Company the amount owed.
	11	Purchased merchandise from McBride Company, $7,000, FOB destination, terms 1/10, n/30.
	23	Paid McBride Company the amount owed.
Aug.	7	Purchased merchandise from Dun Company, $4,000, FOB destination, terms 2/10, n/30.
	9	Returned one-fourth of the merchandise acquired in the August 7 transaction to Dun Company because of detected defects.
	16	Paid Dun Company the balance owed.

Instructions

Prepare the journal entries to record these transactions on the books of the Randy Travis Sales Company.

SOLUTION TO EXERCISE 5-7

July	1	Purchases	3,000	
		Cash..		3,000
		(To record cash purchases)		
	2	Purchases	5,000	
		Accounts Payable.................................		5,000
		(To record goods purchased on account, terms 2/10, n/30)		
	6	Freight-In..	125	
		Cash..		125
		(To record payment of freight, terms FOB shipping point)		
	10	Accounts Payable	5,000	
		Purchase Discounts...............................		100
		Cash..		4,900
		(To record payment within discount period) ($5,000 X .02 = $100; $5,000 - $100 = $4,900)		
	11	Purchases	7,000	
		Accounts Payable.................................		7,000
		(To record goods purchased on account, terms 1/10, n/30)		
	23	Accounts Payable	7,000	
		Cash..		7,000
		(To record payment with no discount taken)		
Aug.	7	Purchases	4,000	
		Accounts Payable.................................		4,000
		(To record goods purchased on account, terms 2/10, n/30)		
	9	Accounts Payable	1,000	
		Purchase Returns and Allowances.....................		1,000
		(To record allowance for damaged goods) (1/4 X $4,000 = $1,000)		
	16	Accounts Payable	3,000	
		Purchase Discounts...............................		60
		Cash..		2,940
		(To record payment within discount period) ($4,000 - $1,000 returned = $3,000; $3,000 X .02 = $60 discount; $3,000 - $60 = $2,940 payment)		

TIP:	A **periodic inventory system** is characterized by no entries being made to the Inventory account during the period. Acquisitions are recorded in a Purchases account. The cost of inventory withdrawals is computed and reflected in the accounts **only** at the end of the period.

*EXERCISE 5-8

Purpose: (L.O. 7) This exercise reviews the journal entries to record sales of merchandise inventory under a periodic inventory system.

A list of transactions for the Randy Travis Sales Company appears below. A periodic inventory system is used.

July 17 Sold merchandise with a cost of $300 to Eric Nelson for cash, $520.

18 Sold merchandise with a cost of $340 to Guy Sellars for $580, terms 2/10, n/30.

23 Issued a credit memo for $80 to Guy Sellars because of a sales allowance granted to him due to the inferior quality of goods sold to him on July 18.

26 Received payment from Guy Sellars for amount due for sale of July 18.

27 Sold merchandise to Jason Zahner, $200, terms n/30. The merchandise cost $120.

Aug. 25 Received payment in full from Jason Zahner.

Sept. 5 Sold merchandise to Andrea Brotherly, $600, terms 2/10, n/30. The merchandise cost $350.

22 Received payment from Andrea Brotherly for amount due for sale of Sept. 5.

Instructions
Prepare the journal entries to record these transactions on the books of the Randy Travis Sales Company.

SOLUTION TO EXERCISE 5-8

July	17	Cash...	520	
		Sales Revenue		520
		(To record cash sales)		
	18	Accounts Receivable...	580	
		Sales Revenue		580
		(To record sales on account, terms 2/10, n/30)		

TIP:	When the periodic inventory system is used, withdrawals from inventory are not recorded as cost of goods sold until the end of the accounting period.

	23	Sales Returns and Allowances....................................	80	
		Accounts Receivable		80
		(To record allowance because of inferior goods)		
	26	Cash...	490	
		Sales Discounts...	10	
		Accounts Receivable		500
		(To record collection within discount period)		
		($580 - $80 allowance = $500; $500 X .02 = $10;		
		$500 - $10 = $490)		
	27	Accounts Receivable...	200	
		Sales Revenue		200
		(To record sales on account, terms n/30)		
Aug.	25	Cash...	200	
		Accounts Receivable		200
		(To record collection on account)		
Sept.	5	Accounts Receivable...	600	
		Sales Revenue		600
		(To record sales on account, terms 2/10, n/30)		
	22	Cash...	600	
		Accounts Receivable		600
		(To record collection, not within the discount period)		

TIP:	The amount was collected after the end of discount period so no discount is allowed.

**EXERCISE 5-9

Purpose: (L.O. 6) This exercise will give you practice in completing a worksheet for a business engaged in merchandising activity.

The trial balance of the Heron Foliage Sales Company at December 31, 2014, has already been entered on the worksheet on the following page.

Adjustment data:
- a. The physical count of inventory reveals there is only $13,500 on hand.
- b. A count of supplies shows $400 to be on hand.
- c. Accrued salaries at year end amount to $750.
- d. Depreciation on the building amounts to $1,500 for the year.

Instructions
Complete the worksheet for the Heron Foliage Sales Company for the year ended December 31, 2014.

HERON FOLIAGE SALES COMPANY
Worksheet
For the Year Ended December 31, 2014

Account Titles	Trial Balance		Adjustments		Adjusted Trial Balance		Income Statement		Balance Sheet	
	Dr.	Cr.	Dr.	Cr.	Dr.	Cr.	Dr.	Cr.	Dr	Cr.
Cash	4,150									
Accounts Receivable	4,000									
Inventory	14,000									
Supplies	1,500									
Buildings	30,000									
Accumulated Deprecia-tion—Buildings		4,500								
Accounts Payable		15,000								
Owner's Capital		26,000								
Owner's Drawings	15,000									
Sales Revenue		78,000								
Sales Returns & Allow.	2,000									
Sales Discounts	500									
Cost of Goods Sold	37,300									
Salaries & Wages Expense	14,250									
Advertising Expense	800									
Totals	123,500	123,500								

SOLUTION TO 5-9

HERON FOLIAGE SALES COMPANY
Worksheet
For the Year Ended December 31, 2014

Account Titles	Trial Balance Dr.	Trial Balance Cr.	Adjustments Dr.	Adjustments Cr.	Adjusted Trial Balance Dr.	Adjusted Trial Balance Cr.	Income Statement Dr.	Income Statement Cr.	Balance Sheet Dr.	Balance Sheet Cr.
Cash	4,150				4,150				4,150	
Accounts Receivable	4,000				4,000				4,000	
Inventory	14,000			(a) 500	13,500				13,500	
Supplies	1,500			(b) 1,100	400				400	
Buildings	30,000				30,000				30,000	
Accumulated Depreciation—Buildings		4,500		(d) 1,500		6,000				6,000
Accounts Payable		15,000				15,000				15,000
Owner's Capital		26,000				26,000				26,000
Owner's Drawing	15,000				15,000				15,000	
Sales Revenue		78,000				78,000		78,000		
Sales Returns & Allow.	2,000				2,000		2,000			
Sales Discounts	500				500		500			
Cost of Goods Sold	37,300		(a) 500		37,800		37,800			
Salaries & Wages Expense	14,250		(c) 750		15,000		15,000			
Advertising Expense	800				800		800			
Totals	123,500	123,500								
Supplies Expense			(a) 1,100		1,100		1,100			
Salaries & Wages Payable				(c) 750		750				750
Depreciation Expense			(d) 1,500		1,500		1,500			
Totals			3,850	3,850	125,750	125,750	58,700	78,000	67,050	47,750
Net Income							19,300			19,300
Totals							78,000	78,000	67,050	67,050

**EXERCISE 5-10

Purpose: (L.O. 5, 6) This exercise will give you practice in preparing a multiple-step income statement from a worksheet for a merchandising company.

A worksheet is a tool to organize accounting data to be reported in external financial statements.

Instructions
Refer to the worksheet in the **Solution for Exercise 5-9** above.

a. Prepare a multiple-step income statement for Heron Foliage Sales Company for the year ended December 31, 2014.
b. Prepare an owner's equity statement for Heron Foliage Sales Company for the year ended December 31, 2014.

SOLUTION TO EXERCISE 5-10

a.

HERON FOLIAGE SALES COMPANY
Income Statement
For the Year Ended December 31, 2014

Sales revenues			
Sales revenue			$78,000
Less: Sales returns and allowances		$ 2,000	
Sales discounts		500	2,500
Net sales			75,500
Cost of goods sold			37,800
Gross profit			37,700
Operating expenses			
Salaries and wages expense	15,000		
Depreciation expense	1,500		
Advertising expense	800		
Supplies expense	1,100		
Total operating expenses			18,400
Net income			$19,300

b.
HERON FOLIAGE SALES COMPANY
Owner's Equity Statement
For the Year Ended December 31, 2014

Owner's capital, January 1	$26,000
Add: Net income	19,300
	45,300
Less: Drawings	15,000
Owner's capital, December 31	$30,300

EXERCISE 5-11

Purpose: (L.O. 1 thru 5) This exercise will quiz you about terminology used in this chapter.

A list of accounting terms with which you should be familiar appear below.

Contra revenue account	Other revenues and gains
Cost of goods sold	Periodic inventory system
FOB destination	Perpetual inventory system
FOB shipping point	Purchase allowance
Gross profit	Purchase discount
Gross profit rate	Purchase invoice
Income from operations	Purchase return
Multiple-step income statement	Sales discount
Net sales	Sales invoice
Nonoperating activities	Sales returns and allowances
Operating expenses	Sales revenue (sales)
Other expenses and losses	Single-step income statement

Instructions
For each item below, enter in the blank the term that is described.

1. _____Freight terms indicating that the seller places the goods free on board to the buyer's place of business, and the seller pays the freight costs.

2. _____Freight terms indicating that the seller places the goods free on board the carrier, and the buyer pays the freight costs.

3. _____The primary source of revenue in a merchandising company.

4. _____Sales revenue less sales returns and allowances and less sales discounts.

5. _____The total cost of merchandise sold during the period. A synonymous term is **cost of sales.**

6. _____The excess of net sales over the cost of goods sold. A synonymous term is **gross margin.**

7. _____Expenses incurred in the process of earning sales revenues.

8. _____A nonoperating section of the income statement that shows expenses from auxiliary operations and losses unrelated to the company's operations.

9. _____A nonoperating activities section of the income statement that shows revenues from auxiliary operations and gains unrelated to the company's operations.

10. _____Income from a company's principal operating activity, determined by subtracting cost of goods sold and operating expenses from net sales.

11. _____An income statement that shows several steps in determining net income.

12. _____An income statement that shows only one step in determining net income.

13. _____An inventory system under which the company does **not** keep detailed inventory records throughout the accounting period, but determines the cost of goods sold only at the end of an accounting period.

14. _____An inventory system under which the company keeps detailed records of the cost of each inventory purchase and sale and the records continuously show the quantity and cost of the inventory that should be on hand.

15. _____A reduction given by a seller for prompt payment of a credit sale.

16. _____A document that supports each credit sale.

17. _____A document that supports each credit purchase.

18. _____A cash discount claimed by a buyer for prompt payment of a balance due.

19. _____An account that is offset against a revenue account on the income statement.

20. _____Gross profit expressed as a percentage, by dividing the amount of gross profit by net sales.

21. _____Various revenues, expenses, gains, and losses that are unrelated to a company's main line of operations.

22. _____A return of goods by the buyer to the seller for a cash or credit refund.

23. _____A deduction (from buyer's viewpoint) made to the selling price of merchandise, granted by the seller so that the buyer will keep the merchandise.

24. _____Purchase returns and allowances from the seller's perspective. (See purchase returns and purchase allowances.)

SOLUTION TO EXERCISE 5-11

1. FOB destination
2. FOB shipping point
3. Sales revenue
4. Net sales
5. Cost of goods sold
6. Gross profit
7. Operating expenses
8. Other expenses and losses
9. Other revenues and gains
10. Income from operations
11. Multiple-step income statement
12. Single-step income statement

13. Periodic inventory system
14. Perpetual inventory system
15. Sales discounts
16. Sales invoices
17. Purchase invoice
18. Purchase discount
19. Contra revenue account
20. Gross profit rate
21. Nonoperating activities
22. Purchase return
23. Purchase allowance
24. Sales returns and allowances

ANALYSIS OF MULTIPLE-CHOICE TYPE QUESTIONS

1. (L.O. 1) Which of the following formulas will yield the net income figure for a merchandising firm?
   a. Gross profit minus cost of goods sold.
   b. Net sales minus cost of goods sold.
   c. Gross profit minus operating expenses.
   d. Net sales minus operating expenses.

   Approach and Explanation: Before you look at the alternative answers, write down the components in the net income computation. Abbreviations for these components will suffice.

	Net Sales
-	**Cost of Goods Sold**
=	**Gross Profit**
-	**Operating Expenses**
=	**Income from Operations**
+/-	**Other Revenues, Gains, Losses, & Expenses**
=	**Net Income**

   Then take each answer selection and see if it describes your model. (Solution = c.)

2. (L.O. 3) The balance in the Sales Discounts account is to be reported on the income statement as a(n):
    a. contra account to Sales Revenue.
    b. expense account.
    c. reduction of the cost of goods sold.
    d. addition to Sales Revenue.

    Approach and Explanation: Write down a sketch of the portion of the income statement that includes sales discounts.

    > Sales revenue
    > Less: Sales returns and allowances
    >   Sales discounts
    > ————————————————
    > Net sales

    Then examine each answer solution to see if it describes what you know about sales discounts. The items which are deducted from sales are called contra revenue items; they are contra type valuation accounts. They are **not** to be called expenses even though they have debit balances and reduce net income in the same fashion as expense accounts. (Solution = a.)

3. (L.O. 3) The purchaser is responsible for the transportation charges on goods that are sold and shipped on terms of:
    a. FOB destination.
    b. FOB shipping point.
    c. FOB common carrier.
    d. FOB buyer.

    Approach and Explanation: Before you look at the alternative answers, write down the two shipping terms and describe who bears the freight cost:

    > FOB shipping point = Buyer bears freight cost
    > FOB destination = Seller bears freight cost

    The question asks for the terms where the purchaser bears the cost, which is FOB shipping point. Look for that answer. (Solution = b.)

TIP:	FOB buyer is another name for FOB destination. FOB common carrier is a nonsense type answer selection.

4.   (L.O. 2) The following amounts relate to the current year for the Ira Company:

Beginning inventory	$ 20,000
Ending inventory	28,000
Purchases	166,000
Purchase returns	4,800
Freight-out	6,000

The amount of cost of goods sold for the period is:
a. $169,200.
b. $162,800.
c. $153,200.
d. $147,200.

Approach and Explanation: Write down the components of the cost of goods sold. Enter the amounts given and solve for the unknown.

	$ 20,000		**Beginning Inventory**
+	166,000	+	**Purchases**
-	4,800	-	**Purchase Returns and Allowances**
		-	**Purchase Discounts**
		+	**Freight-In**
	181,200	=	**Cost of Goods Available for Sale**
-	X	-	**Cost of Goods Sold**
	$ 28,000	=	**Ending Inventory**

Solving for Cost of Goods Sold: $181,200 - $28,000 = X; X = $153,200
(Solution = c.)

TIP: Freight-out is classified as a selling expense, **not** a component of cost of goods sold.

---

5.   (L.O. 1, 2) The following amounts relate to the Crown Sales Company:

Beginning inventory	$12,500
Purchases	42,500
Net sales	45,000
Gross profit	15,000

The amount of ending inventory is:
a. $40,000.
b. $25,000.
c. $30,000.
d. $15,000.

Approach and Explanation: Write down the models for the net sales and cost of goods sold computations. Fill in the amounts given.

$ 45,000		**Net Sales**
- _____	-	Cost of Goods Sold
15,000	=	**Gross Profit**
12,500		**Beginning Inventory**
+ 42,500	+	Cost of Goods Purchased
55,000	=	Cost of Goods Available for Sale
- _____	-	Cost of Goods Sold
X	=	**Ending Inventory**

Solving for Cost of Goods Sold: $45,000 - $15,000 = $30,000 Cost of Goods Sold. $55,000 - $30,000 Cost of Goods Sold = X. Solving for X: $55,000 - $30,000 = $25,000 Ending Inventory. (Solution = b.)

6. (L.O. 2) Abraham Company sold a product to Walsh Company. Abraham finds reason to prepare a credit memorandum related to the sale to Walsh. Abraham will record the credit memorandum by a credit to:
    a. Accounts Receivable.
    b. Sales Returns and Allowances.
    c. Purchase Returns and Allowances.
    d. Accounts Payable.

Explanation: A credit memorandum is prepared by a seller to grant a customer a sales return or allowance. This document informs a customer that a credit has been made to the customer's account receivable for a return or allowance. The document is recorded on the seller's (Abraham) books by a debit to Sales Returns and Allowances and a credit to Accounts Receivable. This credit reduces the balance of the Accounts Receivable account. There is an accompanying entry to record the return of the goods to the Inventory account and a reduction of the Cost of Goods Sold account on the seller's books. The credit memorandum is recorded on the buyer's (Walsh) books by a debit to Accounts Payable and a credit to Inventory. (Solution = a.)

7. (L.O. 3) The following information pertains to the Boot Sales Company:

Sales revenue	$100,000
Sales returns and allowances	4,500
Sales discounts	500
Purchase returns	2,000
Transportation-out	3,200

    The amount of net sales for the period is:
    a. $100,000.
    b. $95,000.
    c. $93,000.
    d. $89,800.

Approach and Explanation: Write down the computation model for net sales. Enter the data given and solve for the unknown.

$100,000		**S**ales **R**evenue	
-	4,500	- **S**ales **R**eturns and **A**llowances	
-	500	- **S**ales **D**iscounts	
$ 95,000	=	**N**et **S**ales	(Solution = b.)

TIP: Purchase returns are a contra-purchases (therefore contra cost of goods sold) item, **not** a contra-sales item. Transportation-out (or freight-out) is a selling expense, **not** a contra-sales item, for classification purposes.

---

8. (L.O. 5) Which of the following is **not** included in the operating expenses section of a multiple-step income statement?
   a. Advertising expense.
   b. Cost of goods sold.
   c. Freight-out.
   d. Supplies expense.

   Approach and Explanation: Operating expenses include those costs incurred in the generation of sales revenue and are deducted from gross profit to determine income from operations. Cost of goods sold is the total cost of the merchandise sold during the period and is deducted from net sales to determine gross profit. Therefore, cost of goods sold is not a part of operating expenses. (Solution = b.)

9. (L.O. 5) Which of the following will **not** appear on a single-step income statement?
   a. Net sales.
   b. Cost of goods sold.
   c. Gain on disposal of plant assets.
   d. Gross profit.

   Approach and Explanation: Write down an outline of the major parts of the single-step income statement: Revenues minus Expenses = Net income (loss). The revenues section includes all forms of revenues and gains. The expense section includes all forms of expenses and losses. Notice there is no subtotal for Gross profit. Therefore, Gross pofit does not appear on the single-step income statement. (Solution = d).

10. (L.O. 1, 2, 3) The net cost of goods purchased is affected by:
    a. Sales returns.
    b. Purchase discounts.
    c. Freight-out.
    d. Sales allowances.

Explanation: The net cost of goods purchased is computed as follows:

Purchases
- Purchase discounts
- Purchase returns and allowances
= Net purchases
+ Freight-in
= Net cost of goods purchased

Sales returns and sales allowances reduce net sales revenue. Freight-out is classified as an operating expense. (Solution = b.)

11. (L.O. 1, 2) The following amounts relate to the current year for the Rod Buckley Company:

Beginning inventory	$ 40,000
Ending inventory	56,000
Purchases	332,000
Purchase returns	9,600
Freight-out	12,000

The amount of cost of goods sold for the period is:
a. $338,400.
b. $325,600.
c. $306,400.
d. $294,400.

Approach and Explanation: Write down the computation model for cost of goods sold. Enter the amounts given and solve for the unknown.

	$ 40,000		Beginning Inventory
+	332,000	+	Purchases
-	9,600	-	Purchase Returns and Allowances
	0	-	Purchase Discounts
	0	+	Freight-in
	362,400	=	Cost of Goods Available for Sale
-	56,000	-	Ending Inventory
	$306,400	=	Cost of Goods Sold

(Solution = c.)

TIP: Freight-out is classified as a selling expense, not a component of cost of goods sold.

12. (L.O. 1, 3) The following amounts relate to the Rachael Avery's Sales Company:

Beginning inventory	$25,000
Purchases	85,000
Net sales	90,000
Gross profit	30,000

The amount of ending inventory is:
a. $80,000.
b. $50,000.
c. $60,000.
d. $30,000.

Approach and Explanation: Write down the models for the net sales and cost of goods sold computations. Fill in the amounts given.

	$ 90,000		Net Sales
-	_____	-	Cost of Goods Sold
	30,000	=	Gross Profit
	25,000		Beginning Inventory
+	85,000	+	Cost of Goods Purchased
	110,000	=	Cost of Goods Available for Sale
-	X	-	Ending Inventory
		=	Cost of Goods Sold

Solving for Cost of Goods Sold: $90,000 - $30,000 = $60,000 Cost of Goods Sold. $110,000 - X = $60,000 Cost of Goods Sold. Solving for X: $110,000 - $60,000 = X = $50,000 Ending Inventory. (Solution = b.)

*13. (L.O. 7) The accountant for the Orion Sales Company is preparing the income statement for 2015 and the balance sheet at December 31, 2015. Orion uses the periodic inventory system. The January 1, 2015 merchandise inventory balance will appear:
a. only as an asset on the balance sheet.
b. only in the cost of goods sold section of the income statement.
c. as a deduction in the cost of goods sold section of the income statement and as a current asset on the balance sheet.
d. as an addition in the cost of goods sold section of the income statement and as a current asset on the balance sheet.

Explanation: The January 1, 2015 inventory amount is the beginning inventory figure. Beginning inventory is a component of the cost of goods available for sale for the period which is a component of cost of goods sold. (Solution = b.)

> **TIP:** If the question asked about the December 31, 2015 merchandise inventory balance (ending inventory) rather than the beginning inventory balance, the correct answer would have been "c" (as a deduction in computing cost of sales and as a current asset).

CHAPTER 6

· ·

*I*NVENTORIES

OVERVIEW

In accounting, the term inventory refers to a stock of goods held for sale in the ordinary course of business or goods that will be used or consumed in the production of goods to be sold. A number of questions regarding inventory are addressed in this chapter. These include: (1) How is the ownership of goods determined? (2) What goods should be included in inventory? (3) How will the selection of a particular cost flow assumption affect the income statement and balance sheet? (4) What is the LCM rule for inventory valuation? (5) How do inventory errors affect the financial statements? (6) How do you compute an estimate of the cost of ending inventory using the gross-profit method? (7) How do you determine the cost of ending inventory using the retail method?

SUMMARY OF LEARNING OBJECTIVES

1. **Determine how to classify inventory and inventory quantities.** The steps in determining inventory quantities are: (1) take a physical inventory of goods on hand, and (2) determine the ownership of goods in transit or on consignment.

2. **Explain the accounting for inventories and apply the inventory cost flow methods.** The primary basis of accounting for inventories is cost. Cost includes all expenditures necessary to acquire goods and to place them in a condition ready for sale. Inventoriable costs include the invoice price plus freight-in less purchase discounts and purchase returns and allowances. Cost of goods available for sale includes (1) cost of beginning inventory and (2) the cost of goods purchased. The inventory cost flow methods are specific identification and three assumed cost flow methods--FIFO, LIFO, and average-cost.

3. **Explain the financial effects of the inventory cost flow assumptions.** Companies may allocate the cost of goods available for sale to cost of goods sold and ending inventory by specific identification or by a method based on an assumed cost flow. These methods have different effects on financial statements during periods of changing prices. When prices are rising, the first-in, first-out method (FIFO) results in lower cost of goods sold and higher net income than the average and the last-in, first-out (LIFO) methods. LIFO results in the lowest income

taxes (because of lower net income). (The reverse is true when prices are falling.) In the balance sheet, FIFO results in an ending inventory that is closest to current value, whereas the inventory under LIFO is the farthest from the current value. Cost of goods sold and ending inventory amounts using the average-cost method fall somewhere between those obtained by the use of LIFO and FIFO.

4. **Explain the lower-of-cost-or-market basis of accounting for inventories.** Companies must apply the lower-of-cost-or-market (LCM) basis to their inventory at year end. A " write down" occurs when the current replacement cost (market) is less than cost. Under LCM, companies recognize the loss in the period in which the price decline occurs.

5. **Indicate the effects of inventory errors on the financial statements.** In the income statement of the current year: (a) an error in beginning inventory will have a reverse effect on net income (overstatement of beginning inventory results in understatement of net income, and vice versa) and (b) an error in ending inventory will have a similar effect on net income (overstatement of ending inventory results in overstatement of net income). If ending inventory errors are not corrected in the next period, their effect on net income for that period is reversed (i.e., opposite of the impact that the error had on the period the error originated), and total net income for the two years will be correct. In the balance sheet, ending inventory errors will have the same effect on total assets and total owner' s equity and no effect on liabilities.

6. **Compute and interpret the inventory turnover.** The inventory turnover is calculated as cost of goods sold divided by average inventory. To convert it to average days in inventory, divide 365 days by the inventory turnover. A higher turnover or lower average days in inventory suggests that management is trying to keep inventory levels low relative to its sales level.

*7. **Apply the inventory cost flow methods to perpetual inventory records.** Under FIFO and a perpetual inventory system, a company charges to cost of goods sold the cost of the earliest goods on hand prior to each sale. Under the moving-average cost method and a perpetual system, a company computes a new weighted-average cost after each purchase. Under LIFO and a perpetual system, a company charges to cost of goods sold the cost of the most recent purchase prior to sale.

8. **Describe the two methods of estimating inventories. The two methods of estimating inventories are the gross profit method and the retail inventory method. Under the gross profit method, companies apply a gross profit rate to net sales to determine estimated gross profit. They deduct estimated gross profit from net sales to determine estimated cost of goods sold. Then they subtract estimated cost of goods sold from cost of goods available for sale to determine the estimated cost of the ending inventory. Under the retail inventory method, companies compute a cost-to-retail ratio by dividing the cost of goods available for sale by the retail value of the goods available for sale. Then they apply this ratio to the ending inventory at retail to determine the estimated cost of the ending inventory.

*This material appears in Appendix 6A in the text.
**This material appears in Appendix 6B in the text.

TIPS ON CHAPTER TOPICS

TIP:	**The cost of an inventory item (inventoriable costs)** includes all costs necessary to acquire the item and bring it to the location and condition for its intended purpose. The cost would include the item's purchase price, freight-in, and any special handling charges. However, freight-out is **not** included in the cost of inventory, it is classified as a selling expense on the income statement for the period in which the expense was incurred.
TIP:	FOB terms designate the time that title passes. **FOB (free on board) shipping point** or seller means the title passes to the buyer when it leaves the seller's dock. **FOB destination** or buyer means the title passes to the buyer when it arrives at the buyer's dock. FOB terms also designate which party is to bear the cost of the freight. If goods are shipped FOB shipping point, the buyer bears the cost; if goods are shipped FOB destination, the seller bears the cost.

EXERCISE 6-1

Purpose: (L.O. 1) This exercise will review how to determine (1) the owner of goods in transit and (2) the owner of goods on consignment at a balance sheet date.

As an auditor for Ryan's Art Company, you discover the following facts when auditing the client's inventory balance as of December 31, 2014.
1. Ryan's Art received goods on January 2, 2015. The goods had been shipped FOB shipping point on December 27, by Wells Company.
2. Ryan's Art received goods on January 4, 2015. The goods had been shipped FOB destination on December 28 by Nanula Company.
3. Ryan's Art sold goods to O'Toole Company on December 29, 2014. The goods were picked up by the common carrier on that same date and shipped FOB shipping point. They were expected to arrive at the buyer's business as early as January 3, 2015.
4. Ryan's Art sold goods to Matheson Company on December 31, 2014. The goods were picked up by the common carrier on that same date and shipped FOB destination. They were expected to arrive at the buyer's store as early as January 2, 2015.
5. Ryan's Art is the consignor for a collection of prints. The prints are hanging in the showroom of Decorator's Den.
6. Ryan's Art is the consignee for some goods on consignment from European Collectibles.

Instructions

For each situation above, indicate whether or not the goods being described should be **Included In** or **Excluded From** the amount to be reported for inventory on the balance sheet for Ryan' s Art at December 31, 2014. Also, briefly explain your reason for each answer.

SOLUTION TO EXERCISE 6-1

1. **Included In**   When the terms of sale are FOB shipping point, ownership of the goods passes to the buyer when the public carrier accepts the goods from the seller. Therefore, title passed to Ryan' s Art on December 27, 2014.

2. **Excluded From**   When the terms of sale are FOB destination, legal title to the goods remains with the seller until the goods reach the buyer. Therefore, title did not pass to Ryan' s Art until January 4, 2015.

3. **Excluded From**   With shipping terms of FOB shipping point, title passed to O' Toole when the goods were picked up by the common carrier on December 29, 2014.

4. **Included In**   With shipping terms of FOB destination, title did not pass to Matheson (the buyer) until the goods were received by the buyer which was expected to be January 2, 2015, or later.

5. **Included In**   Under a consignment arrangement, the holder of the goods (called the **consignee**) does not own the goods. Ownership remains with the shipper of the goods (called the **consignor**) until the goods are sold to a customer. Ryan' s Art, the consignor, should include merchandise held by the consignee as part of its inventory.

6. **Excluded From**   Ryan' s Art does not own the goods which it holds on consignment. Therefore, these goods should be included in the inventory of the consignor, European Collectibles.

EXERCISE 6-2

Purpose: (L.O. 2, 3) This exercise reviews the characteristics and the effects of using various cost flow methods to determine inventory costs.

The selection of an inventory cost flow method is an important one. It affects the computation of net income (and thus the resulting amount of income taxes) as well as the amount of total assets and owner' s equity.

Instructions
Answer each of the following questions by inserting one of these abbreviations in the space provided:

SI   (specific identification)   **FIFO**   (first-in-first-out)
A   (average-cost)   **LIFO**   (last-in-first-out)

_____   1.   Which inventory cost flow method **best** matches current costs with current revenues on the income statement?

_____   2.   Which inventory cost flow method yields the most realistic amount for inventory, compared to replacement cost, on the balance sheet?

_____   3.   Which method results in the most exact ending inventory valuation when inventory items of the same type are **not** homogeneous?

_____   4.   Which method is based on the assumption that inventory flow is " mixed" and therefore " mixes" all acquisition prices?

During a period of **rising prices,** which method yields the:

_____   5.   lowest net income figure?

_____   6.   lowest amount for inventory on the balance sheet?

_____   7.   lowest cost of goods sold figure?

_____   8.   lowest owner' s equity figure?

_____   9.   lowest income tax bill for the current year?

During a period of **declining prices,** which method yields the:

_____   10.   lowest net income figure?

_____   11.   lowest amount for inventory on the balance sheet?

_____ 12.   lowest cost of goods sold figure?

_____ 13.   lowest owner's equity figure?

_____ 14.   lowest income tax bill for the current year?

SOLUTION TO EXERCISE 6-2

1.	LIFO	5.	LIFO	9.	LIFO	12.	LIFO
2.	FIFO	6.	LIFO	10.	FIFO	13.	FIFO
3.	SI	7.	FIFO	11.	FIFO	14.	FIFO
4.	A	8.	LIFO				

TIP: **Inventory pricing method, inventory costing method,** and **inventory cost** method are synonymous terms for **inventory cost flow method.**

TIP: **FIFO (first-in, first-out)** means the cost of the first items put into inventory are used to price the first items out to cost of goods sold. Thus, the earliest acquisition prices are used to price cost of goods sold for the period, and the latest (most current) acquisition prices are used to price items in the ending inventory. **LIFO (last-in, first-out)** uses the most recent costs to price the units sold during the period, and it uses the oldest prices to cost the items in ending inventory. Thus, in a period of rising prices, the method that will yield the lowest net income on the income statement and the lowest ending inventory on the balance sheet is the LIFO method.

TIP: Some corporations prefer to use the LIFO method for purposes of determining taxable income on the entity's tax return because in periods of inflation, LIFO yields a lower taxable income figure than other inventory costing methods. LIFO is said to defer holding gains; therefore, the payment of related income taxes is deferred also. For example, assume two inventory items are purchased for $50. One is sold for $75 and the other is held for awhile. In the meantime, the supplier raises his price to $60. One more item is purchased to keep the inventory quantity at two. Then the old item is sold at a new selling price of $90. There is a $10 gain experienced because an item was purchased at $50 and held while prices (both acquisition and selling) increased. Using the FIFO method, that holding gain will be recognized in the current period as a part of the gross profit figure (Sales of $75 + $90 minus cost of goods sold of $50 + $50 = gross profit of $25 + $40). Whereas if the LIFO method is used, that holding gain is deferred to a future period when the LIFO base inventory is liquidated. Thus, the gross profit would only amount to $55 under LIFO (Sales of $75 + $90 minus cost of goods sold of $50 + $60 = gross profit of $25 + $30). The difference between $65 gross profit under FIFO and $55 gross profit under LIFO is the $10 deferral of holding gain under LIFO.

EXERCISE 6-3

Purpose: (L.O. 2, 3) This exercise reviews the computations that you must make when you use the LIFO, FIFO, and average cost methods to determine inventory cost under a periodic inventory system.

The following information pertains to the inventory of the Sheldon Cooper Sales Company:

Jan. 1	Balance on hand	200 units	@ $26..................	$ 5,200
Mar. 3	Purchase	300 units	@ 27..................	8,100
July 2	Purchase	200 units	@ 28..................	5,600
Sept. 21	Purchase	100 units	@ 30..................	3,000
Oct. 31	Purchase	200 units	@ 31..................	6,200
	Total Goods Available for Sale	1,000 units		$28,100

The selling price of Cooper's product was $48 for the first six months of the year and $50 for the last six months of the year. Total sales amounted to $29,300. A physical count of the inventory on December 31 revealed that 400 units were on hand.

Instructions
Compute the amount of (1) ending inventory for the December 31, 2014 balance sheet, (2) cost of goods sold for the 2014 income statement, and (3) gross profit for the 2014 income statement using each of the following inventory cost flow methods:
(a) FIFO.
(b) LIFO.
(c) Average cost.

SOLUTION TO EXERCISE 6-3

(a) (1)

200	@ $31	$ 6,200	
100	@ 30	3,000	
100	@ 28	2,800	
400	units	$12,000	Ending Inventory

   (2) $28,100 CGAS - $12,000 EI = $16,100 Cost of Goods Sold

   (3) $29,300 NS - $16,100 CGS = $13,200 Gross Profit

(b) (1)

200	@ $26	$ 5,200	
200	@ 27	5,400	
400	units	$10,600	Ending Inventory

   (2) $28,100 CGAS - $10,600 EI = $17,500 Cost of Goods Sold

   (3) $29,300 NS - $17,500 CGS = $11,800 Gross Profit

(c)   (1) $\dfrac{\$28,100}{1,000}$ = $28.10   Average Unit Cost

$28.10 X 400   = $11,240   Ending Inventory

(2) $28,100 CGAS - $11,240 EI   = $16,860   Cost of Goods Sold

(3) $29,300 NS - $16,860 CGS   = $12,440   Gross Profit

Abbreviations:
CGAS   = Cost of Goods Available for Sale
EI   = Ending Inventory
NS   = Net Sales Revenue
CGS   = Cost of Goods Sold

TIP: Examine your solution to the exercise above and judge the reasonableness of your answers. What do you expect the relationship of the answers to be?
(1)   Because the trend of the acquisition costs was upward, the ending inventory and gross profit figures computed under LIFO should be lower than the ending inventory and gross profit figures computed under FIFO.
(2)   The cost of the ending inventory determined by using the average-cost method should be between the amount of the ending inventory determined by using the LIFO method and the amount of the ending inventory determined by using the FIFO method.

TIP: When working a problem which requires the computation of either ending inventory or cost of goods sold, remember that the total of the ending inventory and the cost of goods sold should equal the total cost of goods available for sale during the period (beginning inventory plus the net cost of the purchases).

TIP: Sales revenue represents the **selling prices** of goods sold; whereas, cost of goods sold expense represents the **cost** of items sold.

TIP: The inventory cost flow method selected by an entity does **not** have to correspond to the actual physical flow of goods. Thus, a company can use the LIFO method to determine the cost of ending inventory even though the first goods purchased are the first to be sold.

TIP: In this exercise you can only compute amounts that would pertain to a company using the periodic inventory system because to compute amounts that result from use of the perpetual inventory system, you would have to have information about the dates and quantities of the **individual** sales transactions.

EXERCISE 6-4

Purpose: (L.O. 4) This exercise will review the lower of cost or market rule for inventory valuation.

Electronics Galore had net cost of purchases of $5,000,000 and net sales revenue of $7,200,000 for 2014, its first year of operations. The following information pertains to its inventory at December 31, 2014:

Historical cost (using FIFO)	$420,000
Current replacement cost	$340,000

Instructions

Answer the following questions:
(a) What amount should appear for inventory on the company's balance sheet at December 31, 2014? Why?
(b) What amount should appear for cost of goods sold on the income statement for the year ending December 31, 2014?
(c) What is the theory behind the use of the lower-of-cost-or-market (LCM) rule?

SOLUTION TO EXERCISE 6-4

(a) $340,000 The current replacement cost of $340,000 should be used to value the ending inventory for purposes of reporting the asset on the balance sheet because market value (replacement cost is used here as the appropriate measure of market value) is lower than cost.

(b)
Beginning inventory	$ 0
Net cost of purchases	5,000,000
Cost of goods available for sale	5,000,000
Ending inventory	(340,000)
Cost of goods sold	$4,660,000

(c) The **lower of cost of market (LCM) rule** is based on the accounting convention of **conservatism** which dictates that when choosing among accounting alternatives, the best choice is the treatment that is the least likely to overstate assets and net income. Or to state it another way, in matters of doubt and uncertainty, take the conservative approach (the approach that has the **least** favorable effect on net income and owner's equity).

The current replacement cost (cost of purchasing the same goods at the present time from the usual suppliers in the usual quantities) is lower than original cost. This indicates the supplier has been lowering prices. The same economic forces that caused the supplier to lower its prices are likely to cause Electronics Galore (EG) to lower its selling prices so that EG will end up selling them at a price lower than cost or at a price that cuts down on the normal gross profit experienced by EG. There has been a loss in the utility (value) of the inventory. The LCM rule provides that the loss should be recognized in the period of the decline in utility rather than be deferred and recognized in the period of sale.

By reporting a lower amount for inventory on the December 31, 2014 balance sheet (replacement cost of $340,000 rather than original cost of $420,000), the gross profit figure for 2014 will be $2,540,000 rather than $2,620,000. By using $340,000 for the beginning inventory of 2015 rather than $420,000, cost of goods sold for 2015 will be lower, and gross profit for 2015 will be relatively higher. The loss thus reduces net income for 2014 rather than net income for 2015.

EXERCISE 6-5

Purpose: (L.O. 5) This exercise will test your skill in analyzing inventory errors and determining their effects on the financial statements.

Four separate situations are described below:
1.   An error in the physical count on December 31, 20XA caused the inventory to be overstated.
2.   An error in the physical count on December 31, 20XA caused the inventory to be understated.
3.   An error in the physical count on December 31, 20XB, caused the inventory to be overstated.
4.   An error in the physical count on December 31, 20XB caused the inventory to be understated.

Instructions
For each of the **independent** situations, explain the effect of each error by filling in the matrix with the proper code letters.

O   = Overstatement
U   = Understatement
NE   = No Effect

	Income Statement for 20XA		Balance Sheet at Dec. 31, 20XA		Income Statement for 20XB		Balance Sheet at Dec. 31, 20XB		Income Statement for 20XC		Balance Sheet at Dec. 31, 20XC	
	Cost of Goods Sold	Net Income	Assets	Owner's Equity	Cost of Goods Sold	Net Income	Assets	Owner's Equity	Cost of Goods Sold	Net Income	Assets	Owner's Equity
1												
2												
3												
4												

SOLUTION TO EXERCISE 6-5

	Income Statement for 20XA		Balance Sheet at Dec. 31, 20XA		Income Statement for 20XB		Balance Sheet at Dec. 31, 20XB		Income Statement for 20XC		Balance Sheet at Dec. 31, 20XC	
	Cost of Goods Sold	Net Income	Assets	Owner's Equity	Cost of Goods Sold	Net Income	Assets	Owner's Equity	Cost of Goods Sold	Net Income	Assets	Owner's Equity
1	U	O	O	O	O	U	NE	NE	NE	NE	NE	NE
2	O	U	U	U	U	O	NE	NE	NE	NE	NE	NE
3	NE	NE	NE	NE	U	O	O	O	O	U	NE	NE
4	NE	NE	NE	NE	O	U	U	U	U	O	NE	NE

Explanation: The following points are relevant:

1. The proper determination of the amount to report for inventory is vital to the preparation of both the balance sheet and the income statement. Any misstatement of the ending inventory value has a direct impact on the total of current assets (and total assets) on the balance sheet. This misstatement of inventory will cause a similar misstatement (overstatement or understatement) of the net income calculation on the income statement. The misstated net income figure will cause a similar misstatement of the amount of owner's equity on the balance sheet (because net income is closed to the Owner's Capital account which is an owner's equity account).

2. Due to the manner in which the inventory balance at the balance sheet date is used in the calculation of the cost of goods sold, an inventory error will result in errors in the cost of goods sold, gross profit, and net income figures. As a review, the cost of goods sold and net income computations are:

	Beginning inventory		Net sales
+	Cost of goods purchased	-	Cost of goods sold
=	Cost of goods available for sale	=	Gross profit
-	Ending inventory	-	Operating expenses
=	Cost of goods sold	=	Net income

3. If **ending inventory for Year A is overstated,** the following effects on **Year A** will result:
   (a) Cost of goods sold for Year A will be understated.
   (b) Gross profit for Year A will be overstated.
   (c) Net income for Year A will be overstated.
   (d) Inventory on the balance sheet at the end of Year A will be overstated.
   (e) Owner's equity on the balance sheet at the end of Year A will be overstated.

4. The ending inventory for Year A is the beginning inventory for Year B; thus, if Year A's ending inventory **(Year B's beginning inventory) is overstated,** the following effects on **Year B** will result:
   (a) Cost of goods sold for Year B will be overstated.
   (b) Gross profit for Year B will be understated.
   (c) Net income for Year B will be understated.
   (d) The inventory on the balance sheet at the end of Year B should be correct, as it is determined by a new physical count at that date. If errors are made in this count or in the pricing of this count, additional misstatements will result.
   (e) The owner's equity on the balance sheet at the end of Year B should be correct, as the understated net income for Year B, which was closed to the owner's capital account, counterbalances (offsets) the effect of the overstated net income for Year A (which had previously been closed to the owner's capital account).

5. On the other hand, if the **ending inventory for Year A is understated** the effects on the balance sheet at the end of Year A and on the income statements for Years

A and B would be **opposite** of the effects listed in Points 3 and 4 above. The owner' s equity on the balance sheet at the end of Year B should be correct, as the overstated net income for Year B—which was closed to the owner' s capital account—counterbalances the effect of the understated net income for Year A (which had previously been closed to the owner' s capital account). The inventory on the balance sheet at the end of Year B should be correct unless additional errors are made in the new determination of inventory value at that date.

EXERCISE 6-6

Purpose: (L.O. 5) This exercise will enable you to practice identifying the effects of inventory errors on the financial statements.

The net income per books of Sharon Graham Company was determined without knowledge of the errors indicated.

Year	Net Income Per Books	Error in Ending Inventory	
2011	$100,000	Overstated	$ 6,000
2012	104,000	Overstated	14,000
2013	108,000	Understated	22,000
2014	112,000	No error	

Instructions

Compute the corrected net income figure for each of the four years after taking into account the inventory errors.

SOLUTION TO EXERCISE 6-6

Year	Net Income Per Books	Add Overstate- ment Jan. 1	Deduct Understate- ment Jan. 1	Deduct Overstate- ment Dec. 31	Add Understate- ment Dec. 31	Corrected Net Income
2011	$100,000			$ 6,000		$ 94,000
2012	104,000	$ 6,000		14,000		96,000
2013	108,000	14,000			$22,000	144,000
2014	112,000		$22,000			90,000

Approach and Explanation: When more than one error affects a given year (such as in 2012), analyze each error separately then combine the effects of each analysis to get the net impact of the errors. The beginning inventory for 2012 (ending inventory for 2011) was overstated by $6,000. Therefore, cost of goods sold was overstated by $6,000, and net income for 2012 was understated by $6,000. The ending inventory for 2012 was overstated by $14,000. Therefore, cost of goods sold was understated, and net income for 2012 was overstated by $14,000. An understatement in net income of $6,000 and an overstatement of $14,000 in 2012 net to an overstatement of $8,000 for the net income figure reported for 2012. This overstatement of $8,000 combined with the $104,000 amount reported yields a corrected net income figure of $96,000 for 2012.

Another way of analyzing the effects of an individual error is illustrated below for the $14,000 overstatement of inventory at the end of 2012.

		Effect on 2012	**Effect on 2013**
	Beginning inventory		Overstated 14,000
+	Cost of goods purchased		
=	Cost of goods available for sale		Overstated 14,000
-	Ending inventory	Overstated 14,000	
=	Cost of goods sold	Understated 14,000	Overstated 14,000

		Effect on 2012	**Effect on 2013**
	Sales revenue		
-	Cost of goods sold	Understated 14,000	Overstated 14,000
=	Gross profit	Overstated 14,000	Understated 14,000
-	Operating expenses		
=	Net income	Overstated 14,000	Understated 14,000

Thus, the previously computed net income figure for 2012 must be reduced by $14,000 to correct for this error. Also, the net income figure for 2013 must be increased by $14,000 to correct for the same error.

*EXERCISE 6-7

Purpose: (L.O. 2, 7) This exercise will allow you to practice performing calculations to determine inventory cost under each of three cost flow methods, using both the periodic and the perpetual systems.

The Griggs Company is a multi-product firm. Presented below is information concerning one of their products, Infusion-39.

Date	Transaction	Quantity	Cost
1/1	Beginning inventory	1,000	$12
2/4	Purchase	2,000	18
2/20	Sale	2,500	
4/2	Purchase	3,000	22
11/4	Sale	2,000	

Instructions

Compute the cost of the ending inventory, assuming Griggs uses:

(a)   Periodic system, FIFO cost method.
(b)   Perpetual system, FIFO cost method.
(c)   Periodic system, LIFO cost method.
(d)   Perpetual system, LIFO cost method.
(e)   Periodic system, average-cost method.
(f)   Perpetual system, moving-average cost method.

SOLUTION TO EXERCISE 6-7

(a)   **Periodic-FIFO:**   **Units**
     Beginning inventory   1,000
     Purchases (2,000 + 3,000)   5,000
     Units available for sale   6,000
     Sold (2,500 + 2,000)   4,500
     Goods on hand (assumed)   1,500   1,500 units X $22 = **$33,000**

(b)   **Perpetual-FIFO:** Same as periodic: **$33,000**

TIP:	The use of FIFO with a perpetual system always yields the same results as the use of FIFO with a periodic system. The same does **not** hold true with the LIFO or average cost methods.

(c)   **Periodic-LIFO:**
     1,000 units X $12   = $12,000
       500 units X $18   =   9,000
     1,500 units   **$21,000**

(d)   **Perpetual-LIFO:**

Date	Purchased	Sold	Balance	
1/1			1,000 X $12 =	$12,000
2/4	2,000 X $18 = $36,000		(2,000 X $18) + (1,000 X $12) =	$48,000
2/20		(2,000 X $18) + (500 X $12) = $42,000	500 X $12 =	$ 6,000
4/2	3,000 X $22 = $66,000		(3,000 X $22) + (500 X $12) =	$72,000
11/4		2,000 X $22 = $44,000	(1,000 X $22) + (500 X $12) =	**$28,000**

(e) **Periodic-average:**

1,000 X $12 = $ 12,000
2,000 X $18 = 36,000
3,000 X $22 = 66,000
6,000 $114,000 ÷ 6,000 = $19 each

1,500 units
X $19
$28,500

(f) **Perpetual-average:**

Date	Purchased	Sold	Balance	
1/1			1,000 X $12 =	$12,000
2/4	2,000 X $18 = $36,000		3,000 X $16ᵃ =	$48,000
2/20		2,500 X $16 = $40,000	500 X $16 =	$ 8,000
4/2	3,000 X $22 = $66,000		3,500 X $21.14ᵇ =	$73,990
11/4		2,000 X $21.14 = $42,280	1,500 X $21.14 =	$31,710

ᵃ1,000 X $12 = $12,000
2,000 X $18 =   36,000
3,000 $48,000

ᵇ 500 X $16 = $ 8,000
3,000 X $22 =   66,000
3,500 $74,000

$48,000 ÷ 3,000 = $16.00 average unit cost $74,000 ÷ 3,500 = $21.14 average unit cost

> **TIP:** When using the average-cost method and a perpetual system, a new average unit cost must be computed **only** after each new purchase; a sale will **not** affect the average unit cost.
>
> **TIP:** Examine your solution to the exercise above and judge the reasonableness of your answers. What do you expect the relationship of the answers to be for the **periodic system?**
> (1) Because the trend of the acquisition costs was upward, the ending inventory computed under LIFO should be lower than the ending inventory figure computed under FIFO.
> (2) The cost of the ending inventory determined by using the average-cost method should be between the amount of the ending inventory determined by using the LIFO method and the amount of ending inventory determined by using the FIFO method.

**ILLUSTRATION 6-1
FORMULAS FOR ESTIMATING INVENTORIES (L.O. 8)

GROSS PROFIT METHOD

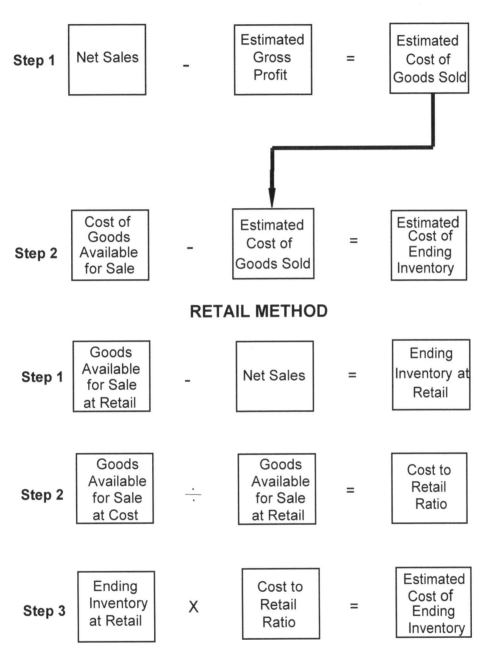

RETAIL METHOD

The retail method can be used as a cost (pricing) method (rather than an estimating technique) if the ending inventory at retail is actually observed rather than estimated. This means a physical count of inventory is taken at the balance sheet date and that actual quantity is priced at selling prices (retail). Then steps 2 and 3 above are applied to determine the actual cost of the inventory at the count date.

**EXERCISE 6-8

Purpose: (L.O. 8) This exercise reviews the relationships and computations involved with methods of estimating inventory.

Information relating to five different situations is as follows:

1.	Net sales	$132,000
	Gross profit	52,800
	Gross profit rate	_____
2.	Net sales	$ 80,000
	Cost of goods sold	52,000
	Net income	12,000
	Gross profit rate	_____
3.	Cost of goods available for sale	$ 74,000
	Estimated cost of goods sold	60,000
	Estimated ending inventory at cost	_____
4.	Beginning inventory at cost	$ 20,000
	Purchases at cost	112,000
	Purchases returns at cost	4,000
	Net sales	200,000
	Gross profit rate	45%
	Estimated cost of goods sold	_____
	Estimated ending inventory at cost	_____
5.	Cost of goods available for sale	$ 52,000
	Selling prices of goods for sale	78,000
	Cost-to-retail ratio	_____
6.	Beginning inventory at cost	$ 12,000
	Beginning inventory at retail	20,000
	Purchases at cost	62,100
	Purchases at retail	94,000
	Ending inventory at retail	17,200
	Operating expenses	38,000
	Cost-to-retail ratio	_____
	Estimated ending inventory at cost	_____

Instructions
Fill in the missing figure(s) for each of the **independent** situations above.

SOLUTION TO EXERCISE 6-8

1.   Gross profit, $52,800 ÷ Net sales, $132,000 = **Gross profit rate, <u>40%</u>.**

2.
Net sales	$ 80,000
Cost of goods sold	(52,000)
Gross profit	$28,000

     Gross profit, $28,000 ÷ Net sales, $80,000 = **Gross profit rate, <u>35%</u>.**

3.
Cost of goods available for sale	$74,000
Estimated cost of goods sold	(60,000)
Estimated ending inventory at cost	**$14,000**

4.
Net sales	$200,000
Gross profit rate	45%
Estimated gross profit	$ 90,000

Net sales	$200,000
Estimated gross profit	(90,000)
Estimated cost of goods sold	**$110,000**

Purchases at cost	$112,000
Purchase returns at cost	(4,000)
Net purchases	108,000
Freight-in	0
Cost of goods purchased	$108,000

Beginning inventory at cost	$ 20,000
Cost of goods purchased	108,000
Cost of goods available for sale	128,000
Estimated cost of goods sold	(110,000)
Estimated ending inventory at cost	**$ 18,000**

5.   Cost of goods available for sale, $52,000 ÷ Selling price of goods available for sale, $78,000 = **Cost-to-retail ratio, <u>66.67%</u>.**

6.
Beginning inventory at cost	$12,000
Cost of goods purchased	62,100
Cost of goods available for sale	$74,100

Beginning inventory at retail	$ 20,000
Net purchases at retail	94,000
Goods available for sale at retail	$114,000

Cost of goods available for sale, $74,100 ÷ Goods available for sale at retail, $114,000 = **Cost-to-retail ratio, <u>65%</u>.**

Ending inventory at retail	$17,200
Cost to retail ratio	<u>65%</u>
Estimated ending inventory at cost	**<u>$11,180</u>**

TIP:	The ending inventory at retail was probably determined by a physical inventory count.
TIP:	Operating expenses are not used in any of the computations requested in this exercise.

****EXERCISE 6-9**

Purpose: (L.O. 8) This exercise will illustrate the use of the gross profit method of inventory estimation.

Carol Morlan requires an estimate of the cost of goods lost by fire on March 9. Merchandise on hand on January 1, was $38,000. Purchases since January 1 were $72,000; freight-in, $3,400; purchase returns and allowances, $2,400. Net sales totaled $100,000 to March 9. All goods on hand on March 9 were destroyed. Prior experience shows that the gross profit rate is 25% of sales.

Instructions
Compute the cost of goods destroyed.

SOLUTION TO EXERCISE 6-9

$36,000 is the estimated fire loss.

Computations:

Step 1   Net Sales - Estimated Gross Profit = Estimated Cost of Goods Sold.

$100,000   - $25,000[1]   = $75,000

Step 2	Cost of Goods Available for Sale	-	Estimated Cost of Goods Sold	=	Estimated Cost of Ending Inventory
	$111,000[2]	-	$75,000	=	**$36,000**

[1]Net sales	$100,000
Gross profit rate	25%
Estimated gross profit	$ 25,000

[2]Inventory, January 1	$ 38,000
Purchases	72,000
Purchase returns and allowances	(2,400)
Freight-in	3,400
Cost of goods available for sale	$111,000

Approach: Follow the two steps as illustrated above (these steps are diagrammed in **Illustration 6-1**). Plug in the amounts known and solve.

OR

If you cannot recall the steps diagrammed in **Illustration 6-1** or do not want to memorize more formulas, write down the basic formulas or equations to compute the cost of goods sold and gross profit. Enter the amounts given and solve for the rest. For example:

	Net sales	$100,000	
-	CGS	(X)	
=	GP	$ 25,000	100,000 X 25%

	Beginning inventory	$38,000	
+	Cost of goods purchased	73,000	(72,000 - $2,400 + $3,400)
=	Cost of goods available for sale	111,000	
-	Ending inventory	(Y)	
=	Cost of goods sold	X	

Solving for X: X = $100,000 Sales - $25,000 Gross profit = $75,000 Estimated cost of goods sold

Solving for Y: $111,000 - X = Y
$111,000 CGAS - $75,000 CGS = $36,000 Estimated ending inventory

****EXERCISE 6-10**

Purpose: (L.O. 8) This exercise illustrates the use of the retail inventory method to estimate ending inventory.

The records of Petite Clothiers report the following figures for the month of September:

Sales	$79,000
Sales returns	1,000
Freight on purchases	2,400
Purchases (at cost)	48,000
Purchases (at sales price)	92,000
Purchase returns (at cost)	2,000
Purchase returns (at sales price)	3,000
Beginning inventory (at cost)	30,000
Beginning inventory (at sales price)	51,000

Instructions
Compute an estimate of the cost of ending inventory by using the retail inventory method.

SOLUTION TO EXERCISE 6-10

		Cost	**Retail**
	Beginning inventory	$30,000	$ 51,000
	Purchases	48,000	92,000
	Purchase returns	(2,000)	(3,000)
	Freight on purchases	2,400	
	Goods available for sale	78,400	140,000
	Net sales ($79,000 - $1,000)		(78,000)
Step 1	Ending inventory at retail		$ 62,000

Step 2   Cost-to-retail ratio = $\dfrac{\$78,400}{\$140,000}$ = <u>56%</u>

Step 3   Estimated cost of ending inventory = $62,000 X 56% = **$34,720**

Approach and Explanation:
Refer to the steps diagrammed in **Illustration 6-1.**

(a)   **Step 1:**   **Compute the ending inventory at retail.** This is done by determining the retail value of goods available for sale and deducting the retail value of goods no longer on hand (sales, estimated theft, etc.).

Step 2: **Compute the cost-to-retail ratio.** This is done by dividing the cost of goods available for sale by the retail value of the goods available for sale. The retail method approximates an average cost amount so both beginning inventory and net purchases information is used in the ratio.

Step 3: **Determine the estimated cost of ending inventory.** Apply the appropriate cost-to-retail ratio (Step 2) to the ending inventory at retail (Step 1).

TIP:	The retail inventory method can be used only if sufficient information is accumulated and maintained. Purchases are recorded in the accounts at cost. Although not recorded in the accounts, the retail value of purchases must be recorded in supplemental records for use in inventory calculations utilizing the retail inventory method.

EXERCISE 6-11

Purpose: (L.O. 1 thru 8) This exercise will quiz you about terminology used in this chapter.

A list of accounting terms with which you should be familiar appears below.

Average-cost method	**Gross profit method
Conservatism	Inventory turnover
Consigned goods	Just-in-time (JIT) inventory
Consistency concept	Last-in, first-out (LIFO) method
Current replacement cost	Lower-of-cost-or-market (LCM)
Days in inventory	**Retail inventory method
Finished goods inventory	Raw materials
First-in, first-out (FIFO) method	Specific identification method
FOB (free on board) destination	Weighted-average unit cost
FOB (free on board) shipping point	Work in process

These items are covered in **Appendix 6B in the text.

Instructions
For each item below, enter in the blank the term that is described.

1. _____An actual inventory physical flow costing method in which items still in inventory are specifically costed to arrive at the total cost of the ending inventory.

2. _____An inventory cost flow method that assumes that the goods available for sale have the same (average) cost per unit; generally they are identical.

3. _____An inventory cost flow method that assumes that the costs of the earliest goods acquired are the first to be recognized as cost of goods sold.

4. _____An inventory cost flow method that assumes that the costs of the latest units purchased are the first to be allocated to cost of goods sold.

5. _____A method of valuing inventory that recognizes the decline in the value of inventory when the current purchase price (market) is less than cost.

6. _____The amount that would be paid at the present time to acquire an identical item.

7. _____A method for estimating the cost of the ending inventory by applying a gross profit rate to net sales to compute the estimated gross profit.

8. _____A method used to estimate the cost of the ending inventory by applying a cost to retail ratio to the ending inventory at retail.

9. _____Freight terms indicating that the goods are placed free on board at the buyer's place of business, and the seller pays the freight cost; goods belong to the seller while in transit.

10. _____Freight terms indicating that the goods are placed free on board the carrier by the seller, and the buyer pays the freight cost; goods belong to the buyer while in transit.

11. _____Measure of the average number of days inventory is held; calculated as 365 divided by inventory turnover.

12. _____Goods shipped by a consignor (who retains ownership) to another party called the consignee.

13. _____Basic goods that will be used in production but have not yet been place in production.

14. _____Manufactured items that are completed and ready for sale.

15. _____That portion of manufactured inventory that has begun the production process but is not yet complete.

16. _____Inventory system in which companies manufacture or purchase goods just in time for use.

17. _____A measure of the number of times the average amount of inventory on hand is sold during the period; computed by dividing cost of goods sold by the average inventory balance during the period.

18. _____Average cost that is weighted by the number of units purchased at each unit cost.

19. _____Convention that dictates that when in doubt, choose the method that will be least likely to overstate assets and net income.

20. _____Dictates that a company use the same accounting principles and methods from year to year.

SOLUTION TO EXERCISE 6-11

1. Specific identification method
2. Average-cost method
3. First-in, first-out method (FIFO)
4. Last-in, first-out method (LIFO)
5. Lower-of-cost-or-market (LCM)
6. Current replacement cost
7. **Gross profit method
8. **Retail inventory method
9. FOB destination
10. FOB shipping point
11. Days in inventory
12. Consigned goods
13. Raw materials
14. Finished goods inventory
15. Work in process
16. Just-in-time (JIT) inventory
17. Inventory turnover
18. Weighted average unit cost
19. Conservatism
20. Consistency concept

ANALYSIS OF MULTIPLE-CHOICE TYPE QUESTIONS

1. (L.O. 1) At December 31, 2014, a physical count of merchandise inventory belonging to Klintworth Corp. showed $500,000 to be on hand. The $500,000 was calculated before any potential necessary adjustments related to the following:
   - Excluded from the $500,000 was $80,000 of goods shipped FOB shipping point by a vendor to Klintworth on December 30, 2014 and received on January 3, 2015.
   - Excluded from the $500,000 was $72,000 of goods shipped FOB destination to Klintworth on December 30, 2014 and received on January 3, 2015.
   - Excluded from the $500,000 was $95,000 of goods shipped FOB destination by Klintworth to a customer on December 28, 2014. The customer received the goods on January 4, 2015.

   The correct amount to report for inventory on Klintworth's balance sheet at December 31, 2014 is:
   a. $572,000.
   b. $595,000.
   c. $675,000.
   d. $747,000.

   Explanation:
   (1) The $80,000 should be added to the $500,000 because FOB shipping point means the title transferred when the goods left the seller's dock on December 30, 2014.
   (2) The $72,000 is properly excluded from the ending inventory because title did not pass to Klintworth until Klintworth received the goods on January 3, 2015.
   (3) The $95,000 should be added to the $500,000 because the goods belong to Klintworth until they are received by the customer (in 2015)

   $500,000
   + 80,000
   + 95,000
   $675,000   Amount to report for ending inventory at December 31, 2014. (Solution = c.)

2.   (L.O. 3)   Which inventory cost flow method most closely approximates current cost for each of the following?

	Ending inventory	Cost of Goods Sold
a.	FIFO	FIFO
b.	FIFO	LIFO
c.	LIFO	FIFO
d.	LIFO	LIFO

Approach and Explanation: Write down which inventory method (LIFO or FIFO) reports current cost for ending inventory and which uses current cost to price cost of goods sold and then look for your answer combination. FIFO uses the first cost in as the first cost out, so the last (more current) costs are used to price the ending inventory. Therefore, FIFO is the answer for the first column. In contrast, LIFO uses the last cost in (current cost) as the first cost out (to cost of goods sold), so LIFO reflects current costs in cost of goods sold. Therefore, LIFO is the answer for the second column. Answer " b" is the determined combination. (Solution = b.)

3.   (L.O. 3) For 2014, Selma Co. had beginning inventory of $75,000, ending inventory of $90,000 and net income of $120,000 using the LIFO inventory method. If the FIFO method had been used, beginning inventory would have been $85,000, ending inventory would have been $105,000, and net income would have been:
a. $125,000.
b. $115,000.
c. $145,000.
d. $95,000.

Approach and Explanation: Develop the answer by analyzing the effects on the cost of goods sold computation and resulting effects on net income.

		LIFO	FIFO	Effect on Cost of Goods Sold		Effect on Net Income
	Beginning inventory	$ 75,000	$ 85,000	Increase	$10,000	Decrease $10,000
+	Cost of goods pur- chased					
=	Cost of goods avail- able for sale					
-	Ending inventory	90,000	105,000	Decrease	15,000	Increase 15,000
=	Cost of goods sold					
	Net income	120,000	?	Decrease	5,000	Increase 5,000

Net income using LIFO	$120,000
Net increase in net income using FIFO	5,000
Net income using FIFO	$125,000

(Solution = a.)

4. (L.O. 3) The following facts pertain to the cost of one product carried in the merchandise inventory of the Herara Store, which uses the periodic system:

Inventory on hand, January 1	200 units @ $20 =	$ 4,000
Purchase, March 18	600 units @ $24 =	14,400
Purchase, July 20	800 units @ $26 =	20,800
Purchase, October 31	400 units @ $30 =	12,000

A physical count of the inventory on December 31 reveals that 500 units are on hand. If the FIFO cost method is used, the inventory should be reported on the balance sheet at:
a. $40,000.
b. $36,600.
c. $14,600.
d. $11,200.
e. None of the above.

Approach and Explanation: Think about what FIFO stands for: the first cost in is the first out to cost of goods sold. Therefore, ending inventory is comprised of the latest costs experienced.

400 units @ $30 =	$12,000
100 units @ $26 =	2,600
Ending inventory at FIFO	$14,600	(Solution = c.)

5. (L.O. 3) Refer to the data in **Question 4** above.

If the average-cost method is used, the cost of goods sold for the year amounts to:
a. $38,400.
b. $37,500
c. $12,800.
d. $12,500.

Approach and Explanation: Read the question carefully. Notice it asks for the cost of goods sold and **not** for the ending inventory as you might expect.

Total cost of all units available for sale:	
Beginning inventory	$ 4,000
Purchases ($14,400 + $20,800 + $12,000)	47,200
Cost of goods available for sale	$51,200

$51,200 Cost of goods available for sale ÷ 2,000[1]
Units available for sale = $25.60 Average unit cost

$25.60 Average unit cost X 500 units =	$12,800 Ending inventory
$25.60 Average unit cost X 1,500[2] units =	$38,400 Cost of goods sold

[1]200 + 600 + 800 + 400 = 2,000 units available.
[2]2,000 units available - 500 units in ending inventory = 1,500 units sold.   (Solution = a.)

6.   (L.O. 3) Refer to the data in **Question 4** above.

If the LIFO cost method is used, the cost of goods sold for the year amounts to:
a. $40,000.
b. $36,600.
c. $14,600.
d. $11,200.

Approach and Explanation: Notice the question asks for the cost of goods sold rather than the cost of the ending inventory. You may approach the solution one of two ways: You may cost the items sold or compute the cost of the ending inventory and deduct that cost from the cost of goods available for sale. Using the first of these two approaches, think of what LIFO stands for: the last cost in is the first cost out to cost of goods sold.

Units available	2,000
Units on hand at end of period	(500)
Units sold	1,500

400	@ $30	=	$12,000			
800	@ $26	=	20,800			
300	@ $24	=	7,200			
1,500 units		=	$40,000	cost of goods sold		(Solution = a.)

TIP: The cost of the ending inventory using LIFO would be:

200 @ $20 =	$ 4,000	
300 @ $24 =	7,200	
500	$11,200	ending inventory

---

7.   (L.O. 3) In a period of rising prices, which of the following inventory cost flow methods will yield the largest reported amount for cost of goods sold?
a.   Specific identification.
b.   FIFO.
c.   LIFO.
d.   Average.

Explanation: In a period of rising prices, the most recent purchase prices are the highest ones experienced by the entity. Using LIFO, the latest costs (the highest ones, in this instance) are used to price cost of goods sold and the earliest ones are used to price ending inventory. FIFO would give the lowest cost of goods sold in a period of rising prices. The results of the average-cost method would fall between the results of the LIFO and FIFO methods. The specific identification method would likely yield a cost of goods sold figure similar to FIFO (but not more than LIFO) because specific identification would use the cost of the specific items sold to price the cost of the goods sold, and the specific items sold usually follow a first-in, first-out physical flow. (Solution = c.)

8. (L.O. 3) Which of the following statements is false regarding an assumption of inventory cost flow?
a. The cost flow assumption need not correspond to the actual physical flow of goods.
b. The assumption selected may be changed each accounting period.
c. The FIFO assumption uses the earliest acquired prices to cost the items sold during a period.
d. The LIFO assumption uses the earliest acquired prices to cost the items on hand at the end of an accounting period.

Explanation: Once a method is selected from acceptable alternative methods, the entity must consistently apply that method for successive periods. The reason for this **consistency concept** is that **comparability** of financial statements for the entity for successive periods is reduced or lost if methods are changed from period to period. However, an entity may change a method if it becomes evident that there is a more appropriate method and proper disclosure of the change is made. (Solution = b.)

9. (L.O. 4) In applying the lower-of-cost-or-market (LCM) for inventories, the most conservative valuation will be derived when LCM is applied to:
a. each individual item in the inventory.
b. categories of inventory.
c. the total inventory.

Explanation: When categories or total inventory is used, situations caused by products whose replacement cost is higher than original cost are allowed to offset situations where replacement cost is lower than original cost. When an item-by-item approach is used, all possible declines in utility are recognized and not offset by inventory items whose replacement cost exceeds original cost. (Solution = a.)

10. (L.O. 4) Peachy Products has an item in inventory with a cost of $85. Current replacement cost is $75. The expected selling price is $100 and estimated selling costs are $18. Using the lower-of-cost-or-market rule, the item should be included in the inventory at:
a. $100.
b. $85.
c. $82.
d. $75.

Approach and Explanation: Write down the two steps in determining LCM and follow them:
(1) **Find market:** Replacement cost = $75
(2) **Compare market with cost and choose the lower:**
   Market of $75 versus cost of $85. Lower = $75   (Solution = d.)

11. (L.O. 5) If the beginning inventory for 2014 is overstated, the effects of this error on cost of goods sold for 2014, net income for 2014, and assets at December 31, 2015, respectively are:
   a. overstatement, understatement, overstatement.
   b. overstatement, understatement, no effect.
   c. understatement, overstatement, overstatement.
   d. understatement, overstatement, no effect.

   Approach and Explanation: For questions dealing with inventory errors, assume a periodic system unless otherwise indicated. Write down the components of the cost of goods sold computation and analyze the resulting effects on net income.

		2014	**2015**
	Beginning inventory	Overstated	No effect
+	Cost of goods purchased		↓
=	Cost of goods available for sale	Overstated	
-	Ending inventory		
=	Cost of goods sold	Overstated	
	Net income	Understated	

   The inventory at the end of 2014 and the inventory at the end of 2015 are both apparently free of error because the inventory at a balance sheet date is determined by a physical count and pricing process. Assume there are no errors in this process unless otherwise indicated. (Solution = b.)

   > **TIP:** The fact that the inventory at the beginning of 2014 was in error indicates that the inventory at the end of 2013 was in error because the ending inventory of one period is the beginning inventory of the next period.

12. (L.O. 5) If beginning inventory is understated by $8,000 and ending inventory is overstated by $3,000, net income for the period will be:
   a. overstated by $11,000.
   b. overstated by $5,000.
   c. understated by $5,000.
   d. understated by $11,000.

   Approach and Explanation: The effect on net income is dependent on the effect on the computation of cost of goods sold (which is an expense affecting net income). Each error's effect on net income should be determined separately. The effects are then combined to compute the **total** effect on net income for the period.

		Effect on Net Income		
		First Error	**Second Error**	**Total (Net) Effect**
	Beginning inventory	Understated $8,000		Understated $ 8,000
+	Purchases			
=	Goods available	Understated $8,000		Understated $ 8,000
-	Ending inventory		Overstated $3,000	Overstated $ 3,000
=	Cost of goods sold	Understated $8,000	Understated $3,000	Understated $11,000
	Net income	Overstated $8,000	Overstated $3,000	Overstated $11,000

(Solution = a.)

TIP: When analyzing a question like this one, it is often helpful to create an example with numbers.

---

13. (L.O. 6) The inventory turnover is computed by dividing:
    a. net sales by cost of goods sold.
    b. cost of goods sold by net sales.
    c. cost of goods sold by average inventory.
    d. average inventory by cost of goods sold.

    Explanation: The inventory turnover ratio measures the number of times on average the inventory balance was sold during the period. Its purpose is to measure the liquidity of the inventory. The inventory turnover is computed by dividing cost of goods sold by the average inventory during the period. Unless seasonal factors are significant, average inventory can be computed from the beginning and ending inventory balances rather than from monthly inventory balances. (Solution = c.)

14. (L.O. 6) The **average days to sell inventory** is computed by dividing:
    a. 365 days by the inventory turnover ratio.
    b. the inventory turnover ratio by 365 days.
    c. net sales by the inventory turnover ratio.
    d. 365 days by cost of goods sold.

    Explanation: The average days to sell inventory is a variant of the inventory turnover ratio. It is computed by dividing 365 days by the inventory turnover ratio. It measures the average number of days an item remains in inventory before it is sold. (Solution = a.)

*15. (L.O. 7) The average-cost method used in a perpetual inventory system is called the moving-average method. Under this method, the company computes a new average
    a. after each purchase.
    b. after each sale
    c. after each purchase and after each sale.

    Explanation: A new average is computed after each new purchase (assuming the new purchase is at a price different than the existing weighted-average cost). A withdrawal of inventory due to a sale is recorded at the weighted-average cost existing at the moment of sale. (Solution = a.)

**16. (L.O. 8) The following data relate to the merchandise inventory of the Hofma Company:

Beginning inventory at cost	$13,800
Beginning inventory at selling price	20,000
Purchases at cost	31,000
Purchases at selling price	50,000

The cost-to-retail percentage (ratio) to be used in calculating an estimate of ending inventory by use of the retail method is:
a. 156%.
b. 145%.
c. 69%.
d. 64%.

Explanation: $\dfrac{\text{Cost} = \$13,800 + \$31,000}{\text{Retail} = \$20,000 + \$50,000} = \dfrac{\$44,800}{\$70,000} = \underline{64\%}$ (Solution = d.)

**17. (L.O. 8) The following information pertains to the Godfrey Company for the six months ended June 30 of the current year:

Merchandise inventory, January 1	$ 700,000
Purchases	5,000,000
Freight-in	400,000
Net sales	6,000,000

Gross profit is normally 25% of sales. What is the estimated amount of inventory on hand at June 30?
a. $100,000.
b. $1,600,000.
c. $2,100,000.
d. $4,600,000.

Approach and Explanation: Use the following steps to solve a gross profit inventory method question:

(1) Determine the **estimated cost of goods sold** during the period:

Net sales	$6,000,000
Estimated gross profit (25%)	(1,500,000)
Estimated cost of goods sold	$4,500,000

(2) Compute the **estimated cost of inventory on hand** at the end of the period:

Beginning inventory	$ 700,000
Purchases	5,000,000
Freight-in	400,000
Cost of goods available for sale	6,100,000
Estimated cost of goods sold	(4,500,000)
Estimated ending inventory	$1,600,000

(Solution = b.)

**18. (L.O. 8) The Ruffier Department Store uses the retail inventory method. The following information is available at December 31, 2014:

	Cost	Retail
Beginning inventory	$ 37,800	$ 60,000
Purchases	200,000	290,000
Freight-in	7,200	
Net sales		275,000

What is the estimated cost of the ending inventory?
a. $47,250.
b. $52,500.
c. $53,586.
d. $192,500.

Computations:

		Cost	Retail
	Beginning inventory	$ 37,800	$ 60,000
	Purchases	200,000	290,000
	Freight-in	7,200	
	Cost of goods available for sale	$245,000	350,000
	Net sales		(275,000)
Step 1:	Ending inventory at retail		$ 75,000
Step 2:	Cost to retail ratio = $245,000 ÷ $350,000 = 70%		
Step 3:	Estimated cost of ending inventory = $75,000 X 70% = $52,500		

(Solution = b.)

CHAPTER 7

. . . .

ACCOUNTING INFORMATION SYSTEMS

OVERVIEW

As transactions increase in number, so do the recordings and postings required to account for business activities. To deal with transactions the accountant employs (1) special journals to efficiently organize and expedite the recording and posting process for transactions which occur frequently and (2) subsidiary ledgers to free the general ledger of details. A business may have a computerized accounting system or it may rely on a manual system. The steps in the accounting cycle remain the same whether or not the system is automated.

SUMMARY OF LEARNING OBJECTIVES

1. **Identify the basic concepts of an accounting information system.** The basic principles in developing an accounting information system are cost effectiveness, useful output, and flexibility. Most companies use a computerized accounting system. Smaller companies use entry-level software such as QuickBooks or Sage50. Larger companies use custom-made software packages which often integrate all aspects of the organization.

2. **Describe the nature and purpose of a subsidiary ledger.** A subsidiary ledger is a group of accounts with a common characteristic. It facilitates the recording process by freeing the general ledger from details of individual balances.

3. **Explain how companies use special journals in journalizing.** Companies use special journals to group similar types of transactions. In a special journal, generally only one line is used to record a complete transaction.

TIPS ON CHAPTER TOPICS

TIP:	It is sometimes confusing for a beginning accounting student to differentiate between subsidiary ledgers and special journals. It may help to think about how **special journals** are used **to record similar transactions** in a common place (such as all sales on account are recorded in the sales journal); thus, special journals are used in the **recording** process. All transactions affect accounts. **Subsidiary ledgers** are used to **group similar accounts** in a common place (such as an account receivable for each customer is included in the accounts receivable ledger); thus, subsidiary ledgers are used in the **posting** process.
TIP:	The **cash payments journal** is often called the **cash disbursements journal.**

EXERCISE 7-1

Purpose: (L.O. 2) This exercise will test your understanding of the postings that appear in a subsidiary ledger.

Presented below is the account for the vendor, Kitchen Plastics Company, as it appears in the accounts payable subsidiary ledger of Great Value Hardware.

KITCHEN PLASTICS COMPANY

Date	Ref.	Debit	Credit	Balance
2014				
Jan. 1				17,000
3	P17		22,000	39,000
8	P18		13,000	52,000
9	CP25	17,000		35,000
11	G5	5,000		30,000
17	CP28	30,000		-0-

Instructions
Explain each amount reflected in this subsidiary account.

SOLUTION TO EXERCISE 7-1

Jan. 1 The account started the period with a beginning balance of $17,000. This balance was the result of unpaid purchases from the prior period.

Jan. 3 A posting of $22,000 from page 17 of the purchases journal (P17) indicates that purchases of $22,000 were made on credit.

Jan. 8 A posting of $13,000 from page 18 of the purchases journal (P18) indicates that purchases of $13,000 were made on credit.

Jan. 9 A posting of $17,000 from page 25 of the cash payments journal (CP25) indicates that a cash payment of $17,000 was made to Kitchen Plastics on account.

Jan. 11 A debit posting of $5,000 from page 5 of the general journal (G5) probably stems from a purchase return or allowance.

Jan. 17 A posting of $30,000 from page 28 of the cash payments journal (CP28) indicates that a cash payment of $30,000 was made to the vendor on account.

TIP:	Think about the normal balance of an account payable—credit balance. Think about common reasons for increases (credits) and for decreases (debits). Identify the source of each posting by the abbreviation in the Ref. column. The transactions being posted should then be fairly evident.
TIP:	In addition to having subsidiary ledgers for accounts receivable and accounts payable, it is not uncommon for a business to also use control accounts and subsidiary ledgers for other accounts such as inventory (when a perpetual system is used), equipment, and selling and administrative expenses.

EXERCISE 7-2

Purpose: (L.O. 3) This exercise will help you identify the journal in which to record specific transactions.

A list of abbreviations and a list of transactions (in random order) follow:

Abbreviations
S = Sales Journal
CR = Cash Receipts Journal
P = Single-Column Purchases Journal
CP = Cash Payments Journal
GJ = General Journal

Instructions
For each transaction, indicate the journal in which it would be recorded.

Transactions

_____   1.   Sold merchandise for cash.

_____   2.   Purchased merchandise for cash.

_____   3.   Made an adjusting entry for accrued salaries.

_____   4.   Made collection on an accounts receivable.

_____   5.   Paid rent for the month.

_____   6.   Accepted a note receivable from a customer in settlement of an account receivable.

_____   7.   Paid salaries for the current period.

_____   8.   Wrote a check for an owner's withdrawal.

_____   9.   Returned merchandise to a supplier for credit.

_____   10.   Sold merchandise on account.

_____   11.   Purchased merchandise on account.

_____   12.   Purchased equipment for cash.

_____   13.   Purchased equipment on account.

_____   14.   Purchased office supplies for cash.

_____ 15. Purchased office supplies on account.

_____ 16. Recorded depreciation on equipment for the period.

_____ 17. Received return of merchandise from a customer who had purchased it on credit. Issued a credit memorandum.

_____ 18. Recorded an adjustment for supplies used.

_____ 19. Recorded an adjustment for insurance which had expired.

_____ 20. Paid freight bill on purchases of merchandise inventory.

_____ 21. Loaned money to an employee.

_____ 22. Paid for merchandise which had been purchased on account. Paid within the discount period.

_____ 23. Recorded accrued revenue.

_____ 24. Paid the utilities bill.

_____ 25. Closed the temporary accounts.

_____ 26. Removed merchandise inventory from stock for owner's personal use.

_____ 27. Paid a creditor after the 2% discount period lapsed.

_____ 28. Gave a cash refund to a customer who returned merchandise.

_____ 29. Paid freight on goods shipped to a customer FOB destination.

_____ 30. Collected revenue in advance.

_____ 31. Paid for an insurance premium one year in advance.

_____ 32. Received an additional investment of cash from an owner.

_____ 33. Sold inventory on credit.

_____ 34. Purchased inventory on credit.

_____ 35. Received a cash refund from a supplier upon return of merchandise.

_____ 36. Collected interest from employee who borrowed money.

SOLUTION TO EXERCISE 7-2

1.	CR	10.	S	19.	GJ	28.	CP
2.	CP	11.	P	20.	CP	29.	CP
3.	GJ	12.	CP	21.	CP	30.	CR
4.	CR	13.	GJ	22.	CP	31.	CP
5.	CP	14.	CP	23.	GJ	32.	CR
6.	GJ	15.	GJ	24.	CP	33.	S
7.	CP	16.	GJ	25.	GJ	34.	P
8.	CP	17.	GJ	26.	GJ	35.	CR
9.	GJ	18.	GJ	27.	CP	36.	CR

Approach and Explanation: Keep in mind that a special journal is used to record similar types of transactions, such as all sales of merchandise or all cash receipts. Write down a brief description of the types of transactions to be recorded in each of the journals used in this exercise. They are:

Sales journal—all sales of merchandise on account.

Cash receipts journal—all receipts of cash (including cash sales).

Purchases journal—all purchases of merchandise on account.

Cash payments (disbursements) journal—all payments of cash (including cash purchases).

General journal—all transactions that do not appropriately fit in a special journal (including adjustments and closing entries).

Identify the transactions that involve sales of merchandise on credit (items 10 and 33). They go in the sales journal. Identify the transactions that involve purchases of merchandise on account (items 11 and 34). They go in the purchases journal. Identify the transactions that involve the receipt of cash (items 1, 4, 30, 32, 35, and 36). They are to be recorded in the cash receipts journal.

Identify the transactions that involve a cash payment (items 2, 5, 7, 8, 12, 14, 20, 21, 22, 24, 27, 28, 29, and 31). They go in the cash payments journal. Identify the transactions that do not fit those first four categories (items 3, 6, 9, 13, 15, 16, 17, 18, 19, 23, 25, and 26). They go in the general journal. (Notice that items 3, 16, 18, 19 and 23 are adjusting entries and item 25 involves closing entries.)

EXERCISE 7-3

Purpose: (L.O. 3) This exercise reviews general ledger accounts and postings to them from special journals.

A list of abbreviations and a list of postings to general ledger accounts (in random order) follow:

Abbreviations
S = Sales Journal
CR = Cash Receipts Journal
P = Single-Column Purchases Journal
CP = Cash Payments Journal
GJ = General Journal

Instructions
For each of the postings to the general ledger accounts listed below, indicate the **most common** source of the posting. Use the appropriate abbreviations to indicate your answer for each. (Assume all purchases of inventory and sales are made on account.)

Postings to General Ledger Accounts

_____ 1. Debits to Inventory

_____ 2. Credits to Sales Revenue

_____ 3. Debits to Accounts Payable

_____ 4. Credits to Accounts Payable

_____ 5. Debits to Cash

_____ 6. Credits to Cash

_____ 7. Debits to Accounts Receivable

_____ 8. Credits to Accounts Receivable

_____ 9. Credits to Interest Payable

_____ 10. Debits to Postage Expense

_____ 11. Debits to Salaries and Wages Expense

_____ 12. Debits to Depreciation Expense

_____ 13. Debits to Prepaid Insurance

_____ 14. Credits to Prepaid Insurance

_____ 15. Debits to Supplies

_____ 16. Credits to Supplies

_____ 17. Credits to Notes Payable

_____ 18. Credits to Unearned Rent Revenue

_____ 19. Debits to Unearned Rent Revenue

_____ 22. Credits to Interest Revenue

_____ 20. Credits to Salaries & Wages Expense

_____ 23. Credits to Inventory

_____ 21. Debits to Maintenance And Repairs Expense

_____ 24. Debits to Cost of Goods Sold

SOLUTION TO EXERCISE 7-3

1.	P	7.	S	13.	CP	19.	GJ
2.	S	8.	CR	14.	GJ	20.	GJ
3.	CP	9.	GJ	15.	CP or GJ*	21.	CP
4.	P	10.	CP	16.	GJ	22.	CR
5.	CR	11.	CP	17.	CR	23.	S and/or CR**
6.	CP	12.	GJ	18.	CR	24.	S and/or CR**

*The answer depends on whether the entity makes most purchases of supplies for cash (entered in the cash payments journal) or on credit (entered in the general journal). Some companies expand their purchases journal to provide columns to record credit purchases of items **other than** merchandise inventory.

**The answer depends on whether the entity makes most sales on credit (entered in the sales journal) or for cash (entered in the cash receipts journal).

Approach and Explanation: Briefly describe the columns typically found in each of the special journals listed. Match them up with the postings in this exercise. The remainder of the postings have to come from the general journal (items 9, 12, 14, 16, 19, and 20).

Sales journal:

Debit to Accounts Receivable
Credit to Sales Revenue
} same column

Debit to Cost of Goods Sold
Credit to Inventory
} same column

Cash receipts journal:

Debit to Cash
Debit to Sales Discounts
Credit to Accounts Receivable
Credit to Sales
Credit to Other Accounts
  (such as Interest Revenue, Notes Receiv-
  able, and Inventory)

Debit to Cost of Goods Sold
Credit to Inventory
} same column

Purchases journal:

Debit to Inventory
Credit to Accounts Payable
} same column

Cash payments journal: Credit to Cash
Credit to Inventory (for purchase discounts)
Debit to Accounts Payable
Debit to Other Accounts (such as Inventory,
   Prepaid Insurance, Owner's Drawings, and various
   expense accounts)

TIP: Keep in mind that posting to a given account describes one-half of the dual effect of one transaction. For example, a posting "Debits to Advertising Expense" describes an increase in advertising expense. The most common transaction increasing advertising expense is the payment for advertising services. All cash payments are recorded in the cash payments journal. Therefore, the most common source of the posting of debits to the Advertising Expense account is the cash payments journal. For a second example, a posting "Credits to Interest Revenue" describes an increase in interest revenue. Although the Interest Revenue account can be increased at the end of a period because of an adjusting entry in the general journal to record accrued interest (revenue that has been earned but not received), the most common reason for having an increase in Interest Revenue is the collection of interest during a period. All cash collections are recorded in the cash receipts journal.

TIP: Remember that all transactions involving a receipt of cash go in the cash receipts journal, and all transactions involving a payment of cash go in the cash payments journal.

EXERCISE 7-4

Purpose: (L.O. 2, 3) This exercise will discuss why a business employs special journals and subsidiary ledgers.

Up until this point, we have assumed that all transactions are recorded in the general journal and posted to the general ledger. In this chapter, we find that even small businesses can expedite the recording process by the use of special journals and subsidiary ledgers.

Instructions
(a)   Explain the advantages of using special journals.
(b)   Explain the advantages of using subsidiary ledgers.

SOLUTION TO EXERCISE 7-4

(a)   The main advantages of using special journals are that they:
  (1)   **Permit greater division of labor** by allowing several individuals to record entries in different journals at the same time. For example, one employee may be responsible for journalizing all cash receipts, and another for journalizing all credit sales.
  (2)   **Reduce the time necessary to record and post transactions** by eliminating the need to repeatedly write out account titles in the general journal and by dramatically cutting down on the number of postings required to the general ledger. Monthly postings to some accounts may be substituted for daily postings.

(b)   The advantages of using subsidiary ledgers are that they:
  (1)   **Show transactions affecting one customer or one creditor in a single account,** thus providing necessary up-to-date information on specific account balances.
  (2)   **Free the general ledger of excessive details.** As a result, a trial balance of the general ledger does not contain a vast number of individual account balances.
  (3)   **Help locate errors in individual accounts** by reducing the number of accounts combined in one ledger and by using controlling accounts.
  (4)   **Make possible a division of labor** in posting by having one employee post to the general ledger and a different employee(s) post to the subsidiary ledgers.

TIP: A company may employ any number of special journals. A special journal can be designed to record any type of transaction that occurs frequently. The four special journals typically found in a merchandising entity are discussed in this chapter: sales journal, cash receipts journal, single-column purchases journal, and the cash payments journal. If a company finds it frequently has a transaction that is not recorded in one of these journals, it can design another special journal. For example, frequent sales returns for credit against the customers' account receivable balances would indicate the usefulness of designing a sales returns journal. Amounts in the one column would get posted as debits to Sales Returns and credits to Accounts Receivable and amounts in a second column would get posted as debits to Merchandise Inventory and credits to Cost of Goods Sold. Each return would also be individually posted to the customer's account in the accounts receivable subsidiary ledger and to the appropriate perpetual inventory records.

EXERCISE 7-5

Purpose: (L.O. 3) This exercise will allow you to practice recording transactions in the sales journal and the cash receipts journal.

PW Company's chart of accounts includes the following **selected** accounts:

101	Cash	401	Sales Revenue
111	Accounts Receivable	415	Sales Discounts
115	Inventory	416	Sales Returns & Allowances
211	Accounts Payable	505	Cost of Goods Sold
311	Owner's Capital	521	Utilities Expense

PW Company has four customers. The following balances appeared in PW Company's accounts receivable subsidiary ledger at July 1, 2014:

Charlie Calhoun	$170
Charlie Daly	0
Bill Jackson	0
Jan Larson	105
Total	$275

A list of selected transactions for July 2014 for PW Company follows. The sales journal and the cash receipts journal follow that list.

Transactions

July 3   Sold merchandise to Charlie Daly for $100 on account; terms 2/10, n/30, Invoice No. 240. The cost of the merchandise sold was $60.

5   Sold merchandise to Charlie Calhoun for $150 cash. The cost of the merchandise sold was $90.

6   Sold merchandise to Jan Larson for $80 on account; terms n/30, Invoice No. 241. The cost of the merchandise sold was $48.

10   Sold merchandise to Charlie Daly for $50 cash. The cost of the merchandise sold was $30.

11   Sold merchandise to Bill Jackson for $200 on account; terms 2/10, n/30, Invoice No. 242. The cost of the merchandise sold was $120.

12   Collected $98 from Charlie Daly for the July 3 transaction.

13   Sold merchandise to Jan Larson for $630 on credit; terms n/30, Invoice No. 243. The cost of the merchandise sold was $378.

14   Sold merchandise to Bill Jackson for $350 on account; terms 2/10, n/30, Invoice No. 244. The cost of the merchandise sold was $210.

15   Sold merchandise to Charlie Daly for $600 on account; terms 2/10, n/30, Invoice No. 245. The cost of the merchandise sold was $360.

18   Collected $105 from Jan Larson on account for a credit sale made in June, no sales discount taken.

19   Collected $170 from Charlie Calhoun on account, no sales discount taken.

20   Collected $80 from Jan Larson on account.

20   Collected $196 from Bill Jackson for the sale on July 11.

23   Collected $343 from Bill Jackson for the sale on July 14.

July 25 Sold merchandise to Charlie Calhoun for $1,420 on credit; terms 2/10, n/30, Invoice No. 246. The cost of the merchandise sold was $852.

28 Deposited additional owner investment, $800 cash, into the company's bank account.

29 Received a $200 cash refund from a vendor for defective merchandise which was returned.

30 Received a $50 cash refund from the utility company because of an error in last month's billing. PW had paid the bill before the error was detected.

PW COMPANY
Sales Journal

S5

Date	Account Debited	Invoice No.	Ref.	Accounts Receivable Dr. Sales Revenue Cr.	Cost of Goods Sold Dr. Inventory Cr.

PW COMPANY
Cash Receipts Journal

CR7

Date	Account Credited	Ref.	Cash Dr.	Sales Discounts Dr.	Accounts Receivable Cr.	Sales Revenue Cr.	Other Accounts Cr.	Cost of Goods Sold Dr Inventory Cr.

Instructions

(a) Journalize the transactions above in the sales journal and the cash receipts journal.

(b) Foot and crossfoot the two journals at July 31, 2014.

SOLUTION TO EXERCISE 7-5

(a)

PW COMPANY
Sales Journal

S5

Date		Account Debited	Invoice No.	Ref.	Accounts Receivable Dr. Sales Revenue Cr.	Cost of Goods Sold Dr. Inventory Cr.
2014						
July	3	Charlie Daly	240		100	60
	6	Jan Larson	241		80	48
	11	Bill Jackson	242		200	120
	13	Jan Larson	243		630	378
	14	Bill Jackson	244		350	210
	15	Charlie Daly	245		600	360
	25	Charlie Calhoun	246		1,420	852
					3,380	2,028

PW COMPANY
Cash Receipts Journal

CR7

Date	Account Credited	Ref.	Cash Dr.	Sales Discounts Dr.	Accounts Receivable Cr.	Sales Cr.	Other Accounts Cr.	Cost of Goods Sold Dr. Inv. Cr.
2014								
July 5			150			150		90
10			50			50		30
12	Charlie Daly		98	2	100			
18	Jan Larson		105		105			
19	Charlie Calhoun		170		170			
20	Jan Larson		80		80			
20	Bill Jackson		196	4	200			
23	Bill Jackson		343	7	350			
28	John Purdy, Capital		800				800	
29	Inventory		200				200	
30	Utilities Expense		50				50	
			2,242	13	1,005	200	1,050	120

TIP:	Purchase returns for cash are recorded in the cash receipts journal. Returns to suppliers on credit are recorded in the general journal unless a special journal for credit returns is established.
TIP:	Nothing appears in the reference column in this solution because no instructions were given regarding postings. Recall, however, that amounts are usually posted to the subsidiary ledger daily. Postings will be illustrated in the next exercise.

(b) **To foot** a journal means to sum each column in the journal. Thus, adding the amounts in the columns in the sales journal constitutes footing the journal. There are six individual columns of figures to be added to foot the cash receipts journal. **To crossfoot** a journal means to prove the equality of the debits and credits recorded therein. Because the columns in the sales journal are posted both as debits and credits, there is nothing to crossfoot. In the cash receipts journal, the totals of the debit columns are added together ($2,242 + $13 + $120 = $2,375) and are compared to the sum of the totals of the credit columns ($1,005 + $200 + $1,050 + $120 = $2,375). Because the two grand totals equal, the journal is said to crossfoot.

EXERCISE 7-6

Purpose: (L.O. 2, 3) This exercise illustrates the relationship of the accounts receivable subsidiary ledger to the Accounts Receivable control account in the general ledger.

PW Company has four customer accounts in its accounts receivable ledger. The following balances appeared in that subsidiary ledger at July 1, 2014:

Charlie Calhoun	$170
Charlie Daly	0
Bill Jackson	0
Jan Larson	105
Total	$275

The cash receipts journal and the sales journal for July are reproduced below (from the **Solution to Exercise 7-5**).

The accounts receivable subsidiary ledger and **selected** accounts from the general ledger appear below. Some accounts have a balance at July 1, 2014 as shown.

Instructions

(a) Post the transactions to both the general ledger and the subsidiary ledger accounts. (Show the appropriate cross references in both the journals and the ledgers.)

(b) Prove the agreement of the subsidiary ledger and its control account.

(c) Explain how an accountant unfamiliar with a company could examine your work and determine the following:

  1. What accounts are to receive postings from the sales journal?
  2. Have the postings been completed to the general ledger accounts?
  3. Have the postings been completed to the subsidiary ledger accounts?
  4. What was the source of the $50 credit to the Utilities Expense account on July 30?

TIP:	If you wish to more closely simulate a real life situation, you will post the transactions in chronological order. If you post all of the transactions in the sales journal before you post the transactions in the cash receipts journal, you should end up with the correct ending balances, but your postings will appear in an order different than the order shown in the solution presented below.
TIP:	All credit sales are recorded in the sales journal, and all cash sales are recorded in the cash receipts journal so all sales transactions for July have been entered in the appropriate journals. However, a number of other transactions are not reflected because they appear in the purchases journal, the cash payments journal, and the general journal and are, therefore, not included in this exercise.

PW COMPANY
Sales Journal

S5

Date		Account Debited	Invoice No.	Ref.	Accounts Receivable Dr. Sales Revenue Cr.	Cost of Goods Sold Dr. Inventory Cr.
2014						
July	3	Charlie Daly	240		100	60
	6	Jan Larson	241		80	48
	11	Bill Jackson	242		200	120
	13	Jan Larson	243		630	378
	14	Bill Jackson	244		350	210
	15	Charlie Daly	245		600	360
	25	Charlie Calhoun	246		1,420	852
					3,380	2,028

PW COMPANY
Cash Receipts Journal

CR7

Date	Account Credited	Ref.	Cash Dr.	Sales Discounts Dr.	Accounts Receivable Cr.	Sales Revenue Cr.	Other Accounts Cr.	Cost of Goods Sold Dr. Inv. Cr.
2014								
July 5			150			150		90
10			50			50		30
12	Charlie Daly		98		100			
18	Jan Larson		105	2	105			
19	Charlie Calhoun		170		170			
20	Jan Larson		80		80			
20	Bill Jackson		196	4	200			
23	Bill Jackson		343	7	350			
28	John Purdy, Capital		800				800	
29	Inventory		200				200	
30	Utilities Expense		50				50	
			2,242	13	1,005	200	1,050	120

ACCOUNTS RECEIVABLE SUBSIDIARY LEDGER

Charlie Calhoun

Date		Explanation	Ref.	Debit	Credit	Balance
July	1	Balance	√			170

Charlie Daly

Date		Explanation	Ref.	Debit	Credit	Balance
July	1	Balance	√			0

Bill Jackson

Date		Explanation	Ref.	Debit	Credit	Balance
July	1	Balance	√			0

Jan Larson

Date		Explanation	Ref.	Debit	Credit	Balance
July	1	Balance	√			105

GENERAL LEDGER

Cash   No. 101

Date		Explanation	Ref.	Debit	Credit	Balance
July	1	Balance	√			1,400

Accounts Receivable   No. 111

Date		Explanation	Ref.	Debit	Credit	Balance
July	1	Balance	√			275

Inventory   No. 115

Date		Explanation	Ref.	Debit	Credit	Balance
July	1	Balance	√			6,100

Owner's Capital   No. 311

Date		Explanation	Ref.	Debit	Credit	Balance
July	1	Balance	√			5,000

Sales Revenue   No. 401

Date	Explanation	Ref.	Debit	Credit	Balance
July 1	Balance	√			24,000

Sales Discounts   No. 415

Date	Explanation	Ref.	Debit	Credit	Balance
July 1	Balance	√			100

Cost of Goods Sold   No. 505

Date	Explanation	Ref.	Debit	Credit	Balance
July 1	Balance	√			15,400

Utilities Expense   No. 521

Date	Explanation	Ref.	Debit	Credit	Balance
July 1	Balance	√			1,300

SOLUTION TO EXERCISE 7-6

PW COMPANY
Sales Journal   S5

Date		Account Debited	Invoice No.	Ref.	Accounts Receivable Dr. Sales Rev. Cr.	Cost of Goods Sold Dr. Inv. Cr.
2014						
July	3	Charlie Daly	240	√	100	60
	6	Jan Larson	241	√	80	48
	11	Bill Jackson	242	√	200	120
	13	Jan Larson	243	√	630	378
	14	Bill Jackson	244	√	350	210
	15	Charlie Daly	245	√	600	360
	25	Charlie Calhoun	246	√	1,420	852
					3,380	2,028
					(111) (401)	(505) (115)

> **TIP:** Practically all states, and cities require a sales tax be charged on items sold, which the company must remit to the state or city. In this case, it is desirable to add an additional credit column to the sales journal for sales tax payable. Sales tax payable is posted in total at the end of the month, similar to sales. Accounting for sales taxes is **not** illustrated in this exercise.

PW COMPANY
Cash Receipts Journal

CR7

Date	Account Credited	Ref.	Cash Dr.	Sales Discounts Dr.	Accounts Receivable Cr.	Sales Cr.	Other Accounts Cr.	Cost of Goods Sold Dr. Inv. Cr.
2014								
July 5			150			150		90
10			50			50		30
12	Charlie Daly	✓	98	2	100			
18	Jan Larson	✓	105		105			
19	Charlie Calhoun	✓	170		170			
20	Jan Larson	✓	80		80			
20	Bill Jackson	✓	196	4	200			
23	Bill Jackson	✓	343	7	350			
28	John Purdy, Capital	311	800				800	
29	Inventory	115	200				200	
30	Utilities Expense	521	50				50	
			2,242	13	1,005	200	1,050	120
			(101)	(415)	(111)	(401)	(X)	(505) (115)

ACCOUNTS RECEIVABLE SUBSIDIARY LEDGER

Charlie Calhoun

Date	Explanation	Ref.	Debit	Credit	Balance
July 1	Balance	√			170
19		CR7		170	0
25		S5	1,420		1,420

Charlie Daly

Date	Explanation	Ref.	Debit	Credit	Balance
July 1	Balance	√			0
3		S5	100		100
12		CR7		100	0
15		S5	600		600

Bill Jackson

Date	Explanation	Ref.	Debit	Credit	Balance
July 1	Balance	√			0
11		S5	200		200
14		S5	350		550
20		CR7		200	350
23		CR7		350	0

Jan Larson

Date	Explanation	Ref.	Debit	Credit	Balance
July 1	Balance	√			105
6		S5	80		185
13		S5	630		815
18		CR7		105	710
20		CR7		80	630

GENERAL LEDGER

Cash   No. 101

Date	Explanation	Ref.	Debit	Credit	Balance
July 1	Balance	√			1,400
31		CR7	2,242		3,642

Accounts Receivable   No. 111

Date		Explanation	Ref.	Debit	Credit	Balance
July	1	Balance	√			275
	31		S5	3,380		3,655
	31		CR7		1,005	2,650

Inventory   No. 115

Date		Explanation	Ref.	Debit	Credit	Balance
July	1	Balance	√			6,100
	31		S5		2,028	4,072
	31		CR7		120	3,952

Owner's Capital   No. 311

Date		Explanation	Ref.	Debit	Credit	Balance
July	1	Balance	√			5,000
	28		CR7		800	5,800

Sales Revenue   No. 401

Date		Explanation	Ref.	Debit	Credit	Balance
July	1	Balance	√			24,000
	31		S5		3,380	27,380
	31		CR7		200	27,580

Sales Discounts   No. 415

Date		Explanation	Ref.	Debit	Credit	Balance
July	1	Balance	√			100
	31		CR7	13		113

Cost of Goods Sold   No. 515

Date		Explanation	Ref.	Debit	Credit	Balance
July	1	Balance	√			15,400
	31		S5	2,028		17,428
	31		CR7	120		17,548

Utilities Expense   No. 521

Date		Explanation	Ref.	Debit	Credit	Balance
July	1	Balance	√			1,300
	30		CR7		50	1,250

TIP: The accounts listed above all have a single balance column. Therefore, the balance is assumed to be a normal balance for that type of account (debit versus credit) unless the balance is in brackets ( ) or is circled or is printed in red ink, in which case the balance is an abnormal one.

TIP: Total debits do not equal total credits in the general ledger accounts shown because only **selected** accounts are being illustrated in this exercise.

TIP: Examine the "Account Credited" column of the cash receipts journal. Notice that a subsidiary ledger account title is entered in that column whenever the entry involves an account receivable. Whereas, a general ledger account title is entered in that column whenever the entry involves an account that is not the subject of a special column (and an amount is entered in the "Other Accounts" column). No account title is entered in the "Account Credited" column if neither of the foregoing apply.

TIP: In this exercise, the balance of the Inventory account continues to decrease throughout the entire month because there was no information about inventory acquisitions during the month. Typically, purchases are made regularly in order to keep a sufficient inventory level to accommodate customers.

(b)   **Accounts Receivable Subsidiary Ledger**

Charlie Calhoun	$1,420
Charlie Daly	600
Bill Jackson	0
Jan Larson	630
	$2,650

Balance at July 31 per the Accounts Receivable account in the
general ledger $2,650

(c)   1.   The accounts to receive postings from the sales journal can be determined by reading the two money column headings in that journal: (1) Accounts Receivable Dr. and Sales Revenue Cr., and (2) Cost of Goods Sold Dr. and Inventory Cr.

2.   An independent reviewer can readily see that the postings have been completed to the general ledger accounts because the relevant general ledger account numbers appear in parentheses below the totals of the money columns in the special journals. For example, the account numbers 111 (Accounts Receivable) and 401 (Sales Revenue) appear below the total of the first money column in the sales journal because that total was posted to both the Accounts Receivable account and the Sales Revenue account in the general ledger. The account numbers 505 (Cost of Goods Sold) and 115 (Inventory) appear below the second money column in the sales journal. The account number 101 (Cash) appears below the "Cash" column of the cash receipts journal, and so forth.

The transactions recorded in the cash receipts journal which affect accounts **other** than the accounts for which there are special money columns have been posted to those other accounts as can be determined by the relevant account numbers appearing in the Ref. column (311 for Owner's Capital, 115 for Inventory, and 521 for Utilities Expense).

3.   The completion of a posting to a subsidiary account is indicated by a "√" in the Ref. column of a special journal. All postings have been completed from the sales journal because there is a √ in the Ref. column on every used line. All postings have been completed from the cash receipts journal because a "√" appears in the Ref. column on every line that contains a **subsidiary ledger account title** in the Account Credited column.

4.   The source of the $50 credit to the Utilities Expense account on July 30 can be determined by looking in the Ref. column in the general ledger account for Utilities Expense. The posting for $50 on July 30 came from CR7 which stands for page 7 of the cash receipts journal.

TIP:	A **control** account in the general ledger is often referred to as the **controlling** account for the related subsidiary ledger. Thus, the Accounts Receivable account is a controlling account for the accounts receivable subsidiary ledger.
TIP:	Regardless of the journal in which it is recorded, a transaction involving a subsidiary ledger account must be posted to that subsidiary ledger account as well as to the control account in the general ledger.
TIP:	The process of reconciling or proving a control account and its related subsidiary ledger consists of three steps: (a) Compute the balance of each account in the subsidiary ledger. (b) Add up (total) the balances of the subsidiary accounts. (c) Compare this total with the control account balance. Any differences between the control account and the subsidiary ledger must be found and corrected.
TIP:	Postings from the special journals are made **daily** to the subsidiary ledgers; postings from the special journals are made **monthly** to the general ledger. For example, postings from the sales journal are made daily to the individual accounts receivable in the accounts receivable subsidiary ledger and monthly to the control account in the general ledger. For a second example, postings from the cash payments journal are made daily to the individual accounts payable in the accounts payable subsidiary ledger and monthly to the Accounts Payable control account in the general ledger. For a third example, postings from the sales journal are made daily to the individual perpetual inventory records and monthly to the Inventory control account in the general ledger.

EXERCISE 7-7

Purpose: (L.O. 3) This exercise will allow you to practice recording transactions in the purchases journal and the cash payments journal.

E & Y Company's chart of accounts includes the following selected accounts:

101	Cash		401	Sales Revenue
111	Accounts Receivable		415	Sales Discounts
115	Inventory		416	Sales Returns
131	Prepaid Insurance		505	Cost of Goods Sold
140	Supplies		521	Utilities Expense
150	Equipment		522	Advertising Expense
211	Accounts Payable		523	Rent Expense
311	Owner's Capital			

A list of selected transactions for June 2014 for E & Y Company appears below. The purchases journal and the cash payments journal follow that list.

Transactions

June 1 Purchased supplies, check no. 103, $800.
   3 Purchased merchandise on account from Ed Hastings, Inc., invoice no. 1272, terms 2/10, n/30, $1,800.
   4 Purchased equipment on credit from Val Edmonds, Inc., $3,000.
   5 Purchased supplies on account from PV Roddy, $300.
   6 Purchased merchandise on account from Earl Elbert, invoice no. 1521, terms 2/10, n/30, $1,500.
   7 Purchased supplies, check no. 104, $1,200.
  10 Purchased merchandise on account from Ed Hastings, Inc., invoice no. 1490, terms 2/10, n/30, $2,000.
  12 Paid Ed Hastings, Inc. for invoice no. 1272, $1,800 less 2% discount, check no. 105, $1,764.
  13 Paid Val Edmonds, Inc., $3,000 on account, check no. 106.
  14 Paid an advertising agency for ads to appear in June, check no. 107, $400.
  15 Purchased merchandise on account from Earl Elbert, invoice no. 1706, terms 2/10, n/30, $1,300.
  16 Paid premium due on a one-year insurance policy, check no. 108, $600.
  17 Paid PV Roddy on account, $300, check no. 109.
  18 Issued check no. 110 for $1,500 to Earl Elbert for payment on account.
  19 Paid Ed Hastings, Inc., in full for invoice no. 1490, $1,960, check no. 111.
  20 Purchased merchandise on account, from Earl Elbert, invoice no. 1811, terms 2/10, n/30, $1,400.
  21 Paid $75 for utilities, check no. 112.
  22 Paid $400 for rent for June, check no. 113.
  23 Purchased supplies on account from PV Roddy, $420.
  24 Paid Earl Elbert for invoice no. 1706, $1,300 less 2% discount, check no. 114, $1,274.
  26 Purchased supplies for cash, check no. 115, $300.
  27 Purchased merchandise for cash, $200, check no. 116.

Purchases Journal

P1

Date	Account Credited	Terms	Ref.	Inventory Dr. Accounts Payable Cr.

Cash Payments Journal

CP1

Date	Ck. No.	Account Debited	Ref.	Other Accounts Dr.	Accounts Payable Dr.	Inventory Cr.	Cash Cr.

Instructions

(a) Journalize the transactions above in the single-column purchases journal and the cash payments journal provided.

(b) Identify any transactions which must be recorded in a journal other than these two special journals.

(c) Foot and crossfoot the two special journals at June 30, 2014.

SOLUTION TO EXERCISE 7-7

Purchases Journal

P1

Date		Account Credited	Terms	Ref.	Inventory Dr. Accounts Payable Cr.
2014					
June	3	Ed Hastings, Inc.	2/10, n/30		1,800
	6	Earl Elbert	2/10, n/30		1,500
	10	Ed Hastings, Inc.	2/10, n/30		2,000
	15	Earl Elbert	2/10, n/30		1,300
	20	Earl Elbert	2/10, n/30		1,400
					8,000

Cash Payments Journal

CP1

Date		Ck. No.	Account Debited	Ref.	Other Accounts Dr.	Accounts Payable Dr.	Inventory Cr.	Cash Cr.
2014								
June	1	103	Supplies		800			800
	7	104	Supplies		1,200			1,200
	12	105	Ed Hastings, Inc.			1,800	36	1,764
	13	106	Val Edmonds, Inc.			3,000		3,000
	14	107	Advertising Exp.		400			400
	16	108	Prepaid Ins.		600			600
	17	109	PV Roddy			300		300
	18	110	Earl Elbert			1,500		1,500
	19	111	Ed Hastings, Inc.			2,000	40	1,960
	21	112	Utilities Exp.		75			75
	22	113	Rent Exp.		400			400
	24	114	Earl Elbert			1,300	26	1,274
	26	115	Supplies		300			300
	27	116	Inventory		200			200
					3,975	9,900	102	13,773

TIP: The cash payments journal is often called the **cash disbursements journal.**

(b)   Transactions which must be recorded in other journals are:

Transactions			**Journal**
June	4	Purchased equipment on credit, $3,000	General Journal
	5	Purchased supplies on account, $300	General Journal
	23	Purchased supplies on account, $420	General Journal

TIP:	Some companies expand the purchases journal to include all types of purchases on account. Instead of one column for purchases of merchandise on credit (requiring postings to both Inventory and Accounts Payable), a multiple-column format is used. The multiple-column format usually includes a credit column for accounts payable and debit columns for purchases of merchandise, purchases of office supplies, purchases of store supplies, and other accounts. A special column can be added for purchases of equipment if the activity warrants it.
TIP:	The general journal is used to record transactions that do not occur with enough frequency to warrant the creation of a special journal.

(c)   Footing is accomplished by adding the amounts of each column and inserting the totals at the bottom of the respective columns. There is nothing to crossfoot in a single-column journal because there is only one column. The cash payments journal is crossfooted by summing the totals of the debit columns ($3,975 +$9,900 = $13,875) and comparing that sum with the sum of the totals of the credit columns ($102 + $13,773 = $13,875). The two sums are equal so the journal crossfoots. This means the equality of the debits and credits entered in that journal has been proven.

EXERCISE 7-8

Purpose: (L.O. 1 thru 3) This exercise will quiz you about terminology used in this chapter.

A list of accounting terms with which you should be familiar appear below.

Accounting information system
Accounts payable (creditors') subsidiary ledger
Accounts receivable (customers') subsidiary ledger
Cash payments (cash disbursements) journal
Cash receipts journal
Control account

Manual accounting system
Purchases journal
Sales journal
Special journal
Subsidiary ledger

Instructions
For each item below, enter in the blank the term that is described.

1. _____A journal that records similar types of transactions, such as all credit sales.

2. _____A special journal used to record all sales of merchandise on account (on credit).

3. _____A special journal that records all cash received.

4. _____A special journal that records all purchases of merchandise on account (on credit).

5. _____A special journal that records all cash paid.

6. _____A group of accounts with a common characteristic.

7. _____A subsidiary ledger that contains accounts with individual creditors.

8. _____A subsidiary ledger that contains individual customer accounts.

9. _____An account in the general ledger that controls a subsidiary ledger.

10. _____A system that collects and processes data, and communicates financial information to interested parties.

11. _____A system in which someone performs each of the steps in the accounting cycle by hand.

SOLUTION TO EXERCISE 7-8

1. Special journal
2. Sales journal
3. Cash receipts journal
4. Purchases journal
5. Cash payments (cash disbursements) journal
6. Subsidiary ledger
7. Accounts payable (creditors') subsidiary ledger
8. Accounts receivable (customers') subsidiary ledger
9. Control account
10. Accounting information system
11. Manual accounting system

ANALYSIS OF MULTIPLE-CHOICE TYPE QUESTIONS

1. (L.O. 1) Which of the following is **not** a principle of accounting information system development?
   a. Automation.
   b. Cost awareness.
   c. Useful output.
   d. Flexibility.

   Approach and Explanation: List the principles that should be followed in designing and developing an accounting system. Identify the answer selection **not** in your list. Not all entities need automated (or computerized) systems. Some entities find a manual system more appropriate. For any entity, however, the following principles should be followed in designing and developing an efficient and effective accounting information system:
   1. **Cost awareness**—the benefits obtained from the information collected and disseminated must outweigh the cost of providing it.
   2. **Useful output**—to be useful, information must be understandable, relevant, reliable, timely, and accurate.
   3. **Flexibility**—the system should be able to accommodate a variety of users and changing information needs.
   (Solution = a.)

2. (L.O. 2) A general ledger account which summarizes the collection of related accounts appearing in a subsidiary ledger is called a:
   a. contra account.
   b. control account.
   c. summary account.
   d. subsidiary ledger account.

   Explanation: The subsidiary ledger reduces the number of accounts that otherwise would appear in the general ledger. The details about an item (such as accounts receivable or accounts payable or equipment, for example) are removed from the general ledger and are replaced by a single account (control account) which summarizes the detail. The details are then grouped and called a subsidiary ledger. A control account is often called the controlling account. (Solution = b.)

3. (L.O. 3) Each of the following likely appears as a column heading in the cash receipts journal **except:**

a. Accounts Receivable Cr.
b. Sales Revenue Dr.
c. Sales Discounts Dr.
d. Other Accounts Cr.

Approach and Explanation: Think about the purpose of the cash receipts journal—to record all transactions involving a receipt of cash. A receipt of cash is recorded by a debit to Cash; therefore, the rest of the entry involves a credit to a noncash account. The credit is (1) to Sales Revenue for a cash sale of merchandise, or (2) to Accounts Receivable for a collection on a customer's account, or (3) to some other account (such as Equipment for a sale of equipment or Interest Revenue for interest earned on money loaned to others).

If a merchandiser offers a cash discount on sales for timely payment of the customer's account, the collection of the account receivable within the discount period results in recording a debit to Sales Discounts (a contra sales account). Thus, a special column in the cash receipts journal for Sales Discounts Dr. is needed to accommodate the recording of this frequent transaction. Debits are made to the Sales Revenue account only to (1) correct erroneous credit entries to the same account, and (2) close the balance of the Sales Revenue account to Income Summary at the end of the period. Therefore, "Sales Dr." does not appear as a column heading in any special journal. (Solution = b.)

4. (L.O. 3) A checkmark entered in the "Ref." column of a single-column purchases journal indicates that the entry:
a. is not to be posted to any ledger.
b. has been posted to the general ledger.
c. has been posted to the appropriate subsidiary ledger.
d. has been posted to the general ledger and to the appropriate subsidiary ledger.

Explanation: Answer selection "a" is incorrect because all transactions recorded in any journal must be posted to the general ledger and all transactions recorded in a single-column purchases journal must also be posted to a subsidiary ledger—the accounts payable ledger. Answer selection "b" is incorrect because the transactions recorded in the single-column purchases journal are posted to the general ledger in total at the end of the month, and the completion of that posting is indicated by placing the general ledger account numbers for Inventory and Accounts Payable beneath the total of the single-money column. Answer selection "d" is incorrect because a checkmark appears by an individual transaction, and purchases are not posted individually to the
general ledger. A checkmark is placed in the Ref. column when the posting has been made to the suppliers' (accounts payable) subsidiary ledger. Postings are to be made to the subsidiary ledger on a daily basis. (Solution = c.)

5.   (L.O. 3) When special journals are used, the return of merchandise to a supplier for credit is usually recorded in the:
     a.   Sales journal.
     b.   Purchases journal.
     c.   Cash receipts journal.
     d.   Cash payments journal.
     e.   General journal.

     Approach and Explanation: List the four special journals discussed in this chapter and briefly describe their function. Also describe the general journal's function.
     1.   **Sales journal**—all sales of merchandise on account.
     2.   **Cash receipts journal**—all receipts of cash (including cash sales).
     3.   **Purchases journal**—all purchases of merchandise on account.
     4.   **Cash payments journal**—all payments of cash (including cash purchases).
     5.   **General journal**—all transactions that do not appropriately fit in a special journal (including adjustments and closing entries).
     The transaction described does not fit the description of any of the four special journals. Thus, it goes into the general journal. (Solution = e.)

6.   (L.O. 3) When special journals are used, the payment to a supplier for merchandise which had previously been purchased on account is usually recorded in the:
     a.   Sales journal.
     b.   Purchases journal.
     c.   Cash receipts journal.
     d.   Cash disbursements journal.
     e.   General journal.

     Approach and Explanation: Mentally review the types of journals and their functions. All cash payments are recorded in the cash payments journal which is often called the cash disbursements journal. (Solution = d.)

7.   (L.O. 3) When special journals are used, the most likely source of a debit posting to the Accounts Receivable account in the general ledger is the:
     a.   Sales journal.
     b.   Purchases journal.
     c.   Cash receipts journal.
     d.   Cash payments journal.
     e.   General journal.

     Approach and Explanation: Identify the most common reason for debits to Accounts Receivable—sales on account (on credit). Mentally review the special journals and the transactions recorded therein. All sales on account are recorded in the sales journal. (Solution = a.)

8. (L.O. 3) When special journals are used, the most likely source of a credit posting to an expense account in the general ledger is the:
a. Sales journal.
b. Purchases journal.
c. Cash receipts journal.
d. Cash payments journal.
e. General journal.

Explanation: The most common reason for a credit to an expense account is a closing entry at the end of the period or possibly from an adjusting entry or a correction. All of these items are recorded in the general journal. (A cash refund for an item previously recorded as an expense would cause a credit posting and would be recorded in the cash receipts journal; however, this would not be as common as adjusting or closing entries.) (Solution = e.)

CHAPTER **8**

. . . .

*F*RAUD, INTERNAL CONTROL AND CASH

OVERVIEW

In previous chapters, you learned the basic formats for general purpose financial statements. In this chapter, you begin your in-depth study of accounting for items reported on the balance sheet: (1) what is to be included in an item classification, (2) related internal control procedures, (3) rules for determining the dollar amount to be reported, (4) disclosure requirements, and (5) special accounting procedures which may be required. In this chapter, you will learn what is to be included with the cash caption on the balance sheet and some key internal controls which should be employed for business activities involving cash.

At the end of an accounting period, after all transactions have been recorded and posted, the balance of the Cash account usually does not reflect the amount of cash available in the checking account per the bank statement. A bank reconciliation should be prepared as one control feature over cash disbursements to determine whether errors have been made or if any unrecorded transactions exist. The adjusted cash balance as determined by the bank reconciliation will be the amount used to report for cash on the balance sheet. (The Cash account in the general ledger often includes cash on hand and cash in the bank, although separate ledger accounts such as Cash in Bank and Cash on Hand may be used. The balance of this account and any other unrestricted cash accounts, such as the Petty Cash account, are added together to report cash on the balance sheet.) Bank reconciliations and petty cash funds are discussed in this chapter.

SUMMARY OF LEARNING OBJECTIVES

1. **Define fraud and internal control.** A fraud involving an employee is a dishonest act by an employee that results in personal benefit to the employee at a cost to the employer. The fraud triangle refers to the three factors that contribute to fraudulent activity by employees: opportunity, financial pressure, and rationalization. Internal control consists of all the related methods and measures adopted within an organization to safeguard its assets, enhance the accuracy and reliability of its

accounting records, increase efficiency of operations, and ensure compliance with laws and regulations.

2. **Identify the principles of internal control.** The principles of internal control are: establishment of responsibility; segregation of duties; documentation procedures; physical controls; independent internal verification; and human resource controls such as bonding and requiring employees to take vacations.

3. **Explain the applications of internal control principles to cash receipts.** Internal controls over cash receipts include: (a) designating personnel to handle cash; (b) assigning different individuals to receive cash, record cash, and maintain custody of cash; (c) using remittance advices for mail receipts, cash register tapes for over-the-counter receipts, and deposit slips for bank deposits; (d) using company safes and bank vaults to store cash with access limited to authorized personnel, and using cash registers in executing over-the-counter receipts; (e) making independent daily counts of register receipts and daily comparing total receipts with total deposits; and (f) bonding personnel that handle cash and requiring them to take vacations.

4. **Explain the applications of internal control principles to cash disbursements.** Internal controls over cash disbursements include: (a) having specific individuals, such as the treasurer, authorized to sign checks and approve invoices; (b) assigning different individuals to approve items for payment, pay the items, and record the payment; (c) using prenumbered checks and accounting for all checks, with each check supported by an approved invoice; (d) storing blank checks in a safe or vault with access restricted to authorized personnel, and using a check-writing machine to imprint amounts on checks; (e) comparing each check with the approved invoice before issuing the check, and making monthly reconciliations of bank and book balances; and (f) bonding personnel who handle cash, requiring employees to take vacations, and conducting background checks.

5. **Describe the operation of a petty cash fund.** Companies operate a petty cash fund to pay relatively small amounts of cash. They must establish the fund, make payments from the fund, and replenish the fund when the cash in the fund reaches a minimum level.

6. **Indicate the control features of a bank account.** A bank account contributes to good internal control by providing physical controls for the storage of cash. It minimizes the amount of currency that a company must keep on hand and creates a double record of a depositor's bank transactions.

7. **Prepare a bank reconciliation.** It is customary to reconcile the balance per books and balance per bank to their adjusted balances. The steps in the reconciling process are to determine deposits in transit, outstanding checks, errors by the depositor or the bank, and unrecorded bank memoranda.

8.   **Explain the reporting of cash.**   Companies list cash first in the current assets section of the balance sheet. In some cases, they report cash together with cash equivalents. Cash restricted for a special purpose is reported separately as a current asset or as a noncurrent asset, depending on when the cash is expected to be used.

TIPS ON CHAPTER TOPICS

TIP:	A **point-of-sale** terminal is a sophisticated cash register that does **not** rely on a tape to accumulate data regarding cash receipts. Rather, it is networked with the company's computing and accounting records, which results in direct documentation of amounts of cash received.
TIP:	Electronic funds transfers (EFT) are disbursement systems that use wire, telephone, or computers to transfer cash amounts from one location to another. For example, many employees receive no formal payroll checks; rather the employer sends electronic payment to the appropriate banks. Also, individuals (and companies) now make many regular monthly payments (such as those for house mortgage, car loan, and utilities) by EFT. Such EFT transactions provide better internal control since no cash or checks are handled by company employees.
TIP:	A **bank memorandum** is often called a **bank memo.** A depositor's checking account is a liability on the bank's books, so a bank debit memo decreases the depositor's cash balance and a bank credit memo increases the depositor's cash balance.
TIP:	If you have a checking account, look at the back of your bank statement. A bank often provides a form there to assist you in reconciling your bank account. Very often that form reconciles the cash balance per bank to the cash balance per books rather than reconciling both the bank cash balance and the book cash balance to the adjusted (correct) cash balance. Use of that alternative format is not illustrated in this book.
TIP:	The "Adjusted cash balance" caption on a bank reconciliation is often replaced with "Correct cash balance" or "True cash balance."
TIP:	Total receipts per bank for a month include all deposits made by the depositor during the month plus any bank credit memos (such as for interest credited by the bank or a customer's note receivable collected by the bank).
TIP:	Total disbursements per bank for a month include all depositor's checks that cleared the banking system during the month plus any bank debit memos originating during the month (such as for bank service charges or a customer's NSF check).
TIP:	Beginning cash balance per bank plus total receipts for the month per bank minus total disbursements for the month per bank equals ending cash balance per bank.
TIP:	Beginning cash balance per books plus total receipts for the month per books minus total disbursements for the month per books equals ending cash balance per books.

EXERCISE 8-1

Purpose: (L.O. 4) This exercise will test your knowledge of internal control procedures related to cash disbursements. The following procedures pertain to cash disbursements for Jon Ron's Surf Shop in Daytona Beach.

1. The company checks come in books of twenty-five each and are unnumbered.
2. The company checks are stored in an unlocked drawer in the manager's office.
3. The assistant manager approves all payments, signs all checks, and distributes all checks.
4. A bank reconciliation is prepared once every six months.
5. Employees are allowed two weeks of vacation after they have been with the company for one full year. An employee can then take the vacation time earned or choose to work continuously and receive regular pay as well as vacation pay for the two "vacation weeks."
6. Most employees are authorized to write company checks.

Instructions

For each procedure, explain the weakness in internal control and identify the internal control principle that is violated.

SOLUTION TO EXERCISE 8-1

Weakness	**Principle**
1. Checks are not prenumbered. (Checks should be prenumbered and subsequently accounted for.)	Documentation procedures.
2. Checks are not stored in a secure area. (Checks should be stored in a safe or locked file drawer.)	Physical controls.
3. The approval and payment of bills is done by the same individual. (One person, such as the store manager, should approve bills for payment and another person, possibly the assistant manager, should sign and issue checks.)	Segregation of duties.
4. The bank reconciliation is not prepared on a timely basis. (It should be prepared monthly soon after the bank statement is received.)	Independent internal verification (also called independent check).
5. Employees who handle cash are allowed to work continuously. A company should rotate employees' duties and require employees to take vacations. These measures deter employees from attempting thefts since they will not be able to permanently conceal their improper actions.	Human resource controls.
6. Most employees are authorized to write company checks.	Establishment of responsibility.

EXERCISE 8-2

Purpose: (L.O. 2, 3, 4) This exercise will illustrate the need for certain internal control procedures.

Four independent situations appear below:

Situation 1: The Broadway Cinema Company operates six movie screens in a local mall. Although the cashier gives a ticket to each customer upon payment of the movie price, no one collects the ticket as the customer enters the theater.

Situation 2: Home Gadgets sells a multitude of housewares. Although there is a register at the check out counter, it has been situated so that the customer cannot see the display and thus has no evidence of what the clerk rings up. (No scanning equipment is used.)

Receipts are allowed to remain on the cash register in a continuous strip unless a customer requests that their receipt be torn from the register.

Situation 3: Better Bath Wear Company hires people based solely on an interview with the store manager.

Situation 4: The individual who is responsible for writing the checks to pay bills for Seafin Seafoods is also the employee who prepares the monthly bank reconciliation.

Instructions
For each situation, identify the internal control principle being violated and briefly describe the risk inherent in the existing circumstances.

SOLUTION TO EXERCISE 8-2

Situation 1: The independent internal verification principle is being violated. The cashier may collect the ticket price from a customer and pocket the cash then not give the customer a ticket. Because sales are tracked by tickets, the theft will most likely occur undetected. On the other hand, the cashier may collect the price of an adult ticket, ring up the price of a child's ticket and pocket the difference in price. Because no one independently verifies the sale, the theft can easily go unnoticed.

Situation 2: The documentation procedures principle is being violated. If the customer cannot see the display and receives no written evidence of the amount rung into the register, the clerk can easily tell the customer the correct total but ring up less than that amount. The difference can be pocketed by the employee and go undetected.

Situation 3: The human resource controls principle is being violated. The company should conduct a thorough background check on the prospective employee before hiring them.

Situation 4: The segregation of duties principle is being violated. The employee can make improper disbursements and have them go undetected because the employee has access to the records and can "doctor" them.

EXERCISE 8-3

Purpose: (L.O. 2, 3, 4) This exercise will help you understand the reasons for implementing a system of internal control. This exercise focuses on the one component of an internal control system—the **control activities.**

Family Grub, a large grocery store in Louisiana has a policy manual which contains the following guidelines:

_____ 1. Customers who pay by check must be identified via a store I.D. card or other means.

_____ 2. Store personnel are prohibited from accepting checks for anything except merchandise sales plus a nominal cash amount.

_____ 3. For each sale, a receipt is to be produced by the cash register and is to be given to the customer.

_____ 4. A reading of each cash register is to be taken periodically by an employee who is independent of the handling of cash receipts.

_____ 5. Cash counts are to be made on a surprise basis by an individual who is independent of the handling of cash receipts.

_____ 6. The reading of each cash register is to be compared regularly to the cash received.

_____ 7. A summary listing of cash register readings is to be prepared by an employee who is independent of personnel physically handling cash receipts.

_____ 8. Receipts are to be forwarded to an independent employee who makes the bank deposits.

_____ 9. Cash receipts are to be deposited in the company's bank account daily.

_____ 10. The summary listing of cash register receipts is to be reconciled to the duplicate deposit slips authenticated by the bank.

_____ 11. Entries to the cash receipts journal are to be prepared from duplicate deposit slips or the summary listing of cash register readings.

_____ 12. The entries to the cash receipts journal are compared to the deposits per bank statement.

_____ 13. Areas involving the physical handling of cash are to be reasonably safeguarded.

_____ 14. Employees who handle cash receipts are to be bonded.

_____ 15. Customer checks charged back by the bank (NSF checks) are to be directed to an employee who does not physically handle cash receipts or have access to the books.

_____ 16. Each cashier works out of a separate cash drawer and begins each shift with a two-hundred dollar change fund.

_____ 17. When a prospective employee completes a job application and lists the phone number of a previous employer, the manager is to search for and independently obtain the phone number of that entity.

_____ 18. Duties for employees are to be rotated periodically.

_____ 19. Each payment from the petty cash fund must be accompanied by a prenumbered petty cash receipt (often called petty cash voucher).

_____ 20. Each petty cash voucher must be signed by the fund custodian (and by the person receiving the payment).

These policies were designed to comply with the following principles of internal control:
a. Establishment of responsibility.   d. Physical controls.
b. Segregation of duties.   e. Independent internal verification.
c. Documentation procedures.   f. Human resource controls.

Instructions
For each policy listed above, indicate to which principle of internal control the procedure is most closely related.

SOLUTION TO EXERCISE 8-3

1.	c	6.	e	11.	c	16.	a
2.	d	7.	b	12.	e	17.	f
3.	c	8.	b	13.	d	18.	f
4.	e	9.	d	14.	f	19.	c
5.	e	10.	e	15.	b	20.	a

TIP: **Internal control** consists of all the related methods and measures adopted within an organization to safeguard its assets, enhance the reliability of its accounting records, increase efficiency of operations, and ensure compliance with laws and regulations. Internal control systems have five primary components as listed below:

- **A control environment.** It is the responsibility of top management to make it clear that the organization values integrity and that unethical activity will not be tolerated. This component is often referred to as the "tone at the top"

- **Risk assessment.** Companies must identify and analyze the various factors that create risk for the business and must determine how to manage these risks.

- **Control activities.** To reduce the occurrence of fraud, management must design policies and procedures to address the specific risks faced by the company.

- **Information and communication.** The internal control system must capture and communicate all pertinent information both down and up the organization, as well as communicate information to appropriate external parties.

- **Monitoring.** Internal control systems must be monitored periodically for their adequacy. Significant deficiencies need to be reported to top management and/or the board of directors.

ILLUSTRATION 8-1
BANK RECONCILIATION FORMAT (L.O. 7)

Balance per bank
- Add positive items per books not on bank's records.
- Deduct negative items per books not on bank's records.
- Add or deduct, whichever is applicable, bank error in recording receipts or disbursements.

Adjusted cash balance per bank.

Balance per books
- Add positive items per bank not on books.
- Deduct negative items per bank not on books.
- Add or deduct, whichever is applicable, depositor error in recording receipts or disbursements.

Adjusted cash balance per books.

Examples of reconciling items:

Positive item per books not on bank's records:
    Deposit in transit
Negative item per books not on bank's records:
    Outstanding check
Positive item per bank not on books:
    Note collected by bank
    Interest paid by bank to depositor on account balance
Negative item per bank not on books:
    Bank service charge
    Customer's NSF check returned by bank
Error by bank:
    In recording receipt
    In recording disbursement
Error by depositor:
    In recording receipt
    In recording disbursement

TIP:	The objective of a bank reconciliation is to explain all reasons why the bank balance differs from the book balance and to identify the errors and omissions in the bank's records and in the depositor's records.
TIP:	In the context of a bank reconciliation, "per bank" refers to the records of the bank pertaining to the depositor's account and "per books" refers to the depositor's records of the same bank account.

> **TIP:** Some items in a bank reconciliation will require adjustments either on the depositor's books or in the bank's records while others will not. All of the reconciling items appearing in the lower half of the reconciliation (balance per books to adjusted cash balance) require adjustment on the depositor's books. All of the reconciling items appearing in the upper half of the reconciliation **except** for deposits in transit and outstanding checks require adjustment on the bank's books.
>
> **TIP:** Unless otherwise indicated, an NSF (nonsufficient funds) check is assumed to be a customer's NSF check; that is, an NSF check from a customer of the depositor rather than a depositor's NSF check.

EXERCISE 8-4

Purpose: (L.O. 5) This exercise reviews the journal entries involved with establishing and maintaining a petty cash fund.

The Kirmani Corporation makes most expenditures by check. The following transactions relate to an imprest fund established by the Kirmani Corporation to handle small expenditures on an expedient basis.

Transactions

May 4 Wrote a $100 check to establish the petty cash fund.
    6 Paid taxi $10 to deliver papers to a branch office.
    6 Purchased stamps, $13.
    8 Paid $15 for advertising posters.
  12 Paid $6 for a charitable contribution.
  12 Paid $8 for coffee supplies.
  13 Paid $17 supplies.
  14 Paid bus charges of $18 to ship goods to a customer.
  15 Counted the remaining coins and currency in the fund, $12. Wrote a check to replenish the fund.

Instructions
(a) Record the transactions in general journal form.
(b) Answer the questions that follow.

Questions

1. How much coin and currency should have been in the petty cash box at the end of the day on May 12? $_____

2. How much coin and currency should have been in the petty cash box on May 15 before replenishment? $_____

3. What was the balance in the Petty Cash ledger account on May 12?
   $_____

4. What was the balance in the Petty Cash ledger account at the end of the day, May 15?
   $_____

TIP:	In order to answer the last two questions, it would be helpful to post the journal entries to a T-account for Petty Cash.

SOLUTION TO EXERCISE 8-4

(a) May 4 Petty Cash... 100
                Cash.. 100
                (To establish a petty cash fund)

    May 15 Miscellaneous Expense ($10 + $8) 18
            Postage Expense 13
            Advertising Expense.. 15
            Charitable Contribution Expense 6
            Supplies... 17
            Freight-out 18
            Cash Over and Short.. 1
                Cash.. 88
                (To replenish the petty cash fund)

(b) 1. There should have been $48 in coin and currency in the fund at the end of the day on May 12. ($100 - $10 - $13 - $15 - $6 - $8 = $48)
    2. There should have been $13 in coin and currency in the fund on May 15 before replenishment. ($100 - $10 - $13 - $15 - $6 - $8 - $17 - $18 = $13)

TIP:	Because only $12 was found in the fund on May 15, there was a shortage of $1 which must be recorded by a debit to the Cash Over and Short account.

    3. $100
    4. $100

TIP:	The balance of the Petty Cash account changes only when the fund is established or the size of the fund is increased or decreased. The Petty Cash account balance is **not** affected by expenditures from the fund nor by replenishments. (No journal entry is made at the time an expenditure is made. Expenditures from the fund are accounted for at the date of replenishment.)
TIP:	Petty Cash is not normally reported separately on the balance sheet. The balance of the Petty Cash account is generally lumped together with all other cash items when a balance sheet is prepared.

EXERCISE 8-5

Purpose: (L.O. 7) This exercise will help you review situations that give rise to reconciling items on a bank reconciliation and identify those which require adjusting entries on the depositor's books.

A sketch of the bank reconciliation at July 31, 20XX for the Ace Electric Company and a list of possible reconciling items appear below.

Ace Electric Co.
BANK RECONCILIATION
July 31, 20XX

Balance per bank statement, July 31		$X,XXX
A. Add	$XXX	
	XXX	X,XXX
		X,XXX
B. Deduct		X,XXX
Adjusted cash balance, July 31, per bank		$X,XXX
Balance per books, July 31		$X,XXX
C. Add	$XXX	
	XXX	X,XXX
		X,XXX
D. Deduct:	XXX	
	XXX	
	XXX	
	XXX	X,XXX
Adjusted cash balance, July 31, per books		$X,XXX

(a)   **Items**

_____   1. Deposits of July 30 amounting to $1,582 have not reached the bank as of July 31.

_____   2. A customer's check for $140 that was deposited on July 20 was returned NSF by the bank; return has not been recorded by Ace.

_____   3. Bank service charge for July amounts to $3.

_____   4. Included with the bank statement was check No. 422 for $702 as payment of an account payable. In comparing the check with the cash disbursement records, it was discovered that the check was incorrectly entered in the cash disbursements journal for $720.

_____   5. Outstanding checks at July 31 amount to $1,927.

_____   6. The bank improperly charged a check of the Ace Plumbing Co. for $25 to Ace Electric Co.'s account.

_____   7. The bank charged $8 during July for printing checks.

_____   8. During July, the bank collected a customer's note receivable for the Ace Electric Co.; face amount $1,000, interest $20, and the bank charged a $2 collection fee. This transaction has not been recorded by Ace.

_____   9. A check written by Ace in June for $180 cleared the bank during July.

_____ 10. Deposits of June 30 for $1,200 were recorded by the company on June 30 but were not recorded by the bank until July 2.

Instructions

(a)   Indicate how each of the 10 items listed above would be handled on the bank reconciliation by placing the proper code letter in the space provided. The applicable code letters appear in the sketch of the bank reconciliation. Use the code "NR" for any item which is not a reconciling item on July 31.

(b)   Assume that the July 31 balance per bank statement was $4,232. Complete the bank reconciliation using the items given and answer the questions that follow:

1. What is the adjusted (correct) cash balance at July 31?
    $_____

2. What is the balance per books **before** adjustment at July 31?
    $_____

3. What reconciling items require an adjusting entry on Ace Electric Company's books? (Identify by item numbers.) _____

4. What item(s) requires a special entry on the bank's records to correct an error(s)?
    _____

SOLUTION TO EXERCISE 8-5

(a) 1. A   6. A
     2. D   7. D
     3. D   8. C, D
     4. C   9. NR
     5. B   10. NR

TIP:	Items 9 and 10 would have been reconciling items of cash balances on the June 30 bank reconciliation (the prior month).

(b) 1. $3,912* ($4,232 + $1,582 + $25 - $1,927 = $3,912)
     2. $3,027* [X + $18 + $1,020 - $140 - $3 - $8 - $2 = $3,912 (answer to question 1)]
         X = $3,027
     3. 2; 3; 4; 7; 8
     4. 6
     *See the completed bank reconciliation on the following page.

Approach to part (b) 2: You can compute the correct cash balance by completing the top half of the bank reconciliation (balance per bank to correct cash balance). The correct cash balance can then be entered on the last line of the bottom half of the reconciliation and used along with certain reconciling items to "work backwards" to compute the $3,027 cash balance per books before adjustment.

Ace Electric Co.
BANK RECONCILIATION
July 31, 20XX

Balance per bank statement, July 31			$4,232
Add:	Deposits in transit on July 31	$1,582	
	Check improperly charged by bank	25	1,607
			5,839
Deduct: Checks outstanding as of July 31			1,927
Adjusted cash balance per bank at July 31			$3,912
Balance per books, July 31			$3,027
Add:	Error in recording check No. 422	$ 18	
	Collection of customer's note receivable and interest		
	by bank	1,020	1,038
			4,065
Deduct: Customer's NSF check		140	
	Bank service charge for July	3	
	Cost of printing checks	8	
	Bank collection fee	2	153
Adjusted cash balance per books at July 31			$3,912

TIP:	The required adjusting entries on the depositor's books would be:		
Cash		18	
Accounts Payable...			18
(To correct error in recording check No. 422)			
Cash		1,020	
Note Receivable			1,000
Interest Revenue			20
(To record collection of note receivable by bank)			
Accounts Receivable		140	
Cash			140
(To record customer's NSF check)			
Miscellaneous Expense		13	
Cash			13
(To record bank service charges); ($3 + $8 + $2 = $13)			

EXERCISE 8-6

Purpose: (L.O. 7) This exercise will illustrate how to determine the amount of deposits in transit and outstanding checks at a given date.

Shown below for Molly's Folly are the
- (1) bank reconciliation at September 30, 2014.
- (2) listing of deposits for October per the bank statement.
- (3) listing of deposits for October per the books.
- (4) listing of checks paid by the bank during October.
- (5) listing of checks written by the depositor during October.

Molly's Folly
BANK RECONCILIATION
September 30, 2014

Cash balance per bank statement		$15,000
Add: Deposits in transit		
September 29	$2,000	
September 30	1,600	3,600
		18,600
Less: Outstanding checks		
No. 514	650	
No. 516	410	
No. 520	560	
No. 521	740	
No. 522	1,000	3,360
Adjusted cash balance per bank		$15,240
Cash balance per books		$15,690
Less: Customer's NSF check	$400	
Bank service charge	50	450
Adjusted cash balance per books		$15,240

Bank Statement for October—Deposits

Date	Amount	Date	Amount
10/1	$2,000	10/21	$ 700
10/2	1,600	10/22	900
10/3	500	10/25	100
10/5	300	10/27	600
10/11	1,100	10/28	800
10/11	1,200	10/29	1,300
10/15	200	Total	$11,700
10/18	400		

Cash Receipts Journal

Date	Amount	Date	Amount
10/1	$ 500	10/21	$ 900
10/4	300	10/23	100
10/8	1,100	10/25	600
10/10	1,200	10/27	800
10/13	200	10/28	1,300
10/16	400	10/30	1,400
10/20	700	10/31	2,050
		Total	$11,550

Bank Statement for October—Checks Paid and Debit Memos

Date	Check No.	Amount	Date	Check No.	Amount
10/1	514	$ 650	10/12	533	$ 190
10/1	520	560	10/13	534	220
10/4	521	740	10/14	535	240
10/4	522	1,000	10/18	538	380
10/5	525	120	10/18	536	250
10/5	526	140	10/18	537	320
10/6	528	230	10/18	539	430
10/8	529	310	10/19	540	510
10/8	527	210	10/23	541	330
10/8	530	420	10/25	542	340
10/11	532	160	10/29	545	540
10/11	531	130	10/29	546	470
			10/31	DM	30
			Total		$8,920

Cash Payments Journal—Checks Issued

Date	Check No.	Amount	Date	Check No.	Amount
10/1	525	$120	10/14	538	$ 380
10/1	526	140	10/15	539	430
10/3	527	210	10/17	540	510
10/4	528	230	10/20	541	330
10/5	529	310	10/23	542	340
10/5	530	420	10/25	543	110
10/7	531	130	10/26	544	160
10/7	532	106	10/27	545	540
10/7	533	190	10/28	546	470
10/11	534	220	10/31	547	590
10/11	535	240	10/31	548	640
10/12	536	250	Total		$7,386
10/14	537	320			

Instructions
(a)   Prepare a list of deposits in transit at October 31, 2014.
(b)   Prepare a list of outstanding checks at October 31, 2014.
(c)   Locate any errors per books assuming information recorded in the bank's records is correct.
(d)   Locate any bank memoranda that will need to be recorded on the books.

SOLUTION TO EXERCISE 8-6

(a) Deposits in transit at October 31, 2014:

October 30	$1,400
October 31	2,050
Total	$3,450

(b) Outstanding checks at October 31, 2014:

No.	Amount
516	$ 410
543	110
544	160
547	590
548	640
	$1,910

(c) Check No. 532 was recorded on the depositor's books for $106 when it should have been recorded for the correct amount of $160.

(d) The DM for $30 on October 31 will need to be recorded on the depositor's books. (The DM is likely for bank service charges for October.)

Approach and Explanation:

(a) To identify the deposits in transit at October 31:

(1) Compare the deposits in transit at September 30 (per the company's bank reconciliation at that date) with the October bank statement. If the deposit did not get recorded by the bank during October, it is to be considered a deposit in transit at October 31. (It would be extremely rare for a particular deposit to be listed as a deposit in transit on two successive bank reconciliations because it would indicate the deposit was lost in the mail or lost in the bank's facilities or a victim of some strange fate or possibly related to an irregularity.)

For Molly's Folly, the $2,000 and $1,600 items deposited at the end of September (deposits in transit at September 30, 2014) both were recorded by the bank in early October as expected.

(2) Compare the deposits made during October per company records with the October deposits per the bank's records. Deposits not recorded by the bank represent **deposits in transit.** As can be expected, the items deposited at the very end of October have not had enough time to be processed by the bank by the end of the day on October 31. These include the deposits made by Molly's Folly on October 30 ($1,400) and October 31 ($2,050).

(b)   To identify the outstanding checks at October 31, 2014:

(1)   Compare the checks outstanding at September 30, 2014 (per the September 30th bank reconciliation) with the paid checks shown on the October bank statement. If a September check remains unpaid at the end of October, it is an outstanding check at October 31. For Molly's Folly, check numbers 514, 520, 521, and 522 all cleared the bank during October but check number 516 ($410) remains unpaid at October 31, 2014. (The check could be lost in the mail or lost in the banking system. More likely, the check is still in the hands of the payee who, for some reason, has not yet deposited it to his account.)

(2)   Compare the checks written by Molly's Folly during October with the checks paid by the bank. Issued checks that have not been paid by the bank represent **outstanding checks.**

For Molly's Folly, October check numbers 543 ($110), 544 ($160), 547 ($590) and 548 ($640) were written during October and are outstanding at October 31.

(c)   To identify errors on either the bank's records or the depositor's books, compare all of the figures on the October bank statement with their source on the depositor's records. If there are any discrepancies, determine which is in error. For Molly's Folly, check number 532 correctly cleared the bank for $160 but was entered in the cash payments journal as $106 (the facts of the problem state that the bank's records are correct). This transposition type error caused the depositor's bank balance per ledger to be overstated by $54 ($160 - $106 = $54).

TIP:	Recall that a transposition error (reversing the order of numbers) will cause a difference that is divisible by 9.

EXERCISE 8-7

Purpose: (L. O. 7) This exercise will allow you to practice preparing a bank reconciliation.

A bank reconciliation should be prepared by a depositor every month.

The cash balance per bank at October 31 is $17,780, and the cash balance per Molly's Folly books at October 31 is $19,404.

Instructions
(a) Using the data in **Exercise 8-6** and the solution to that exercise, prepare a bank reconciliation for Molly's Folly at October 31, 2014.
(b) Prepare the adjusting entries at October 31 for the depositor's books. Assume check No. 532 was issued to the power company for utilities.

SOLUTION TO EXERCISE 8-7

(a)
Molly's Folly
BANK RECONCILIATION
October 31, 2014

Cash balance per bank statement		$17,780*
Add: Deposits in transit (Answer (a) Exercise 8-6)		3,450
		21,230
Deduct: Outstanding checks (Answer (b) Exercise 8-6)		1,910
Adjusted cash balance per bank		$19,320
Cash balance per books		$19,404**
Deduct: Bank service charge	$30	
Error in recording check No. 532	54	84
Adjusted cash balance per books		$19,320

*To add to the complexity of this exercise, you could be asked to solve for the $17,780 cash balance per bank statement. The computation would be as follows:

Balance per bank statement at September 30, 2014	$15,000
Add: Deposits recorded during October and credit memoranda	11,700
Deduct: Checks paid during October and debit memoranda	8,920
Balance per bank statement at October 30, 2014	$17,780

**To add to the complexity of this exercise, you could be asked to solve for the $19,404 cash balance per books at October 31, 2014. The computation would be as follows:

Balance per books at September 30, 2014, before adjustment	$15,690
Deduct: NSF check recorded by an adjusting entry	400
Deduct: Bank service charge for September recorded by an adjusting entry	50
Adjusted cash balance at September 30	15,240
Add: Deposits made during October	11,550
Deduct: Checks written (issued) during October	7,386
Balance per books at October 31, 2014	$19,404

An alternate approach to solving for the balance per books before adjustment is illustrated in the **Solution to Exercise 8-5** part (b) 2.

TIP:	Keep in mind that deposits in transit and outstanding checks are reconciling items but do **not** require adjusting entries on either the bank's books or the depositor's books.

(b) Oct. 31 Miscellaneous Expense...   30
                    Cash...   30
                    (To record the bank service charges for October)

       Oct. 31 Utilities Expense...   54
                    Cash...   54
                    (To correct error in recording check no 532)

EXERCISE 8-8

Purpose: (L.O. 1 thru 8) This exercise will quiz you about terminology used in this chapter.

A list of accounting terms with which you should be familiar appears below:

Bank reconciliation	Fraud triangle
Bank service charge	Internal auditors
Bank statement	Internal control
Bonding	NSF check
Cash	Outstanding checks
Cash equivalents	Petty cash fund
Check	Restricted cash
Deposits in transit	Sarbanes-Oxley Act (SOX)
Electronic funds transfer (EFT)	Voucher
Fraud	Voucher system

Instructions
For each item below, enter in the blank the term that is described.

1. _____Resources that consist of coins, currency, checks, money orders, and money on hand or on deposit in a bank or similar depository.

2. _____Short-term, highly liquid investments that can be converted to a specific amount of cash.

3. _____A cash fund used to pay relatively small amounts.

4. _____All of the related methods and measures adopted within an organization to safeguard its assets and enhance the accuracy and reliability of its accounting records.

5. _____A fee charged by a bank for the use of its services.

6. _____A monthly statement from the bank that shows the depositor's bank transactions and balances.

7. _____A written order signed a bank depositor directing the bank to pay a specified sum of money to a designated recipient.

8. _____Checks issued and recorded by a company not yet paid by the bank.

9. _____Deposits recorded by the depositor but not yet recorded by the bank.

10. _____A check that is not paid by a bank because of insufficient funds in a customer's bank account.

11. _____A disbursement system that uses wire, telephone, telegraph, or computer to transfer funds from one location to another.

12. _____Company employees who continually evaluate the effectiveness of the company's internal control system.

13. _____An extensive network of approvals by authorized individuals acting independently to ensure that all disbursements by check are proper.

14. _____An authorization form prepared for each payment in a voucher system.

15. _____Obtaining insurance protection against misappropriation of assets by employees.

16. _____The process of comparing the bank's balance of an account with the company's recorded cash balance and explaining any differences to make them agree.

17. _____Cash that must be used for a special purpose.

18. _____Regulations passed by Congress to try to reduce unethical corporate behavior.

19. _____A dishonest act by an employee that results in personal benefit to the employee at a cost to the employer.

20. _____The three factors that contribute to fraudulent activity by employees: opportunity, financial pressure, and rationalization.

SOLUTION TO EXERCISE 8-8

1.	Cash	8.	Outstanding checks	15.	Bonding
2.	Cash equivalents	9.	Deposits in transit	16.	Bank reconciliation
3.	Petty cash fund	10.	NSF check	17.	Restricted cash
4.	Internal control	11.	Electronic funds transfer (EFT)	18.	Sarbanes-Oxley Act (SOX)
5.	Bank service charge	12.	Internal auditors		
6.	Bank statement	13.	Voucher system	19.	Fraud
7.	Check	14.	Voucher	20.	Fraud triangle

ANALYSIS OF MULTIPLE-CHOICE TYPE QUESTIONS

1.   (L.O. 1) One of the main objectives of a good system of internal control is to:
      a.   increase sales.
      b.   provide a means of gathering information about competitors.
      c.   prevent errors and irregularities in the accounting records.
      d.   prosecute employees who embezzle from the company.

      Approach and Explanation: Mentally define internal control before you look at the answer selections. **Internal control** consists of the plan of organization and all the related methods and measures adopted within a business to:
      1. Safeguard its assets from employee theft, robbery, and unauthorized used.
      2. Enhance the accuracy and reliability of its accounting records by reducing the risks of errors (unintentional mistakes) and irregularities (intentional mistakes and misrepresentations) in the accounting process.
      3. Increase efficiency of operations.
      4. Ensure compliance with laws and regulations. (Solution = c.)

2.   (L.O. 1) Irregularities are also known as:
      a.   errors.
      b.   unintentional mistakes.
      c.   fraud.
      d.   defects in internal control.

      Explanation: Errors are unintentional mistakes. Irregularities are intentional mistakes and misrepresentations; irregularities are also called fraud. Irregularities can occur even in a company with adequate internal control when a situation such as collusion exists. (Solution = c.)

3.   (L.O. 2) The basic internal control principle that is being applied when the work assignment for one employee is designed to check on the work of another employee is:
      a.   independent internal verification.
      b.   documentation procedures.
      c.   separation of duties.
      d.   double duties.

      Explanation: Independent internal verification (or independent check) involves the review, comparison, and reconciliation of data prepared by one or several employees. To be effective, the verification should (1) be made periodically or on a surprise basis, (2) be done by an employee who is independent of the personnel responsible for the information, and (3) have discrepancies reported to a management level that can take appropriate corrective action. (Solution = a.)

4.   (L.O. 3) The best way to discourage a sales clerk from using a sales invoice to make a cash sale to a customer and then pocketing the cash and destroying the company's copy of the sales invoice is to require:
      a.   verification of sales invoices.
      b.   authorization of sales invoices.
      c.   serialization of sales invoices.
      d.   separation of duties for making the sale and recording the sale in the journal.
      Explanation: Whenever possible, documents should be prenumbered, and all documents should be accounted for. Prenumbering helps to prevent a transaction from being

recorded more than once, or conversely, to prevent the transaction from not being recorded. Serialization of sales invoices refers to prenumbering. (Solution = c.)

5. (L.O. 4) An extensive network of approvals by authorized individuals acting independently to ensure that all disbursements by check are proper is called a(n):
    a. electronic funds transfer system.
    b. computerized system.
    c. verifiable system.
    d. voucher system.

    Explanation: A voucher system is an extensive network of approvals by authorized individuals acting independently to ensure that all disbursements by check are proper. A voucher system may or may not include electronic transfer of fund as a mode of disbursement. A computerized system for cash disbursements may or may not be a voucher system. (Solution = d.)

6. (L.O. 5) The journal entry to record the replenishment of a petty cash fund that was established at $200 and is replenished at a date when petty cash vouchers in the fund amount to $172 and coins and currency in the fund amount to $30 will contain:
    a. debits to various expense accounts, a debit to Cash Over and Short, and a credit to Cash.
    b. debits to various expense accounts, a credit to Cash Over and Short, and a credit to Cash.
    c. a debit to Petty Cash, a credit to Cash Over and Short, and a credit to Cash.
    d. a debit to Cash and a credit to Petty Cash.

    Approach and Explanation: Reconstruct the journal entry in question:

Miscellaneous Expenses	172	
Cash Over and Short		2
Cash		170

    The amount of expense receipts ($172) and the amount of coins and currency ($30) exceed the fund balance ($200) which indicates there is $2 too much in the fund. This $2 overage is recorded in the Cash Over and Short account. A credit balance in the Cash Over and Short account is classified as a revenue item on the income statement. (Solution = b.)

7. (L.O. 6) A debit memorandum issued by a bank will:
   a. not affect the depositor's account balance.
   b. increase the depositor's account balance.
   c. decrease the depositor's account balance.
   d. be recorded as a debit to Cash on the depositor's books.

   Approach and Explanation: Think about what a bank debit memorandum is used for. Think about how it affects the bank's books and the depositor's books. A depositor's bank account balance is a liability on the bank's books. Therefore, the bank uses a debit memorandum (memo), often abbreviated as DM on a bank statement, to indicate the bank has reason to debit the depositor's account. This debit reduces the bank's liability. Therefore, the bank debit memorandum reduces the depositor's bank balance and is recorded by the depositor as a credit to Cash. (Solution = c.)

8. **Question**
   (L.O. 6) Which of the following items would **not** accompany a monthly bank statement?
   a. Depositor's checks paid by the bank during the month (or copies thereof).
   b. Copies of outstanding checks at the end of the month.
   c. Copies of bank debit memos issued during the month.
   d. Copies of bank credit memos issued during the month.

   Explanation: A bank statement is usually accompanied by the paid checks (checks which were paid by the bank during the month), bank debit memoranda, and bank credit memoranda. Copies of outstanding checks would **never** be included because the bank is unaware of any information related to checks outstanding at the date a bank statement is prepared. (Solution = b.)

9. (L.O. 7) Which of the following would most likely **not** appear as a reconciling item on a bank reconciliation prepared at the end of August?
   a. Deposits in transit at August 31.
   b. Checks which were disbursed and recorded by the depositor in July and were paid by the bank during August.
   c. Bank service charges for the month of August.
   d. Error in the depositor's account made by the bank during August and discovered by the depositor when examining the bank statement.

   Approach and Explanation: Think about the possible reconciling items (refer to **Illustration 8-1**): deposits in transit, outstanding checks, bank debit memoranda, bank credit memoranda, bank errors, and depositor errors. Bank debit memoranda are issued for items such as bank service charges, customers' NSF checks deposited, and wire transfers. Checks disbursed in July and paid by the bank in August would be outstanding checks at July 31, but they are not outstanding at August 31; thus, they are not a reconciling item at August 31. (Solution = b.)

10. (L.O. 7) The term "outstanding checks" refers to
   a. checks that have been lost in the mail or for some other reason have been misplaced.
   b. depositor checks which have been processed by the bank but have not yet been recorded by the depositor.
   c. customer checks which have been returned by the bank because the customer's bank would not honor them.
   d. depositor checks which have not yet cleared the banking system.

Explanation: There is a lag in time between the date a check is issued and the date the check clears the banking system. During the time between these two dates, the checks are referred to as "outstanding checks." (Solution = d.)

11. (L.O. 7) The following information pertains to Honeybee Co. at December 31, 2014

Bank statement balance	$40,000
Checkbook balance	56,400
Deposits in transit	20,000
Outstanding checks	4,000
Bank service charges for December	400

In Honeybee's balance sheet at December 31, 2014 cash should be reported as:
   a. $36,000.
   b. $40,000.
   c. $56,000.
   d. $60,000.

Approach and Explanation: When a question relates to data used in a bank reconciliation, you should sketch out the format for a bank reconciliation, put in the information given, and solve for the unknown piece.

Cash balance per bank statement	$40,000
Deposits in transit	20,000
Outstanding checks	(4,000)
Adjusted cash balance per bank	$56,000
Cash balance per books	$56,400
Bank service charges	(400)
Adjusted cash balance per books	$56,000

In this particular question, the completion of either the top half or the bottom half of the reconciliation using the bank-to-adjusted balance format would be enough to solve for the answer requested. (Solution = c.)

12. (L.O. 7) The following information pertains to the Berry Bear Corporation at December 31, 2014

Balance per bank	$20,000
Deposits in transit	6,000
Outstanding checks	16,000
Bank service charges for December	400
Bank erroneously charged Berry Bear's account for Sonny-Bear's check written for $1,400. As of December 31, the bank had not corrected this error	1,400

Berry Bear's cash balance per ledger (books) before adjustment at December 31, 2014 is
a. $28,200.
b. $11,800.
c. $11,000.
d. $8,200.

Approach and Explanation: The balance per books (before adjustment) can easily be computed by putting the data into the format for a bank reconciliation. Solve for the unknown.

Cash balance per bank statement	$20,000
Deposits in transit	6,000
Outstanding checks	(16,000)
Bank error in charge for check	1,400
Adjusted cash balance per bank	$11,400
Cash balance per books	$ X
Bank service charges	(400)
Adjusted cash balance per books	$11,400

X = $11,800 (Solution = b.)

13. (L.O. 7) The following data relate to the bank account of Springfield Cleaners:

Cash balance, September 30 per bank	$10,000
Cash balance, October 31 per bank	21,500
Checks paid during October by bank	5,900
Checks written during October per books	6,800
Cash balance, October 31 per books	22,200
Bank service charge for October, not recorded on books	100
Deposits per books for October	19,000

The amount of deposits recorded by the bank in October is
a. $19,000.
b. $17,500.
c. $11,500.
d. $5,700.

Approach and Explanation: Think about how deposits recorded by the bank affect the cash balance per bank and other items that cause that balance to change. Plug in the figures given and solve for the unknown.

Balance per bank, September 30	$10,000
Deposits per bank during October	X
Bank credit memoranda	-0-
Checks paid by bank during October	(5,900)
Bank service charge for October and other bank debit memoranda	(100)
Balance per bank, October 31	$21,500

Solving for X: $10,000 + X - $5,900 - $100 = $21,500
                  X = $21,500 - $10,000 + $5,900 + $100

                  X = $17,500 (Solution = b.)

14. (L.O. 8) When financial statements are prepared, the balance of the Petty Cash account is:
  a. not reflected in the financial statements.
  b. reported along with other unrestricted cash items in the current asset section of the balance sheet.
  c. reported as restricted cash in the balance sheet.
  d. reported as a miscellaneous expense item on the income statement.

Explanation: Cash on hand, cash in banks, and petty cash are usually combined and reported simply as Cash in the current asset section of the balance sheet. (Solution = b.)

15. (L.O. 8) Which of the following items should **not** be included in the Cash caption on the balance sheet?
  a. Coins and currency in the cash register.
  b. Checks from other parties presently in the cash register.
  c. Amounts on deposit in checking account at the bank.
  d. Postage stamps on hand.

Explanation: Cash on hand, unrestricted cash in banks, and petty cash are usually combined and reported simply as Cash. Postage stamps on hand are classified as office supplies (a prepaid expense). Cash on hand consists of coins, currency (paper money), checks, and money orders. The general rule is that if a bank will accept it for deposit, it is cash. (Solution = d.)

CHAPTER 9

ACCOUNTING FOR RECEIVABLES

OVERVIEW

Receivables are claims that are expected to be collected in cash. Three major types of receivables are usually recognized; they are accounts, notes, and other receivables. Receivables can be (a) held until they are collected, (b) sold before they are collected, or (c) held and never collected. Many businesses grant credit to customers; hence, they have accounts receivable. They know that, when making sales "on account," a risk exists because some accounts will never be collected. However, the cost of these bad debts is more than offset by the profit from the extra sales made because of the attraction of granting credit. The collections department may make many attempts to collect an account before "writing-off" a bad debtor. Frequently an account is deemed to be uncollectible a year or more after the date of the credit sale. In this chapter, we will discuss the allowance method of accounting for bad debts. The allowance method permits the accountant to estimate the amount of bad debts expense that should be matched with revenues rather than waiting to book expense at the time of an actual write-off.

SUMMARY OF LEARNING OBJECTIVES

1. **Identity the different types of receivables.** Receivables are frequently classified as (1) accounts, (2) notes, and (3) other. Accounts receivable are amounts customers owe on account. Notes receivable are claims for which lenders issue formal instruments of credit as proof of the debt. Other receivables include nontrade receivables such as interest receivable, loans to company officers, advances to employees, and income taxes refundable.

2. **Explain how companies recognize accounts receivable.** Companies record accounts receivable when they provide a service on account or at the point of sale of merchandise on account. Accounts receivable balances are reduced by sales returns and allowances. Cash discounts also reduce the amount received on accounts receivable. When interest is charged on a past due receivable, the company adds this interest to the accounts receivable balance and recognizes it as interest revenue.

3. **Distinguish between the methods and bases companies use to value accounts receivable.** There are two methods of accounting for uncollectible accounts: the allowance method and the direct write-off method. The allowance method is required for financial reporting purposes when bad debts are material (significant) in size. Companies may use either the percentage-of-sales or the percentage-of-receivables basis to estimate uncollectible accounts using the allowance method. The percentage-of-sales basis emphasizes the expense recognition (matching) principle. The percentage-of-receivables basis emphasizes the cash realizable value of the accounts receivable. An aging schedule is often used with this basis.

4. **Describe the entries to record the disposition of accounts receivable.** When a company collects an account receivable, it credits Accounts Receivable. When a company (factors) an account receivable, a service charge is assessed which reduces the amount of cash collected.

5. **Compute the maturity date of and interest on notes receivable.** For a note stated in months, the maturity date is found by counting the months from the date of issue. For a note stated in days, the number of days is counted, omitting the issue date and counting the due date. The formula for computing interest is Face value X Interest rate X Time.

6. **Explain how companies recognize notes receivable.** Companies record notes receivable at face value. In some cases, it is necessary to record accrued interest prior to maturity. In this case, companies debit Interest Receivable and credit Interest Revenue.

7. **Describe how companies value notes receivable.** As with accounts receivable, companies report notes receivable at their cash (net) realizable value. The notes receivable allowance account is the Allowance for Doubtful Accounts. The computation and estimations involved in valuing notes receivables at cash realizable value, and in recording the proper amount of bad debt expense and related allowance, are similar to those involved in accounting for accounts receivable.

8. **Describe the entries to record the disposition of notes receivable.** Notes can be held to maturity. At that time the face value plus accrued interest is due, and the note is removed from the accounts. In many cases, the holder of the note speeds up the conversion to cash by selling the receivable to another party (a factor). In some situations, the maker of the note dishonors the note (defaults), in which case the company transfers the note and accrued interest to an account receivable or writes off the note.

9. **Explain the statement presentation and analysis of receivables.** Companies should identify in the balance sheet or in the notes to the financial statements each major type of receivable. Companies report short-term receivables as current assets. They report the gross amount of receivables and the allowance for doubtful accounts. They report bad debt expense and service charge expense in the multiple-step income statement as operating (selling) expenses. Interest revenue appears as other revenue in the nonoperating section of the income statement. Managers and investors evaluate accounts receivable for liquidity by computing a turnover ratio and an average collection period.

TIPS ON CHAPTER TOPICS

TIP: **Trade accounts receivable** result from the sale of products or services to customers. **Nontrade accounts receivable** (amounts that are due from nontrade customers who do not buy goods or services in the normal course of the company's main business activity) should be listed separately on the balance sheet from the trade accounts receivable balance.

TIP: Notice how the subjects of this chapter affect the balance sheet and the income statement. The balance of the Accounts Receivable account and its contra account—Allowance for Doubtful Accounts—are reported in the current asset section of the balance sheet. The balance of Notes Receivable (assuming the notes are due within one year of the balance sheet date) is also classified in the current asset section of the balance sheet. The balance of Bad Debt Expense is usually reported in the operating expense section of the multiple-step income statement.

TIP: Assets such as current receivables and inventories should never be reported at more than their net (cash) realizable value. Thus, if some uncollectible accounts are expected, receivables are reduced by these uncollectible amounts when presented on the balance sheet.

TIP: The **carrying value** (or **book value** or **carrying amount**) of accounts receivable is equal to the balance of the Accounts Receivable account less the balance of the related valuation account (Allowance for Doubtful Accounts).

TIP: In the event that a customer's account has a credit balance on the balance sheet date, it should be classified as a current liability and **not** be offset against other accounts receivable with debit balances.

TIP: Even though special journals were discussed in a prior chapter, simplicity requires that the general journal be used to illustrate all journal entries in the remainder of the book.

ILLUSTRATION 9-1
ENTRIES FOR THE ALLOWANCE METHOD (L.O.3)

Journal Entry		Effect on Net Income	Effect on Current Assets	Effect on Allowance Account	Effect on Net Receivables
Entry to record bad debts expense, $1,000					
		Decrease			
Bad Debt Expense	1,000	$1,000	No effect	No effect	No effect
Allowance for Doubtful Accounts	1,000	No effect	Decrease $1,000	Increase $1,000	Decrease $1,000
Net effect of entry		Decrease $1,000	Decrease $1,000	Increase $1,000	Decrease $1,000
Entry to write-off a customer's account, $200					
			Increase	Decrease	Increase
Allowance for Doubtful Accounts	200	No effect	$200	$200	$200
Accounts Receivable	200	No effect	Decrease $200	No effect	Decrease $200
Net effect of entry		No effect	No effect	Decrease $200	No effect
Entries to record collection of account receivable previously written off, $120					
			Increase		Increase
Accounts Receivable	120	No effect	$120	No effect	$120
Allowance for Doubtful Accounts	120	No effect	Decrease $120	Increase $120	Decrease $120
			Increase		
Cash	120	No effect	$120	No effect	No effect
Accounts Receivable	120	No effect	Decrease $120	No effect	Decrease $120
Net effect of entries		No effect	No effect	Increase $120	Decrease $120

TIP: Study the effects of the journal entries related to accounting for accounts receivable using the allowance method. Those entries and their effects are clearly shown above. Notice that the entry to record bad debts reduces current assets and reduces net income. The entry to record the write off of an individual account has no net effect on the amount of current assets nor does it affect income. It merely reduces Accounts Receivable and the Allowance for Doubtful Accounts account (which is a contra item); thus, the entry has no net effect on the carrying value of the accounts receivable. Thus, it is the entry to record the bad debt expense that impacts **both** the balance sheet and the income statement.

ILLUSTRATION 9-1 (Continued)

TIP:	Bad Debt Expense is often called Uncollectible Accounts Expense or Doubtful Accounts Expense or Provision for Bad Debts.
TIP:	Allowance for Doubtful Accounts is often called Allowance for Uncollectible Accounts or Allowance for Bad Debts. Notice that these account titles all start with "Allowance for" which typically indicates a contra type balance sheet account.

EXERCISE 9-1

Purpose: (L.O. 3) This exercise will identify the two approaches of applying the allowance method of accounting for uncollectible accounts receivable.

Howell's Department Store offers a store credit card for the convenience of its customers. Even though the store follows up on delinquent accounts, past experience indicates that a predictable amount of credit sales will ultimately result in uncollectible accounts. Howell uses the allowance method of accounting for uncollectible accounts. Bad debts are a material amount.

Instructions
(a) Describe the two methods available for determining the amount of the adjusting entry to record bad debt expense and to adjust the allowance account. Also discuss the emphasis of each method.
(b) Explain why the direct write-off method is not a generally accepted accounting method for Howell's Department Store.

SOLUTION TO EXERCISE 9-1

(a) When using the allowance method of accounting for bad debts, there are two methods available for determining the amount of the adjusting entry to record bad debts expense and to adjust the allowance account. They are:
   (1) **The percentage-of-sales basis:** This method focuses on estimating bad debts expense. The average percentage relationship between actual bad debt losses and net credit sales (or total credit sales) of the period is used to determine the amount of expense for the period. This method focuses on the matching of current bad debts expense with revenues of the current period and thus emphasizes the income statement. The amount of bad debts expense is simply calculated and recorded; a by-product of this approach is the increase in the allowance account.

(2) **The percentage-of-receivables basis:** This method focuses on estimating the cash (net) realizable value of the current receivables and thus emphasizes the balance sheet. It only incidentally measures bad debts expense; the expense reported may not be the best figure to match with the amount of credit sales of the current period. If this method is to be used, the aging technique is preferable to the use of a simple percentage times total accounts receivable. An aging analysis takes into consideration the age of a receivable. The older the age, the lower the probability of collection.

(b) Under the direct write-off method, bad debt losses are not estimated and no allowance account is used. No entry regarding bad debts is made until a specific account has definitely been established as uncollectible. Then the loss is recorded by a debit to Bad Debt Expense and a credit to Accounts Receivable.

When the direct write-off method is used, Accounts Receivable will be reported at its gross amount and bad debt expense is often recorded in a period different from the period in which the revenue was recorded. Thus, no attempt is made to match bad debt expense to sales revenues in the income statement or to show the cash (net) realizable value of the accounts receivable in the balance sheet. Consequently, unless bad debt losses are insignificant, the direct write-off method is **not** acceptable for financial reporting purposes. Howell's bad debts are material (significant) in amount so the allowance method must be used for financial reporting purposes. The direct write-off method is, however, used for tax purposes.

EXERCISE 9-2

Purpose: (L.O. 3) This exercise will review the two bases for determining the dollar amount of the adjusting entry to recognize bad debt expense and to adjust the Allowance for Doubtful Accounts account.

The trial balance before adjustment at December 31, 2014 for the Liz Company shows the following balances:

	Debit	Credit
Accounts Receivable	$82,000	
Allowance for Doubtful Accounts	2,120	
Sales Revenue (all on credit)		$410,000
Sales Returns and Allowances	7,600	

Instructions
Using the data above, give the journal entries to record each of the following cases (each situation is **independent**):
(a) The company expects bad debts to be 1 3/4% of net credit sales.
(b) Liz performs an aging analysis at December 31, 2014 which indicates an estimate of $6,000 uncollectible accounts.

SOLUTION TO EXERCISE 9-2

(a) Bad Debt Expense 7,042
    Allowance for Doubtful Accounts [($410,000 - $7,600) X
       1.75%] 7,042

(b) Bad Debt Expense 8,120
    Allowance for Doubtful Accounts 8,120

Explanation

(a) The percentage-of-net-credit-sales approach to applying the allowance method of accounting for bad debts focuses on determining an appropriate expense figure. The existing balance in the allowance account is **not** relevant in the computation.

(b) An aging analysis provides the best estimate of the net realizable value of accounts receivable. By using the results of the aging to adjust the allowance account, the amount reported for net receivables on the balance sheet is the cash (net) realizable value of accounts receivable. It is important to notice that the balance of the allowance account before adjustment is a determinant in the adjustment required. The following T-account reflects the facts used to determine the necessary adjustment.

Allowance for Doubtful Accounts

Unadjusted balance	2,120	**Adjustment needed**	**8,120**
		Desired balance at 12/31/14	6,000

TIP: Notice that in this particular instance, the allowance account has an abnormal balance before adjustment. The normal balance of the Allowance for Doubtful Accounts is a credit. Therefore, a debit balance in this account indicates an abnormal balance. It is not uncommon to have a debit balance in the allowance account before adjusting entries are prepared because individual accounts may be written off at various times during a period, and the entry to adjust the allowance account is made at the end of the period before financial statements are prepared. After adjustment, the allowance account should have a credit balance.

TIP: Refer to the **Solution to Exercise 9-1** (a) to review the emphasis of both the percentage-of-sales basis and the percentage-of-receivables basis for estimating uncollectible accounts using the allowance method.

> **TIP:** When it is time to prepare the adjusting entry for bad debts (at the end of an accounting period), the existing balance in the Allowance for Doubtful Accounts account (that is, the balance before adjustment) is **NOT** considered in determining the amount of the adjusting entry **IF** the percentage-of-sales-basis is used. However, the balance of the allowance account before adjustment **IS** used in determining the amount of the adjusting entry when the percentage-of-receivables-basis is used to implement the allowance method of accounting for bad debts. The use of an aging analysis is one approach to using the percentage-of-receivables basis.

EXERCISE 9-3

Purpose: (L.O. 4) This exercise will illustrate the journal entries related to credit card sales.

Bubba's Bed & Bath Shop accepts MasterCard, VISA, and its own Bubba's Bed & Bath Shop (BB&BS) credit cards. MasterCard and VISA sales slips are deposited in the bank daily; the bank charges a 3% fee. The following transactions occurred on May 3, 2014.

1. Made sales of $7,200 to customers who presented MasterCard and VISA cards.
2. Made sales to the following who used their BB&BS cards:
   a. Nadine Adam, $120
   b. Connie Dawson, $240
   c. Dale Bandy, $500

Instructions
(a) Prepare the journal entries to record the transactions above for Bubba's Bed and Bath Shop.
(b) Prepare the journal entry to record collections of $120, $40, and $100 from Nadine Adam, Connie Dawson, and Dale Bandy, respectively.
(c) Prepare the journal entry to record interest charged to customer accounts at the rate of 1.5% per month as follows: Connie Dawson, $3; Dale Bandy, $6.

SOLUTION TO EXERCISE 9-3

(a) 1. Cash 6,984
          Service Charge Expense (3% X $7,200) 216
               Sales Revenue   7,200
               (To record MasterCard and VISA sales)

     2. Accounts Receivable—Nadine Adam 120
         Accounts Receivable—Connie Dawson 240
         Accounts Receivable—Dale Bandy 500
               Sales Revenue   860
               (To record company credit card sales)

(b) Cash 260
          Accounts Receivable—Nadine Adam   120
          Accounts Receivable—Connie Dawson   40
          Accounts Receivable—Dale Bandy   100
          (To record collections on account)

(c) Accounts Receivable—Connie Dawson 3
     Accounts Receivable—Dale Bandy 6
          Interest Revenue   9
          (To record interest on amounts due)

EXERCISE 9-4

Purpose: (L.O. 4) This exercise will illustrate the factoring of accounts receivable.

The Tuscawilla Tailgate Company often factors its accounts receivable. On May 1, 2014, the company factored $250,000 of customer accounts receivable to Fagan Factors, Inc. which charged a 3% service charge.

Instructions
(a) Prepare the journal entry to record the sale of the accounts receivable to the factor.
(b) Explain how the service charge will affect Tuscawilla Tailgates' financial statements.

SOLUTION TO EXERCISE 9-4

(a) Cash.. 242,500
    Service Charge Expense... 7,500
        Accounts Receivable 250,000
        (To record the sale of accounts receivable)

(b) The service charge expense incurred should be reported as a selling expense (operating expense) on the income statement because the company often sells its receivables. If receivables were sold infrequently, the service charge expense may be classified in the Other Expenses and Losses section of the income statement.

EXERCISE 9-5

Purpose: (L.O. 6) This exercise reviews the journal entries for various transactions involving notes receivable.

The following transactions occurred during 2014 and pertain to the Aaron Retail Company.

June 1   Accepted a note from R. Greenblatt in settlement of his $2,000 account. The note is due in six months and bears interest at 12%.

July 1   Sold merchandise to C. Lynn for $5,000. Accepted a note due in nine months at 10%.

Oct. 1   Accepted a note from D. Gioia for $6,000 in settlement of his account receivable. The 10% note is due in 180 days.

Instructions
(a) Prepare the journal entries to record the receipt of each of the three notes.
(b) Indicate the due date of each note.
(c) Assume the first note is collected on its due date. Prepare the appropriate journal entry to record its collection.
(d) Assume the accounting period ends on December 31. Prepare the appropriate adjusting entry(s) at December 31, 2014, to record accrued interest on the second and third notes.
(e) Assume the second note is honored on its maturity date. Prepare the journal entry to record this transaction.
(f) Assume the third note is dishonored on its due date. Aaron expects eventual collection. Prepare the appropriate journal entry.

SOLUTION TO EXERCISE 9-5

(a) 2014

June	1	Notes Receivable—R. Greenblatt......................		2,000	
		Accounts Receivable—R. Greenblatt..........			2,000
		(To record acceptance of R. Greenblatt note)			
July	1	Notes Receivable—C. Lynn.............................		5,000	
		Sales Revenue			5,000
		(To record sale of merchandise and			
		acceptance of C. Lynn note)			
Oct.	1	Notes Receivable—D. Gioia		6,000	
		Accounts Receivable—D. Gioia			6,000
		(To record acceptance of D. Gioia note)			

(b) R. Greenblatt note is due on December 1, 2014.
    C. Lynn note is due on April 1, 2015.
    D. Gioia note is due on March 30, 2015.
        Computations for due date of D. Gioia note:

October (31 - 1 = 30)	30
November	30
December	31
January	31
February	28
Subtotal	151
March	30
Total	180

TIP: When the life of a note is expressed in terms of months, the due date is found by counting the months from the date of issue. A note drawn on the last day of a month matures on the last day of a subsequent month. When the due date is stated in terms of days, it is necessary to count the exact number of days to determine the maturity date. In counting, the day the note was issued is omitted but the due date is included.

(c) Dec. 1 Cash... 2,120
           Notes Receivable—R. Greenblatt..................... 2,000
           Interest Revenue 120
           (To record collection of note at maturity);
           ($2,000 X 12% X 6/12 = $120)

TIP: The formula for computing interest on an interest-bearing note is:

Face Value		Annual		Time in		
of	X	Interest	X	Terms of	=	Interest
Note		Rate		One Year		

(d) Dec.31 Interest Receivable 400

                        Interest Revenue 400

                        (To record six months of accrued interest on
                        the Lynn note and three months interest on the
                        Gioia note) ($5,000 X 10% X 6/12 = $250);
                        ($6,000 X 10% X 3/12 = $150); ($250 + $150
                        = $400)

TIP:	An interest rate is always stated in terms of an annual basis, unless otherwise indicated.

(e) 2015
    Apr. 1 Cash... 5,375

                   Notes Receivable—C. Lynn 5,000
                   Interest Receivable................................... 250
                   Interest Revenue 125
                   (To record collection of note at maturity);
                   ($5,000 X 10% X 9/12 = $375 interest for
                   9 mos.); ($5,000 + $375 = $5,375 total
                   cash collected); ($375 - $250 accrued
                   last year = $125 interest earned this year)

TIP:	A note is said to be **honored** when it is paid in full at its maturity date.

(f) 2015
    Mar. 30 Accounts Receivable—D. Gioia 6,300

                   Notes Receivable....................................... 6,000
                   Interest Revenue 150
                   Interest Receivable................................... 150
                     (To record the dishonor of the D. Gioia
                   note);
                   ($6,000 X 10% X 180/360 = $300);
                   ($300 - $150 = $150)

TIP:	A **dishonored note** is a note that was **not** paid in full at its maturity date. The maker defaulted on the note.
TIP:	No interest revenue would be recorded at this date if collection of the note was **not** expected.
TIP:	Review the terminology related to notes receivable: **Promissory note** is a written promise to pay a specified amount of money on demand or at a definite time. **Face value** is the principal amount of a note. **Maker** is the person who promises to pay money later. **Payee** is the person to whom the money is owed.
TIP:	**Interest** is always a function of time, rate, and balance. Always assume a 360-day year when computing interest (unless a 365-day year is specified). This assumption makes computations easier.

EXERCISE 9-6

Purpose: (L.O. 9) This exercise will review the measures used to evaluate the liquidity of accounts receivable.

The management of M. F. Specie Company is analyzing the entity's recent financial statements to determine the efficiency of the company's credit policies for customers. The following information is extracted from the statements:

Sales revenue	$930,000
Sales returns	30,000
Accounts receivable, 12/31/14	85,000
Accounts receivable, 12/31/13	60,000

Instructions
1.   Assuming all sales are credit sales (on account), compute the receivables turnover for 2014.
2.   Assuming the company's policy is to require payment within 30 days of invoicing a customer and invoices are sent within two days of a sale, explain whether the company's average collection period suggests that the company has weak or strong controls surrounding its credit-granting activity.

SOLUTION TO EXERCISE 9-6

1.   Receivables turnover $= \dfrac{\text{Net credit sales}}{\text{Average accounts receivable}}$

   Receivables turnover $= \dfrac{\$930,000 \ - \ \$30,000}{1/2(\$85,000 \ + \ \$60,000)} = 12.41$ times

2.   The average collection period of 29.41 days when compared to the typical 32 days between a sale date and the payment due date suggests that the company has adequate to strong controls surrounding its credit-granting activity.

   The average number of days to collect an account receivable is computed as follows:

   $$\dfrac{365 \text{ days}}{\text{Accounts receivable turnover ratio}} = \dfrac{365}{12.41 \text{ times}} = 29.41 \text{ days}$$

TIP: A **ratio** is an expression of the relationship of one item (or group of items) to a second item (or group of items). It is determined by dividing the first item (amount) by the second item (amount). The relationship may be expressed either as a percentage, a rate, or a simple proportion.

For example: If A is $100,000 and B is $25,000 the ratio of A to B can be expressed in several ways, such as the following:

A:B	A/B
4:1	4.00
4 to 1	$4.00
4 times	400%

The way in which the ratio is expressed depends on the particular ratio. If it is the current ratio, it would likely be expressed as a proportion (4:1 or 4 to 1) or as a rate (4 times). If it is the debt to stockholders' equity ratio, it would likely be expressed as a percentage (400%).

TIP: In this chapter we look at the financial ratio used to assess the liquidity of receivables-- the receivables turnover ratio. In **Chapter 6** we looked at the financial ratio used to assess the liquidity of inventory—the inventory turnover ratio. In the remaining chapters of this book, be alert for discussions of other financial ratios.

TIP: The **average collection period** is not very meaningful until it is compared with the company's credit terms.

TIP: The denominator of a turnover ratio (such as for receivables) always involves an **average** balance. That average can be determined by adding the balance at the end of the period to the balance at the beginning of the period and dividing by 2. However, if seasonal variances are significant, the annual average should be determined by adding together the balances at the end of each month and dividing by 12.

EXERCISE 9-7

Purpose: (L.O. 1 thru 9) This exercise will quiz you about terminology used in this chapter.

A list of accounting terms with which you should be familiar appears below.

Accounts receivable	Maker
Accounts receivable turnover	Notes receivable
Aging the accounts receivable	Other receivables
Allowance method	Payee
Average collection period	Percentage-of-receivables basis
Bad Debts Expense	Percentage-of-sales basis
Cash (net) realizable value	Promissory note
Direct write-off method	Receivables
Dishonored (defaulted) note	Trade receivables
Factor	

Instructions
For each item below, enter in the blank the term that is described.

1. _____Amounts due from individuals and other companies.

2. _____Amounts owed by customers on account.

3. _____Written promise from another party (as evidenced by a formal instrument) for an amount to be received from them.

4. _____Various forms of nontrade receivables, such as interest receivable and income taxes refundable.

5. _____The analysis of customer balances by the length of time they have been unpaid.

6. _____Management establishes a percentage relationship between the expected losses from uncollectible accounts and the amount of receivables.

7. _____Management establishes a percentage relationship between expected losses from uncollectible accounts and the amount of credit sales.

8. _____The net amount expected to be received in cash.

9. _____A written promise to pay a specified amount of money on demand or at a definite time.

10. _____The party in a promissory note who is making the promise to pay.

11. _____The party to whom payment of a promissory note to be made.

12. _____A note that is not paid in full at maturity.

13. _____A finance company or bank that buys receivables from businesses and then collects the payments directly from the customers.

14. _____Notes and accounts receivable that result from sales transactions.

15. _____A measure of the liquidity of accounts receivables, computed by dividing net credit sales by average net accounts receivables.

16. _____The average amount of time that a receivable is outstanding, calculated by dividing 365 days by the accounts receivable turnover.

17. _____An expense account used to record the cost of uncollectible receivables.

18. _____A method of accounting for bad debts that involves expensing accounts at the time they are determined to be uncollectible.

19. _____A method of accounting for bad debts that involves estimating uncollectible accounts at the end of each period.

SOLUTION TO EXERCISE 9-7

1. Receivables
2. Accounts receivable
3. Notes receivable
4. Other receivables
5. Aging the accounts receivable
6. Percentage-of-receivables basis
7. Percentage-of-sales basis
8. Cash (net) realizable value
9. Promissory note
10. Maker
11. Payee
12. Dishonored (defaulted) note
13. Factor
14. Trade receivables
15. Accounts receivable turnover
16. Average collection period
17. Bad Debts Expense
18. Direct write-off method
19. Allowance method

ANALYSIS OF MULTIPLE-CHOICE TYPE QUESTIONS

1.   (L.O. 3) The journal entry to record the write-off of an individual customer's account receivable using the allowance method involves a debit to:
a.   Allowance for Doubtful Accounts and a credit to Accounts Receivable.
b.   Bad Debt Expense and a credit to Accounts Receivable.
c.   Accounts Receivable and a credit to Allowance for Doubtful Accounts.
d.   Bad Debt Expense and a credit to Allowance for Doubtful Accounts.

Approach and Explanation: Write down the journal entry to record the write-off of an individual customer's account:

Allowance for Doubtful Accounts   XXX
        Accounts Receivable   XXX

Find the answer selection that describes this entry. Answer selection "d" describes the journal entry to record bad debts expense and to adjust the allowance account. (Solution = a.)

2.   (L.O. 3) The balances of the Accounts Receivable account and Allowance for Doubtful Accounts account, before adjustment, are $60,000 and $1,200 respectively. Bad debt expense for the period is estimated to be $3,100. What amount should be reported for net accounts receivable on the balance sheet?
a. $58,100.
b. $58,800.
c. $56,900.
d. $55,700.

Approach and Explanation: One approach is to draw T-accounts, enter the balances before adjustment, reflect in the accounts the entry to record bad debt expense, balance the accounts, and deduct the balance of the contra account from the balance of the Accounts Receivable account to determine net accounts receivable at the balance sheet date.

Accounts Receivable	Allowance for Doubtful Accounts	Bad Debt Expense
60,000	1,200	Adjust. 3,100
	Adjust. 3,100	
	Bal. 4,300	

$60,000 Accounts receivable - $4,300 Allowance = $55,700 Net accounts receivable. (Solution = d.)

3.   (L.O. 3) The journal entry to record uncollectible accounts expense using the allowance method will:
a.   reduce net income and total current assets.
b.   reduce net income but will not affect total current assets.
c.   not affect net income but will reduce total current assets.
d.   not affect net income or total current assets.

Approach and Explanation: Before you read all of the answer choices, write down the journal entry to record bad debt expense (uncollectible accounts expense is synonymous to bad debt expense). Analyze both parts of the entry (one part at a time) to determine the impact on (1) net income and (2) current assets.

		Effect on Net Income	Effect on Current Assets
Bad Debt Expense	5,000	Decrease $5,000	No Effect
Allowance for Doubtful Accounts	5,000	No Effect	Decrease $5,000
Net effect of entry		Decrease $5,000	Decrease $5,000

The amount used in the entry can be any assumed amount since no amount was specified. (Solution = a.)

4.   (L.O. 3) The journal entry to write off an individual customer's account receivable using the allowance method will:
a.   reduce net income and total current assets.
b.   reduce net income but will not affect total current assets.
c.   not affect net income but will reduce total current assets.
d.   not affect net income or total current assets.

Approach and Explanation: Write down the journal entry to write off an individual customer's account. Analyze each part of the entry to determine its impact on (1) net income and (2) current assets. Summarize the effects and locate the correct answer selection. Assume any amount you want for the entry since no amount was specified in the question.

		Effect on Net Income	Effect on Current Assets
Allowance for Doubtful Accounts	5,000	No Effect	Increase $5,000
Accounts Receivable	5,000	No Effect	Decrease $5,000
Net effect of entry		No Effect	No Effect

(Solution = d.)

5.   (L.O. 3) The balance of the Allowance for Doubtful Accounts account represents the:
a.   total amount of uncollectible accounts written off to date.
b.   amount of credit sales made this period that has not been collected.
c.   amount of cash that has been set aside in a special fund to make up for bad debt losses.
d.   portion of total accounts receivable that is not expected to be converted to cash.

Approach and Explanation: Think about what prompts entries to the valuation (allowance) account for accounts receivable. The allowance is increased when the provision for bad debt (expense) is recorded. The allowance is decreased when an individual account is ultimately deemed to be uncollectible. The provision is recorded because some yet unidentified portion of receivables arising from credit sales will never be collected (hence, will never be converted to cash). Selection "c" is false because cash is not involved in the entry to set up the allowance; no fund is set aside for this purpose. (Solution = d.)

6. (L.O. 3) The balance of the Allowance for Doubtful Accounts account at January 1, 2014 was $5,900. During 2014, accounts receivable amounting to $8,000 were written off. Estimated uncollectible accounts expense for 2014 amounts to $7,100. The balance of the Allowance for Doubtful Accounts account to be reported on the balance sheet at December 31, 2014 is:
    a. $13,000.
    b. $ 7,100.
    c. $ 6,800.
    d. $ 5,000.

    Approach and Explanation: Draw a T-account for the account in question. Visualize the journal entries to write off accounts and to estimate bad debt expense. Enter the resulting postings as they would be reflected in the allowance account.

    Allowance for Doubtful Accounts

Write-offs, 2014	8,000	Balance, 1/1/14	5,900
		Expense, 2014	7,100
		Balance, 12/31/14	5,000

    It is evident that the company is using the percentage-of-sales basis of applying the allowance method because its entry to the allowance account is based on the amount of bad debts expense rather than an appropriate ending balance for the allowance account. (Solution = d.)

7. (L.O. 3) The following data are available for 2014:

Sales, cash	$200,000
Sales, credit	500,000
Accounts Receivable, January 1	80,000
Accounts Receivable, December 31	72,000
Allowance for Doubtful Accounts, January 1	4,000
Accounts written off during 2014	4,600

    The journal entry to record bad debt expense for the period and to adjust the allowance account is to be based on an estimate of 1% of credit sales. The entry to record the uncollectible accounts expense for 2014 would include a debit to the Bad Debt Expense account for:
    a. $7,200.
    b. $5,600.
    c. $4,400.
    d. $5,000.

    Approach and Explanation: Think about the emphasis of the entry when the percentage-of-sales basis is used. This basis emphasizes the income statement. Therefore, 1% times credit sales equals expense. $500,000 X 1% = $5,000. The balance of the allowance account before adjustment does **not** affect this computation or entry. (Solution = d.)

8. (L.O. 3) The following data are available for 2014:

Sales, cash	$200,000
Sales, credit	500,000
Accounts Receivable, January 1	80,000
Accounts Receivable, December 31	72,000
Allowance for Doubtful Accounts, January 1	4,000
Accounts written off during 2014	4,600

The journal entry to record bad debt expense for the period and to adjust the allowance account is to be based on an aging analysis of accounts receivable. The aging analysis of accounts receivable at December 31, 2014, reveals that $5,200 of existing accounts receivable are estimated to be uncollectible. The entry to record the uncollectible accounts expense for 2014 will involve a debit to the Bad Debt Expense account for:

a. $9,800.
b. $5,800.
c. $5,200.
d. $4,600.

Approach and Explanation: An aging analysis is performed to determine the best figure to represent the cash (net) realizable value for accounts receivable in the balance sheet. Thus, $5,200 is the desirable balance for the allowance account at the reporting date. Determine the existing balance in the allowance account and the adjusting entry needed to arrive at the predetermined balance.

Allowance for Doubtful Accounts

Write-offs, 2014	4,600	Balance, 1/1/14	4,000	
				Entry
Balance before adjustment	600	Adjustment needed	X	←needed.
		Desired bal. at 12/31/14	5,200	

Solving for X: X - $600 = $5,200
X = $5,200 + $600
X = $5,800 (Solution = b.)

9. (L.O. 3) Gatorland recorded bad debt expense of $30,000 and wrote off accounts receivable of $25,000 during 2014. The net effect of these two transactions on net income was a decrease of:

a. $55,000.
b. $30,000.
c. $25,000.
d. $5,000.

Approach and Explanation: Reconstruct both entries referred to in the question. Then analyze each debit and each credit separately as to its effect on net income.

			Effect on Net Income
Bad Debt Expense	30,000		Decrease $30,000
Allowance for Doubtful Accounts		30,000	No Effect
Allowance for Doubtful Accounts	25,000		No Effect
Accounts Receivable		25,000	No Effect
Net effect of entries			Decrease $30,000

(Solution = b.)

10. (L.O. 3) Chelser Corporation performed an analysis and an aging of its accounts receivable at December 31, 2014 which disclosed the following:

Accounts receivable balance	$100,000
Allowance for doubtful accounts balance	5,000
Accounts deemed uncollectible	7,400

The cash (net) realizable value of the accounts receivable at December 31 is:
a. $87,600.
b. $92,600.
c. $95,000.
d. $97,600.

Approach and Explanation: Read the last sentence of the question. "The cash (net) realizable value of the accounts receivable at December 31 is." Underline cash (net) realizable value of accounts receivable. Write down the definition of cash (net) realizable value of accounts receivable—amount of accounts receivable ultimately expected to be converted into cash. Read the details of the question. If an aging shows $7,400 of the $100,000 accounts receivable are deemed uncollectible, then the remaining $92,600 are expected to be converted into cash. (Because the balance of the allowance account does not agree with the amount of uncollectibles per the aging, the allowance for doubtful accounts balance must be the unadjusted balance or the percentage of sales method is being used to determine the amount to record as bad debts expense.) (Solution = b.)

11. (L.O. 5) The term "maker" as it applies to a promissory note refers to the:
a. payee.
b. lender.
c. borrower.
d. seller.

Approach and Explanation: Think about the terminology related to a promissory note:
Face value or face amount: Denomination of note. Principal.
Maker or borrower: Entity promising to pay face amount plus interest.
Payee: Entity to receive face value plus interest.
(Solution = c.)

12. (L.O. 5) A note receivable with a face value of $20,000 was received from a customer. The note was dated April 1, 2014 and becomes due on April 1, 2015. Interest of 12% is payable at the maturity date. The income statement for the calendar year of 2014 should report interest income (or interest revenue) for this note of:
   a. $0.
   b. $600.
   c. $1,800.
   d. $2,400.

   Approach and Explanation: Write down the formula for the computation of interest. Fill in the amounts known and solve for the unknown.

$$\text{Face Value X Rate X Time} \quad = \text{Interest}$$
$$\$20,000 \ X \ 12\% \ X \ 9/12 \quad = \$1,800$$

   Interest would be accrued for the time between April 1, 2014 and December 31, 2014, which is nine months. (Solution = c.)

13. (L.O. 6) The journal entry to adjust for the accrued interest on a note receivable involves:
   a. a debit to Interest Revenue and a credit to Notes Receivable.
   b. a debit to Interest Receivable and a credit to Notes Receivable.
   c. a debit to Interest Receivable and a credit to Interest Revenue.
   d. a debit to Interest Expense and a credit to Interest Payable.

   Approach and Explanation: Recall that an accrued revenue is revenue that has been earned but not received. The adjusting entry to record an accrued revenue will increase revenue (record earned revenue) and increase a receivable (record the fact that the earned revenue has not been received.) Therefore, debit a receivable account and credit a revenue account. (Solution = c.)

14. (L.O. 8) If a maker of a note fails to pay the amount due on the due date (defaults), the note is said to be:
   a. uncollectible.
   b. discounted.
   c. dishonored.
   d. due on demand.

   Explanation: A note is said to be honored when it is paid in full at the maturity date. A dishonored note is a note that is **not** paid in full at maturity. (Solution = c.)

15. (L.O. 8) A note receivable with a face value of $10,000 was received from a customer in connection with a sale of merchandise on October 1, 2014. The note has a stated interest rate of 12% and the principal and interest are both due on October 1, 2015. An appropriate adjusting entry was made on December 31, 2014, the end of the annual accounting period. No reversing entry was recorded on January 1, 2015. The journal entry to record the collection of the principal plus interest on October 1, 2015 will involve a credit to:
  a. Notes Receivable for $11,200.
  b. Interest Revenue for $1,200.
  c. Interest Revenue for $900.
  d. Cash for $11,200.

Approach and Explanation: Prepare the journal entry to record the collection of the principal plus interest on October 1, 2015. That entry is as follows:

Cash	11,200	
Notes Receivable		10,000
Interest Receivable...		300
Interest Revenue		900

$10,000 X 12% X 3/12 = $300 interest accrued at December 31, 2014:
$10,000 X 12% X 9/12 = $900 interest earned in 2015.
$10,000 + ($10,000 X 12%) = $11,200 total cash collected.
(Solution = c.)

TIP: If a reversing entry had been made on January 1, 2015, to reverse the prior period's accrual, the entry on October 1, 2015, would include a credit to Interest Revenue for $1,200 and no credit to Interest Receivable.

---

16. (L.O. 9) When the multiple-step format is used by Petite Clothiers Company for the income statement, bad debt expense (arising from sales to customers using the Petite Clothiers credit card) and service charge expense (arising from sales to customers using the VISA credit card) are to be:
  a. included with cost of goods sold.
  b. reported as selling expenses.
  c. reported as contra sales revenue items.
  d. reported as "other expenses" in the nonoperating section.

Explanation: Bad debt expense and service charge expense are to be classified as selling expenses; the "selling expenses" classification is a subsclassification of operating expenses. Thus, bad debt expense and service charge expense are **not** included with cost of goods sold expense or with nonoperating expenses and losses. (Solution = b.)

17. (L.O. 9) Zollo Corporation's net accounts receivable were $500,000 at December 31, 2013 and $600,000 at December 31, 2014. The accounts receivable turnover was 5.0 for 2014 and net cash sales for 2014 were $200,000. Zollo's total net sales for 2014 were:
  a. $2,750,000.
  b. $2,950,000.
  c. $3,200,000.
  d. $5,000,000.

Approach and Explanation: Write down the formula for computing the accounts receivable turnover. Enter the data given and solve for the unknown (net credit sales). Add net cash sales ($200,000) to net credit sales ($2,750,000) to obtain total net sales ($2,950,000). The formula for the accounts receivable turnover ratio is:

$$\frac{\text{Net credit sales}}{\text{Average accounts receivable}} = \frac{X}{1/2(\$500,000 + \$600,000)} = 5.0$$

$$\frac{X}{\$550,000} = 5.0 \qquad X = \$2,750,000$$

(Solution = b.)

CHAPTER 10

· ·

*P*LANT ASSETS, NATURAL RESOURCES, AND INTANGIBLE ASSETS

OVERVIEW

Assets that have physical existence and that are expected to be used in revenue-generating operations for more than one year or operating cycle, whichever is longer, are classified as plant assets. Some problems may arise in determining the acquisition cost of a plant asset. For example, the initial acquisition may be the result of several expenditures or additional expenditures may be involved subsequent to acquisition.

Expenses arise from the cost of goods or services that are consumed in the process of generating revenue. When a long-term tangible asset (plant asset) is acquired, it actually represents a bundle of future asset services. The total cost of these services equals the acquisition cost of the asset minus the asset's expected market value at the end of its useful life. As a productive asset is used, services (benefits) are consumed; therefore, a portion of the original asset cost should be charged to expense, in order to comply with the expense recognition (matching principle). The process of allocating (expensing) the cost of long-term tangible assets over the accounting periods during which the asset is used is called depreciation.

An entity commonly disposes of plant assets before or at the end of their estimated service lives. The disposal may be by retirement, sale or exchange. The asset's fair value will usually differ from its book value at the date of disposal, and this difference usually results in recognizing a gain or loss on disposal.

Companies which extract natural resources from the earth must account for the acquisition cost of the wasting assets and determine the cost of units extracted and sold during the period.

Intangible means "lack of physical substance." The balance sheet classification for intangible assets is used to report assets which lack physical existence and are not properly classifiable elsewhere. For instance (1) bank deposits and accounts receivable both are intangible by a legal definition but they are properly classifiable as current assets for accounting purposes, and (2) investment in stock is intangible in nature but should be classified as either a current asset or a long-term investment for accounting purposes. Assets such as patents, trademarks, copyrights, franchises, licenses, and goodwill are intangible in nature and are classified in the intangible asset section of a balance sheet.

The subjects mentioned above along with other issues involved in accounting for plant assets, natural resources, and intangible assets are discussed in this chapter.

SUMMARY OF LEARNING OBJECTIVES

1. **Describe how the historical cost principle applies to plant assets.** The cost of a plant asset includes all expenditures necessary to acquire the asset and make it ready for its intended use. Once cost is established, the company uses that amount as the basis of accounting for the plant asset over its useful life.

2. **Explain the concept of depreciation, and how to compute it.** Depreciation is the allocation of the cost of a plant asset to expense over its limited useful (service) life in a rational and systematic manner. Depreciation is **not** a process of valuation, and it is **not** a process that results in an accumulation of cash. A limited service life for an asset (and the resulting depreciation) is caused by wear and tear or by obsolescence.

   Three depreciation methods are:

Method	Effect on Annual Depreciation	Formula
Straight-line	Constant amount	Depreciable cost ÷ Useful life (in years)
Units-of-activity	Varying amount	Depreciable cost per unit X Units of activity during the year
Declining-balance	Decreasing amount	Book value at beginning of year X Declining-balance rate

   Companies make revisions of periodic depreciation in present and future periods, not retroactively. When the straight-line depreciation method is used, they determine the new annual depreciation by dividing the depreciable cost at the time of the revision by the remaining useful life.

3. **Distinguish between revenue and capital expenditures, and explain the entries for each.** Companies incur **revenue expenditures** to maintain the operating efficiency and expected productive life of the asset. They debit these expenditures to Repair Expense as incurred. **Capital expenditures** add new asset services or increase the operating efficiency, productive capacity, or expected useful life of the asset. Companies generally debit these expenditures to the plant asset affected.

4. **Explain how to account for the disposal of a plant asset.** The accounting for disposal of a plant asset through retirement or sale is as follows:
   (a) Eliminate the book value of the plant asset at the date of disposal.

(b)   Record cash proceeds, if any.

(c)   Account for the difference between the book value and the cash proceeds as a gain or loss on disposal.

5.   **Compute periodic depletion of natural resources.**   Companies compute depletion cost per unit by dividing the total cost of the natural resources minus salvage value by the number of units estimated to be in the tract of natural resources. They then multiply the depletion cost per unit by the number of units extracted and sold.

6.   **Explain the basic issues related to accounting for intangible assets.**   The term used to describe the allocation of the cost of an intangible asset to expense is **amortization.** The cost of an intangible asset with an indefinite life is **not** amortized. Companies generally use the straight-line method for amortizing intangible assets.

7.   **Indicate how plant assets, natural resources, and intangible assets are reported.**   Usually, companies combine plant assets and natural resources under the property, plant, and equipment classification. They show intangibles separately under intangible assets. Either within the balance sheet or in the notes, companies should disclose: (1) the balances of the major classes of assets, such as land, buildings, and equipment, and (2) accumulated depreciation by major classes or in total. In addition, they should describe the depreciation and amortization methods used and the amount of depreciation and amortization expense for the period. The asset turnover measures the productivity of a company's assets in generating sales.

*8.   **Explain how to account for the exchange of plant assets.** Ordinarily companies record a gain or loss on the exchange of plant assets. The rationale for recognizing a gain or loss is that most exchanges have commercial substance. An exchange has commercial substance if the future cash flows change significantly as a result of the exchange.

*This material appears in the **Appendix 10A** in the text.

TIPS ON CHAPTER TOPICS

TIP: **Plant assets** is a balance sheet classification that is often referred to as **fixed assets** or **property, plant and equipment.** Included in this section should be long-lived tangible assets that are currently being used in operations (to generate goods and services for customers). Examples include land, land improvements, buildings, and equipment.

TIP: In determining the cost of a plant asset, keep in mind the guideline used for inventory, the asset's **cost** includes all costs necessary to get the item to the condition and location for its intended use.

TIP: In determining the cost of a plant asset, keep in mind the historical cost principle. **Cost** is measured by the cash paid or cash equivalent value. When cash is given to acquire an asset, it is a relatively simple matter to determine the asset's cost. However, when a noncash asset is given in exchange, more thought is required to determine the newly acquired asset's cost.

TIP: The cost of tearing down an old building should be charged (debited) to the Land account if the building was someone else's old building and was acquired along with a parcel of land in a case where the land was intended to be used as a site for another structure. This cost is charged to Land because it is necessary to get the land in the condition for its intended purpose—to provide space upon which to erect a new building. (Any proceeds from material salvaged in the removal is considered to be a reduction of land cost.) The cost of tearing down an old building is **never** charged to the Building account.

TIP: In the context of accounting for property, plant, and equipment, the term **"to capitalize"** means to record and carryforward into one or more periods expenditures from which benefits or proceeds will be realized; thus, a balance sheet account is debited for capital expenditures.

TIP: **Salvage value** is often referred to as **residual value,** and sometimes is called **estimated scrap value.**

TIP: Salvage value is used in the computation of depreciation for each year of life of an asset whenever the straight-line method or the units-of-activity method is used. Salvage value is **not** a factor in determining depreciation for the early years of life if a declining-balance method is used; however, salvage value can effect the amount computed for depreciation in the last year(s) of an asset's life because an asset should **not** be depreciated below its salvage value.

TIP: Most plant assets have a limited service (useful) life because the asset will lose its utility or usefulness over time due to wear and tear and/or obsolescence. Land does not lose its utility; thus, it has an unlimited life and is **not** depreciated.

TIP: The **units-of-activity method** is often called the **units-of-output method** or the **units-of-production method.**

TIP: The **book value** of a plant asset is determined by deducting the balance of accumulated depreciation from the balance of the related asset account. The balance in the related asset account is generally the asset's original cost. Thus, the estimated salvage value does not directly affect the book value computation. Book value for a plant asset is often called **carrying value** or **carrying amount** or **undepreciated cost**. An asset's book value at a given date may be far different than its market value at the same date.

TIP: Depreciable cost or depreciation base is a term that refers to the total amount to be depreciated over the useful life of the asset. It is determined by deducting the estimated salvage value from the cost of the asset.

TIP: The **declining-balance depreciation method** applies a constant rate to a declining book value to calculate depreciation. The rate used is often twice the straight-line rate in which case the method is then referred to as the **200% declining-balance method** or the **double-declining-balance method.** Sometimes the rate is one and one-half times the straight-line rate in which case the method is called the **150% declining-balance method.**

TIP: For each class of depreciable plant assets, an entity must select the most appropriate depreciation method. The same method should then be used for subsequent periods for financial reporting purposes in order to comply with the **consistency concept.** However, a different method may be used for the same assets for tax purposes.

TIP: The annual rate of depreciation using the straight-line method can be determined by dividing 100% by the estimated service life. For example, an asset with a 5-year life will be depreciated 20% (100% ÷ 5 = 20%) per year.

TIP: When a plant asset is retired from service or sold, it must be removed from the accounts; hence, the appropriate asset account is credited for the amount of the asset's original cost, and the related accumulated depreciation account is debited for the total depreciation recorded on that asset to date. Cash is debited for the amount of net proceeds, if any, from the disposal. An excess of book value over cash proceeds is recorded by a debit to a loss account; an excess of cash proceeds over book value is recorded by a credit to a gain account.

TIP: Depreciation must be updated before an asset disposal can be properly recorded. Additional depreciation recorded in such an update impacts the determination of the amount of gain or loss experienced on disposal.

TIP: A gain on disposal of plant assets is reported in the Other Revenues and Gains section of the income statement. A loss on disposal of plant assets is reported in the Other Expenses and Losses section of the income statement.

TIP: **Fair market value** is a term that refers to an item's current value; the price at which a seller who is willing to sell at a fair price and a buyer who is willing to buy at a fair price will trade, assuming both parties have knowledge of the facts and bargain in his or her own self-interest. The terms **market value** or **fair value** are often used to indicate fair market value.

TIP: **Natural resources** are often called **wasting assets.** They include tracts of resources still attached to the earth, such as oil in an oil well, minerals in a mine, and trees in a forest.

TIP: Research and development (R & D) costs are to be expensed in the period incurred. The Financial Accounting Standards Board established this guideline after a study revealed that very few R & D projects ever culminate in a successfully marketed product. When great uncertainty exists, the **conservatism convention** dictates that we choose the alternative with the least favorable effect on net income and on assets.

ILLUSTRATION 10-1
CAPITAL EXPENDITURES VS. REVENUE EXPENDITURES (L.O. 3)

The terms, capital expenditure and revenue expenditure, are used in the context of accounting for property, plant, and equipment. A **capital expenditure** is one which is expected to benefit two or more accounting periods. A **revenue expenditure** is one whose benefits are not expected to extend beyond the current period. Thus a revenue expenditure benefits only the current period or no period at all.

Capital expenditures are recorded by increasing an asset account (or by decreasing the balance of the Accumulated Depreciation account). If an asset is of limited life, its cost is depreciated (expensed) over the periods which will be benefited (to comply with the matching principle). Because a revenue expenditure does not yield benefits beyond the current period, it is recorded as an expense in the period it is made.

The distinction between capital and revenue expenditures is of significance because it involves the timing of the recognition of expense and, consequently, the determination of periodic net income. This distinction also affects the costs reflected in asset accounts which will be recovered from future periods' revenues.

Examples of capital expenditures include the acquisition of land, land improvements, building and/or equipment. Examples of revenue expenditures include outlays for maintenance and repair services.

The **acquisition cost for a plant asset** includes all costs necessary to acquire the item and get it in the location and condition for its intended use.

The **acquisition cost of land** may include costs such as:
(1)   purchase price.
(2)   survey fees.
(3)   attorney fees and escrow fees.
(4)   delinquent property taxes and interest assumed by buyer.
(5)   real estate broker's commission.

(6)   title search fees and recording fees.
(7)   cost of clearing, grading, filling, and draining).
(8)   cost of removing old building (less salvage).
(9)   landscaping of a permanent nature.

TIP:	Typically, the cost of land includes the cost of elements that occur prior to excavation for a new building. Costs related to the foundation of the building are elements of building cost.

The acquisition cost of land improvements may include costs such as:
(1)   parking lots.
(2)   fencing.
(3)   lighting.
(4)   driveways.
(5)   underground sprinklers.

The **acquisition cost of a building** may include costs such as:
(1)   construction costs.
(2)   excavation fees.
(3)   architectural fees and building permit fees.
(4)   cost of insurance during construction (if paid by property owner).
(5)   property taxes and interest during construction.
(6)   purchase price plus all costs incurred to make building ready for intended use.

The **acquisition cost of equipment** may include costs such as:
(1)   purchase price (less discounts allowed).
(2)   sales tax.
(3)   freight charges and installation charges.
(4)   insurance during transit.
(5)   cost of labor and materials for test runs (breaking-in costs).
(6)   cost of special platforms.

An expenditure that relates to property, plant, and equipment already in use (often called an **expenditure subsequent to acquisition**) should be capitalized (recorded by a debit to a balance sheet account rather than an income statement account) if the expenditure is:
(1)   Material in nature and
(2)   Nonrecurring in nature and
(3)   Of benefit to future periods by doing one of the following:
   a.   Extending the useful life of an existing plant asset.
   b.   Enhancing the quality of existing services or increasing the productive capacity of an existing asset.
   c.   Adding new asset services.
   d.   Reducing the operating costs of existing assets thereby increasing operating efficiency.

Examples of expenditures subsequent to acquisition that should be capitalized are additions, improvements, and betterments. These expenditures should be debited to an asset account.

EXERCISE 10-1

Purpose: (L.O. 1, 3) This exercise will help you identify which expenditures should be capitalized (debited to a balance sheet account) and which should be expensed (charged to an income statement account).

TIP:	Remember that expenditures which benefit the company for more than the current accounting period should be capitalized in order to properly match expenses with revenues over successive accounting periods. Expenditures for items that do **not** yield benefits beyond the current accounting period should be expensed.

Instructions

Assume all amounts are material (significant). For each of the following independent items, indicate by use of the appropriate letter if it should be:

C for Capitalized

or

E for Expensed

_____   1.   Invoice price of drill press.

_____   2.   Sales tax on computer.

_____   3.   Costs of permanent partitions constructed in office building.

_____   4.   Installation charges for new conveyer system.

_____   5.   Costs of trees and shrubs planted in front of office building.

_____   6.   Cost of surveying new land site to determine property boundaries.

_____   7.   Costs of major overhaul of delivery truck which extends the life of the truck.

_____   8.   Costs of constructing new counters for show room.

_____   9.   Costs of powders, soaps, and wax for office floors.

_____   10.   Cost of janitorial services for office and show room.

_____   11.   Costs of carpets in a new office building.

_____   12.   Costs of annual termite inspection of warehouse.

_____ 13. Insurance charged for new equipment while in transit.

_____ 14. Property taxes on land used for parking lot.

_____ 15. Cost of a fan installed to help cool an old factory machine.

_____ 16. Cost of exterminator's services.

_____ 17. Costs of major redecorating of executive's offices.

_____ 18. Cost of fertilizers for shrubs and trees.

_____ 19. Cost of labor services for self-constructed machine.

_____ 20. Costs of materials used and labor services expended during trial runs of new machine.

SOLUTION TO EXERCISE 10-1

1.	C	6.	C	11.	C	16.	E
2.	C	7.	C	12.	E	17.	C
3.	C	8.	C	13.	C	18.	E*
4.	C	9.	E*	14.	E	19.	C
5.	C	10.	E	15.	C	20.	C

*This answer assumes the products were consumed during the current period. Material (significant) amounts of unused supplies on hand at the balance sheet date should be reported as a prepaid expense on the balance sheet.

Approach: Refer to **Illustration 10-1** for a discussion of capital expenditures versus revenue expenditures.

EXERCISE 10-2

Purpose: (L.O. 1, 3) This exercise will give you practice in identifying capital expenditures and revenue expenditures.

Sellen Supply Company, a newly formed corporation, incurred the following expenditures related to Land, Buildings, and Equipment.

Abstract company's fee for title search		$ 520
Architect's fees		10,200
Cash paid for land and dilapidated building thereon		100,000
Removal of old building	$20,000	
Less salvage	5,500	14,500
Surveying before construction		370
Excavation before construction for basement		19,000
Machinery purchased		55,000
Freight on machinery purchased		1,340
New building constructed		500,000
Assessment by city for drainage project		1,600
Installation of machinery		2,000
Trees, shrubs, and other landscaping after completion of building (permanent in nature)		5,400

Instructions
(a) Identify the amounts that should be debited to Land.
(b) Identify the amounts that should be debited to Buildings.
(c) Identify the amounts that should be debited to Equipment.

SOLUTION TO EXERCISE 10-2

	(a) Land	(b) Buildings	(c) Equipment
Abstract fees	$ 520		
Architect's fees		$ 10,200	
Cash paid for land and old building	100,000		
Removal of old building ($20,000 - $5,500)	14,500		
Surveying before construction		370	
Excavation before construction		19,000	
Machinery purchased			$55,000
Freight on machinery			1,340
New building		500,000	
Assessment by city	1,600		
Installation—machinery			2,000
Landscaping	5,400		
Totals	$122,020	$529,570	$58,340

Approach: Refer to **Illustration 10-1** and review the common cost elements for land, building, and equipment.

EXERCISE 10-3

Purpose: (L.O. 2) This exercise will allow you to practice using various depreciation methods and it will also give you the opportunity to compare the results of using one method to the results of using another method.

On January 1, 2014, Kinka Company, a manufacturer, acquires for $230,000 a piece of new equipment. The new equipment has a useful life of five years and the salvage value is estimated to be $30,000. Kinka estimates that the new equipment can produce a total of 80,000 units. Kinka expects it to produce 20,000 units in its first year, 18,000 units in its second year, 32,000 units in its third year, and 5,000 units each in its last two years.

The following depreciation methods are being considered:
*   Straight-line
*   Declining-balance using double the straight-line rate
*   Units-of-activity

Instructions
(a) Prepare depreciation schedules for the equipment using the following methods:
   (1)   straight-line
   (2)   double-declining-balance
   (3)   units-of-activity
   Each schedule should display the annual depreciation expense for each year of service life and the resulting amounts of accumulated depreciation and book value. Round to the nearest dollar.

(b) Identify the depreciation method which would result in the maximization of profits for financial reporting for the three-year period ending December 31, 2016. Explain why.

(c) Identify the depreciation method which would result in the highest book value at the end of the third year of service life.

(d) Identify the depreciation method which would result in the lowest book value at the end of the third year of service life.

SOLUTION TO EXERCISE 10-3

(a) (1)

KINKA COMPANY
Depreciation Schedule Using Straight-Line Method

	Computation			End of Year	
Year	Depreciable Cost[a]	X Depreciation Rate[b]	= Annual Depreciation Expense	Accumulated Depreciation[c]	Book Value[d]
2014	$200,000	20%	$ 40,000	$ 40,000	$190,000
2015	200,000	20%	40,000	80,000	150,000
2016	200,000	20%	40,000	120,000	110,000
2017	200,000	20%	40,000	160,000	70,000
2018	200,000	20%	40,000	200,000	30,000
			$200,000		

[a]Depreciable cost is original cost ($230,000) less estimated salvage ($30,000).
[b]Depreciation rate (straight-line) equals 100% divided by the estimated service life (5 years).
[c]Accumulated depreciation is the total depreciation expense reported to date. Thus, the accumulated depreciation at the end of the first year is equal to the depreciation expense for that first year. The accumulated depreciation at the end of the second year is equal to the total of the depreciation expense figures for the first and second years.
[d]Book value is determined by the original cost less the depreciation taken to date (accumulated depreciation). Thus, book value at the end of the first year is $230,000 - $40,000 = $190,000. Book value at the end of 2018 is $230,000 - $200,000 = $30,000 (the $30,000 is the estimated salvage value).

(2)

KINKA COMPANY
Depreciation Schedule Using Double-Declining-Balance Method

	Computation			End of Year	
Year	Book Value Beginning of Year[a]	X Depreciation Rate[b]	= Annual Depreciation Expense	Accumulated Depreciation	Book Value
2014	$230,000	40%	$ 92,000	$ 92,000	$138,000
2015	138,000	40%	55,200	147,200	82,800
2016	82,800	40%	33,120	180,320	49,680
2017	49,680	40%	19,680[c]	200,000	30,000
2018	30,000		-0- [c]	200,000	30,000
			$200,000		

[a]Book value is original cost less accumulated depreciation. The book value of the asset at the beginning of the asset's first year is the asset's acquisition cost.
[b]The depreciation rate is a multiple of the straight-line rate. The straight-line rate is 100% divided by the 5-year service life which is 20%. The depreciation rate for the double declining-balance method is twice the straight-line rate. 2 X 20% = 40%.
[c]An asset is not to be depreciated below its residual value.

> **TIP:** An asset is not depreciated below its residual (salvage) value. Because of the relatively high salvage value in this case, use of the double-declining-balance method resulted in reaching a book value equal to the residual value by the end of the fourth year of service. Because it makes good accounting sense to match some cost with every year of service, it is a common practice (in cases such as this) to use the double-declining-balance method to the mid-point in the asset's life (through 2016 in this case) and then spread the remaining depreciable cost equally (straight-line) over the remaining useful life. This procedure applied to the asset in question would result in depreciation of $9,840 for 2017 and $9,840 for year 2018.

(3)

KINKA COMPANY
Depreciation Schedule Using Units-of-Activity Method

	Computation			End of Year	
Year	Units of X Activity	Depreciation = Cost Per Unit[a]	Annual Depreciation Expense	Accumulated Depreciation	Book Value
2014	20,000	$2.50	$ 50,000	$ 50,000	$180,000
2015	18,000	2.50	45,000	95,000	135,000
2016	32,000	2.50	80,000	175,000	55,000
2017	5,000	2.50	12,500	187,500	42,500
2018	5,000	2.50	12,500	200,000	30,000
	80,000		$200,000		

[a]Depreciation per unit = Depreciable cost of $200,000 (cost of $230,000 less salvage of $30,000) divided by the 80,000 total estimated units to be produced during the total service life of the asset.

> **TIP:** Notice that none of the depreciation methods depreciate the asset below the amount recoverable through sale of the asset at the end of the asset's estimated economic service life. That recoverable amount is called **salvage value** or **residual value.**

(b) The **straight-line method** will report the most net income for the three years (2014-2016) combined because the straight-line method results in the lowest amount of accumulated depreciation at the end of 2016. Total depreciation expense for the three year period is summarized as follows:

Straight-line method	$120,000
Double-declining-balance method	180,320
Units-of-activity method	175,000

(c) The **straight-line method** will result in reporting the highest book value at the end of 2016 because it is the method that yields the lowest total depreciation expense over the first three years of the asset's life.

(d) The **double-declining-balance method** will result in the lowest book value at the end of 2016 because it is the method that yields the greatest total depreciation expense over the first three years of the asset's life.

EXERCISE 10-4

Purpose: (L.O. 2) This exercise will provide an illustration of the computations for depreciation of partial periods using two common methods.

Scanlan Company purchased a new plant asset on April 1, 2014, at a cost of $690,000. It was estimated to have a service life of 20 years and a salvage value of $60,000. Scanlan's accounting period is the calendar year.

Instructions
(a) Compute the amount of depreciation for this asset for 2014 and 2015 using the straight-line method.
(b) Compute the amount of depreciation for this asset for 2014 and 2015 using the double-declining-balance method.
(c) Briefly define depreciation as the term is used in accounting.

SOLUTION TO EXERCISE 10-4

(a) $\dfrac{\$690,000 - \$60,000}{20 \text{ years}} \times \dfrac{9}{12} = \underline{\$23,625}$ depreciation for 2014

$\dfrac{\$690,000 - \$60,000}{20 \text{ years}} = \underline{\$31,500}$ depreciation for 2015

(b) Straight - line rate $= \dfrac{100\%}{20} = 5\%$; 5% X 2 = 10% double the straight-line rate.

$690,000 X 10% X 9/12 = \underline{\$51,750}$ depreciation for 2014

($690,000 - $51,750) X 10% = $\underline{\$63,825}$ depreciation for 2015

(c) Depreciation is the accounting process of allocating an asset's historical cost (recorded amount) to the accounting periods benefited by the use of the asset. It is a process of cost allocation, **not** valuation. Depreciation is **not** intended to provide funds for an asset's replacement; it is merely an application of the matching principle.

Approach and Explanation:

(a)   Write down and apply the formula for straight-line depreciation. Then multiply the annual depreciation amount by the portion of the asset's year of service that falls in the given accounting period.

$$\frac{\text{Cost} \quad - \quad \text{Salvage Value}}{\text{Estimated} \quad \text{Service Life}} = \text{Depreciation Expense for Full Asset Year}$$

Only nine months of the first asset year falls in 2014 so the fraction 9/12 (or 3/4) must be applied to the annual depreciation amount calculated to arrive at the depreciation expense for the income statement for 2014.

(b)   Write down and apply the formula for the declining-balance method.

$$\begin{array}{l}\text{Book Value} \\ \text{at Beginning} \\ \text{of Asset Year}\end{array} \text{X Constant Percentage} = \text{Depreciation for Asset Year}$$

Only nine months of the first asset year falls in 2014 so the fraction of 3/4 must be applied to the annual depreciation amount calculated to arrive at the depreciation for the income statement for 2014.

After the first partial year, depreciation can be calculated for a full **accounting year** by multiplying the constant percentage by the **book value of the asset at the beginning of the accounting period.** Thus, the computation for 2015 for this asset is as follows: ($690,000 - $51,750) X 10% = $63,825.

EXERCISE 10-5

Purpose: (L.O. 2, 3) This exercise will provide you with an illustration of how to handle a change in the estimated service life and salvage value of a plant asset due to an expenditure subsequent to acquisition.

The Royal Company purchased a machine at the very end of 2004 for $210,000. The machine was being depreciated using the straight-line method over an estimated life of 20 years, with a $30,000 salvage value. At the beginning of 2015, the company paid $50,000 to overhaul the machine. As a result of this improvement, the company estimated that the useful life of the machine would be extended an additional 5 years, and the salvage value would be reduced to $20,000.

Instructions
Compute the depreciation charge for 2015.

SOLUTION TO EXERCISE 10-5

Approach: Whenever you have a situation that involves a change in the estimated service life and/or salvage value of a depreciable asset, use the format shown below to compute the remaining depreciable cost and allocate that amount over the remaining useful life using the given depreciation method.

Cost	$210,000
Accumulated depreciation	(90,000)[a]
Book value (before overhaul)	120,000
Additional expenditure capitalized[c] (if any)	50,000
Revised book value (after overhaul)	170,000
Current estimate of salvage	(20,000)
Remaining depreciable cost	150,000
Remaining years of useful life at 1/1/15	÷ 15[b]
Depreciation expense for 2015	$ 10,000

[a]Cost	$210,000
Original estimate of salvage	(30,000)
Original depreciable cost	180,000
Original service life in years	÷ 20
Original depreciation per year	9,000
Number of years used	X 10
Accumulated depreciation at 1/1/15	$ 90,000

[b]Original estimate of life in years	20
Number of years used	(10)
Additional years	5
Remaining years of useful life at 1/1/15	15

[c]The term capitalized refers to being recorded by a debit to a balance sheet account—Accumulated Depreciation in this case.

TIP: **A change in the estimated useful life and/or salvage value** of an existing depreciable asset is to be accounted for prospectively; that is, there is no correction of previously recorded depreciation expense. Therefore, the book value at the beginning of the period of change, less the current estimate of salvage, is to be allocated over the remaining periods of life using the appropriate depreciation method. The book value at the beginning of the period of change is calculated using the original estimates of service life and salvage value. Using the straight-line method, the new annual depreciation is determined by dividing the remaining depreciable cost by the remaining useful life.

TIP: The $50,000 cost of overhaul is capitalized in this case because the cost benefits the future periods by extending the useful life of the machine.

TIP: Be careful when computing the length of time between two dates. The length of time between the **end** of 2004 and the **beginning** of 2015 is 10 years; whereas, the length of time between the **beginning** of 2004 and the **beginning** of 2015 is 11 years and the length of time between the **beginning** of 2004 and the **end** of 2015 is 12 years. It is a common mistake to deduct one year from the other (2015 - 2004 = 11 years). As you can see from the foregoing, that will not always work. It is wise to write down the years that fall between the two dates and then count those years on your list. For example, the length of time between the **end** of 2011 and the **beginning** of 2015 is three years and is determined as follows:

2012	1
2013	2
2014	3

EXERCISE 10-6

Purpose: (L.O. 4) This exercise will help you to understand how the sale of a plant asset compares with the sale of inventory.

Houston Merchandising Company sold two items. The following facts pertain:

	Item 1	**Item 2**
Sales price	$10,000	$10,000
Cost/book value	5,200	5,200
Sales commission	400	400

Item 1 is an inventory item. Item 2 is a plant asset.

Instructions
Explain the manner of reporting each item on a multiple-step income statement.

SOLUTION TO EXERCISE 10-6

Item 1: Sale of an inventory item:
The sale of inventory is Houston's main line of business. The $10,000 sales price is included in sales revenue on the income statement. The cost, $5,200, is included in cost of goods sold. Therefore, this transaction causes $4,800 to be reflected in the gross profit figure for the period. The $400 commission is reported as a selling expense (operating expense) on the income statement. The net impact is a $4,400 increase in the net income amount for the period.

Item 2: Sale of a plant asset:

The sale of a plant asset is incidental to the main focus of Houston's business (to sell goods to customers). Therefore, the $10,000 sales price, $5,200 book value, and $400 commission are all netted off of the income statement; one line item, a gain of $4,400, is reported in the Other Revenues and Gains section of the income statement.

TIP:	Notice both transactions have the same net impact on net income.

EXERCISE 10-7

Purpose: (L.O. 4) This exercise will (1) illustrate several different ways in which you may dispose of property, and (2) discuss the appropriate accounting procedures for each.

Presented below is a schedule of property dispositions for Barbara Steiner Co. during 2014:

SCHEDULE OF PROPERTY DISPOSITIONS

	Cost	Accumulated Depreciation at 12/31/13	Cash Proceeds	Fair Market Value	Nature of Disposition
Furniture	$10,000	$ 8,800	--	--	Abandonment
Automobile	8,000	3,500	3,100	3,100	Sale
Land	40,000	--	92,000	100,000	Sale

The following additional information is available:

Furniture. On January 1, 2014, furniture was tossed out in the dumpster because it was no longer adequate to serve the company's needs. It cost $10,000 when it was acquired. Depreciation of $8,800 was taken in prior years.

Automobile. On January 2, 2014, an automobile was sold for $3,100 cash. It had a cost of $8,000, and total depreciation recorded prior to the sale date amounted to $3,500.

Land. On February 15, 2014, land previously used in operations was subdivided and a section was sold for $100,000. A commission of $8,000 went to a real estate agent. The original cost of that land segment was $40,000.

Instructions

Prepare the appropriate journal entry for each of the dispositions. Show computations where appropriate.

TIP:	The **disposal of property, plant, and equipment** should be accounted for as follows:
	(1) The book (carrying) value at the date of the disposal (cost of the property, plant, and equipment less the accumulated depreciation) should be removed from the accounts.
	(2) The cash (or other assets), if any, recovered should be recorded.
	(3) The difference between (1) and (2) should be recorded:
	(a) An excess of cash (or other dissimilar assets) over the book value removed is accounted for as a gain on the disposal.
	(b) An excess of book value removed over the cash (or other assets) from the disposal is accounted for as a loss on the disposal.

SOLUTION TO EXERCISE 10-7

Jan.	1	Loss on Disposal of Plant Assets.............................	1,200	
		Accumulated Depreciation	8,800	
		Furniture...		10,000
		(To record abandonment of furniture)		
Jan.	2	Cash	3,100	
		Accumulated Depreciation	3,500	
		Loss on Disposal of Plant Assets.............................	1,400	
		Automobile...		8,000
		(To record the sale of an automobile at a loss)		
Feb.	15	Cash	92,000	
		Land...		40,000
		Gain on Disposal of Plant Assets		52,000[a]
		(To record sale of land at a gain)		

[a]Sales price of land	$100,000
Commission	(8,000)
Net proceeds	92,000
Book value of land	(40,000)
Gain on sale	$ 52,000

Explanations:

Furniture. There is no salvage (residual) value; hence, the book value ($1,200) is written off as a loss.

Automobile. The book value ($8,000 - $3,500 = $4,500) is removed from the accounts. The cash recovered ($3,100) is recorded. The book value exceeds the cash; therefore, a loss is recorded for the difference.

Land. The book value ($40,000) is removed from the accounts. The net proceeds ($100,000 - $8,000 = $92,000) is recorded. The commission is a cost of the disposal rather than an operating expense; hence, it is a reduction of the gain or increase in the loss on disposal. (In this case, it is a decrease in gain.) The excess of the net proceeds ($92,000) over the book value ($40,000) is recorded as a gain.

EXERCISE 10-8

Purpose: (L.O. 5) This exercise will give you practice in computing depletion.

During 2014, Alston Corporation acquired a mineral mine for $2,000,000 of which $450,000 is attributable to the land value after the mineral has been removed. Alston spent $700,000 to prepare the mine for removal of the minerals. Engineers estimate that 15 million units of mineral can be recovered from this mine. During 2014, 1,200,000 units were extracted and sold.

Instructions
Compute the depletion for 2014.

SOLUTION TO EXERCISE 10-8

$$\frac{\$2,000,000 \; + \; \$700,000 \; - \; \$450,000}{15,000,000} = \$.15 \text{ per unit}$$

$.15 X 1,200,000 = $180,000 Depletion for 2014

Approach and Explanation: Write down the formulas to compute depletion, enter the data given, and solve.

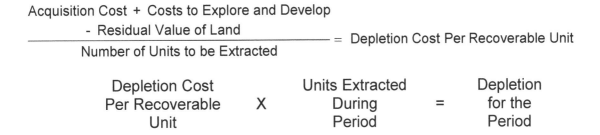

TIP:	The depletion cost is the amount to be removed from the property, plant, and equipment classification ($180,000 in this case). It is based on the units extracted from the earth during the period. The portion of this $180,000 which appears on the income statement is dependent upon the number of units sold. The depletion costs related to units sold—depletion expense—is classified as part of cost of goods sold expense on the income statement. When the number of units extracted exceed the number sold, a portion of the depletion costs goes into the inventory account on the balance sheet.

EXERCISE 10-9

Purpose: (L.O. 6) This exercise illustrates the steps in estimating the value of goodwill.

Mr. Judski is contemplating the sale of his business, Classic Vettes. The following data are available.

Book value of tangible & identifiable intangible assets less liabilities	$135,000
Fair market value of tangible & identifiable intangible assets less liabilities	200,000
Estimated fair market value of the business as a whole	240,000

Instructions
(a) Compute the estimated value of goodwill.
(b) Assume Tom Benyon Enterprises purchases the business for $240,000 cash. Explain how Tom Benyon Enterprises should account for the goodwill at the purchase date and in the future as well as the reasons why.

TIP:	Companies record goodwill **only** when an entire business is purchased (that is, what some people call "internally generated" goodwill cannot be recorded). When an entire business is purchased, **goodwill** is the excess of cost over the fair market value of the net identifiable assets acquired. Net identifiable assets are determined by deducting total liabilities from total identifiable (tangible and intangible) assets.

SOLUTION TO EXERCISE 10-9

(a)		
	Purchase price (cost)	$240,000
	Fair market value of net assets acquired other than goodwill	(200,000)
	Goodwill	$ 40,000

(b) Tom Benyon would record a credit to Cash for $240,000, debits to individual asset accounts for the inventory, plant assets, identifiable intangible assets and other assets acquired for their fair market values, credits to liability accounts (at market value) for any liabilities assumed, and a debit to Goodwill for $40,000.

Goodwill is **not** to be amortized (written off) because it is considered to have an indefinite life, but goodwill must be written down if its value is determined to have declined (been permanently impaired). Goodwill appears on the balance sheet under Intangible Assets.

*ILLUSTRATION 10-2
SUMMARY OF REQUIREMENTS FOR RECORDING GAINS AND LOSSES ON EXCHANGES OF PLANT ASSETS (When the Exchange has Commercial Substance) (L.O. 8)

1. Eliminate the book value of the asset given up.

2. Record the cost of the asset acquired. The cost is equal to the fair value of the asset given up plus the cash (if any) given in the exchange or minus any cash received in the exchange. (This should equal the fair value of the asset received in the exchange.)

3. Recognize the gain or loss on disposal. The total gain or loss experienced on the transaction is equal to the difference between the fair market value of the asset given up and the book value of the asset given up. An excess of fair market value over book value indicates a **gain**; an excess of book value over fair market value indicates a **loss.**

TIP:	An exchange has commercial substance if the future cash flows expected to be generated by use of the asset being acquired (referred to as the new asset) are significantly different than the future cash flows that would be expected to be generated by use of the asset being relinquished (the old asset).
TIP:	An asset exchange may be one of similar or dissimilar assets. An exchange of dissimilar assets is almost sure to be one of commercial substance. An exchange of similar assets may or may not be one of commercial substance. Examples of a dissimilar asset exchange are the exchange of land for equipment and the exchange of office equipment for manufacturing equipment. An example of a similar asset exchange is the exchange of an old delivery truck for a new delivery truck. Most exchanges have commercial substance even those of similar assets.

*EXERCISE 10-10

Purpose: (L.O. 8) This exercise will allow you to practice recording the exchange of plant assets when the exchange has commercial substance.

Soon Yoon Company exchanged equipment used in its manufacturing operations plus $5,000 in cash for delivery equipment used in the operations of Peggy Gunshanan Company. The exchange is determined to have commercial substance because the timing and the amount of the cash flows arising from the delivery equipment will likely differ significantly from the cash flows arising from the manufacturing equipment. The following information pertains to the exchange.

	Soon Yoon Co.	**Peggy Gunshanan Co.**
Equipment (cost)	$28,000	$28,000
Accumulated depreciation	22,000	10,000
Fair market value of equipment	10,500	15,500
Cash given up	5,000	

Instructions
(a) Prepare the journal entries to record the exchange on the books of Soon Yoon Co.
(b) Prepare the journal entries to record the exchange on the books of Soon Yoon Co. assuming the fair value of Soon Yoon Co.'s old asset is $5,500 (rather than $10,500) and the fair value of Peggy Gunshanan's old equipment is $10,500 (rather than $15,500). (Assume the rest of the facts are unchanged.)

SOLUTION TO EXERCISE 10-10

(a) **Soon Yoon Company:**

Delivery Equipment (New)..	15,500	
Accumulated Depreciation (Old)	22,000	
Manufacturing Equipment (Old).................................		28,000
Cash..		5,000
Gain on Disposal of Plant Assets		4,500
(To record exchange of manufacturing equipment		
for delivery equipment)		

Computation of book value:

Cost of old asset	$28,000
Accumulated depreciation	(22,000)
Book value of old asset	$ 6,000

Computation of gain:

Fair market value of equipment given	$10,500
Book value of equipment given	(6,000)
Gain experienced on old asset	$ 4,500

Valuation of new equipment:

Fair market value of equipment given	$10,500
Cash given	5,000
Cost of new equipment	$15,500

TIP: When plant assets are exchanged where the exchange has commercial substance and cash is given and a gain is experienced on disposal of the old asset, there are two other ways of computing the cost of the new equipment. They are as follows:

Book value of equipment given	$ 6,000		Fair value of equip. received is	
Cash given	5,000	**OR**	Cost of new equipment	$15,500
Gain on old asset	4,500			
Cost of new equipment	$15,500			

Approach and Explanation: Refer to **Illustration 10-2** which summarizes the rules for recognizing gains and losses on exchanges of plant assets where the exchange has commercial substance.

Soon Yoon has experienced a gain of $4,500 on the exchange of its old asset. It is an exchange of plant assets where cash is given and the exchange has commercial substance. This is an application of the cost principle in determining the cost of the new asset.

TIP: The parties will bargain so that the total fair value given equals the total fair value received. Therefore, since Peggy Gunshanan is giving up equipment worth $15,500 but Soon Yoon's equipment is only worth $10,500, Soon Yoon is also giving $5,000 cash to Peggy Gunshanan.

(b) **Soon Yoon Company:**

Delivery Equipment (New)	10,500	
Accumulated Depreciation (Old)	22,000	
Loss on Disposal of Plant Assets	500	
Manufacturing Equipment (Old)		28,000
Cash		5,000

Computation of loss:

Fair market value of equipment given	$5,500
Book value of equipment given	(6,000)
Loss on disposal	$ (500)

Valuation of new equipment:

Fair market value of equipment given	$ 5,500
Cash given	5,000
Cost of new equipment	$10,500

OR

Book value of equipment given	$ 6,000
Loss recognized on old asset	(500)
Cash given	5,000
Cost of new equipment	$10,500

Explanation: Soon Yoon has experienced a loss on the disposal of the old plant asset; the loss is to be recognized. The cost principle is followed in determining the cost of the new plant asset.

TIP:	The rules for recording the exchange of **plant** assets where the exchange does **not** have commercial substance are not illustrated in this book or your text. They are complex and are reserved for a more advanced accounting course.
TIP:	Peggy Gunshanan Company would also have to record the exchange. The guidelines to be followed when cash is **received** in a transaction involving the exchange of plant assets are not discussed in this book or your text. They are reserved for a more advanced accounting course.

EXERCISE 10-11

Purpose: (L.O. 1 thru 8) This exercise will quiz you about terminology used in this chapter.

A list of accounting terms with which you should be familiar appears below:

Accelerated-depreciation method
Additions and improvements
Amortization
Asset turnover
Capital expenditures
Copyright
Declining-balance method
Depletion
Depreciation
Depreciable cost
Franchise (license)
Going-concern assumption
Goodwill
Intangible assets

Materiality concept
Natural resources
Ordinary repairs
Patent
Plant assets
Research and development (R & D) costs
Revenue expenditures
Salvage value
Straight-line method
Trademark (trade name)
Units-of-activity method
Useful life

Instructions
For each item below, enter in the blank the term that is described.

1. _____Expenditures that increase the company's investment in productive facilities. Expenditures that relate to plant assets and benefit more than the current period.

2. _____Expenditures related to plant assets that are immediately charged against revenues as expense.

3. _____An estimate of an asset's value at the end of its useful life.

4. _____Tangible resources that are used in the operations of the business and are not intended for sale to customers.

5. _____Costs incurred to increase the operating efficiency, productive capacity, or expected useful life of a plant asset.

6. _____The process of allocating to expense the cost of a plant asset over its useful (service) life in a rational and systematic manner.

7. _____The cost of a plant asset less its salvage value.

8. _____A depreciation method in which periodic depreciation is the same for each year of the asset's useful life.

9. _____A depreciation method that produces higher depreciation expense in the early years than in the later years of an asset's useful life.

10. _____A depreciation method that applies a constant rate to the declining book value of the asset and produces a decreasing annual depreciation expense over the useful life of the asset.

11. _____A depreciation method in which useful life is expressed in terms of the total units of production or use expected from an asset.

12. _____Expenditures to maintain the operating efficiency and productive life of the asset.

13. _____Rights, privileges, and competitive advantages that result from the ownership of long-lived assets that do not posses physical substance.

14. _____An exclusive right granted from the federal government that allows the owner to reproduce and sell an artistic or published work.

15. _____The value of all favorable attributes that relate to a business enterprise.

16. _____An exclusive right issued by the U.S. Patent Office that enables the recipient to manufacture, sell or otherwise control his or her invention for a period of 20 years from the date of the grant.

17. _____A work, phrase, jingle, or symbol that identifies a particular enterprise or product.

18. _____A contractual arrangement under which the franchisor grants the franchisee the right to sell certain products, render specific services, or use certain trademarks or trade names, usually within a designated geographic area.

19. _____The allocation of the cost of an intangible asset to expense over its useful life in a systematic and rational manner.

20. _____Expenditures that may lead to patents, copyrights, new processes, and new products.

21. _____Assets that consist of standing timber and underground deposits of oil, gas, and minerals.

22. _____The process of allocation of the cost of a natural resource to expense in a rational and systematic manner over the resource's useful life.

23. _____An estimate of the expected productive life, also called service life, of an asset.

24. _____A measure of how efficiently a company uses its assets to generate sales, calculated as net sales divided by average total assets.

25. _____States that the company will continue in operation for the foreseeable future.

26. _____If an item would **not** make a difference in decision making, a company does not have to follow GAAP in reporting it.

SOLUTION TO EXERCISE 10-11

1. Capital expenditures
2. Revenue expenditures
3. Salvage value
4. Plant assets
5. Additions and improvements
6. Depreciation
7. Depreciable cost
8. Straight-line method
9. Accelerated-depreciation method
10. Declining-balance method
11. Units-of-activity method
12. Ordinary repairs
13. Intangible assets
14. Copyright

15. Goodwill
16. Patent
17. Trademark (trade name)
18. Franchise (license)
19. Amortization
20. Research and development (R & D) costs
21. Natural resources
22. Depletion
23. Useful life
24. Asset turnover
25. Going concern assumption
26. Materiality principle

ANALYSIS OF MULTIPLE-CHOICE TYPE QUESTIONS

1. (L.O. 1) The Jupiter Company purchased a parcel of land to be used as the site of a new office complex. The following data pertain to the purchase of the land and the beginning of construction for the new building:

Purchase price of land	$200,000
Attorney's fees for land transaction	1,000
Title insurance cost	2,000
Survey fees to determine the boundaries of the lot	800
Excavation costs for the building's foundation	8,000
Costs of clearing and grading the land	1,400

The total acquisition cost of the land is:
a. $213,200.
b. $205,200.
c. $203,800.
d. $202,400.
e. $200,000.

Approach and Explanation: Think about how the cost of land is determined: an asset's cost includes all costs necessary to acquire the asset and get it to the location and condition for its intended purpose. When land has been purchased for the purpose of constructing a building, all costs incurred up to the excavation for the new building are considered land costs. Think of the common components of land cost (refer to the listing in **Illustration 10-1).** The cost is computed as follows:

Purchase price	$200,000
Attorney's fees	1,000
Title insurance	2,000
Survey fees	800
Costs of clearing and grading	1,400
Total cost of land	$205,200

The $8,000 excavation costs for the building's foundation should be charged (debited) to the Building account. (Solution = b.)

2. (L.O. 1) The Venus Company hired an architect to design plans and a construction firm to build a new office building on a parcel of land it owns. The following data relates to the building:

Price paid to the construction firm	$320,000
Architect fees	18,000
Permit fees	1,200
Interest paid during the construction period	800
Insurance premium for first year of operations	3,000
Property taxes during the first year of operations	6,000

The total acquisition cost of the new building is:
a. $349,000.
b. $340,000.
c. $338,000.
d. $320,000.

Approach and Explanation: Think about how the cost of a building is determined: an asset's cost includes all costs necessary to acquire the asset and get it to the location and condition for its intended purpose. Think of the common components of building cost (refer to the listing in **Illustration 10-1).** The cost is computed as follows:

Price paid to construction firm	$320,000
Architect fees	18,000
Permit fees	1,200
Interest paid during construction	800
Total cost of building	$340,000 (Solution = b.)

3. (L.O. 1) The Patty Company purchased a piece of office equipment to be used in operations. The following expenditures and other data relate to the equipment:

Invoice price excluding sales tax	$12,000
Sales tax	600
Delivery charges	200
Installation costs	300
Cost of a special platform	400
Cost of supplies used in testing	80
Insurance premium for first year of use	60

The total acquisition cost of this piece of equipment is:
a. $13,640.
b. $13,580.
c. $13,100.
d. $12,700.

Approach and Explanation: Apply the cost principle: the cost of equipment includes all costs necessary to acquire the equipment, transport it to the place where it will be used, and prepare it for use. Thus, all costs related to equipment incurred prior to use in regular operations are charged to the Equipment account. Recurring costs (such as for insurance and maintenance) incurred after the equipment is ready for use should be expensed in the period incurred. Refer to the list of common elements of equipment cost in **Illustration 10-1**. The cost of the equipment is determined as follows:

Invoice price	$12,000
Sales tax	600
Delivery charges	200
Installation costs	300
Costs of special platform	400
Costs of supplies used in testing	80
	$13,580 (Solution = b.)

4. (L.O. 3) In accounting for plant assets, which of the following subsequent outlays should be fully expensed in the period the expenditure is made?
a. Expenditure made to increase the efficiency or effectiveness of an existing asset.
b. Expenditure made to extend the useful life of an existing asset beyond the time frame originally anticipated.
c. Expenditure made to maintain an existing asset so that it can function in the manner intended.
d. Expenditure made to add new asset services.

Explanation: If an expenditure benefits future periods, it should be capitalized (debited to a balance sheet account); if the expenditure does not yield benefits to a future period, it should be recorded by a debit to an income statement account. An expenditure made to maintain an existing asset in good working condition does not provide any benefits other than those that were in potential when the original asset was acquired. Hence, it should be expensed. Answer selections "a", "b", and "d", all represent future economic benefits; hence, they should be debited to an asset account or to an accumulated depreciation account, depending on whether or not an asset's life is increased by the expenditure subsequent to acquisition. (Solution = c.)

5. (L.O. 2) The term depreciable cost, as it is used in accounting for a plant asset, refers to:
   a. the total amount to be charged (debited) to expense over the asset's useful life.
   b. cost of the asset less the related depreciation recorded to date.
   c. the estimated market value of the asset at the end of its useful life.
   d. the acquisition cost of the asset.

   Approach and Explanation: Write down a definition of depreciable cost **before** you read any of the answer selections. **Depreciable cost** is the total amount of asset cost that can be expensed over the useful life of the asset; thus, it is original cost less estimated residual (salvage) value. Answer selection "b" describes the term book value. Answer "c" describes salvage value or residual value. Selection "d" represents total cost of the asset. (Solution = a.)

6. (L.O. 2) The book value of a plant asset is:
   a. the fair market value of the asset at a balance sheet date.
   b. the asset's acquisition cost less the total related depreciation recorded to date.
   c. equal to the balance of the related accumulated depreciation account.
   d. the assessed value of the asset for property tax purposes.

   Approach and Explanation: Write down the definition for the term book value: **book value** is the asset's original cost (acquisition cost) less accumulated depreciation. Look for the answer selection that agrees with your definition. Book value is often called **carrying value** or **carrying amount.** (Solution = b.)

7. (L.O. 2) A machine is purchased by the Dunnagin Company for $18,000. Dunnagin pays $6,000 in cash and gives a note payable for $12,000 that is payable in installments over a four-year period. Dunnagin estimates that the machine could physically last for 12 years even though Dunnagin expects to use it in its business for only 9 years. The period of time to be used by Dunnagin for depreciation purposes is:
   a. 4 years.
   b. 5 years.
   c. 9 years.
   d. 12 years.

   Approach and Explanation: Think about the objective of the depreciation process—to comply with the matching principle. The process of depreciation serves to allocate an asset's cost to the periods benefited in order to match the cost of asset services consumed with the revenues the asset services helped to generate. The asset should be depreciated over its useful life, which is the length of time the asset will be of service to the entity using it in operations. (Solution = c.)

8. (L.O. 2) A machine was purchased for $8,000,000 on January 1, 2014. It has an estimated useful life of 8 years and a residual value of $800,000. Depreciation is being computed using the straight-line method. What amount should be shown for this machine, net of accumulated depreciation, in the company's December 31, 2015 balance sheet?
   a. $5,400,000.
   b. $6,200,000.
   c. $7,100,000.
   d. $7,200,000.

   Approach and Explanation: Write down the formula to compute book value and the formula to compute depreciation using the straight-line method. Fill in the data from the scenario at hand and solve. Be careful that you don't get so involved with the computation of depreciation that you lose sight of the question—and that is, to compute the book value of the equipment. It would be helpful to underline the middle of the last sentence of the stem of the question in order to keep your focus on what is being asked.

   $$\text{Cost - Accumulated Depreciation} = \text{Book Value}$$

   $$\frac{\text{Cost - Salvage Value}}{\text{Estimated Service Life}} = \text{Depreciation for Full Asset Year}$$

   ($8,000,000 - $800,000) ÷ 8 = $900,000 depreciation for one year.

Depreciation for 2014	$ 900,000
Depreciation for 2015	900,000
Accumulated depreciation	$1,800,000
Cost	$8,000,000
Accumulated depreciation	(1,800,000)
Book value	$6,200,000

   (Solution = b.)

9. (L.O. 2) Tammy Company purchased a machine on July 1, 2014 for $900,000. The machine has an estimated life of five years and a salvage value of $120,000. The machine is being depreciated by the declining-balance method using double the straight-line rate. What amount of depreciation should be recorded for the year ended December 31, 2015?
   a. $360,000.
   b. $288,000.
   c. $249,600.
   d. $180,000.

   Approach and Explanation: Write down the formula to use for the declining-balance approach. (Notice the facts indicate there is a partial period for the first year (2014) and the question asks for the depreciation for the 2015 reporting period.) Compute the rate that is double the straight-line rate. Apply the formula to the facts given. Remember that salvage value is **not** used with this method in computing depreciation in the early years of the asset's life.

Book Value at Beginning of Year X Declining-Balance Rate = Depreciation

$$\frac{100\%}{\text{Life}} = \frac{100\%}{5 \text{ years}} = 20\% \qquad 20\% \times 2 = 40\% \text{ constant percentage}$$

$900,000 X 40% X 1/2 = $180,000 for 2014
($900,000 - $180,000) X 40% = $288,000 for 2015   (Solution = b.)

10. (L.O. 2) A machine was purchased at the beginning of 2012 for $68,000. At the time of its purchase, the machine was estimated to have a useful life of six years and a salvage value of $8,000. The machine was depreciated using the straight-line method of depreciation through 2014. At the beginning of 2015, the estimate of useful life was revised to a total life of eight years and the expected salvage value was changed to $5,000. The amount to be recorded for depreciation for year 2015, reflecting these changes in estimates, is:
   a. $7,875.
   b. $7,600.
   c. $6,600.
   d. $4,125.

Approach and Explanation: Write down the model to compute depreciation whenever there has been a change in the estimated service life and/or salvage value of a plant asset. Fill in the data of the case at hand and solve:

Cost	$68,000
Accumulated depreciation	(30,000)[a]
Book value	38,000
Additional expenditure capitalized	-0-
Revised book value	38,000
Current estimate of salvage	(5,000)
Remaining depreciable cost	33,000
Remaining years of useful life at 1/1/15	÷ 5[b]
Depreciation expense for 2015	$ 6,600 (Solution = c.)

[a]Cost	$68,000
Original estimate of salvage	(8,000)
Original depreciable cost	60,000
Original service life in years	÷ 6
Original depreciation per year	10,000
Number of years used	3
Accumulated depreciation—1/1/15	$30,000

[b]Total life as revised	8
Number of years used	(3)
Remaining part of useful life at 1/1/15	5

11. (L.O. 4) A van has an original cost of $42,000 and accumulated depreciation of $11,000. It is sold for $27,000 cash. The journal entry to record the sale will include a:
   a. debit to Loss on Disposal of Plant Assets for $4,000.
   b. credit to Gain on Disposal of Plant Assets for $4,000.
   c. credit to Vans for $27,000.
   d. debit to Loss on Disposal of Plant Assets for $15,000.

   Approach and Explanation: Prepare the journal entry to record the sale. Begin with the cash received so debit Cash. Remove the old asset from the books; credit Vans for $42,000 and debit Accumulated Depreciation for $11,000. Examine the entry and determine what is needed to balance the entry; a debit balancing figure represents a loss or a credit balancing figure represents a gain.

   In this case, a debit of $4,000 is needed to balance; hence, a loss of $4,000 is recorded. (Solution = a.)

Cash	27,000	
Accumulated Depreciation—Vans	11,000	
Loss on Disposal of Plant Assets	4,000	
Vans..		42,000

12. (L.O. 6) Which of the following items would **not** be classified as an intangible asset for accounting purposes:
   a. Patent.
   b. Goodwill.
   c. Trade name.
   d. Advertising to promote long-term relationship with customers.

   Explanation: Patent, trade name (or trademark) and goodwill are all examples of intangible assets. Advertising and other costs to promote goodwill must be expensed in the period incurred. (Solution = d.)

13. **Question**
   (L.O. 6) A company has recorded purchased goodwill at a cost of $200,000. What is the maximum amount which may be recorded as amortization expense for the full year immediately following its acquisition?
   a. $0.
   b. $4,000.
   c. $5,000.
   d. $20,000.

   Approach and Explanation: Goodwill is considered to have an indefinite life; therefore, it is not to be amortized. In the case where a permanent impairment is determined to have occurred, a write down is required. (Solution = a.)

14. (L.O. 6) Which of the following items conveys the legal right to perform a service or to sell a product in a defined geographical area?
a. Copyright.
b. Trademark.
c. Patent.
d. Franchise.

Explanation: A **copyright** gives the owner the exclusive right to reproduce and sell an artistic or published work. A **trademark** or **trade name** is a word, phrase, jingle, or symbol that distinguishes a particular enterprise or product. A **patent** is an exclusive right that enables the recipient to manufacture, sell, or otherwise control his or her invention. A **franchise** is a contractual arrangement under which the franchisor grants the **franchisee** the right to sell certain products, to render specific services, or to use certain trademarks or trade names, usually within a designated geographic area. (Solution = d.)

15. (L.O. 6) In 2014, Barney Stinson Corporation incurred $600,000 of research and development costs. The costs relate to a product that will be marketed beginning in 2015 when the patent is obtained. It is estimated that these costs will be recouped by December 31, 2016. What is the amount of research and development costs that should be charged to income in 2014?
a. $0.
b. $150,000.
c. $200,000.
d. $600,000.

Explanation: All R & D costs are to be expensed in the period incurred. (Solution = d.)

16. (L.O. 6) Paws Inn is for sale. The following facts pertain:

	Book Value	**Fair Market Value**
Current assets	$100,000	$170,000
Plant assets	400,000	700,000
Intangible assets	60,000	90,000
Liabilities	300,000	300,000

Cousin Vinnie Resorts purchases Paws Inn for $825,000. The value of goodwill amounts to:
a. $30,000.
b. $165,000.
c. $300,000.
d. $370,000.

Approach and Explanation:
(1) **Compute the total fair market value of the identifiable assets:**
$170,000 + $700,000 + $90,000 = $960,000
(2) **Compute the fair market value of the net identifiable assets:**
$960,000 - $300,000 liabilities = $660,000
(3) **Compute the excess of cost over the fair market value of the net identifiable assets.** That excess represents goodwill.
$825,000 - $660,000 = $165,000 goodwill   (Solution = b.)

17. (L.O. 6) A patent was acquired in early 2010. Its useful life was determined to be 12 years even though its legal life is 20 years. At the beginning of 2014, a large sum was spent for legal costs to successfully defend the patent rights. Those legal costs should be:
   a. expensed in 2014.
   b. amortized over 20 years.
   c. amortized over 12 years.
   d. amortized over 8 years.
   e. none of the above.

   Explanation: The legal costs are necessary to establish the validity of the patent. They should be amortized over the periods benefited which are the remaining years of the useful life of the patent (12 - 4 = 8). (Solution = d.)

18. (L.O. 7) All of the following must be disclosed **except:**
   a. depreciation method(s) used.
   b. amount of depreciation expense for the period.
   c. balances of the major classes of plant assets.
   d. service lives of plant assets.

   Explanation: Either within the balance sheet or in the notes to the financial statements, there should be disclosure of the balances of the major classes of assets, such as land, buildings, and equipment, and accumulated depreciation by major classes or in total. In addition, the depreciation and amortization methods used should be described, and the amount of depreciation and amortization expense for the period should be disclosed. (Solution = d.)

19. (L.O. 7) The asset turnover may be used to determine:
   a. the average service life of plant assets.
   b. the average age of plant assets.
   c. the dollars of sales produced for each dollar invested in assets.
   d. the number of times you can divide depreciation expense into total assets.

   Explanation: The asset turnover is computed by dividing average assets into net sales; it measures the productivity of a company's total assets. (Solution = c.)

*20. (L.O. 8) The King-Kong Corporation exchanges one plant asset for another plant asset and gives cash in the exchange. If a gain on the disposal of the old asset is indicated, and the exchange has commercial substance, the gain will:
   a. be reported in the Other Revenues and Gains section of the income statement.
   b. effectively reduce the amount to be recorded as the cost of the new asset.
   c. be credited directly to the owner's capital account.

   Explanation: The gain results from an excess of fair value over book value of the asset relinquished. The gain is reported like other gains from nonoperating sources. (Solution = a.)

*21. (L.O. 8) Two home builders agree to exchange plant assets. The exchange has commercial substance.. An appraiser was hired and the following information is available.

	Batson	Beamer
Book value of asset given up	$50,000	$108,000
Fair market value of asset given up	80,000	100,000
Cash paid	20,000	

In recording this exchange, Batson should recognize:
a.   a loss of $20,000.
b.   a gain of $20,000.
c.   a gain of $30,000.
d.   no gain or loss.

Approach and Explanation:
Determine if a gain or loss is experienced. Fair market value ($80,000) exceeds book value ($50,000) for Batson's old asset so Batson has experienced a gain of $30,000. The gain is recognized in an exchange that has commercial substance. (Solution = c.)

*22. (L.O. 8) Refer to the facts of **Question 21.** The amount to be recorded by Batson for the acquisition cost of the new plant asset is:
a. $50,000.
b. $70,000.
c. $80,000.
d. $100,000.
e. $108,000.

Approach and Explanation:

The cost of the new asset can be determined as follows:

Fair market value of asset given	$ 80,000
Cash given	20,000
Cost of new asset	$100,000 (Solution = d.)

A journal entry approach can also be used (the debit to the new asset account is a plug figure):

Plant Asset (New)	100,000		**Plug last.**
Plant Asset (Old)		50,000	**Do second.**
Cash		20,000	**Do first.**
Gain on Disposal of Plant Assets		30,000	**Do third.**

CHAPTER 11

· ·

CURRENT LIABILITIES AND PAYROLL ACCOUNTING

OVERVIEW

Initially, the resources (assets) of a business have to come from an entity outside of the particular organization. Two main sources of resources are creditor sources (liabilities) and owner's sources (owner's equity). In this chapter, we begin our in-depth discussion of liabilities.

Due to the nature of some business activities, an entity will commonly receive goods and services and not pay for them until days or weeks later. Therefore, at a specific point in time, such as a balance sheet date, we may find that a business has obligations for merchandise received from suppliers (accounts payable), for money it has borrowed (notes payable), for interest incurred (interest payable), for sales tax charged to customers which has not yet been remitted to the government (sales taxes payable), for salaries and wages (salaries and wages payable), and for amounts due to government agencies in connection with employee compensation (Federal Income Tax Withholdings Payable, FICA Taxes Payable, Federal Unemployment Taxes Payable, and State Unemployment Taxes Payable). Such payables are reported as current (short-term) liabilities because they will fall due within the next 12 months and will require the use of current assets (cash, in most cases) to liquidate them. Accounting for current liabilities is discussed in this chapter.

SUMMARY OF LEARNING OBJECTIVES

1. **Explain a current liability and identify the major types of current liabilities.** A current liability is a debt that a company can reasonably expect to pay (1) from existing current assets or through the creation of other current liabilities, and (2) within one year or the operating cycle, whichever is longer. The major types of current liabilities are notes payable, accounts payable, sales taxes payable, unearned revenues, and accrued liabilities such as taxes, salaries and wages, and interest payable.

2. **Describe the accounting for notes payable.** When a promissory note is interest-bearing, the amount of assets received upon the issuance of the note is generally equal to the face value of the note. Interest expense accrues over the life of the note. At maturity, the amount paid equals the face value of the note plus accrued interest.

3. **Explain the accounting for other current liabilities.** Companies record sales taxes payable at the time the related sales occur. The company serves as a collection agent for the taxing authority. Sales taxes are not an expense to the company. Companies initially record unearned revenues (advances from customers) in an Unearned Revenue account. As a company recognizes revenue, a transfer from unearned revenue to revenue occurs. Companies report the current maturities of long-term debt as current liabilities in the balance sheet.

4. **Explain the financial statement presentation and analysis of current liabilities.** Companies should report the nature and amount of each current liability in the balance sheet or in schedules in the notes accompanying the financial statements. The liquidity of a company may be analyzed by computing working capital and the current ratio.

5. **Describe the accounting and disclosure requirements for contingent liabilities.** If it is **probable** (likely to occur) that the contingency will happen and the amount is reasonably estimable, the company should record the liability in the accounts. However, if the contingency is only **reasonably possible** (it could occur), then it need be disclosed only in the notes to the financial statements. If the possibility that the contingency will happen is **remote** (unlikely to occur), it need not be recorded or disclosed.

6. **Compute and record the payroll for a pay period.** The computation of the payroll involves gross earnings, payroll deductions, and net pay. In recording the payroll, companies debit Salaries and Wages Expense for gross earnings, credit individual tax and other liability accounts for payroll deductions, and credit Salaries and Wages Payable for net pay. When the payroll is paid, companies debit Salaries and Wages Payable and credit Cash.

7. **Describe and record employer payroll taxes.** Employer payroll taxes consist of FICA, federal unemployment taxes, and state unemployment taxes. The taxes are usually accrued at the time the company records the payroll by debiting Payroll Tax Expense and crediting separate liability accounts for each type of tax.

8. **Discuss the objectives of internal control for payroll.** The objectives of internal control for payroll are (1) to safeguard company assets against unauthorized payments of payrolls, and (2) to ensure the accuracy of the accounting records pertaining to payrolls.

*9. **Identify additional fringe benefits associated with employee compensation.** Additional fringe benefits associated with wages are paid absences (paid vacations, sick pay benefits, and paid holidays), postretirement benefits (pensions and health care and life insurance).

   *This material is discussed in the **Appendix 11A** in the text.

TIPS ON CHAPTER TOPICS

TIP:	**Current liabilities** are also called **short-term liabilities** or **short-term debt. Non-current liabilities** are often called **long-term liabilities** or **long-term debt.**
TIP:	**Current liabilities** are obligations which come due within one year (or the company's operating cycle, if longer than a year) and whose liquidation is reasonably expected to require the use of existing resources properly classifiable as current assets, or the creation of other current liabilities. **Noncurrent liabilities** (or **long-term liabilities**) are obligations which do **not** meet the criteria to be classified as current.
TIP:	Companies often have a portion of long-term debt that is due each year. At a balance sheet date, any portion of long-term debt that is due within one year of that balance sheet date is referred to as "current maturities of long-term debt" or "current portion of long-term debt" or "long-term debt due within one year" and is classified as a current liability.
TIP:	A liability is recognized (recorded) when a legally binding obligation is incurred. Examples include: (a) When cash is received. (b) When legal title to some asset other than cash is received (change in legal title usually occurs at the point that the asset is delivered to the buyer) and payment is deferred. (c) When services are received and payment is deferred. (d) As time passes (for example, interest accrues with passage of time).
TIP:	The amount of a liability is determined in one of three ways: (a) By the amount of cash when cash is exchanged (for example, when money is borrowed from a bank). (b) By the negotiated or fair market value of noncash assets or services involved in a transaction. (c) By estimate.
TIP:	Computing the weekly, biweekly, or monthly payroll involves four basic steps: (a) Determining the amount of employee compensation. (b) Calculating deductions from employee compensation. (c) Calculating employer tax liabilities based on employee compensation. (d) Maintaining proper employee payroll records.

EXERCISE 11-1

Purpose: (L.O. 1) This exercise tests your ability to distinguish between current and noncurrent (long-term) liabilities.

_____ 1. Obligation to supplier for merchandise purchased on credit. (Terms 2/10, n/30).

_____ 2. Note payable to bank maturing 90 days after balance sheet date.

_____ 3. Note payable due January 1, 2017.

_____ 4. Property taxes payable.

_____ 5. Interest payable on note payable.

_____ 6. Sales taxes payable.

_____ 7. Portion of mortgage obligation due in years 2016 through 2020.

_____ 8. Revenue received in advance, to be earned over the next six months.

_____ 9. Salaries and wages payable.

_____ 10. Rent payable.

_____ 11. Short-term notes payable.

_____ 12. Pension obligations maturing in ten years.

_____ 13. Installment loan payments due three months after the balance sheet date.

_____ 14. Installment loan payments due more than one year after the balance sheet date.

_____ 15. Portion of mortgage obligation due within a year after the December 31, 2014 balance sheet date.

_____ 16. Note payable maturing March 1, 2015.

Instructions:
Indicate whether each of the above items would be reported as a current liability (CL) or a long-term liability (LT) on a balance sheet prepared at December 31, 2014.

Approach: Review the definition of a current liability. Analyze each situation above and determine if the liability will fall due within a year (or operating cycle) of the balance sheet date and whether it will require the use of current assets or the incurrence of another current liability to liquidate. If so, it is current; if not, it is long-term.

SOLUTION TO EXERCISE 11-1

1.	C	5.	C	9.	C	13.	C
2.	C	6.	C	10.	C	14.	LT
3.	LT	7.	LT	11.	C	15.	C
4.	C	8.	C	12.	LT	16.	C

EXERCISE 11-2

Purpose: (L.O. 2) This exercise will review the journal entries involved for an interest-bearing note payable.

On November 1, 2014, Bono Company borrowed $80,000 from National Bank and signed a note stipulating that $80,000 was to be repaid in 6 months with interest at 12%. Bono Company adjusts its accounts and prepares financial statements annually on December 31. (Reversing entries are not used.)

Instructions
(a) Prepare the journal entry on November 1, 2014, to record the loan.
(b) Prepare the adjusting entry on December 31, 2014.
(c) Prepare the journal entry at maturity (May 1, 2015).
(d) Determine the total financing cost (interest expense) for the six-month period.

SOLUTION TO EXERCISE 11-2

(a)	2014
	Nov. 1
		Cash..
		    Notes Payable...
		      (To record issuance of 12%, six-month note
		      to National Bank)
			80,000	80,000

(b)	2014
	Dec. 31
		Interest Expense ....
		    Interest Payable ....
		      (To accrue interest for two months on
		      National Bank note)
		      ($80,000 X 12% X 2/12 = $1,600)
			1,600	1,600

(c)	2014
	May 1
		Notes Payable..
		Interest Payable ....
		Interest Expense ....
		    Cash...
		      (To record payment of National Bank interest-
		      bearing note and accrued interest at maturity)
		      ($80,000 X 12% X 4/12 = $3,200 interest expense)
			80,000
			1,600
			3,200
				84,800

(d) $1,600 + $3,200 = $\underline{$4,800}$

TIP:	Interest rates are stated on an annual basis (per annum) unless otherwise indicated. Thus, the 12% rate in this exercise is an annual rate.

EXERCISE 11-3

Purpose: (L.O. 3) This exercise will provide an example of the proper accounting for an obligation to an agency of the state government—unremitted sales taxes.

During the month of June, Chelsea's Boutique had cash sales of $234,000 and credit sales of $137,000, both of which include the 6% sales tax that must be remitted to the state by July 15. Sales taxes on June sales were lumped with the sales price and recorded as a credit to the Sales Revenue account.

During the month of July, Chelsea's Boutique set up a new cash register that rings up sales and the 6% sales tax separately. The register totals for July were cash sales of $220,000 and credit sales of $110,000. The related sales tax is not due to be paid until August 15.

Instructions
(a) Prepare the journal entry to record June's sales at June 30 (assuming the total sales for June are recorded at June 30).
(b) Prepare the adjusting entry that should be recorded to fairly present the financial statements at June 30.
(c) Prepare the journal entry to record the remittance of the sales taxes on July 12.
(d) Prepare the journal entry to record July's sales at July 31.

SOLUTION TO EXERCISE 11-3

(a) June 30 Cash... 234,000
        Accounts Receivable.. 137,000
            Sales 371,000
            (To record sales revenue including sales
            taxes)

(b) June 30 Sales Revenue... 21,000
            Sales Taxes Payable 21,000
            (To record the sales tax liability on June
            sales)
            Computation:
            Sales plus sales tax ($234,000 + $137,000) $371,000
            Sales exclusive of tax ($371,000 ÷ 1.06)   350,000
            Sales tax $ 21,000

(c) July 12   Sales Taxes Payable   21,000
                    Cash...   21,000
                        (To record payment of sales taxes collected
                        in June)

(d) July 31   Cash ($220,000 X 1.06)   233,200
                    Accounts Receivable ($110,000 X 1.06)   116,600
                        Sales Revenue...   330,000
                        Sales Taxes Payable   19,800
                        (To record sales revenue and sales taxes)

EXERCISE 11-4

Purpose: (L.O. 3) This exercise will illustrate the accounting for unearned revenue.

Soap Opera Summarized is published by Viewer Publishers. Subscriptions to the magazine are sold for a one-year, two-year, or three-year period. Cash receipts from subscribers are credited to Unearned Subscription Revenue, and this account had a balance of $3,000,000 at December 31, 2014, before adjustment. Outstanding subscriptions at December 31, 2014, expire as follows:

During 2015	$ 600,000
During 2016	400,000
During 2017	300,000
Total	$1,300,000

Instructions
(a) Prepare the journal entry to adjust the Unearned Subscription Revenue account at December 31, 2014.
(b) Explain how relevant amounts will be reported on the annual financial statements prepared at the end of 2014.

SOLUTION TO EXERCISE 11-4

(a) Unearned Subscription Revenue   1,700,000
            Subscription Revenue   1,700,000
                (To record subscription revenues earned)

(b) Subscription revenue of $1,700,000 will appear on the income statement for the year ending December 31, 2014.

Unearned subscription revenue of $600,000 will appear as a current liability on the December 31, 2014, balance sheet because Viewer Publishers has an obligation to deliver magazines (or refund $600,000) to subscribers within one year of the balance sheet date because of revenues collected in advance.

Unearned subscription revenue of $700,000 will appear as a long-term liability on the December 31, 2014, balance sheet because of collections from customers for services to be performed in periods beyond one year from the balance sheet date.

Approach and Explanation: Draw a T-account. Enter the information given. Solve for the missing link.

Unearned Subscription Revenue

		12/31/14 Bal. before adjustment	3,000,000
Adjustment required	1,700,000		
		12/31/14 Desired balance	1,300,000

A magazine company often collects cash from subscribers before it provides magazines to them. Thus, at the point of receipt of cash, the company has an obligation to publish and deliver magazines for a number of months that follow the cash receipts.

Revenue is to be recognized in the period services are performed. If cash collections of $3,000,000 have been received and credited to the unearned revenue account during the period and the only unearned amount at the end of the period is $1,300,000, $1,700,000 must be removed from the liability account (unearned revenue) and transferred to an earned revenue account.

TIP:	Synonymous terms for **unearned revenue** are **deferred revenue, revenue collected in advance,** and **revenue received in advance.** Unearned revenue is a liability until the point in time when the revenue is earned or a refund is made.

EXERCISE 11-5

Purpose: (L.O. 5) This exercise will test your ability to properly account for situations involving contingent liabilities.

As the accountant for the Blow-Dry Manufacturing Company you are to analyze the following situations in preparing the balance sheet at December 31, 2014:

1. The Blow-Dry Manufacturing Company grants a six-month warranty on each of the hair dryers it sells. Based on past experience, it is estimated that 3% of all hair dryers sold are returned; it costs the company an average of $4.40 to satisfy the warranty obligation for each unit returned. The company sold 77,000 hair dryers in the last half of 2014 and has spent $3,000 for warranty work on those units.

2. The Speedy-Dry Manufacturing Company has filed a lawsuit for $100,000 in damages against the Blow-Dry Manufacturing Company for infringement of patent rights. Legal counsel for Blow-Dry states that it is reasonably possible, but not likely, that there will be an unfavorable outcome of the case because the Blow-Dry Company has good evidence to support its position.

3. The Internal Revenue Service is currently auditing a tax return of the Blow-Dry Company for a prior year. It is remotely possible that the IRS may disallow a deduction of $4,200 on the tax return.

4. The Blow-Dry Company is a defendant in a lawsuit. A former executive filed suit on November 7, 2014 based on his claim that the Blow-Dry Company did not comply with a written promise to pay him a $50,000 bonus for 2013. The company did not make the bonus payment because the executive resigned the last week of December 2013. Legal counsel for the company states that the written agreement will probably be held to apply even though the executive resigned. The suit is expected to be settled early in 2015.

Instructions
Explain how to account for each of the situations. Should a liability be included on the face of the balance sheet at December 31, 2014 or should there only be disclosure in the notes accompanying the financial statements or should the item not be recorded or disclosed? Justify your answer.

SOLUTION TO EXERCISE 11-5

1. Blow-Dry Manufacturing should **include** an estimated warranty **liability in the** current liability section of the **balance sheet** for $7,164 [(77,000 X 3% X $4.40) - $3,000]. Based on past experience, it is probable the company will have to expend goods and services to satisfy the warranty and the cost to do so is estimable.

2. Blow-Dry Manufacturing should **only disclose** this contingent liability **by a note** to accompany the financial statements. It is only reasonably possible that a liability exists at the balance sheet date due to the patent infringement lawsuit.

3. Blow-Dry Manufacturing Company **need not disclose** the IRS audit in the notes or include it in the body of the statements. It is only remotely possible that Blow-Dry will owe tax for the deduction in question.

4. Blow-Dry Company should **include** a $50,000 **liability in the** current liability section of the **balance sheet.** It appears probable that Blow-Dry will lose the suit and the amount is estimable. A journal entry should be made to accrue the loss to the current period (2014). The entry will include a debit to Loss from Lawsuit and a credit to Lawsuit Payable for $50,000.

Approach: Think about the definition of a contingent liability and how to account for one. A **contingent liability** is a potential liability that may become an actual liability in the future based on the outcome of some future event. The following guidelines apply:

1. If it is **probable** (likely) that a liability has been incurred and the amount is estimable, the liability should be recorded in the accounts. (The corresponding debit goes to an income statement account—expense or loss).

2. If it is only **reasonably possible** (less than likely and more than remote) that a liability exists, the potential liability should simply be disclosed in the notes that accompany the financial statements. That is, the potential liability will not appear in the body of the financial statements.

3. If it is only **remotely possible** (unlikely) that the future event will occur to substantiate a liability, the situation can be ignored. No liability is to be included in the balance sheet, and no note disclosure is required.

EXERCISE 11-6

Purpose: (L.O. 5) This exercise will provide an example of how to account for the sale of a product that includes a warranty.

Colleen Mahla Company sells portable tables to be used for massage therapy. Each table has a built-in stereo system and carries a one-year warranty contract that requires the company to replace defective parts and to provide the necessary repair labor. During 2014, the company sold 300 tables at a unit price of $2,500. Sales occurred evenly throughout the year. The one-year warranty costs to repair defective tables are estimated to average $240 per unit. Approximately 10% of the tables sold are estimated to require warranty service. During 2014, the company's first year of operations, 11 units were submitted for warranty work at a total cost of $2,750.

Instructions
(a) Record the adjusting journal entry at the end of 2014 to accrue the estimated warranty costs on the 2014 sales.
(b) Prepare the entry to record repair costs incurred in 2014 to honor warranty contracts on 2014 sales.
(c) Explain how all of the relevant amounts would be reflected on the financial statements prepared at the end of 2014.
(d) Why are warranty costs accrued in the period of sale? Explain.

SOLUTION TO EXERCISE 11-6

(a) 2014   Warranty Expense..   7,200
     Dec. 31   Warranty Liability...   7,200
                          (To accrue estimated warranty costs)
                          (300 X 10% X [$110 + $130] = $7,200)

(b) 2014   Warranty Liability...   2,750
     Jan. 1-   Repair Parts   2,750
     Dec. 31   (To record honoring of 11 warranty contracts
                          on 2014 sales)

> **TIP:** The entry in part (b) is shown in summary form. Throughout the year, customers will bring in units for warranty service and an entry to record the performance of the warranty work will be recorded at that time. The entry in part (a) is made only once a period, in the adjusting process at the end of the period, so the entry(s) in (b) is actually recorded chronologically before the entry illustrated in (a).

(c) Warranty expense of $7,200 is reported in the selling expense classification (which is part of operating expenses) in the income statement for the year ending December 31, 2014. The balance of $4,450 ($7,200 - $2,750) in the Warranty Liability account is to be classified as a current liability on the balance sheet at December 31, 2014.

(d) The accounting for warranty costs is based on the matching principle. To comply with this principle, the estimated cost of honoring product warranty contracts should be recognized as an expense in the period in which the sale occurs.

EXERCISE 11-7

Purpose: (L.O. 6, 7) This exercise will review the computations and journal entries relating to payroll accounting.

Hunt Enterprises has six salaried office employees who get paid on the last day of each month. Information about employee earnings for the current month (December 2014) and cumulative earnings for the first eleven months of 2014 appear on the next page. Data on federal income tax withholdings and health insurance withholdings is also provided.

The tax rates in effect are as follows:
     FICA: 8% on gross earnings of up to $90,000
     Federal unemployment taxes: 0.8% on gross earnings of up to $7,000
     State unemployment taxes: 5.4% on gross earnings of up to $7,000

Instructions
(a) Compute the following items for December 2014 for each employee listed and fill in your answers on the schedule provided.
    1. Employee FICA tax.
    2. Employee's take-home pay.
    3. Employer FICA tax.
    4. Federal unemployment tax.
    5. State unemployment tax.
(b) Prepare the journal entries to record:
    1. The December 31, 2014 payroll.
    2. The payroll tax expense associated with the December 31, 2014 payroll.
    3. The payment of the December 31, 2014, payroll.
(c) Explain how the balances of the payable accounts will be reported on the financial statements.

TIP:	Fixed amounts of compensation paid per week, month, or even per year, regardless of the number of hours worked during the designated period, are referred to as **salaries**. When an employee is paid a certain amount per hour, per day, or per unit, the compensation is referred to as **wages**. The wage rate multiplied by actual employee activity equals the amount of an employee's earnings for the period.

(a)

EMPLOYEE	Cumulative Earnings for Year up to Current Period	Earnings for Current Period (Mo. of Dec.)	Federal Income Tax Withheld This Period	Health Insurance Premiums Withheld This Period	(1) Employee FICA Tax	(2) Employee Take-home Pay	(3) Employer FICA Tax	(4) Federal Unemploy-ment Tax	(5) State Unemploy-ment Tax
James	$121,000.00	$ 11,000.00	$3,300.00	$100.00					
Mary Ann	8,800.00	800.00	140.00	50.00					
Ryan	1,500.00	500.00	100.00	50.00					
Cathy	2,100.00	700.00	80.00	100.00					
Margaret	16,500.00	1,500.00	200.00	100.00					
Diane	88,000.00	8,000.00	1,720.00	100.00					
Totals		$22,500.00	$5,540.00	$500.00					

SOLUTION TO EXERCISE 11-7
(a)

EMPLOYEE	Cumulative Earnings for Year up to Current Period	Earnings for Current Period (Mo. of Dec.)	Federal Income Tax Withheld This Period	Health Insurance Premiums Withheld This Period	(1) Employee FICA Tax	(2) Employee Take-home Pay	(3) Employer FICA Tax	(4) Federal Unemployment Tax	(5) State Unemployment Tax
James	$121,000.00	$11,000.00	$3,300.00	$100.00	$ 0[a]	$7,600.00	$ 0[a]	$ 0[b]	$ 0[b]
Mary Ann	8,800.00	800.00	140.00	50.00	64.00	546.00	64.00	0[b]	0[b]
Ryan	1,500.00	500.00	100.00	50.00	40.00[c]	310.00[d]	40.00[c]	4.00[e]	27.00[f]
Cathy	2,100.00	700.00	80.00	100.00	56.00	464.00	56.00	5.60	37.80
Margaret	16,500.00	1,500.00	200.00	100.00	120.00	1,080.00	120.00	0[b]	0[b]
Diane	88,000.00	8,000.00	1,720.00	100.00	160.00[g]	6,020.00	160.00[g]	0[b]	0[b]
Totals		$22,500.00	$5,540.00	$500.00	$440.00	$16,020.00	$440.00	$9.60	$64.80

[a] Cumulative earnings this year exceed $90,000.00 limit.
[b] Cumulative earnings this year exceed $7,000.00 limit.
[c] $500.00 X 8% = $40.00
[d] $500.00 - $100.00 - $50.00 - $40.00 = $310.00
[e] $500.00 X .8% = $4.00
[f] $500.00 X 5.4% = $27.00
[g] $90,000 - $88,000 = $2,000
$2,000.00 X 8% = $160.00

(b) 1. Dec. 31 Salaries and Wages Expense 22,500.00
              Federal Income Taxes Payable.............   5,540.00
              Health Insurance Payable 500.00
              FICA Taxes Payable 440.00
              Salaries and Wages Payable 16,020.00
              (To record payroll for the month ending
              December 31)

     2. Dec. 31 Payroll Tax Expense................................. 514.40
              FICA Taxes Payable 440.00
              Federal Unemployment Taxes Payable   9.60
              State Unemployment Taxes Payable 64.80
              (To record employer's payroll taxes on
              December 31 payroll)

     3. Dec. 31 Salaries and Wages Payable 16,020.00
              Cash...   16,020.00
              (To record payment of payroll)

(c) At December 31, 2014, the balances in Federal Income Taxes Payable, Health Insurance Payable, FICA Taxes Payable, Federal Unemployment Taxes Payable, and State Unemployment Taxes Payable will be classified in the current liability section of the balance sheet because they are all obligations that become due shortly after the balance sheet date and will require the use of current assets to liquidate them.

Explanation:

• An amount equal to 8% of an employee's gross earnings is withheld from the employee's paycheck and is remitted to the federal government for FICA taxes. This represents the employee's share of the FICA tax.

• An employee's **net pay** (or **take-home pay**) is calculated by the following:
      Employee's gross earnings for the current period
      - Federal income tax withholdings
      - FICA tax withholdings
      - Withholdings for voluntary deductions such as for charitable contributions, group health and life insurance premiums, savings, retirement fund contributions, and loan repayments
      = Net (or take-home) pay

• The employer must also bear a portion of the FICA tax. The FICA tax applies on earnings up to a certain level ($90,000 in this exercise). The employee, James, had surpassed this level prior to December so no FICA taxes are due on him for December. The employee Diane has only $2,000 ($90,000 - $88,000) of her December pay subject to the FICA tax because her December earnings put her cumulative earnings over the $90,000 threshold.

- The employer must bear the federal unemployment tax which is .8% on the employee's first $7,000 of gross earnings from that employer for the current year. Only Ryan and Cathy are still subject to that tax in this exercise.

- The employer must bear the state unemployment tax which is 5.4% on the employee's first $7,000 of gross earnings from that employer for the current year. Only the earnings of Ryan and Cathy are still subject to that tax in this exercise.

TIP:	State income tax withholdings are treated in the same manner as the federal income tax withholdings. Voluntary deductions for union dues, charitable contributions, and the like are handled in the same manner as the health insurance premiums above.
TIP:	The tax rate and earnings base for the FICA tax that are used in this exercise do **not** represent what is currently in effect. The rate and base for this tax changes so frequently that an assumed rate and base are used here for simplicity. The same can be said for the tax rate and earnings base for the unemployment taxes. The Medicare portion of the FICA tax typically has a higher earnings base than the Social Security portion; that has been ignored in this exercise.

EXERCISE 11-8

Purpose: (L.O. 1 thru 9) This exercise will quiz you about terminology used in this chapter.

A list of accounting terms with which you should be familiar appears below:

Bonus	Payroll deductions
Contingent liability	Payroll register
Current ratio	*Pension plan
Employee earnings record	*Postretirement benefits
Federal unemployment taxes	Salaries
Fees	Statement of earnings
FICA taxes	State unemployment taxes
Full-disclosure principle	Wage and Tax Statement (Form W-2)
Gross earnings	Wages
Net pay	Working capital
Notes payable	

Instructions
For each item below, enter in the blank the term that is described.

1. _____A potential liability that may become an actual liability in the future.

2. _____Employee pay that is based on a fixed amount per month or per year rather than an hourly rate.

3. _____Amounts paid to employees based on a rate per hour or on a piece-work basis.

4. _____Compensation to management and other personnel based on factors such as increased sales or the amount of net income.

5. _____Total compensation earned by an employee. Sometimes called **gross pay.**

6. _____Deductions from gross earnings to determine the amount of a paycheck.

7. _____A payroll record that accumulates the gross earnings, deductions, and net pay by employee for each pay period.

8. _____Gross earnings less payroll deductions. Sometimes called **take-home pay.**

9. _____Requires that companies disclose all circumstances and events that would make a difference to financial statement users.

10. _____Taxes imposed on the employer by the federal government that provide benefits for a limited time period to employees who lose their jobs through no fault of their own; the taxing authority is the federal government.

11. _____Taxes designed to provide workers with supplemental retirement, employment disability, and medical benefits.

12. _____A cumulative record of each employee's gross earnings, deductions, and net pay during the year.

13. _____Taxes imposed on the employer by states that provide benefits to employees who lose their jobs; the taxing authority is a state government.

14. _____A form showing gross earnings, FICA taxes withheld, and income taxes withheld which is prepared annually by an employer for each employee.

15. _____A document attached to a paycheck that indicates the employee's gross earnings, payroll deductions, and net pay.

16. _____An agreement whereby an employer provides benefits to employees after they retire.

17. _____Payments by an employer to retired employees for health care, life insurance, and pensions.

18. _____A measure of a company's liquidity; computed as current assets minus current liabilities.

19. _____A measure of a company's liquidity; computed by dividing current assets by current liabilities.

20. _____Obligations in the form of written promissory notes.

21. _____Payments made for the services of professionals.

SOLUTION TO EXERCISE 11-8

1. Contingent liability
2. Salaries
3. Wages
4. Bonus
5. Gross earnings
6. Payroll deductions
7. Payroll register
8. Net pay
9. Full-disclosure principle
10. Federal unemployment taxes
11. FICA taxes

12. Employee earnings record
13. State unemployment taxes
14. Wage and Tax Statement (Form W-2)
15. Statement of earnings
16. *Pension plan
17. *Postretirement benefits
18. Working capital
19. Current ratio
20. Notes payable
21. Fees

ANALYSIS OF MULTIPLE-CHOICE TYPE QUESTIONS

1. (L.O. 1) A current liability is an obligation that:
   a. was paid during the current period.
   b. will be reported as an expense within the year or operating cycle that follows the balance sheet date, whichever is longer.
   c. will be converted to a long-term liability within the next year.
   d. is expected to require the use of current assets or the creation of another current liability to liquidate it.

   Approach and Explanation: Before you read the answer selections, write down the definition for current liability. Compare each answer selection with your definition. A **current liability** is an obligation which will come due within one year and whose liquidation is reasonably expected to require the use of existing resources properly classifiable as current assets or the creation of other current liabilities. (Solution = d.)

2. (L.O. 1) Included in Jurassick Company's liability accounts at December 31, 2014, was the following:

12% note payable issued in 2011 for cash and due in May 2015	$200,000
Sales taxes payable	16,000
Interest payable	11,000
Federal income tax withholdings	6,000

   How much of the above should be included in the current liability section of Jurassick's balance sheet at December 31, 2014?
   a. $27,000.
   b. $33,000.
   c. $227,000.
   d. $233,000.

   Explanation: All of the obligations will become due within a year of the balance sheet date and will require the use of current assets to liquidate them ($200,000 + $16,000 + $11,000 + $6,000 = $233,000). (Solution = d.)

3. (L.O. 1) John Craig Clothiers has an obligation coming due on July 1, 2015, which will be settled by transferring assets which are properly classified as a long-term investment. The obligation should be classified on the company's December 31, 2014 balance sheet as:
a. a current liability.
b. a long-term liability.
c. a contra current liability item.
d. a contra current asset item.

Approach and Explanation: Write down the definition of current liability and determine if the obligation described meets the criteria contained in that definition. A **current liability** is an obligation which will come due within a year of the balance sheet date and is expected to require the use of assets properly classifiable as current assets or the creation of other current liabilities to liquidate it. The obligation described in the question is coming due within a year of the balance sheet date, but a noncurrent asset will be used to settle the debt; thus the obligation is properly classifiable as a long-term liability. (Solution = b.)

4. (L.O. 1, 3) Which of the following should be reported as a current liability at December 31, 2014?
a. Revenue received in advance to be earned in 2015.
b. Installment loan payments due after December 31, 2015.
c. Pension obligations estimated to mature in ten years.
d. Note payable due in 2016.

Approach and Explanation: Define current liability. A **current liability** is an obligation that comes due within one year of the balance sheet date (and thus will be paid within one year) and is expected to require the use of current assets or the incurrence of another current liability to liquidate it. Analyze each answer selection to see if it meets the definition. Revenue received in advance represents an obligation to perform services or to deliver goods or to provide a refund to the customer. If the revenue will be earned in the period that immediately follows the balance sheet date, it is a current liability; if it will be earned beyond that one year mark, it is to be classified as a long-term liability. Selections "b", "c", and "d", are all incorrect because they do not meet the definition. (Solution = a.)

5. (L.O. 2) Which of the following is true regarding a situation where the accounting period ends on a date that does not coincide with an interest payment date for a note payable that is outstanding?
    a. No adjusting entry is required. The interest expense will be recorded in the period it is paid.
    b. An adjusting entry is required and it contains a debit to Interest Expense and a credit to Interest Payable.
    c. An adjusting entry is required and it contains a debit to Note Payable and a credit to Interest Expense.
    d. An adjusting entry is required and it contains a debit to Income Summary and a credit to Interest Expense.

    Explanation: An adjusting entry is required to properly match the interest expense with the time period for which the interest was incurred. Interest is payment for use of someone else's money. The cost of that use should be matched with the period to which the interest pertains. (Solution = b.)

6. (L.O. 2) A note payable dated October 1, 2014 has a face value of $10,000, an interest rate stipulated at 10%, and a maturity date of April 1, 2015. Interest expense (pertaining to this note) to appear on the income statement for the year ending December 31, 2014 amounts to:
    a. $0.
    b. $125.00.
    c. $166.67.
    d. $250.00.

    Approach and Explanation: Write down the formula for computing interest. Plug in the amounts given and solve.

Face Value of Note	X	Annual Interest Rate	X	Time in Terms of One Year	= Interest
$10,000	X	10%	X	3/12 =	$250.00 (Solution = d.)

7. (L.O. 3) McGuire Company sells a product on credit for $200. The sale is subject to a 5% state sales tax which is not included in the $200. The entry to record the sale would include a:
    a. debit to Accounts Receivable for $200.
    b. credit to Sales for $210.
    c. credit to Sales Taxes Payable for $10.
    d. debit to Sales Taxes for $10.

    Approach and Explanation: Before looking at the alternative answers, prepare the journal entry on paper (or mentally). Then find the solution that agrees with your entry. The entry is:

Accounts Receivable	210	
Sales Revenue..		200
Sales Taxes Payable		10

The sales tax is levied by the state government. The company making the sale acts as an agent for the state government as it collects the tax and remits it to the taxing authority. (Solution = c.)

8. (L.O. 4) The current ratio is calculated by dividing:
    a. current assets by total liabilities.
    b. current assets by current liabilities.
    c. quick assets by current liabilities.
    d. total assets by total liabilities.

    Approach and Explanation: Write down the formula for the current ratio **before** you read the answer selections. Choose the answer that matches the formula.

    $$\text{Current ratio} = \frac{\text{Current assets}}{\text{Current liabilities}}$$

    (Solution = b.)

9. (L.O. 4) Which of the following items would **not** be used in calculating the current ratio?
    a. Accounts payable.
    b. Inventory.
    c. Accounts receivable.
    d. Furniture purchased during the current period.

    Approach and Explanation: Think about the current ratio and write down the formula to compute it. Then read the answer selections and determine which selection does not fit into the formula. The current ratio is determined by dividing total current assets by total current liabilities at a point in time. Answer selection "d" would be classified under the property, plant, and equipment classification and would therefore not be included in the calculation of the working capital ratio. (Solution = d.)

10. (L.O. 4) Which of the following will **increase** the amount of working capital?
    a. Collection of accounts receivable.
    b. Sale of a long-term investment at book value.
    c. Purchase of inventory on account.
    d. Payment of a short-term note payable.

    Approach: Write down the formula for determining working capital. Write down the journal entry for each transaction mentioned. Analyze the accounts in each entry to determine the effect on the elements of the working capital computation.

    Working Capital = Current Assets - Current Liabilities

Explanation:

a. Cash.. XX

        Accounts Receivable.. XX

There is no net effect on total current assets (Cash increases by the same amount that Accounts Receivable decreases) and no effect on current liabilities; hence, there is no effect on working capital.

b. Cash.. XX

        Long-term Investment.. XX

There is an increase in Cash (a current asset) and no effect on any other component of working capital; hence, working capital increases.

c. Inventory.. XX

        Accounts Payable.. XX

Current assets increase (Inventory increases) by the same amount that current liabilities increase (Accounts Payable increases); therefore, there is no net effect on working capital.

d. Short-term Note Payable.. XX

        Cash.. XX

Current liabilities decrease by the same amount that current assets decrease; hence, there is no net effect on working capital.

(Solution = b.)

11. (L.O. 5) A company has a contingency. If it is probable that an actual liability exists at the balance sheet date, but the amount is **not** reasonably estimable, the contingent liability should be:
   a. ignored and not disclosed.
   b. reported on the face of the balance sheet without an amount.
   c. disclosed only in the notes accompanying the financial statements.
   d. reported only in the following period.

Approach and Explanation: Briefly review in your mind the guidelines for reporting contingent liabilities:

    If it is **probable** that a loss will occur and the amount is estimable, accrue the loss and report the liability on the face of the balance sheet.

    If it is only **reasonably possible** a loss will occur, or if it is probable but not estimable, disclose only in the notes.

    If the loss is **remotely possible,** it need not be disclosed or accrued.

(Solution = c.)

TIP: In the context of accounting for contingencies, **probable** means "likely;" **remotely possible** means "not likely"; **reasonably possible** means "less than likely and more than remote."

12. (L.O. 5) An example of a contingent liability is:
    a. Sales taxes payable.
    b. Accrued salaries.
    c. Property taxes payable.
    d. A pending lawsuit.

    Approach and Explanation: Mentally define contingent liability and think of examples before you read the alternative answer selections. A **contingent liability** is a situation involving uncertainty as to possible loss or expense that will ultimately be resolved when one or more future events occur or fail to occur. Examples are pending or threatened lawsuits, pending IRS audits, and product warranties. Accrued salaries result in an actual liability. Sales taxes payable and property taxes payable are both actual liabilities if they exist at a balance sheet date. (Solution = d.)

13. (L.O. 5) Warranty costs are accrued in the period of sale to comply with the:
    a. expense recognition principle.
    b. revenue recognition principle.
    c. cost principle.
    d. concept of conservatism.

    Explanation: Revenues are recognized in the period they are earned to comply with the revenue recognition principle. Then the expense recognition principle dictates that all costs incurred in generating the revenue recognized should be reported in the same time period as the revenue. Therefore, warranty costs are to be matched with the revenue from the sale of the product under warranty. (Solution = a.)

14. (L.O. 5) A contingent loss which is judged to be reasonably possible and estimable should be:

	Accrued	**Disclosed**
a.	Yes	Yes
b.	Yes	No
c.	No	Yes
d.	No	No

    Explanation: A contingent loss that is probable and estimable is to be accrued. A contingent loss that is reasonably possible should be disclosed, but it should not be accrued. A contingent loss that is remotely possible can be ignored. (Solution = c.)

15. (L.O. 5) D. Scott Corporation provides a two-year warranty with the sale of its product. Scott estimates that warranty costs will equal 4% of the selling price the first year after sale and 6% of the selling price the second year after the sale. The following data are available:

	2013	**2014**
Sales	$400,000	$500,000
Actual warranty expenditures	10,000	38,000

    The balance of the warranty liability at December 31, 2014 should be:
    a. $12,000.
    b. $42.000.
    c. $44,000.
    d. $50,000.

    Approach and Explanation: Draw a T-account for the liability and enter the amounts that would be reflected in the account and determine its balance.

Warranty Liability

(2)	Expenditures in 2013	10,000	(1)	Expense for 2013	40,000
(4)	Expenditures in 2014	38,000	(3)	Expense for 2014	50,000
				12/31/14 Balance	42,000

(1) $400,000 X (4% + 6%) = $40,000 expense for 2013.
   The total warranty cost related to the products sold during 2013 should be recognized in the period of sale (matching principle).
(2) Given data. Actual expenditures during 2013.
(3) $500,000 X (4% + 6%) = $50,000 expense for 2014.
(4) Given data. Actual expenditures during 2014.

(Solution = b.)

TIP: Because some items are sold near the end of the year and the warranty is for two years, a portion of the warranty liability should be classified as a current liability (the amount pertaining to the actual expenditures estimated to occur in 2015) and the remainder as a long-term liability.

---

16. (L.O. 6) An employee's net pay is determined by gross earnings minus amounts for income tax withholdings,
   a. employee's portion of FICA taxes, and unemployment taxes.
   b. employee's and employer's portion of FICA taxes, and unemployment taxes.
   c. employee's portion of FICA taxes, unemployment taxes, and any voluntary deductions.
   d. employee's portion of FICA taxes, and any voluntary deductions.

   Approach and Explanation: Before you read the answer selections, write down the model for the net pay (take-home pay) computation. Then find the answer selection that agrees with your model.

   Employee's gross earnings for the current period
   - Federal income tax withholdings
   - FICA tax withholdings
   - Withholdings for voluntary deductions such as for charitable contributions, group health and life insurance premiums, savings, retirement fund contributions, and loan repayments
   = Net (or take-home) pay

   (Solution = d.)

17. (L.O. 7) Which group of items would be recorded in the Payroll Tax Expense account?
    a. Employer's share of FICA taxes, federal unemployment tax, state unemployment tax.
    b. Federal and state income tax withholdings, all FICA taxes, federal unemployment tax, state unemployment tax.
    c. Federal and state income tax withholdings, employer's share of FICA taxes, federal and state unemployment taxes, union dues.
    d. Employer's share of FICA, federal and state unemployment taxes, union dues, insurance premiums, contributions to charitable organizations.

    Approach and Explanation: Think of the payroll taxes the employer must bear; they are the ones recorded in the Payroll Tax Expense account. Payroll taxes borne by the employer include the employer's share of FICA tax and all unemployment taxes (both federal and state). Taxes withheld from an employee's payroll check (employee's share of FICA and income tax withholdings) represent a portion of the employee's total earnings (gross pay); therefore, they are in effect charged (debited) to a wages and salaries expense account. (Solution = a.)

18. (L.O. 7) Which group of items represents a cost burden for the employer rather than the employee?
    a. Federal income tax withholdings, employer's portion of FICA tax, state unemployment tax.
    b. Employer's portion of FICA tax, state unemployment tax, federal unemployment tax.
    c. Employer's and employee's portions of FICA tax, federal unemployment tax, state unemployment tax.
    d. Federal income tax withholdings, state income tax withholdings, employer's share of FICA taxes, federal unemployment tax, state unemployment tax.

    Explanation: The items to be borne by the employer include the employer's share of FICA tax and all unemployment taxes (both state and federal). Items which must be borne by an employee include the employee's share of FICA tax, federal income tax withholdings, state income tax withholdings, city income tax withholdings, and voluntary deductions. (Solution = b.)

19. (L.O. 6) Deductions from an employee's earnings may include:
    a. withholdings for federal and state income tax.
    b. FICA tax.
    c. union dues.
    d. amounts for purchase of savings bonds for employee.
    e. all of the above.

    Explanation: See **Explanation to Question 18** above. (Solution = e.)

*20. (L.O. 9) A 401(k) plan is often referred to as a:
   a. defined-contribution plan.
   b. defined-benefit plan.
   c. post-retirement care plan.
   d. post-retirement living plan.

Explanation: A 401(k) plan is often referred to as a **defined-contribution type pension plan**. In a defined-contribution plan, the plan defines the contribution that an employer will make but not the benefit that the employee will receive at retirement. The other type of pension plan is a defined-benefit plan in which the employer agrees to pay a defined amount to retirees, based on employees meeting certain eligibility standards. (Solution = a.)

CHAPTER 12

. . . .

ACCOUNTING FOR PARTNERSHIPS

OVERVIEW

There are three forms of business organization: proprietorship, partnership, and corporation. Accounting for the revenues, expenses, assets, and liabilities is the same for all three forms of business organization; however, these three forms differ in accounting for owners' equity. Thus far in this book, we have been referring to a sole proprietorship when our discussions involved owner's equity. Accounting for owners' equity of a corporation will be discussed in Chapters 13 and 14. In this chapter, we will examine accounting for owners' equity in a partnership. The procedures are the same ones that are used in accounting for a proprietorship—with the exception that separate capital and drawing accounts must be maintained for each partner.

SUMMARY OF LEARNING OBJECTIVES

1. **Identify the characteristics of the partnership form of business organization.** The principal characteristics of a partnership are: (a) association of individuals, (b) mutual agency, (c) limited life, (d) unlimited liability, and (e) co-ownership of property.

2. **Explain the accounting entries for the formation of a partnership.** When formed, a partnership records each partner's initial investment at the fair market value of the invested assets at the date of their transfer to the partnership.

3. **Identify the bases for dividing net income or net loss.** Partnerships divide net income or net loss on the basis of the income ratio, which may be (a) a fixed ratio, (b) a ratio based on beginning or average capital balances, (c) salaries to partners and the remainder on a fixed ratio, (d) interest on partners' capital and the remainder on a fixed ratio, and (e) salaries to partners, interest on partners' capital, and the remainder on a fixed ratio.

4. **Describe the form and content of partnership financial statements.** The financial statements of a partnership are similar to those of a proprietorship. The principal differences are as follows: (a) The partnership shows the division of net income on the income statement. (b) The owners' equity statement is called a partners' capital statement. (c) The partnership reports each partner's capital on the balance sheet.

5. **Explain the effects of the entries to record the liquidation of a partnership.** When a partnership is liquidated, it is necessary to record the (a) sale of noncash assets, (b) allocation of the gain or loss on realization, (c) payment of partnership liabilities, and (d) distribution of cash to the partners on the basis of their capital balances.

*6. **Explain the effects of the entries when a new partner is admitted.** The entry to record the admittance of a new partner by purchase of a partner's interest affects only partners' capital accounts. The entries to record the admittance by investment of assets in the partnership (a) increases both net assets and total capital and (b) may result in recognition of a bonus to either the old partners or the new partner.

*7. **Describe the effects of the entries when a partner withdraws from the firm.** The entry to record a withdrawal from the firm when the partners pay from their personal assets affects only partners' capital accounts. The entry to record a withdrawal when payment is made from partnership assets (a) decreases net assets and total capital and (b) may result in recognizing a bonus either to the retiring partner or the remaining partners.

*This material is discussed in **Appendix 12A** in the text.

TIPS ON CHAPTER TOPICS

TIP: There are various ways in which the partnership income ratio (income-sharing ratio) may be stated. For example: Walt and his brother Roy have a partnership where Walt is to receive 75% of the partnership profits, and Roy is to receive 25%. This relationship can be expressed in the following equivalent ways: **Walt : Roy** **75% : 25%** **3 : 1** **3/4 : 1/4** Notice how the 3 : 1 was determined by dividing 75% by 25%. Also, notice how the 3/4 : 1/4 was derived by looking at the 3 : 1 expression and adding them (the 3 and the 1) together to get the denominator of 4 and then using the 3 and 1 as separate numerators (3/4 : 1/4). The percentages (75% + 25%) add up to 100%; the fractions (3/4 + 1/4) sum to 1.

TIP:	The partnership **income ratio** is often called the **income and loss ratio, profit and loss ratio, income-sharing agreement, income-sharing ratio,** or the **P & L ratio.**
TIP:	Partners must agree on a manner in which partnership income is to be divided. They may agree to share profits based on a simple ratio or they may have more complicated arrangements. When partners do not contribute equal services (or time) to the business and/or do not have equal investments (capital balances) in the business, they may acknowledge and compensate for these differences in their profit-and-loss-sharing agreement. "Salaries" may be used to reflect the relative amounts of talent or time contributed by the partners. "Interest" on capital account balances or a ratio based on relative sizes of the balances of partners' capital accounts may be used to give effect to the different investment amounts of partners.
TIP:	General partners can share business profits and losses in any mutually agreeable way. If they do not mutually agree in writing to a nonequal sharing, most state laws provide for an equal allocation.
TIP:	By law, death, bankruptcy, or any event that takes away the ability of one partner to contract, automatically ends a partnership. A partnership may also be dissolved for any reason when the partners decide it best to discontinue the partnership. Some of the most frequent reasons are the retirement of a partner, incompatibility among the partners, the completion of the purpose for which the business was formed, or a history of unprofitable operations.
TIP:	The dissolution of a partnership involves the distribution of the partnership assets to the partners. All noncash assets that the partners do not wish to accept in their present form are converted to cash, and the resulting cash is distributed to the partners. Gains and losses from the sale (liquidation) of the partnership assets are allocated to the partners' capital accounts in accordance with the same **income ratio** that is used to allocate other business profits or losses. Assets (cash and any assets not converted to cash) are then distributed to partners according to the **remaining balances in their respective capital accounts.**

ILLUSTRATION 12-1
DIFFERENT FORMS OF ORGANIZATIONS WITH PARTNERSHIP CHARACTERISTICS (L.O. 1)

	Major Advantages	**Major Disadvantages**
Regular partnership	Simple and inexpensive to create and operate.	Owners (partners) personally liable for business debts.
Limited partnership	Limited partners have limited personal liability for business debts as long as they do not participate in management. General partners can raise cash without involving outside investors in management of the business.	General partners personally liable for business debts. More expensive to create than regular partnership. Suitable mainly for companies that invest in real estate
Limited liability partnership	Mostly of interest to partners in old-line professions such as law, medicine, and accounting. Owners (partners) are not personally liable for the malpractice of other partners.	Unlike a limited liability company, owners (partners) remain personally liable for many types of obligations owed to business creditors, lenders, and landlords. Often limited to a short list of professions.
Limited liability company	Owners have limited personal liability for business debts even if they participate in management.	More expensive to create than regular partnership.

Source: www.nolo.com--ownership structures (accessed June 2010).

EXERCISE 12-1

Purpose: (L.O. 1) This exercise will review the advantages and disadvantages of the partnership form of business organization.

Groucho, Harpo, and Marko are making plans to enter into a new business together. They come to you for advice as to whether they should form a corporation or operate as a partnership.

Instructions
(a) List and briefly describe the advantages of the partnership form over the corporate form of business organization.
(b) List and briefly describe the disadvantages of the partnership form over the corporate form of business organization.

SOLUTION TO EXERCISE 12-1

(a) The **advantages of the partnership form** as compared to a corporation include:
   1. **A partnership is more easily formed.** A partnership is created by a contract expressing the voluntary agreement of two or more individuals. (The agreement should be written and is referred to as the **partnership agreement or articles of co-partnership.**) There is much more effort and "red tape" involved in forming a corporation.
   2. **A partnership has more freedom from governmental regulations and restrictions.** For example, a partnership is not a taxable entity; it files only an information tax return, and the partners pick up their share of business income on their personal income tax returns. A corporation is a taxable entity. Income of a corporation is taxed once at the corporate level and again as owners receive dividends which must be reported as income on their personal income tax returns.
   3. **There is more ease of decision making with a partnership.** Decisions can be made quickly by a partnership on substantive matters affecting the firm, whereas in a corporation, formal meetings with the board of directors are often needed.

(b) The **disadvantages of the partnership form** as compared to a corporation include:
   1. **Mutual agency exists in a partnership.** Mutual agency means that each partner acts on behalf of the partnership when engaging in partnership business. The act of any partner is binding on all other partners, even when partners act beyond the scope of their authority, so long as the act appears to be appropriate for the partnership. In a corporation, an owner's (stockholder's) acts are not binding on the organization if the owner's acts are beyond the scope of the individual's authority.

2. **A partnership has a limited life.** A partnership may be ended voluntarily at any time through the acceptance of a new partner into the firm or the withdrawal of an old partner. A partnership may be ended involuntarily by the death or incapacity of a partner. The life of a corporation is unlimited.

3. **Each partner has unlimited liability.** Each partner is personally and individually liable for all partnership liabilities. Creditors' claims attach first to partnership assets and then to the personal resources of any partner, irrespective of that partner's equity in the partnership. Some states allow **limited partnerships** in which the liability of a limited partner is limited to that partner's equity in the partnership. However, there must always be at least one partner with unlimited liability, often referred to as the **general partner.**

TIP: It is often harder for a partnership to raise money than it is for a corporation. Also, depending on the articles of co-partnership, it may be more difficult to transfer ownership of the business when the partnership form is used rather than the corporate form.

EXERCISE 12-2

Purpose: (L.O. 2) This exercise will illustrate the accounting involved when three individuals pool their assets to form a partnership.

Malcolm, Blackford, and Aaron combine their proprietorships to start a new partnership named Pet Specialists. The partners invest the following assets in the business:

	Book Value			Market Value		
	Malcolm	**Blackford**	**Aaron**	**Malcolm**	**Blackford**	**Aaron**
Cash	$ 8,800	$11,500	$4,000	$ 8,800	$11,500	$4,000
Accounts receivable	4,000			4,000		
Allowance for doubtful accounts	(300)			(800)		
Equipment		1,000	3,000		500	2,000
Accumulated deprecia-tion		(800)	(600)			
	$12,500	$11,700	$6,400	$12,000	$12,000	$6,000

Instructions
Prepare the journal entries to record the investments of Malcolm, Blackford, and Aaron.

SOLUTION TO EXERCISE 12-2

Cash...	8,800	
Accounts Receivable..	4,000	
Allowance for Doubtful Accounts..........................		800
Malcolm, Capital...		12,000
(To record investment of Malcolm)		

Cash...	11,500	
Equipment..	500	
Blackford, Capital..		12,000
(To record investment of Blackford)		
Cash...	4,000	
Equipment..	2,000	
Aaron, Capital		6,000
(To record investment by Aaron)		

TIP: Notice the accounting treatment of the equipment invested by Blackford. Neither the original cost ($1,000) nor its book value ($200) on Blackford's books is recorded by the partnership. The equipment is recorded on the partnership's books at its fair market value ($500) at the acquisition date, which is consistent with the cost principle.

Since the equipment has not been used by the partnership, there can be no accumulated depreciation when the asset is initially acquired by the partnership entity. In contrast, the gross claims on customers represented by Malcolm's accounts receivable ($4,000) are carried to the partnership, and the Allowance for Doubtful Accounts is established at $800 to arrive at a cash (net) realizable value of $3,200.

TIP: Appropriate liability accounts are credited for any debts assumed by the partnership.

TIP: Care must be taken to ensure that appropriate valuation of assets is made when the partners invest them. Otherwise, when disposition is later made of the assets, improper allocation of gains and losses may result. (This is because the gains and losses would then be allocated among the partners according to their income ratio rather than being reflected in the capital account of the partner who contributed the asset.)

EXERCISE 12-3

Purpose: (L.O. 4) This exercise will test your knowledge of the reasons for changes in the balance of a partner's capital account.

A partner's capital account balance can change for several reasons.

Instructions
In the T-account below, insert each code letter on the appropriate side of the account to indicate how each of the following items would be reflected in a partner's capital account.

Ken Dixon, Capital

(a)   Balance at beginning of the period.
(b)   Additional investment of assets in partnership by the partner.
(c)   Partner's share of net income for the period.
(d)   Partner's drawings for the period.
(e)   A disinvestment by the partner.
(f)   Balance at end of the period.

SOLUTION TO EXERCISE 12-3

Ken Dixon, Capital

(d) Drawings	(a) Balance at beginning of the period
(e) Disinvestment	(b) Additional investment
	(c) Share of net income
	(f) Balance at end of the period

> **TIP:**   As in a proprietorship, changes in capital may result from four causes: additional capital investment, results of operations (net income or net loss), drawings, and capital disinvestment.

EXERCISE 12-4

Purpose: (L.O. 4) This exercise illustrates the entries involved with closing the Income Summary and Drawings accounts in a partnership business.

The following selected accounts appear in the ledger of the Wizzard Services Company. The business is owned by three partners named Ginkel, Grindstaff, and Yount. The amounts shown appear at December 31, 2014, **after** all revenue and expense accounts have been closed, but **before** any other closing entries have been prepared. The partners share all profits and losses equally.

Chip Ginkel, Capital		
	Bal. 1/1/14	50,000
	Aug. 1	3,200

Chip Ginkel, Drawings		
Mar. 31	3,000	
June 30	3,000	
Sept. 30	4,000	
Dec. 30	2,500	

Mickey Grindstaff, Capital		
	Bal. 1/1/14	58,000

Mickey Grindstaff, Drawings		
Apr. 30	4,000	
Aug. 31	4,000	
Dec. 30	4,800	

Eric Yount, Capital		
	Bal. 1/1/14	65,000
	May 1	2,700

Eric Yount, Drawings		
Mar. 31	3,000	
June 30	3,000	
Sept. 30	3,000	
Dec. 30	4,200	

Income Summary		
Dec. 31 234,000	Dec. 31 279,000	

Instructions
(a) Record the remaining necessary closing entries in general journal form.
(b) Post the entries to the ledger accounts.
(c) Calculate the balances of the capital accounts that will appear in the owners' equity section of the balance sheet at December 31, 2014.
(d) Prepare the partners' capital statement for the year ended December 31, 2014.

SOLUTION TO EXERCISE 12-4

(a)
2014

Dec.	31	Income Summary	45,000	
		Chip Ginkel, Capital		15,000
		Mickey Grindstaff, Capital		15,000
		Eric Yount, Capital		15,000
	31	Chip Ginkel, Capital	12,500	
		Chip Ginkel, Drawings		12,500
	31	Mickey Grindstaff, Capital	12,800	
		Mickey Grindstaff, Drawings		12,800
	31	Eric Yount, Capital	13,200	
		Eric Yount, Drawings		13,200

(b)

Chip Ginkel, Capital			
Dec. 31	12,500	Bal. 1/1/14	50,000
		Aug. 1	3,200
		Dec. 31	15,000
		Bal. Dec. 31	55,700

Chip Ginkel, Drawings			
Mar. 31	3,000	Dec. 31 Clos. 12,500
June 30	3,000	
Sept. 30	4,000	
Dec. 30	2,500	

Mickey Grindstaff, Capital			
Dec. 31	12,800	Bal. 1/1/14	58,000
		Dec. 31	15,000
		Bal. Dec. 31	60,200

Mickey Grindstaff, Drawings			
Apr. 30	4,000	Dec. 31 Clos. 12,800
Aug. 31	4,000	
Dec. 30	4,800	

Eric Yount, Capital			
Dec. 31	13,200	Bal. 1/1/14	65,000
		May 1	2,700
		Dec. 31	15,000
		Bal. Dec. 31	69,500

Eric Yount, Drawings			
Mar. 31	3,000	Dec. 31 Clos. 13,200
June 30	3,000	
Sept 30	3,000	
Dec. 30	4,200	

Income Summary			
Dec. 31	234,000	Dec. 31	279,000
Dec. 31 Clos.	45,000		

(c) Ending balances for the balance sheet:

Chip Ginkel, Capital	$ 55,700
Mickey Grindstaff, Capital	60,200
Eric Yount, Capital	69,500
Total	$185,400

(d)

WIZZARD SERVICES COMPANY
Partners' Capital Statement
For the Year Ended December 31, 2014

	Chip Ginkel	Mickey Grindstaff	Eric Yount	Total
Capital, January 1	$50,000	$58,000	$65,000	$173,000
Add: Additional investment	3,200		2,700	5,900
Net income	15,000	15,000	15,000	45,000
	68,200	73,000	82,700	223,900
Less: Drawings	12,500	12,800	13,200	38,500
Capital, December 31	$55,700	$60,200	$69,500	$185,400

TIP:	The function of a partners' capital statement is to explain the changes in each partner's capital account and in total partnership capital during the year. As in a proprietorship, changes in capital may result from four causes: additional capital investment, net income or net loss, drawings, and capital disinvestment.

EXERCISE 12-5

Purpose: (L.O. 3) This exercise will give your practice in allocating partnership net income (or net loss) among partners under various arrangements.

The following balances pertain to the partnership equity accounts of the Haveard Vegetable Market at January 1, 2014:

Lew, Capital	$16,000
Sybil, Capital	12,000
Mike, Capital	8,000

Instructions

Compute the division of partnership net income (or net loss) in each of the **independent** situations described below.

(a) Net income is $36,000. No written agreement on profit distribution exists.

(b) Net income is $36,000. Salaries are $10,000 to Lew, $8,000 to Sybil, and $6,000 to Mike. Any remaining profits are shared equally.

(c) Net income is $54,000. Net income is divided on the basis of relative beginning capital account balances.

(d) Net income is $48,000. Salaries are $12,000 to Lew, $11,000 to Sybil and $11,000 to Mike. Interest of 6% on beginning capital account balances is to be allocated. Any remaining income is to be divided equally.

(e) Net income is $48,000 and is to be divided on a 2:1:1 ratio (2/4 to Lew, 1/4 to Sybil, and 1/4 to Mike).

(f) Net income is $48,000. Salaries are $26,000 to Lew, $20,000 to Sybil and $11,000 to Mike. The remainder is to be divided equally.

(g) Net loss is $9,000 and is to be divided equally.

(h) Net loss is $15,000. Salaries are $10,000 to Lew, $8,000 to Sybil, and $6,000 to Mike. The remainder is divided equally.

SOLUTION TO EXERCISE 12-5

Approach: Allocate salary allowances, then interest allowances, and then apportion the remainder using the appropriate ratio.

(a)   **Division of Net Income**

	Lew	Sybil	Mike	Total
Equally: Lew ($36,000 X 1/3)	$12,000			$12,000
Sybil ($36,000 X 1/3)		$12,000		12,000
Mike ($36,000 X 1/3)			$12,000	12,000
Total division	$12,000	$12,000	$12,000	$36,000

(b)

Division of Net Income

	Lew	**Sybil**	**Mike**	**Total**
Salary allowance	$10,000	$ 8,000	$ 6,000	$24,000
Remaining income, $12,000 ($36,000 - $24,000)				
Lew ($12,000 X 1/3)	4,000			
Sybil ($12,000 X 1/3)		4,000		
Mike ($12,000 X 1/3)			4,000	
Total remainder				12,000
Total division	$14,000	$12,000	$10,000	$36,000

(c)

Division of Net Income

	Lew	**Sybil**	**Mike**	**Total**
Lew: 4/9a X $54,000	$24,000			$24,000
Sybil: 3/9b X $54,000		$18,000		18,000
Mike: 2/9c X $54,000			$12,000	12,000
Total division	$24,000	$18,000	$12,000	$54,000

aLew, Capital	$16,000	$16,000/$36,000 = 4/9
bSybil, Capital	12,000	$12,000/$36,000 = 3/9
cMike, Capital	8,000	$8,000/$36,000 = 2/9
Total capital	$36,000	

(d)

Division of Net Income

	Lew	**Sybil**	**Mike**	**Total**
Salary allowance	$12,000	$11,000	$11,000	$34,000
Interest allowance				
Lew ($16,000 X 6%)	960			
Sybil ($12,000 X 6%)		720		
Mike ($8,000 X 6%)			480	
Total interest				2,160
Total salaries and interest	12,960	11,720	11,480	36,160
Remaining income, $11,840 ($48,000 - $36,160)				
Lew ($11,840 X 1/3)	3,947			
Sybil ($11,840 X 1/3)		3,947		
Mike ($11,840 X 1/3)			3,946	
Total remainder				11,840
Total division	$16,907	$15,667	$15,426	$48,000

TIP: Interest on partnership capital is determined by multiplying the appropriate interest rate by the balance in the individual partner's capital account. Usually, the balance at the beginning of the period is used.

(e)

Division of Net Income

	Lew	Sybil	Mike	Total
2:1:1 ratio:				
Lew: 2/4 X $48,000	$24,000			$24,000
Sybil: 1/4 X $48,000		$12,000		12,000
Mike: 1/4 X $48,000			$12,000	12,000
Total division	$24,000	$12,000	$12,000	$48,000

(f)

Division of Net Income

	Lew	Sybil	Mike	Total
Salary allowance	$26,000	$20,000	$11,000	$57,000
Remaining deficiency, $9,000				
($48,000 - $57,000)				
Lew: ($9,000 X 1/3)	(3,000)			
Sybil: ($9,000 X 1/3)		(3,000)		
Mike: ($9,000 X 1/3)			(3,000)	
Total deficiency				(9,000)
Total division	$23,000	$17,000	$8,000	$48,000

> **TIP:** If the salary and interest allocations exceed the total profits to be divided, the resulting negative figure (deficiency) must be divided among the partners, thereby reducing the net amounts to be credited to the partners' capital accounts in the process of closing the Income Summary account.

(g)

Division of Net Loss

	Lew	Sybil	Mike	Total
Equally:				
Lew: ($9,000 X 1/3)	$(3,000)			$(3,000)
Sybil: ($9,000 X 1/3)		$(3,000)		(3,000)
Mike: ($9,000 X 1/3)			$(3,000)	(3,000)
Total division	$(3,000)	$(3,000)	$(3,000)	$(9,000)

(h)

Division of Net Loss

	Lew	Sybil	Mike	Total
Salary allowance	$10,000	$ 8,000	$ 6,000	$24,000
Remaining deficiency, $39,000				
($24,000 + $15,000)				
Lew ($39,000 X 1/3)	(13,000)			
Sybil ($39,000 X 1/3)		(13,000)		
Mike ($39,000 X 1/3)			(13,000)	
Total deficiency				(39,000)
Total division	$(3,000)	$(5,000)	$(7,000)	$(15,000)

TIP: When the income-sharing agreement provides for "salaries" and/or "interest" on capital account balances, these allocations must also be made in determining the amount of a **net loss** that is to be allocated to each partner.

TIP: When you have arrived at an answer for the amount of net income (or net loss) to be allocated to each partner, double check to see that the total amount allocated to all partners according to your computations equals the total amount you set out to allocate. If the amounts are not equal, you have made an error in your calculations.

TIP: Partners must agree on the manner in which the partnership income is to be divided; otherwise the law says it will be divided equally.

TIP: In determining an equitable distribution of the partnership income, the partners should consider the following factors:

(a) Salary allowances to the partners for services they perform for the partnership.

(b) Interest allowances to the partners for the capital they have invested in the partnership.

(c) The allocation of any remaining income (or deficiency) after allocations (a) and (b) have been made based on a fixed ratio.

TIP: Partners' salaries are **not** true salaries (since owners can't pay themselves), in the legal sense of the term, and do **not** represent an expense to be deducted from revenues on the business books. They are used **only** as a means of computing a partner's share of the partnership income. The same is true regarding interest allowances for partners. The amount of "interest" allocated to the partners is **not** recorded as interest expense; it is simply a directive in determining the portion of partnership profits allocable to individual partners.

EXERCISE 12-6

Purpose: (L.O. 5) This exercise will test your ability to compute both the cash to be received by each partner and the entries to be made when a partnership is dissolved.

Chip and Dale are partners who share profits and losses in a 60%:40% ratio, respectively. Before liquidation of the noncash assets, the following amounts pertain to the partnership:

Cash	$ 8,000
Noncash assets	82,000
Total assets	90,000
Chip, Capital	48,000
Dale, Capital	30,000

Instructions
(a) Compute the amount of cash that each partner will receive under the following **independent** situations:
1. The noncash assets are sold for $82,000 cash, the liabilities are paid, and the remaining cash is distributed to the partners.
2. The noncash assets are sold for $100,000 cash, the liabilities are paid, and the remaining cash is distributed to the partners.
3. The noncash assets are sold for $60,000 cash, the liabilities are paid, and the remaining cash is distributed to the partners.
4. The noncash assets are sold for $6,000 cash, Dale makes payment of his capital deficiency, the liabilities are paid, and the remaining cash is distributed.

(b) Prepare the journal entries for the partnership books for the dissolution of the partnership under each of the situations listed in (a) above.

TIP: In a real-life business, there would be separate accounts for each noncash asset and each type of liability. These items were combined in this exercise to simplify the solution and to highlight the main points being illustrated.

TIP: Total liabilities ($12,000) can be determined by deducting total owners' equity ($48,000 + $30,000 = $78,000) from total assets ($90,000).

SOLUTION TO EXERCISE 12-6

(a) 1. $82,000 cash proceeds - $82,000 book value of noncash assets = no gain or loss on sale of assets
        $48,000 cash to Chip
        $30,000 cash to Dale

2. $100,000 cash proceeds - $82,000 book value of noncash assets = $18,000 gain on sale of assets
   $48,000 + 60% ($18,000) = $58,800 cash to Chip
   $30,000 + 40% ($18,000) = $37,200 cash to Dale

3. $60,000 cash proceeds - $82,000 book value of noncash assets = $22,000 loss on sale of assets
   $48,000 - 60% ($22,000) = $34,800 cash to Chip
   $30,000 - 40% ($22,000) = $21,200 cash to Dale

4. $6,000 cash proceeds - $82,000 book value of noncash assets = $76,000 loss on sale of assets
   $48,000 - 60% ($76,000) = $2,400 cash to Chip
   $30,000 - 40% ($76,000) = ($400) capital deficiency for Dale

(b) 1.

Cash	82,000	
Noncash Assets		82,000
(To record realization of noncash assets)		
Liabilities	12,000	
Cash		12,000
(To record payment of partnership liabilities)		
Chip, Capital	48,000	
Dale, Capital	30,000	
Cash		78,000
(To record distribution of cash to partners)		

2.

Cash	100,000	
Noncash Assets		82,000
Gain on Realization		18,000
(To record realization of noncash assets)		
Gain on Realization	18,000	
Chip, Capital		10,800
Dale, Capital		7,200
(To record allocation of gain to partners)		
Liabilities	12,000	
Cash		12,000
(To record payment of partnership liabilities)		
Chip, Capital	58,800	
Dale, Capital	37,200	
Cash		96,000
(To record distribution of cash to partners)		

3. Cash.. 60,000
    Loss on Realization.. 22,000
        Noncash Assets   82,000
        (To record realization of noncash assets)

    Chip, Capital.. 13,200
    Dale, Capital.. 8,800
        Loss on Realization..   22,000
        (To allocate loss on realization to partners)

    Liabilities 12,000
        Cash...   12,000
        (To record payment of partnership liabilities)

    Chip, Capital.. 34,800
    Dale, Capital.. 21,200
        Cash...   56,000
        (To record distribution of cash to partners)

4. Cash.. 6,000
    Loss on Realization.. 76,000
        Noncash Assets   82,000
        (To record realization of noncash assets)

    Chip, Capital.. 45,600
    Dale, Capital.. 30,400
        Loss on Realization..   76,000
        (To allocate loss on realization to partners)

    Cash..   400
        Dale, Capital..   400
        (To record payment of capital deficiency by Dale)

    Liabilities 12,000
        Cash...   12,000
        (To record payment of partnership liabilities)

    Chip, Capital.. 2,400
        Cash...   2,400
        (To record distribution of cash to partner)

TIP:	If Dale had **not** made payment for his capital deficiency, the last three entries would have been as follows:	
	Chip, Capital	400
	Dale, Capital..	400
	(To record write-off of capital deficiency)	
	Liabilities	12,000
	Cash	12,000
	(To record payment of partnership liabilities)	
	Chip, Capital	2,000
	Cash	2,000
	(To record distribution of cash to partner)	

Approach and Explanation: The liquidation of a partnership entails performing the following steps in order:
1. Sell noncash assets for cash and recognize a gain or loss on realization.
2. **Allocate the gain or loss on realization** to the partners **using their income ratio.**
3. Pay partnership liabilities in cash.
4. **Distribute the remaining cash** to partners **on the basis of their capital balances.**

In liquidation of a partnership, the sale of noncash assets for cash is called **realization,** and the difference between the book value of the assets and the cash proceeds is called the **gain or loss on realization.**

When gains and losses on realization are divided among the partners, the capital accounts of all partners may have credit (normal) balances in their capital accounts (a situation called **no capital deficiency)** or one (or more) partner(s) may end up with a debit (negative) balance instead of a normal credit balance (a situation referred to as a **capital deficiency).** When a capital deficiency occurs, that partner must contribute the amount of his (her) negative balance to the partnership. If a partner is unable to pay the amount owed to the partnership, the partners with credit balances must absorb the loss. The loss is allocated on the basis of the income ratio that exists between the partners with credit balances.

Notice that assumption 1 resulted in no gain or loss on realization. Assumption 2 resulted in a gain on realization. Assumption 3 resulted in a loss on realization. Assumption 4 resulted in a loss on realization and a capital deficiency.

*ILLUSTRATION 12-2
ADMISSION OF A NEW PARTNER IN A
BONUS SITUATION (L.O. 6)

A **bonus to old partners** results when the new partner's capital credit on the date of admittance is less than his or her investment in the firm. A **bonus to a new partner** results when the new partner's capital credit is greater than his or her investment of net assets in the firm. The procedure for determining the new partner's capital credit and the bonus is as follows:

1. **Determine the total capital of the new partnership** by adding the new partner's investment to the total capital of the old partnership.
2. **Determine the new partner's capital credit** by multiplying the total capital of the new partnership by the new partner's ownership interest.
3. **Determine the amount of bonus** by comparing the new partner's capital credit with the new partner's investment.
4. **Allocate the bonus** to the old partners on the basis of their income ratio or allocate the bonus to the new partner, whichever is appropriate.
   a. **If the new partner's capital credit exceeds the new partner's investment,** the bonus is allocated to the new partner, which means the capital account balances of the old partners should be **decreased** by their respective portion of the bonus allocation. This decrease is based on the income ratio of the old partners before admission of the new partner.
   b. **If the partner's capital credit is less than the new partner's investment,** the bonus is allocated to the old partners, which means the capital account balances of the old partners will be **increased** by their respective portion of the bonus allocation. This increase is also based on the income ratio of the old partners before admission of the new partner.

*EXERCISE 12-7

Purpose: (L.O. 6) This exercise will test your knowledge of the various situations in which a new partner is admitted to a partnership.

The following represent various arrangements (situations) which may be present when a new partner is admitted to a partnership:
a. A new partner is admitted by purchasing all or part of the interest of an existing partner or partners.
b. A new partner is admitted by investment and no bonus is granted.
c. A new partner is admitted by investment and a bonus is granted to the old partners.
d. A new partner is admitted by investment and a bonus is granted to the new partner.

_____ 1. A new partner is admitted, the only entry on the company books is an entry to record the transfer of a portion of an old partner's capital interest to the new partner's capital account.

_____ 2. A new partner is admitted and contributes assets to the partnership.

_____ 3. There is no change in total assets or total owners' equity of a partnership when a new partner is admitted.

_____ 4. Total assets and total owners' equity of a partnership are increased when a new partner is admitted.

_____ 5. The increase in total owners' equity is equal to the value of the assets that a new partner invests in the partnership, and the new partner's capital account is credited for the value of the new assets contributed.

_____ 6. The increase in total owners' equity equals the value of the assets that a new partner invests, but the new partner's capital account is credited for an amount less than the value of the assets contributed.

_____ 7. The increase in total owners' equity equals the value of the assets that a new partner invests, but the new partner's capital account is credited for an amount greater than the value of the assets contributed.

_____ 8. The capital account of one or more of the old partners is debited when a new partner is admitted.

_____ 9. A new partner's capital account is credited for an amount that does not equal the amount recorded for the assets contributed to the partnership.

_____ 10. The cash (or other assets) given by a new partner to acquire an interest in the partnership is not recorded on the partnership books.

Instructions
The above are descriptions of situations involving the admission of a new partner to a partnership. For each of the statements, identify the arrangement or arrangements to which the statement would apply by using the appropriate code letter(s). There may be more than one answer for each of them.

SOLUTION TO EXERCISE 12-7

1.	a	6.	c
2.	b, c, d	7.	d
3.	a	8.	a, d
4.	b, c, d	9.	c, d
5.	b	10.	a

Approach: Review **Illustration 12-2** for a description of situations involving a bonus.

Explanation:

Situation a: A new partner is admitted by purchasing all or part of the interest of an existing partner or partners.

- When a new partner purchases an interest from one of the established partners, the appropriate amount of interest in the business is transferred from the existing partner's capital account to the new partner's capital account. Thus, there is **no change in the total assets or total owners' equity of the business.** (The exact amount paid by the new partner is determined by the new partner and the old partner and does not appear on the partnership's books.)

- When an old partner sells his partnership interest (or a portion of it), he records the sale on his **personal** books by a debit to Cash for the sales price, and a credit to the asset, Interest in Partnership, for his book value of the interest. If the situation warrants, he may also record a debit to Loss on Sale of Investment or a credit to Gain on Sale of Investment for the difference between his book value and the sales price.

- When a new partner purchases the interest (or a portion thereof) of an existing partner, all partners must agree on a new manner in which to divide partnership profits and losses. If they do not reach a mutual agreement, the law assumes that they share equally.

Situation b: A new partner is admitted by investment and no bonus is granted.

- When a new partner is admitted to the business by investment (rather than by purchase of an existing interest), the new partner contributes assets (cash and/or noncash) to the partnership. Thus, the total assets and total owners' equity of the partnership are increased through the creation of a capital interest for the new partner.

- If the increase in the total amount of owners' equity is equal to the value of the assets that the new partner invests in the partnership and if the new partner is to receive credit for that exact amount, there is no bonus payment involved. The entry on the partnership's books is a simple debit to Cash (or other assets contributed by the new partner) and a credit to the new owner's capital for the fair market value of the assets contributed.

Situation c: A new partner is admitted by investment and a bonus is granted to the old partners.

- At the time a new partner is being admitted by investment, the fair market values of old partnership assets such as land and buildings may be higher than their book values or unrecorded goodwill may exist and, therefore, the new partner is willing to pay a bonus to the old partners in order to become a partner.

- A bonus payment is made to the old partners when their capital accounts are credited with a portion of the amount that would normally be credited to the capital account of the new partner.

- When a new partner is admitted by investment and a bonus payment to the old partners is recognized, the following events occur:
    (a) The increase in assets is equal to the cash and noncash assets invested by the new partner.
    (b) The increase in total owners' equity is equal to the cash and noncash assets invested by the new partner less any liabilities assumed by the partnership.
    (c) The new partner's capital account is credited with an amount less than the net amount of cash and noncash assets the new partner invested.
    (d) The bonus to the old partners is allocated to them on the basis of their income ratio before the admission of the new partner.

Situation d: A new partner is admitted by investment and a bonus is granted to the new partner.

- At the time a new partner is being admitted by investment, the fair market values of old partnership assets may be lower than their books values or the new partner may have some special expertise for which the old partners are willing to pay a bonus to the new partner.

- A bonus payment is made to the new partner when the new partner's capital account is credited with amounts transferred from the capital accounts of the old partners.

- When a new partner is admitted by investment and a bonus payment to the new partner is recognized, the following events occur:
    (a) The increase in assets is equal to the cash and noncash assets invested by the new partner.
    (b) The increase in total owners' equity is equal to the amount of cash and noncash assets invested by the new partner less any liabilities assumed by the partnership.
    (c) The new partner's capital account is credited with an amount more than the amount of cash and noncash assets the new partner invested.
    (d) The bonus to the new partner results in a decrease in the capital balances of the old partners based on their income ratio before the admission of the new partner.

*EXERCISE 12-8

Purpose: (L.O. 6) This exercise will give you practice in recording the entry for the admittance of a new partner, given different agreements for admittance.

M.F. Specie, his wife Annabelle, and their son, Gary, are partners in a family business. They have respective capital account balances of $100,000, $60,000, and $40,000. They share profits and losses equally.

Instructions
Prepare the journal entry to record Karen Kinkennon's admittance to the partnership under each of the following **independent** assumptions:

(a) Karen acquires a 20% interest in the partnership by purchasing one-fifth of M.F.'s investment and one-third of Annabelle's interest. Karen pays cash of $25,000 to M.F. and $25,000 to Annabelle. The new partnership of M.F., Annabelle, Gary, and Karen will share profits and losses by the ratio of 2:1:1:1.

(b) Karen acquires a 20% interest in the partnership for a $50,000 cash investment. No bonus is recognized. The new partnership will share profits and losses equally.

(c) Karen acquires a 10% interest in the partnership for a $40,000 investment. A bonus is granted to the old partners. The new partnership of M.F., Annabelle, Gary, and Karen will share profits and losses equally.

(d) Karen acquires a 10% interest in the partnership for a $20,000 investment. A bonus is granted to the new partner. The new partnership of M.F., Annabelle, Gary, and Karen will share profits and losses equally.

SOLUTION TO EXERCISE 12-8

(a) M.F. Specie, Capital 20,000
     Annabelle Specie, Capital 20,000
         Karen Kinkennon, Capital..   40,000
         (To record admission of Kinkennon by purchase)
         (1/5 X $100,000 = $20,000; 1/3 X $60,000 = $20,000)

(b) Cash... 50,000
         Karen Kinkennon, Capital...   50,000
         (To record admission of new partner)
         ($100,000 + $60,000 + $40,000 + $50,000 = $250,000;
         $250,000 X 20% = $50,000)

(c) Cash... 40,000
         Karen Kinkennon, Capital...   24,000
         M.F. Specie, Capital...   5,334
         Annabelle Specie, Capital   5,333
         Gary Specie, Capital   5,333
         (To record admission of Kinkennon and bonus to old partners)

Approach: Apply the steps in **Illustration 12-1:**
Step 1: $100,000 + $60,000 + $40,000 + $40,000 = $240,000.
Step 2: $240,000 X 10% = $24,000
Step 3: Investment = $40,000; new partner's capital credit = $24,000 (Step 2); so bonus = $16,000.
Step 4 (b): $16,000 ÷ 3 = $5,333 per old partner so increase old partners' capital accounts.

(d) Cash...   20,000
     M. F. Specie, Capital...   667
     Annabelle Specie, Capital   667
     Gary Specie, Capital   666
         Karen Kinkennon, Capital..............................   22,000
         (To record Kinkennon's admission and bonus)

Approach: Apply the steps in **Illustration 12-1:**
Step 1: $100,000 + $60,000 + $40,000 + $20,000 = $220,000.
Step 2: $220,000 X 10% = $22,000
Step 3: Investment = $20,000; new partner's capital credit = $22,000 (Step 2); so bonus = $2,000.
Step 4 (a): $2,000 ÷ 3 = $667 per old partner so decrease old partners' capital accounts.

*EXERCISE 12-9

Purpose: (L.O. 7) This exercise will illustrate the accounting for the withdrawal of a partner under different assumptions.

On December 31, 2014, the capital account balances and income-sharing percentages in Wiley Books, a partnership, are as follows:

Partner	Capital Account	Income Ratio
K. Hawkins	$40,000	50%
D. Kear	30,000	30%
M. Reynolds	10,000	20%

Instructions
Prepare the journal entry on the partnership books to record the withdrawal of Reynolds under each of the following assumptions:
(a) Each of the remaining partners agrees to pay $6,500 in cash from personal funds to purchase Reynolds' ownership equity. Each receives 50% of Reynolds' partnership interest.
(b) Joe Wright agrees to purchase Reynolds' ownership interest for $14,000 cash.
(c) Reynolds is paid $12,000 from partnership assets and a bonus to the retiring partner is recognized.
(d) Reynolds is paid $9,000 from partnership assets, and bonuses to the remaining partners are recorded.

SOLUTION TO EXERCISE 12-9

(a) M. Reynolds, Capital 10,000
        K. Hawkins, Capital   5,000
        D. Kear, Capital   5,000
            (To record purchase of Reynolds' interest)
            ($10,000 X 50% = $5,000)

TIP: The withdrawal of a partner when **payment is made from partners' personal assets** is the direct opposite of admitting a new partner who purchases a partner's interest. Payment to the retiring partner is made directly from the remaining partners' personal assets. Partnership assets are not involved in any way, and total capital does not change. Thus, the effect on the partnership is limited to a realignment of the partners' capital balances. The amount paid for the retiring partner's interest does **not** impact the journal entry on the partnership books.

(b) M. Reynolds, Capital 10,000
        Wright, Capital   10,000
            (To record admission of Wright by purchase)

(c) M. Reynolds, Capital 10,000
      K. Hawkins, Capital 1,250
      D. Kear, Capital   750
        Cash   12,000
            (To record withdrawal of and bonus to Reynolds)
            ($12,000 - $10,000 = $2,000 bonus);
            (50% : 30% = 5/8 : 3/8); (5/8 X $2,000 = $1,250);
            (3/8 X $2,000 = $750)

(d) M. Reynolds, Capital 10,000
        Cash   9,000
        K. Hawkins, Capital   625
        D. Kear, Capital   375
            (To record withdrawal of Reynolds and bonus to
            remaining partners); ($10,000 - $9,000 = $1,000
            bonus); (50% : 30% = 5/8 : 3/8); (5/8 X $1,000 =
            $625); (3/8 X $1,000 = $375)

Approach and Explanation: When a partner withdraws, determine whether partnership assets are affected or not affected. In assumption (a), the retiring partner is bought out by the other partners, but the other partners use their **personal** assets rather than partnership assets to accomplish the buyout. Therefore, only capital accounts are affected in the journal entry to record assumption (a), and the amount of assets received by the retiring partner is **not** reflected on the partnership books. In assumption (b), two individuals (the retiring partner and an outsider named Wright) make a deal that again does **not** affect the partnership's assets. Only the capital accounts on the partnership's books are affected when a new partner purchases an old partner's ownership interest. In assumptions (c) and (d), partnership assets are used to payoff the withdrawing partner. If the amount of partnership assets being distributed to the retiring partner differs from the balance of that partner's capital account before withdrawal, there is a bonus situation and the procedure for determining and allocating the bonus as follows:

1. **Determine the amount of the bonus** by comparing the assets disbursed to the retiring partner with the retiring partner's capital account balance.

2. (a) **If the amount of assets distributed exceed the retiring partner's capital account balance,** the excess is a bonus to the retiring partner. The bonus is deducted from the remaining partners' capital balances on the basis of their income ratio.

    (b) **If the amount of assets distributed is less than the retiring partner's capital account balance,** the difference is a bonus to the remaining partners and will be allocated (credited) to the capital accounts of the remaining partners on the basis of their income ratio.

Assumption (c) is an example of a bonus paid to the retiring partner and assumption (d) is an example of a bonus paid to the remaining partners.

A bonus may be paid to a retiring partner when (1) the fair market values of partnership assets are more than their book values; (2) there is unrecorded goodwill resulting from the partnership's superior earnings record; or (3) the remaining partners are anxious to remove the withdrawing partner from the firm.

A retiring partner may give a bonus to the remaining partners when (1) partnership assets have book values in excess of their fair market values; (2) the partnership has a poor earnings record; or (3) the withdrawing partner is anxious to leave the partnership.

EXERCISE 12-10

Purpose: (L.O. 1 thru 7) This exercise will quiz you about terminology used in this chapter.

A list of accounting terms with which you should be familiar appears below:

*Admission by investment	Partnership
*Admission by purchase of an interest	Partnership agreement
Capital deficiency	Partnership dissolution
General partner	Partnership liquidation
Income ratio	Schedule of cash payments
Limited liability company	*Withdrawal by payment from partners'
Limited liability partnership	personal assets
Limited partners	*Withdrawal by payment from partnership
Limited partnership	assets
No capital deficiency	
Partners' capital statement	

Instructions
For each item below, enter in the blank the term that is described.

1. _____An association of two or more persons to carry on as co-owners of a business for profit.

2. _____A written contract expressing the voluntary agreement of two or more individuals in a partnership.

3. _____Admission of a partner in a personal transaction between one or more existing partners and the new partner; does not change total partnership assets or total capital.

4. _____Admission of a partner by investing assets in the partnership, causing both partnership net assets and total capital to increase.

5. _____The basis for dividing net income and net loss in a partnership.

6. _____The owners' equity statement for a partnership which shows the changes in each partner's capital balance and in total partnership capital during the year.

7. _____A debit balance in a partner's capital account after allocation of gain or loss on realization.

8. _____All partners have credit balances after allocation of gain or loss on realization.

9. _____A change in partners, due to withdrawal or admission, which does not necessarily terminate the business.

10. _____Withdrawal of a partner in a personal transaction between partners; does not change total partnership assets or total capital.

11. _____Withdrawal of a partner in a transaction involving the partnership, causing both partnership net assets and total capital to decrease.

12. _____A schedule showing the distribution of cash to the partners in the liquidation of a partnership. (Sometimes called a **safe cash payments schedule**).

13. _____An event that ends both the legal and economic life of a partnership.

14. _____A partner who has unlimited liability for the debts of the firm.

15. _____Partners whose liability for the debts of the firm is limited to their investment in the firm.

16. _____A partnership in which one or more general partners have unlimited liability and one or more partners have limited liability for the obligations of the firm.

17. _____A partnership of professionals in which partners are given limited liability and the public is protected from malpractice by insurance carried by the partnership.

18. _____A form of business organization, usually classified as a partnership and usually with limited life, in which partners, who are called members, have limited liability.

SOLUTION TO EXERCISE 12-10

1. Partnership
2. Partnership agreement
3. *Admission by purchase of an interest
4. *Admission by investment
5. Income ratio
6. Partners' capital statement
7. Capital deficiency
8. No capital deficiency
9. Partnership dissolution
10. *Withdrawal by payment from partners' personal assets
11. *Withdrawal by payment from partnership assets
12. Schedule of cash payments
13. Partnership liquidation
14. General partner
15. Limited partners
16. Limited partnership
17. Limited liability partnership
18. Limited liability company

*This material is covered in the Appendix to Chapter 12 in the text.

ANALYSIS OF MULTIPLE-CHOICE TYPE QUESTIONS

1. (L.O. 1) A limited partnership is a partnership in which:
   a. one or more, but not all, of the partners assume a limited liability in the operations of the business.
   b. creditors cannot claim the personal assets of any of the partners.
   c. all partners invest a limited amount of assets.
   d. profit distributions to partners are limited to a set sum.

   Approach and Explanation: Mentally define limited partnership before you read the answer selections. Some states allow limited partnerships in which the liability of a partner is limited to the partner's equity in the partnership. However, there must always be at least one partner with unlimited liability, often referred to as the general partner. (Solution = a.)

2. (L.O. 1) Which of the following is **not** a characteristic of the partnership form of business organization?
   a. Unlimited liability of general partners.
   b. Mutual agency relationship of owners.
   c. Limited life.
   d. Separate taxable entity.

   Explanation: A partnership is **not** a taxable entity. However, a partnership is required to file an information tax return showing partnership net income and each partner's share. The partners then pick up their share of the business income on their personal tax returns and pay taxes at personal tax rates. Taxes are due on a partner's share of the partnership income, regardless of the amount of the partner's withdrawals from the business during the year. (Solution = d.)

3. (L.O. 4) The following items may be reflected in a partner's capital account:
1. The partner's investments in the business.
2. The partner's share of business profits.
3. The partner's share of business losses.
4. The partner's drawings.
5. The partner's disinvestments.

Which of the above items (by reference numbers) are reflected as credits in the partner's capital account?
a. 1, 2, and 5.
b. 2 and 5.
c. 1 and 2.
d. 3, 4, and 5.
e. none of the above.

Approach and Explanation: Draw a T-account and enter the items above. Notice the credits are for the items that cause increases in a partner's capital account. (Solution = c.)

Partner's Capital

Debits	**Credits**
3. Partner's share of losses.	1. Partner's investment
4. Partner's drawings.	2. Partner's share of profits
5. Partner's disinvestments.	

4. (L.O. 2) In starting a partnership, the noncash assets contributed to the business by the partners should be recorded on the business books at:
a. the fair market values.
b. the amounts the assets originally cost the individual partners.
c. proportional amounts that correspond to the income-sharing agreement.
d. the amount at which the assets were reported on the partner's old books (the partner's book value).

Explanation: Each partner's initial investment in a partnership should be recorded at the fair market value of the assets at the date of their transfer to the partnership. (Solution = a.)

5. (L.O. 3) Salaries allocated to the owners of a partnership are:
   a. recorded as an operating expense and reported on the income statement.
   b. always equal for each general partner within the partnership.
   c. never allowed for limited partners.
   d. used only as a means of computing a partner's share of the business income and do not get reported as an expense.

   Explanation: Partners' salaries are **not** an expense on the partnership's books; they are used **only** as a means of determining a partner's share of partnership net income or net loss. (Solution = d.)

6. (L.O. 3) When salary and interest allocations to partners are provided for in a partnership income-sharing agreement, these allocations:
   a. must also be made in determining the amount of net loss that is to be allocated to each partner.
   b. are reported as expenses on the income statement of the business.
   c. need not be made if they exceed the amount of net income for the period.
   d. must be paid in cash.

   Explanation: Salary and interest allowances for partners are used in the determination of a partner's share of partnership profits and losses. They are **not** expenses in determining partnership net income or net loss. (Solution = a.)

7. (L.O. 4) Mike invested $80,000 in a partnership named M & J Printers at the beginning of 2013. Mike and his partner Jane share profits and losses equally. The business reported net income of $22,000 and $28,000 for the year 2013 and 2014, respectively. Mike's drawings totaled $10,000 and $16,000 for 2013 and 2014, respectively. What is the balance of Mike's capital account to be reported on the partnership's balance sheet at the end of 2014?
   a. $131,000.
   b. $105,000.
   c. $104,000.
   d. $79,000.

   Approach and Explanation: Draw a T-account for Mike's capital account. Enter the data given.

Mike, Capital			
2013 Drawings	10,000	Investment	80,000
2014 Drawings	16,000	2013 Profits	11,000
		2014 Profits	14,000
		Balance, 12/31/14	79,000

   (Solution = d.)

8. (L.O. 3) Partners Steve, Bev, and Connie are to share partnership income in a 3 : 1 : 1 ratio. If the net income of the partnership for one year is $90,000, Steve's share amounts to:
a. $67,500.
b. $54,000.
c. $30,000.
d. $27,000.

Approach and Explanation: Add the items in the ratio: 3 + 1 + 1 = 5. Use the five as the denominator of three fractions and the 3, 1, and 1 as numerators. Thus, the fractions are 3/5, 1/5, and 1/5 for Steve, Bev, and Connie, respectively.

$$3/5 \text{ X } \$90,000 = \$54,000 \text{ for Steve's share (Solution = b.)}$$

9. (L.O. 3) Partners Kent, Jill, and Mark have the following income-sharing agreement for their partnership: $20,000 Salary allowance for Kent; $14,000 Salary allowance for Jill; $8,000 Salary allowance for Mark. Remaining profits and losses are to be divided equally. If the results of operations for 2014 show a **net loss** of $12,000, the journal entry to close the Income Summary account will include a:
a. debit to Kent, Capital for $4,000.
b. credit to Mark, Capital for $10,000.
c. credit to Kent, Capital for $2,000.
d. debit to Income Summary for $12,000.

Approach and Explanation: Compute each partner's share of the net loss and prepare the journal entry to close the Income Summary account.

Division of Net Loss

	Kent	**Jill**	**Mark**	**Total**
Salary allowance	$20,000	$14,000	$ 8,000	$ 42,000
Remaining deficiency, $54,000				
($12,000 + $42,000)				
Kent ($54,000 X 1/3)	(18,000)			
Jill ($54,000 X 1/3)		(18,000)		
Mark ($54,000 X 1/3)			(18,000)	
Total deficiency				(54,000)
Total division	$ 2,000	$(4,000)	$(10,000)	$(12,000)

Jill, Capital...	4,000	
Mark, Capital..	10,000	
Income Summary..		12,000
Kent, Capital		2,000

(Solution = c.)

10. (L.O. 5) Diane and Emmett are partners in the D & E Store. Daniel is being admitted as a new partner by the purchase of part of the interests of the existing partners. Which of the following is true?
    a. The balances of the old partners' capital accounts will change by the same amount.
    b. The total assets of the partnership are increased by this transaction.
    c. The total amount of owner's equity of the partnership is not changed by this transaction.
    d. The capital account for Diane will increase in amount.

    Explanation: Admission of a new partner by having the new partner purchase an interest of one or more of the existing partners results in no change in total assets and no change in total owners' equity of the partnership. The capital account for Diane will decrease in amount. The capital accounts of the old partners may or may not decrease by the same amount, depending on what portion of the partners' interests is purchased by the new partner. (Solution = c.)

11. (L.O. 5) Samantha is being admitted as a new partner into a partnership business. If the increase in total owners' equity is equal to the fair market value of the assets that Samantha invests in the partnership and Samantha's capital account is credited for an amount less than the value of the new assets contributed, the arrangement for Samantha's admittance is by:
    a. purchase of all or part of the interest of an existing partner or partners.
    b. investment and no bonus is granted.
    c. investment and a bonus is granted to the old partners.
    d. investment and a bonus is granted to the new partner.

    Explanation: The excess of the fair market value of the assets contributed over the new partner's capital credit is a bonus that is granted to the old partners. It should be allocated to them by their respective income ratios. (Solution = c.)

12. (L.O. 5) If a bonus is granted to a new partner upon admittance to a partnership, this bonus will result in a(an):
    a. increase in the capital accounts of the old partners.
    b. decrease in the capital accounts of the old partners.
    c. operating expense to be reported on the income statement of the partnership.
    d. amount to be recorded in the new partner's drawing account.

    Explanation: A bonus is granted to a new partner when the new partner's capital credit exceeds the new partner's investment. Thus, in the entry to record the new partner's admittance, the credit to the new partner's capital account is greater than the debit(s) to assets. The remaining debits needed to balance the entry come from decreases in the capital accounts of the old partners. The bonus to the new partner is allocated to the old partners (as a reduction in their equity) based on the income-sharing ratio **before** admission of the new partner. (Solution = b.)

*13. (L.O. 7) The following balances exist at December 31, 2014, for the Food Court, a partnership.

Cash	$ 35,000	Liabilities	$45,000
Noncash assets	110,000	B. Bean, Capital	50,000
		H. Burger, Capital	10,000
		I. Lamb, Capital	40,000

The partners share profits in a ratio of 3 : 2 : 1. In the process of liquidating the partnership in January 2015, the noncash assets are sold for $50,000 cash. Assuming any resulting capital deficiency is allocated to the remaining partners, the amount of cash to be distributed to B. Bean amounts to:

a. $12,500.
b. $15,000.
c. $25,000.
d. $27,500.

Approach and Explanation: Work through the steps in the liquidation process:
1.   **Sell noncash assets for cash and recognize a gain or loss on realization.**
      $50,000 cash proceeds - $110,000 book value = $60,000 loss on realization
2.   **Allocate the gain or loss on realization to the partners using their income ratio.**
      3 : 2 : 1 = 3/6 : 2/6 : 1/6
      $60,000 X 3/6 = $30,000 loss allocated to B. Bean; $60,000 X 2/6 = $20,000 loss allocated to H. Burger; $60,000 X 1/6 = $10,000 loss allocated to I. Lamb.
      The resulting $10,000 deficiency for H. Burger is allocated to the remaining partners by their respective ratios (3 : 1 means 3/4 of $10,000 is allocated to B. Bean and 1/4 of $10,000 is allocated to I. Lamb). The capital accounts would then reflect the following:

B. Bean		H. Burger		I. Lamb	
	Bal. 50,000	Bal. 10,000			Bal. 40,000
Loss 30,000		Loss 20,000		Loss 10,000	
	Bal. 20,000	Deficiency 10,000	Deficiency Allocation 10,000		Bal. 30,000
Deficiency Allocation 7,500				Deficiency Allocation 2,500	
	Bal. 12,500	Bal. 0			Bal. 27,500

3.   **Pay partnership liabilities in cash. The Cash account will then reflect the following:**

Cash			
December 31, 2014, Balance	35,000	Payment of liabilities	45,000
Sales of noncash assets	50,000		
Balance to distribute	40,000		

4.   **Distribute the remaining cash to partners on the basis of their capital balances.**
      $12,500 to B. Bean and $27,500 to I. Lamb

(Solution = a.)

*14. (L.O. 7) In the process of dissolving a partnership, any cash that remains after the noncash assets have been liquidated and all liabilities have been paid is distributed to the partners:
   a.   in accordance with their income ratio.
   b.   in proportion to the relative amount of time the partners have devoted to the business.
   c.   according to the remaining balances in their respective capital accounts.
   d.   in proportion to their relative original investments in the partnership.

   Explanation: The balance of a partner's capital account represents that partner's claim against partnership assets. Thus, in liquidation, a partner receives assets equal to the balance of that partner's capital account. Be careful **not** to confuse this issue with the question of how to allocate gains and losses on realization which is part of the liquidation process. When the noncash assets are sold (converted to cash), they are usually exchanged for an amount of cash unequal to their book (carrying) values. Thus, gains and losses on realization are recognized. These gains and losses are allocated to the partners' capital accounts based on their income ratio. The resulting balances in the partners' capital accounts dictate the amount of cash due each partner. (Solution = c.)

*15. (L.O. 7) In the process of dissolving a partnership, if the allocation of the losses from liquidation of the noncash assets results in a debit balance in the capital account of one partner, this indicates that:
   a.   an error was made in the recording process.
   b.   creditors will not be paid the full amounts due them.
   c.   the partner with the debit balance should contribute cash to the partnership equal in amount to the negative balance.
   d.   an amount of cash equal to the debit balance is owed to that partner by the partnership.

   Explanation: The debit balance in the partner's capital account is called a capital deficiency. That partner should pay the partnership the amount of the capital deficiency. In the event of nonpayment, however, the capital deficiency is eliminated by reductions of the capital accounts of the remaining partners (in the proportion of their respective income ratios). (Solution = c.)

Lightning Source UK Ltd.
Milton Keynes UK
UKHW03f0416280918

329610UK00004B/61/P